This book was made possible through partial support provided by the United States Agency for International Development (USAID) for the Sustainable Agriculture and Natural Resources Management Collaborative Research Support

Program (SANREM CRSP) under terms of Cooperative Agreement Award No. EPP-A-00-04-00013-00 to the Office of International Research and Development (OIRED) at Virginia Polytechnic Institute and State University (Virginia Tech); terms of sub-agreement 19070A-425632 between Virginia Tech and North Carolina Agricultural and Technical State University (NCA&T).

Following agencies and individual are co-publishers of this book. We highly appreciate their willingness to share their resources and manpower in this promising endeavor of SWAT.

# Scientific modeling

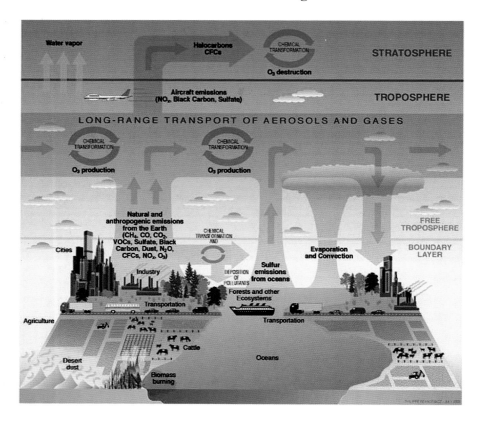

**Scientific modeling** is the process of generating abstract, <u>conceptual</u>, <u>graphical</u> and/or <u>mathematical</u> models. Science offers a growing collection of <u>methods</u>, techniques and <u>theory</u> about all kinds of specialized scientific modeling.

Modeling is an essential and inseparable part of all scientific activity, and many scientific disciplines have their own ideas about specific types of modeling. There is little general theory about scientific modeling, offered by the <u>philosophy of science</u>, <u>systems theory</u>, and new fields like <u>knowledge visualization</u>.

*From* Wikipedia, the free encyclopedia

<u>http://en.wikipedia.org/wiki/Model_(abstract)</u>

# SOIL AND WATER ASSESSMENT TOOL (SWAT): GLOBAL APPLICATIONS

## Editors

**Jeff Arnold, Raghavan Srinivasan, Susan Neitsch, Chris George,
Karim Abbaspour, Philip Gassman, Fang Hua Hao, Ann van Griensven,
Ashvin Gosain, Patrick Debels, Nam Won Kim, Hiroaki Somura,
Victor Ella, Luis Leon, Attachai Jintrawet, Manuel Reyes,
and Samran Sombatpanit**

*Published as* **Special Publication No. 4** *by*

The World Association of Soil and Water Conservation (WASWC)
http://waswc.soil.gd.cn, www.waswc.org

*With following institutions/agencies/societies/associations as co-publishers*

Virginia Polytechnic Institute and State University (Virginia Tech), VA, U.S.A. www.vt.edu/,
dillaha@vt.edu

Texas AgriLife Research, Texas A&M University, College Station, TX 77843, U.S.A.
http://agresearch.tamu.edu/, r-srinivasan@tamu.edu

Spatial Sciences Laboratory, Texas A&M University, Texas, U.S.A. www-ssl.tamu.edu,
r-srinivasan@tamu.edu

North Carolina Agricultural and Technical State Univ., NC 27695-7625, U.S.A. www.ncat.edu,
mannyreyes@nc.rr.com

Biological and Agricultural Engineering, North Carolina State University, Box 7625, Raleigh,
NC 27695-7625, U.S.A. www.bae.ncsu.edu, mohamed_youssef@ncsu.edu

USDA-Agricultural Research Service, Temple, Texas, U.S.A. www.ars.usda.gov,
jgarnold@spa.ars.usda.gov

USDA, NRCS, 1400 Independence Ave., SW, Washington, D.C. 20250, U.S.A.
www.nrcs.usda.gov, tim.sweeney@ar.usda.gov

University of Arkansas, Arkansas, U.S.A. www.uark.edu, dsaraswat@uaex.edu

Texas Institute for Applied Environmental Research (TIAER), Tarleton State University,
Stephenville, TX 76402, U.S.A. http://tiaer.tarleton.edu/, saleh@tiaer.tarleton.edu

International Erosion Control Association (IECA), 3401 Quebec St., Suite 3500, Denver,
CO 80207, U.S.A. www.ieca.org, ecinfo@ieca.org

Mars Incorporated, 6885 Elm St., McLean, VA 22101-3883, U.S.A. www.mars.com

SonTek YSI Incorporated, 9940 Summers Ridge Road, San Diego, CA 92121-3091, U.S.A. www.sontek.com, inquiry@sontek.com, support@sontek.com

Swiss Federal Institute for Aquatic Science and Technology (Eawag), Ueberlandstr. 133, P.O. Box 611, 8600 Duebendorf, Switzerland. www.eawag.ch/index_EN, k_abbaspour@yahoo.com

Korea Institute of Construction Technology (KICT), S. Korea. www.kict.re.kr, nwkim@kict.re.kr

21C Frontier R&D Program, South Korea. http://www.water21.re.kr/en/index.asp

UNESCO-IHE Institute for Water Education, Delft, The Netherlands. www.unesco-ihe.org, A.vanGriensven@unesco-ihe.org

International Center for Tropical Agriculture (CIAT), Cali, Colombia. www.ciat.cgiar.org, a.jarvis@CGIAR.ORG

European Society of Agricultural Engineers (EurAgEng), Barton Road, Silsoe, Bedford, MK45 4FH, U.K. www.eurageng.eu, secgen@eurageng.eu

World Overview of Conservation Approaches and Technologies (WOCAT), Univ. of Bern, Bern, Switzerland. www.wocat.net, hanspeter.liniger@cde.unibe.ch

Combating Desertification Unit, ENEA CR-Casaccia, Via Anguillarese n. 301, 00123 Rome, Italy. www.riade.net, miannetta@casaccia.enea.it

Syngenta, Basel, Switzerland. www.syngenta.com, franz.doppmann@syngenta.com

UNU Int. Network on Water, Environment and Health (UNU-INWEH), Hamilton, Ontario L8P 0A1, Canada. www.inweh.unu.edu, contact@inweh.unu.edu, grovervi@inweh.unu.edu

United Nations University International Institute for Software Technology, Macau, China. www.iist.unu.edu, cwg@iist.unu.edu

Deutsche Gesellschaft für Technische Zusammenarbeit (GTZ), Eschborn, Germany. www.gtz.de, alexander.schoening@gtz.de

Dr. Shabbir Shahid, WASWC Vice President for the Middle East, Dubai, U.A.E. s.shahid@biosaline.org.ae

Sociedad Colombiana Ciencia del Suelo (Colombian Soil Science Society), Carrera 11 # 66-34 Of. 202, Bogota D.C., Colombia scsuelo@cable.net.co, ivalenbal@hotmail.com

SEMEATO S/A, Rua Camilo Ribeiro, 190 - Bairro São Cristóvão - CEP 99060-000, Passo Fundo RS, Brazil. www.semeato.com.br, tiago.martelli@semeato.com.br

Chile Centre for Environmental Sciences EULA-CHILE, University of Concepción, Concepción, Chile. http://www.eula.cl/, pdebels@gmail.com, pdebels@udec.cl

The University of Agricultural Sciences and Veterinary Medicine of Cluj-Napoca, Cluj, Romania. www.fao.org/regional/SEUR/ClujWS/UnivAgrVet.htm, rusuteodor23@yahoo.com

Forestry Faculty, Belgrade University, Belgrade, Serbia. www.bg.ac.yu, miodrag.zla@sbb.rs

Institut für Ingenieurbiologie und Landschaftsbau, Universität für Bodenkultur, A-1190 Wien, Austria. www.boku.ac.at/iblb, hp.rauch@boku.ac.at

Food and Agriculture Organization (FAO), Rome, Italy. www.fao.org, yuji.niino@fao.org

APAD - Association pour la Promotion d'une Agriculture Durable (APAD), 7 rue Surcouf, F-35170 Bruz, France. www.apad.asso.fr, apad.asso@laposte.net, gerard.rass@wanadoo.fr

Universidad de Caldas, Manizales, Caldas, Colombia. www.ucaldas.edu.co, fobando1@yahoo.com

Egerton University, P.O. Box 536-20115 Egerton, Kenya. www.egerton.ac.ke, joowin@yahoo.com

Soil Science Society of Iran, Teheran, I.R. Iran. www.soiliran.org, gh_roshani@yahoo.com

Centre for Integrated Mountain Research (CIMR), University of the Punjab, Lahore, Pakistan. www.pu.edu.pk, cimrpu@yahoo.com

SCSI Soil Conservation Society of India, NASC Complex, Dev Prakash Shastri Marg, New Delhi 110012, India. www.soilcsi.org, soilcsi@yahoo.com.in, helpdesk@soilcsi.org

Beijing Normal University, Beijing, P.R. China. www.bnu.edu.cn, fanghua@bnu.edu.cn

Institute of Soil and Water Conservation, Chinese Academy of Sciences, Yangling, Shaanxi, China. www.iswc.ac.cn, lirui@ms.iswc.ac.cn

Monitoring Center of Soil and Water Conservation, Ministry of Water Resources, Beijing, China. www.cnscm.org, sglu@mwr.gov.cn

Institute of Eco-Environmental and Soil Sciences, Guangzhou, China. www.soil.gd.cn, dqli@soil.gd.cn

Erecon Institute of Environment Rehabilitation and Conservation (ERECON), Tokyo, Japan. www.erecon.jp, hq-erecon@nifty.com

Shimane University, Shimane, Japan. www.shimane-u.ac.jp, som-hiroaki@life.shimane-u.ac.jp

Nong Lam University, Ho Chi Minh City, Vietnam. www.hcmuaf.edu.vn, nguyenkimloi@yahoo.com

Vietnam Society of Soil Science, Hanoi, Vietnam. vsss1991@yahoo.com.vn, chauthu_9lvh@yahoo.co.uk

University of the Philippines, Los Baños, Philippines. www.uplb.edu.ph, vbella100@yahoo.com

Mariano Marcos State University, Ilocos Norte, Philippines. www.mmsu.edu.ph, natzalibuyog@yahoo.com

International University of Business Agriculture and Technology (IUBAT), Dhaka 1230, Bangladesh. www.iubat.edu, info@iubat.edu, miyan@iubat.edu

Institute Pertanian Bogor, Bogor, Indonesia. www.ipb.ac.id, wgar.ipb@gmail.com,

Mountainous Terrain Development Research Center, Faculty of Engineering, University Putra Malaysia, Selangor, Malaysia. www.upm.edu.my, husaini@eng.upm.edu.my

Chiangmai University, Chiang Mai, Thailand. www.cmu.ac.th, attachai@chiangmai.ac.th

Thailand Research Fund, Bangkok, Thailand. www.trf.or.th/en

Department of Soil Science, Kasetsart University, Bangkok 10900, Thailand. www.ku.ac.th, agrpik@ku.ac.th

Land Development Department (LDD), Ministry of Agriculture, Bangkok 10900, Thailand. www.ldd.go.th, ddga@ldd.go.th, ddgt@ldd.go.th, dgldd@ldd.go.th

## WASWC Secretariat

**Secretary General:** *Henry Lu Shunguang*, Monitoring Center of Soil and Water Conservation, Ministry of Water Resources, Beijing 100053, China. Phone +86-10-69826108 sglu@mwr.gov.cn, lushunguang0709@sina.com
**Deputy Secretary General:** *Li Dingqiang*, Guangdong Institute of Eco-Environmental and Soil Sciences, Guangzhou, China. Phone: +86-20-87024766, dqli@soil.gd.cn.
With other offices in China (Yangling), India (New Delhi, Ludhiana, Dehra Dun), Japan (Tokyo), Philippines (Quezon City) and Thailand (Bangkok)

## WASWC Websites

**Guangzhou Website:** http://waswc.soil.gd.cn; Webmaster: *Guo Zhixing* guozx@soil.gd.cn
**Tokyo Website:** www.waswc.org; Webmaster: *Hiromu Okazawa* waswc@nifty.com
**Bangkok Website (for photos):** http://community.webshots.com/user/waswc & http://community.webshots.com/user/waswc1; Webmaster: *Samran Sombatpanit* sombatpanit@yahoo.com

**For general matters** please contact Samran Sombatpanit, WASWC Thailand Office, 67/141, Amonphant 9, Soi Sena 1, Bangkok 10230, Thailand. Phone/Fax: +66-(0)25703641; Phone: +66-(0)25703854 sombatpanit@yahoo.com

**Cover photo credits:** *Front cover:* Main picture is from the paper of Neitsch et al., pp. 3-23, this volume. Inset: upper from SonTek YSI Incorporated.; lower, from a website.

**Cover design:** Prayud Chamaplin

*Suggested citation:* Arnold, J., Srinivasan, R., Neitsch, S., George, C., Abbaspour, K.C., Gassman, P., Fang H.H., van Griensven, A., Gosain, A., Debels, P., Kim, N.W., Somura, H., Ella, V., Leon, L., Jintrawet, A., Reyes, M.R. and Sombatpanit, S. (eds) 2009. *Soil and Water Assessment Tool (SWAT): Global Applications*. Special Publication No. 4., World Association of Soil and Water Conservation, Bangkok. ISBN: 978-974-613-722-5, 415 pp. (With one DVD)

**Printed** at FUNNY PUBLISHING, 549/1-2 Soi Phaholyothin 32, Phaholyothin Rd. Chatuchak District, Bangkok 10900, Thailand. Phone: +66-(0)25793352; Fax: +66-(0)5611933; funnyint@yahoo.com, funnyint@truemail.co.th

*"Assessment efforts should not be concerned about valuing what can be measured but, instead, about measuring that which is valued."*

*From:* Banta, T.W., Lund, J.P., Black, K.E., and Oblander, F.W. 1996. *Assessment in practice: Putting principles to work on college campuses.* San Francisco: Jossey-Bass. p. 5.

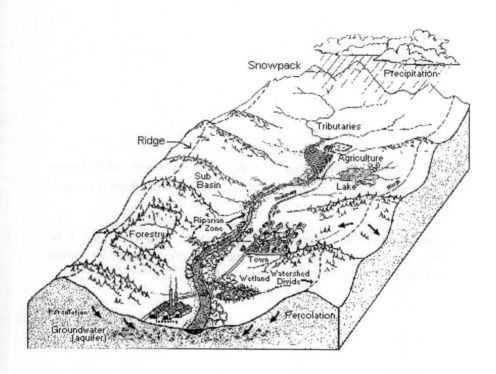

**General view of a watershed, catchment or river basin, the main subject of this book**

*The illustration was produced by the Lane Council of Governments (LCOG), Lane County, Oregon State, U.S.A. (www.lcog.org) and posted on the website of Casper City, Wyoming, U.S.A.*
www.casperwy.gov/content/departments/kcb/watershed.asp

*We thank the LCOG for permitting us to use the drawing in this book.*

# Foreword

For the past 25 years since WASWC was established, we have been trying to gather information concerning technologies for use in studying soil and water and managing them for agricultural production. Apart from several publications that we worked with our publishing partner, Science Publishers, Inc. U.S.A. (see the end part of this book), we have also been producing Special Publications by stressing on the current subjects of much interest. The first one, *Pioneering Soil Erosion Prediction – USLE Story,* was published in 2003 as a small booklet, to record the history of this attempt, and followed with *Carbon Trading, Agriculture and Poverty,* also a booklet, in 2004.

Lately, we tried to identify subjects that have been studied widely and successfully, so a technical book of conventional length, *No-Till Farming Systems,* has come out in 2008 and proved a success since such practice has been widely known to be useful for crop production in many ways, and, importantly, can help reduce soil loss due to erosion down to only a small fraction of those occurring from normal tillage. The book has been distributed at a low price, thus enabling professionals and academics to have access to such publication that otherwise would be available only from publishers that produce textbooks with relatively high prices. We expect that *No-Till Farming Systems* will be used as a platform where researchers and practitioners may work from, so that some new advancements about the farming system that "park the plow" can be achieved.

SWAT, an acronym for "Soil and Water Assessment Tool", a river basin, or watershed, scale model, has come around for some years, but its origin stemmed from those hydrological models in operation during the 1980s. According to Neitsch et al. (2005), SWAT was developed to predict the impact of land management practices on water, sediment and agricultural chemicals yields in large complex watersheds with varying soils, land use and management conditions over long periods of time. Dr. Jeff Arnold of the United States Department of Agriculture – Agricultural Research Service (USDA-ARS) in Temple, Texas, has the credit for being largely responsible for its development.

From a good number of papers on SWAT appearing in the literature world at this time, we are certain there is much information available that when in the book form will make such subject better understood and utilized, thus enhancing more systematic actions to be done for land management and conservation. WASWC therefore has accepted to produce this book by using the same principle as the previous volume, so that it can be distributed to worldwide readers for their immediate use at an affordable price. The book comes with a DVD that contains some computer models that readers may work to learn and experiment with. As a major benefit for being in the digital age, readers at this time are eligible to seek advice from all editors and contributors in any matters that they want to learn more or have problem with. Such privilege is a unique benefit that is always available for WASWC members, as well as other readers of WASWC books.

WASWC will strive to do more works in this line, in order to find the right methods to tackle problems that have occurred to land and soil and help make these resources suitable to sustainably serve humanity with all their functions.

Miodrag Zlatic

President, World Association of Soil and Water Conservation
Faculty of Forestry, Belgrade University
Belgrade, Serbia

# Preface and Acknowledgments

The Soil and Water Assessment Tool (SWAT) is an open source watershed model that is continuously developed and refined by the USDA-Agricultural Research Service and scientists at universities and research agencies around the world. It was developed originally to operate with databases available in the United States but has evolved to run with limited data sets now available throughout the world. The model is routinely used in the U.S. by the US-Environmental Protection Agency for developing watershed management strategies to attain water quality standards in impaired water bodies. It is also used for national conservation assessment by the USDA-Natural Resources Conservation Service and in numerous climate change studies. SWAT has been modified and refined by European scientists and used in numerous projects. European development and application was advanced by four international conferences held between 2001 and 2007. In recent years, SWAT has been successfully applied to assess water availability in the African continent, to study the impact of climate change on water resources in India, and to assess water supply and sedimentation issues in the Yellow River and other major rivers in China. Routine application has not occurred in Southeast Asia although SWAT was applied in the Mekong River downstream of China. Dr. Phil Gassman and colleagues recently published an article providing an excellent overview of historical development, applications, and future research directions. There are currently over 400 SWAT related papers in the referred literature.

There are several requirements for successful applications in Southeast Asia including: 1) readily accessible technology – hardware and software, 2) readily available data to input and calibrate the model, 3) the need (i.e. governments requiring assessment of water supply, water quality and climate change), and 4) local support and a critical mass of scientists working in the region. All of these pieces are now in place and the International SWAT Conference held in Chiang Mai in January 2009 is a critical step in the successful application of SWAT and other ecohydrological models in Southeast Asia.

In gathering the works from many years and from many scientists to be in a book, several persons have been involved in it, for which we recognize and appreciate their important role. We thank several specialists who had worked with the models and other accessory programs for allowing us to put in the DVD that accompanies the book. The long and continued service of Katherine Suda of the Biological Engineering Program, North Carolina A&T State University, has been instrumental in acquiring all these essential digital stuffs that are the heart of SWAT - therefore we are very grateful to her for that. Last, but not least, we acknowledge the kind cooperation from various publishers of scientific journals in permitting us to use most papers in this volume that had first appeared in their publications, without which this book would not have been produced. We appreciate the World Association of Soil and Water Conservation for accepting to put various SWAT stuffs together within one cover as WASWC Special Publication No. 4 and within a short time. This is considered an important milestone of the SWAT endeavor, i.e. in distributing the publication as a low-cost part of the assessment tool to be used for managing and conserving land, soil and water in many parts of the world.

Lastly, it would have been hard to accomplish all these things had we not received the grant from the United States Agency for International Development (USAID) for the Sustainable Agriculture and Natural Resources Management Collaborative Research Support Program (SANREM CRSP, with Dr. Theo A. Dillaha as its Director) to Virginia Polytechnic Institute and State University (Virginia Tech), which we have our high appreciation for.


The Editors

December 2008

# Contents

## PART 1. Overview of SWAT

## PART 2. Worldwide Applications of SWAT

# Part 1
# Overview of SWAT

# 1.1 Overview of
# Soil and Water Assessment Tool (SWAT) Model

## Susan L. Neitsch, Jeff G. Arnold[*], James R. Kiniry and James R. Williams

## Preamble

**SWAT** is the acronym for **S**oil and **W**ater **A**ssessment **T**ool, a river basin, or watershed, scale model developed by Dr. Jeff Arnold for the USDA Agricultural Research Service (ARS). SWAT was developed to predict the impact of land management practices on water, sediment and agricultural chemical yields in large complex watersheds with varying soils, land use and management conditions over long periods of time. To satisfy this objective, the model

Is physically based. Rather than incorporating regression equations to describe the relationship between input and output variables, SWAT requires specific information about weather, soil properties, topography, vegetation, and land management practices occurring in the watershed. The physical processes associated with water movement, sediment movement, crop growth, nutrient cycling, etc. are directly modeled by SWAT using this input data.

> Benefits of this approach are:
> • watersheds with no monitoring data (e.g. stream gage data) can be modeled
> • the relative impact of alternative input data (e.g. changes in management practices, climate, vegetation, etc.) on water quality or other variables of interest can be quantified

uses readily available inputs. While SWAT can be used to study more specialized processes such as bacteria transport, the minimum data required to make a run are commonly available from government agencies.

is computationally efficient. Simulation of very large basins or a variety of management strategies can be performed without excessive investment of time or money.

*Corresponding author: Agricultural Engineer, USDA-ARS Grassland, Soil and Water Research Laboratory, Temple, Texas, U.S.A. jgarnold@spa.ars.usda.gov *(Continued on next page)*

3

enables users to study long-term impacts. Many of the problems currently addressed by users involve the gradual buildup of pollutants and the impact on downstream water bodies. To study these types of problems, results are needed from runs with output spanning several decades.

SWAT is a continuous time model, i.e. a long-term yield model. *The model is not designed to simulate detailed, single-event flood routing.*

# 1. Development of SWAT

SWAT incorporates features of several ARS models and is a direct outgrowth of the SWRRB[1] model (Simulator for Water Resources in Rural Basins) (Williams et al., 1985; Arnold et al., 1990).

Specific models that contributed significantly to the development of SWAT were CREAMS[2] (Chemicals, Runoff, and Erosion from Agricultural Management Systems) (Knisel, 1980), GLEAMS[3] (Groundwater Loading Effects on Agricultural Management Systems) (Leonard et al., 1987), and EPIC[4] (Erosion-Productivity Impact Calculator) (Williams et al., 1984).

Development of SWRRB began with modification of the daily rainfall hydrology model from CREAMS. The major changes made to the CREAMS hydrology model were: a) the model was expanded to allow simultaneous computations on several subbasins to predict basin water yield; b) a groundwater or return flow component was added; c) a reservoir storage component was added to calculate the effect of farm ponds and reservoirs on water and sediment yield; d) a weather simulation model incorporating data for rainfall, solar radiation, and temperature was added to facilitate long-term simulations and provide temporally and spatially representative weather; e) the method for predicting the peak runoff rates was improved; f) the EPIC crop growth model was added to account for annual variation in growth; g) a simple flood routing component was added; h) sediment transport components were added to simulate sediment movement through ponds, reservoirs, streams and valleys; and i) calculation of transmission losses was incorporated.

---

[1]SWRRB is a continuous time step model that was developed to simulate non-point source loadings from watersheds.
[2]In response to the Clean Water Act, ARS assembled a team of interdisciplinary scientists from across the U.S. to develop a process-based, non-point source simulation model in the early 1970s. From that effort CREAMS was developed. CREAMS is a field-scale model designed to simulate the impact of land management on water, sediment, nutrients and pesticides leaving the edge of the field. A number of other ARS models such as GLEAMS, EPIC, SWRRB and AGNPS trace their origins to the CREAMS model.
[3]GLEAMS is a non-point source model which focuses on pesticide and nutrient groundwater loadings.
[4]EPIC was originally developed to simulate the impact of erosion on crop productivity and has now evolved into a comprehensive agricultural management, field scale, non-point source loading model.

4

The primary focus of model use in the late 1980s was water quality assessment and development of SWRRB reflected this emphasis. Notable modifications of SWRRB at this time included incorporation of: a) the GLEAMS pesticide fate component; b) optional SCS technology for estimating peak runoff rates; and c) newly developed sediment yield equations. These modifications extended the model's capability to deal with a wide variety of watershed management problems.

In the late 1980s, the Bureau of Indian Affairs needed a model to estimate the downstream impact of water management within Indian reservation lands in Arizona and New Mexico. While SWRRB was easily utilized for watersheds up to a few hundred sq km in size, the Bureau also wanted to simulate streamflow for basins extending over several thousand sq km. For an area this extensive, the watershed under study needed to be divided into several hundred subbasins.

Watershed division in SWRRB was limited to ten subbasins and the model routed water and sediment transported out of the subbasins directly to the watershed outlet. These limitations led to the development of a model called ROTO (Routing Outputs to Outlet) (Arnold et al., 1995), which took output from multiple SWRRB runs and routed the flows through channels and reservoirs. ROTO provided a reach routing approach and overcame the SWRRB subbasin limitation by 'linking' multiple SWRRB runs together. Although this approach was effective, the input and output of multiple SWRRB files was cumbersome and required considerable computer storage. In addition, all SWRRB runs had to be made independently and then input to ROTO for the channel and reservoir routing. To overcome the awkwardness of this arrangement, SWRRB and ROTO were merged into a single model, SWAT. While allowing simulations of very extensive areas, SWAT retained all the features that made SWRRB such a valuable simulation model.

Since SWAT was created in the early 1990s, it has undergone continued review and expansion of capabilities. The most significant improvements of the model between releases include:

SWAT94.2: Multiple hydrologic response units (HRUs) incorporated.

SWAT96.2: Auto-fertilization and auto-irrigation added as management options; canopy storage of water incorporated; a $CO_2$ component added to crop growth model for climatic change studies; Penman-Monteith potential evapotranspiration equation added; lateral flow of water in the soil based on kinematic storage model incorporated; in-stream nutrient water quality equations from QUAL2E added; in-stream pesticide routing.

SWAT98.1: Snow melt routines improved; in-stream water quality improved; nutrient cycling routines expanded; grazing, manure applications, and tile flow drainage added as management options; model modified for use in Southern Hemisphere.

SWAT99.2: Nutrient cycling routines improved, rice/wetland routines improved, reservoir/pond/wetland nutrient removal by settling added; bank storage of water in reach added; routing of metals through reach added; all year references in model changed from last 2 digits of year to 4-digit year; urban build up/ wash off equations from SWMM added along with regression equations from USGS.

SWAT2000: Bacteria transport routines added; Green & Ampt infiltration added; weather generator improved; allow daily solar radiation, relative humidity, and wind speed to be read in or generated; allow potential ET values for watershed to be read in or calculated; all potential ET methods reviewed; elevation band processes improved; enabled simulation of unlimited number of reservoirs; Muskingum routing method added; modified dormancy calculations for proper simulation in tropical areas.

SWAT2005: Bacteria transport routines improved; weather forecast scenarios added; subdaily precipitation generator added; the retention parameter used in the daily CN calculation may be a function of soil water content or plant evapotranspiration

In addition to the changes listed above, interfaces for the model have been developed in Windows (Visual Basic), GRASS, and ArcView. SWAT has also undergone extensive validation.

## 2. Overview of SWAT

SWAT allows a number of different physical processes to be simulated in a watershed. These processes will be briefly summarized in this section. For more detailed discussions of the various procedures, please consult the chapter devoted to the topic of interest.

For modeling purposes, a watershed may be partitioned into a number of subwatersheds or subbasins. The use of subbasins in a simulation is particularly beneficial when different areas of the watershed are dominated by land uses or soils dissimilar enough in properties to impact hydrology. By partitioning the watershed into subbasins, the user is able to reference different areas of the watershed to one another spatially. Figure 2 shows a subbasin delineation for the watershed shown in Figure 1.

Input information for each subbasin is grouped or organized into the following categories: climate; hydrologic response units or HRUs; ponds/wetlands; groundwater; and the main channel, or reach, draining the subbasin. Hydrologic response units are lumped land areas within the subbasin that are comprised of unique land cover, soil, and management combinations.

No matter what type of problem studied with SWAT, water balance is the driving force behind everything that happens in the watershed. To accurately predict the movement of pesticides, sediments or nutrients, the hydrologic cycle as simulated by the model must conform to what is happening in the watershed.

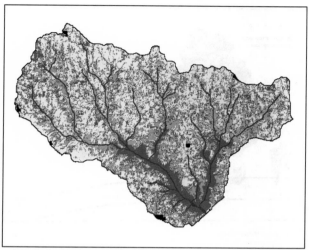

**Figure 1.** Map of the Lake Fork watershed in northeast Texas showing the land use distribution and stream network.

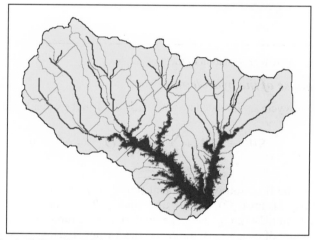

**Figure 2.** Subbasin delineation of the Lake Fork watershed.

Simulation of the hydrology of a watershed can be separated into two major divisions. The first division is the land phase of the hydrologic cycle, depicted in Figure 3. The land phase of the hydrologic cycle controls the amount of water, sediment, nutrient and pesticide loadings to the main channel in each subbasin. The second division is the water or routing phase of the hydrologic cycle which can be defined as the movement of water, sediments, etc. through the channel network of the watershed to the outlet.

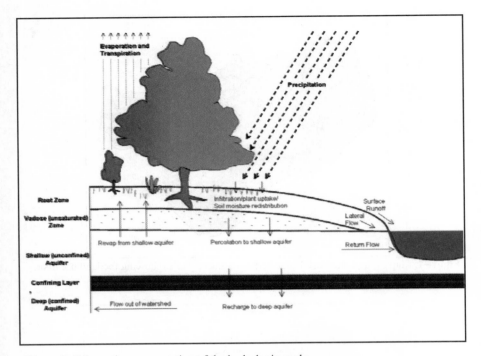

**Figure 3.** Schematic representation of the hydrologic cycle.

## 2.1 Land phase of the hydrologic cycle

The hydrologic cycle as simulated by SWAT is based on the water balance equation:

$$SW_t = SW_0 + \sum_{i=1}^{t} (R_{day} - Q_{surf} - E_a - w_{seep} - Q_{gw})$$

where $SW_t$ is the final soil water content (mm $H_2O$), $SW_0$ is the initial soil water content on day $i$ (mm $H_2O$), $t$ is the time (days), $R_{day}$ is the amount of precipitation on day $i$ (mm $H_2O$), $Q_{surf}$ is the amount of surface runoff on day $i$ (mm $H_2O$), $E_a$ is the amount of evapotranspiration on day $i$ (mm $H_2O$), $w_{seep}$ is the amount of water entering the vadose zone from the soil profile on day $i$ (mm $H_2O$), and $Q_{gw}$ is the amount of return flow on day $i$ (mm $H_2O$).

The subdivision of the watershed enables the model to reflect differences in evapotranspiration for various crops and soils. Runoff is predicted separately for each HRU and routed to obtain the total runoff for the watershed. This increases accuracy and gives a much better physical description of the water balance.

Figure 4 shows the general sequence of processes used by SWAT to model the land phase of the hydrologic cycle. The different inputs and processes involved in this phase of the hydrologic cycle are summarized in the following sections.

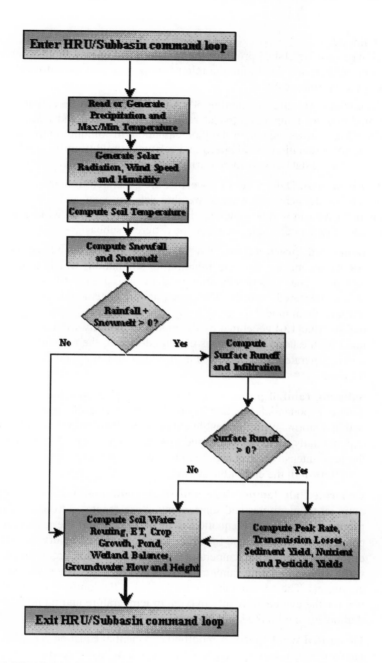

**Figure 4.** HRU/Subbasin command loop.

## 2.1.1 Climate

The climate of a watershed provides the moisture and energy inputs that control the water balance and determine the relative importance of the different components of the hydrologic cycle.

The climatic variables required by SWAT consist of daily precipitation, maximum/minimum air temperature, solar radiation, wind speed and relative humidity. The model allows values for daily precipitation, maximum/minimum air temperatures, solar radiation, wind speed and relative humidity to be input from records of observed data or generated during the simulation.

*Weather generator.* Daily values for weather are generated from average monthly values. The model generates a set of weather data for each subbasin. The values for any one subbasin will be generated independently and there will be no spatial correlation of generated values between the different subbasins.

**Generated precipitation.** SWAT uses a model developed by Nicks (1974) to generate daily precipitation for simulations which do not read in measured data. This precipitation model is also used to fill in missing data in the measured records. The precipitation generator uses a first-order Markov chain model to define a day as wet or dry by comparing a random number (0.0-1.0) generated by the model to monthly wet-dry probabilities input by the user. If the day is classified as wet, the amount of precipitation is generated from a skewed distribution or a modified exponential distribution.

**Subdaily rainfall patterns.** If subdaily precipitation values are needed, a double exponential function is used to represent the intensity patterns within a storm. With the double exponential distribution, rainfall intensity exponentially increases with time to a maximum, or peak, intensity. Once the peak intensity is reached, the rainfall intensity exponentially decreases with time until the end of the storm.

**Generated air temperature and solar radiation.** Maximum and minimum air temperatures and solar radiation are generated from a normal distribution. A continuity equation is incorporated into the generator to account for temperature and radiation variations caused by dry vs. rainy conditions. Maximum air temperature and solar radiation are adjusted downward when simulating rainy conditions and upwards when simulating dry conditions. The adjustments are made so that the long-term generated values for the average monthly maximum temperature and monthly solar radiation agree with the input averages.

**Generated wind speed.** A modified exponential equation is used to generate daily mean wind speed given the mean monthly wind speed.

**Generated relative humidity.** The relative humidity model uses a triangular distribution to simulate the daily average relative humidity from the monthly average. As with temperature and radiation, the mean daily relative humidity is adjusted to account for wet- and dry-day effects.

*Snow.* SWAT classifies precipitation as rain or freezing rain/snow using the average daily temperature.

**Snow cover.** The snow cover component of SWAT has been updated from a simple, uniform snow cover model to a more complex model which allows non-uniform cover due to shading, drifting, topography and land cover. The user defines a threshold snow depth above which snow coverage will always extend over 100% of the area. As the snow depth in a subbasin decreases below this value, the snow coverage is allowed to decline non-linearly based on an areal depletion curve.

**Snow melt.** Snow melt is controlled by the air and snow pack temperature, the melting rate, and the areal coverage of snow. If snow is present, it is melted on days when the maximum temperature exceeds 0°C using a linear function of the difference between the average snow pack-maximum air temperature and the base or threshold temperature for snow melt. Melted snow is treated the same as rainfall for estimating runoff and percolation. For snow melt, rainfall energy is set to zero and the peak runoff rate is estimated assuming uniformly melted snow for a 24 hour duration.

**Elevation bands.** The model allows the subbasin to be split into a maximum of ten elevation bands. Snow cover and snow melt are simulated separately for each elevation band. By dividing the subbasin into elevation bands, the model is able to assess the differences in snow cover and snow melt caused by orographic variation in precipitation and temperature.

*Soil temperature.* Soil temperature impacts water movement and the decay rate of residue in the soil. Daily average soil temperature is calculated at the soil surface and the center of each soil layer. The temperature of the soil surface is a function of snow cover, plant cover and residue cover, the bare soil surface temperature, and the previous day's soil surface temperature. The temperature of a soil layer is a function of the surface temperature, mean annual air temperature and the depth in the soil at which variation in temperature due to changes in climatic conditions no longer occurs. This depth, referred to as the damping depth, is dependent upon the bulk density and the soil water content.

## 2.1.2 Hydrology

As precipitation descends, it may be intercepted and held in the vegetation canopy or fall to the soil surface. Water on the soil surface will infiltrate into the soil profile or flow overland as runoff. Runoff moves relatively quickly toward a stream channel and contributes to short-term stream response. Infiltrated water may be held in the soil and later evapotranspired or it may slowly make its way to the surface-water system via underground paths. The potential pathways of water

11

movement simulated by SWAT in the HRU are illustrated in Figure 5.

***Canopy storage.*** Canopy storage is the water intercepted by vegetative surfaces (the canopy) where it is held and made available for evaporation. When using the curve number method to compute surface runoff, canopy storage is taken into account in the surface runoff calculations. However, if methods such as Green &

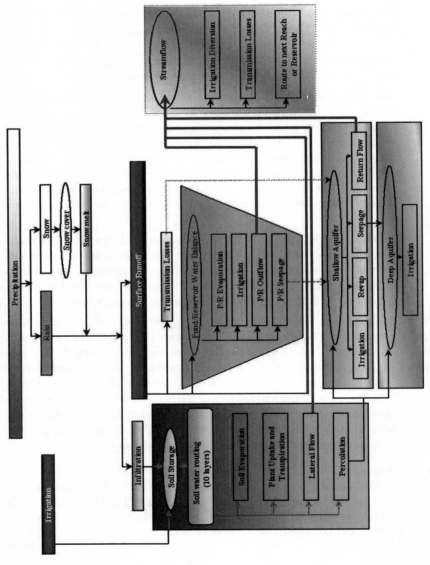

**Figure 5.** Schematics of pathways available for water movement in SWAT.

Ampt are used to model infiltration and runoff, canopy storage must be modeled separately. SWAT allows the user to input the maximum amount of water that can be stored in the canopy at the maximum leaf area index for the land cover. This value and the leaf area index are used by the model to compute the maximum storage at any time in the growth cycle of the land cover/crop. When evaporation is computed, water is first removed from canopy storage.

*Infiltration.* Infiltration refers to the entry of water into a soil profile from the soil surface. As infiltration continues, the soil becomes increasingly wet, causing the rate of infiltration to decrease with time until it reaches a steady value. The initial rate of infiltration depends on the moisture content of the soil prior to the introduction of water at the soil surface. The final rate of infiltration is equivalent to the saturated hydraulic conductivity of the soil. Because the curve number method used to calculate surface runoff operates on a daily time-step, it is unable to directly model infiltration. The amount of water entering the soil profile is calculated as the difference between the amount of rainfall and the amount of surface runoff. The Green & Ampt infiltration method does directly model infiltration, but it requires precipitation data in smaller time increments.

*Redistribution.* Redistribution refers to the continued movement of water through a soil profile after input of water (via precipitation or irrigation) has ceased at the soil surface. Redistribution is caused by differences in water content in the profile. Once the water content throughout the entire profile is uniform, redistribution will cease. The redistribution component of SWAT uses a storage routing technique to predict flow through each soil layer in the root zone. Downward flow, or percolation, occurs when field capacity of a soil layer is exceeded and the layer below is not saturated. The flow rate is governed by the saturated conductivity of the soil layer. Redistribution is affected by soil temperature. If the temperature in a particular layer is 0°C or below, no redistribution is allowed from that layer.

*Evapotranspiration.* Evapotranspiration is a collective term for all processes by which water in the liquid or solid phase at or near the earth's surface becomes atmospheric water vapor. Evapotranspiration includes evaporation from rivers and lakes, bare soil, and vegetative surfaces; evaporation from within the leaves of plants (transpiration); and sublimation from ice and snow surfaces. The model computes evaporation from soils and plants separately as described by Ritchie (1972). Potential soil water evaporation is estimated as a function of potential evapotranspiration and leaf area index (area of plant leaves relative to the area of the HRU). Actual soil water evaporation is estimated by using exponential functions of soil depth and water content. Plant transpiration is simulated as a linear function of potential evapotranspiration and leaf area index.

**Potential evapotranspiration.** Potential evapotranspiration is the rate at which evapotranspiration would occur from a large area completely and uniformly covered with growing vegetation that has access to an unlimited supply of soil water. This rate is assumed to be unaffected by micro-climatic processes such as advection or heat-storage effects. The model offers three options for estimating potential evapotranspiration: Hargreaves (Hargreaves et al., 1985), Priestley-Taylor (Priestley and Taylor, 1972), and Penman-Monteith (Monteith, 1965).

*Lateral subsurface flow.* Lateral subsurface flow, or interflow, is streamflow contribution that originates below the surface but above the zone where rocks are saturated with water. Lateral subsurface flow in the soil profile (0-2 m) is calculated simultaneously with redistribution. A kinematic storage model is used to predict lateral flow in each soil layer. The model accounts for variation in conductivity, slope and soil water content.

*Surface runoff.* Surface runoff, or overland flow, is the flow that occurs along a sloping surface. Using daily or subdaily rainfall amounts, SWAT simulates surface runoff volumes and peak runoff rates for each HRU.

**Surface runoff volume** is computed using a modification of the SCS curve number method (USDA Soil Conservation Service, 1972) or the Green & Ampt infiltration method (Green and Ampt, 1911). In the curve number method, the curve number varies non-linearly with the moisture content of the soil. The curve number drops as the soil approaches the wilting point and increases to near 100 as the soil approaches saturation. The Green & Ampt method requires subdaily precipitation data and calculates infiltration as a function of the wetting front matric potential and effective hydraulic conductivity. Water that does not infiltrate becomes surface runoff. SWAT includes a provision for estimating runoff from frozen soil where a soil is defined as frozen if the temperature in the first soil layer is less than 0°C. The model increases runoff for frozen soils but still allows significant infiltration when the frozen soils are dry.

**Peak runoff rate.** Predictions are made with a modification of the rational method. In brief, the rational method is based on the idea that if a rainfall of intensity $i$ begins instantaneously and continues indefinitely, the rate of runoff will increase until the time of concentration, $t_c$, when all of the subbasin is contributing to flow at the outlet. In the modified Rational Formula, the peak runoff rate is a function of the proportion of daily precipitation that falls during the subbasin $t_c$, the daily surface runoff volume, and the subbasin time of concentration. The proportion of rainfall occurring during the subbasin $t_c$ is estimated as a function of total daily rainfall using a stochastic technique. The subbasin time of concentration is estimated using Manning's Formula considering both overland and channel flow.

*Ponds.* Ponds are water storage structures located within a subbasin which intercept surface runoff. The catchment area of a pond is defined as a fraction of the total area of the subbasin. Ponds are assumed to be located off the main channel

14

in a subbasin and will never receive water from upstream subbasins. Pond water storage is a function of pond capacity, daily inflows and outflows, seepage and evaporation. Required inputs are the storage capacity and surface area of the pond when filled to capacity. Surface area below capacity is estimated as a non-linear function of storage.

*Tributary channels.* Two types of channels are defined within a subbasin: the main channel and tributary channels. Tributary channels are minor or lower order channels branching off the main channel within the subbasin. Each tributary channel within a subbasin drains only a portion of the subbasin and does not receive groundwater contribution to its flow. All flow in the tributary channels is released and routed through the main channel of the subbasin. SWAT uses the attributes of tributary channels to determine the time of concentration for the subbasin.

**Transmission losses** are losses of surface flow via leaching through the streambed. This type of loss occurs in ephemeral or intermittent streams where groundwater contribution occurs only at certain times of the year, or not at all. SWAT uses Lane's method described in Chapter 19 of the SCS Hydrology Handbook (USDA Soil Conservation Service, 1983) to estimate transmission losses. Water losses from the channel are a function of channel width and length and flow duration. Both runoff volume and peak rate are adjusted when transmission losses occur in tributary channels.

*Return flow.* Return flow, or base flow, is the volume of streamflow originating from groundwater. SWAT partitions groundwater into two aquifer systems: a shallow, unconfined aquifer that contributes return flow to streams within the watershed and a deep, confined aquifer that contributes return flow to streams outside the watershed (Arnold et al., 1993). Water percolating past the bottom of the root zone is partitioned into two fractions - each fraction becomes recharge for one of the aquifers. In addition to return flow, water stored in the shallow aquifer may replenish moisture in the soil profile in very dry conditions or be directly removed by plant. Water in the shallow or deep aquifer may be removed by pumping.

### 2.1.3 Land cover/plant growth

SWAT utilizes a single plant growth model to simulate all types of land covers. The model is able to differentiate between annual and perennial plants. Annual plants grow from the planting date to the harvest date or until the accumulated heat units equal the potential heat units for the plant. Perennial plants maintain their root systems throughout the year, becoming dormant in the winter months. They resume growth when the average daily air temperature exceeds the minimum, or base, temperature required. The plant growth model is used to assess removal of water and nutrients from the root zone, transpiration, and biomass/yield production.

*Potential growth.* The potential increase in plant biomass on a given day is defined as the increase in biomass under ideal growing conditions. The potential increase in biomass for a day is a function of intercepted energy and the plant's efficiency in converting energy to biomass. Energy interception is estimated as a function of solar radiation and the plant's leaf area index.

*Potential and actual transpiration.* The process used to calculate potential plant transpiration is described in the section on evapotranspiration. Actual transpiration is a function of potential transpiration and soil water availability.

*Nutrient uptake.* Plant use of nitrogen and phosphorus are estimated with a supply and demand approach where the daily plant nitrogen and phosphorus demands are calculated as the difference between the actual concentration of the element in the plant and the optimal concentration. The optimal concentration of the elements varies with growth stage as described by Jones (1983).

*Growth contraints.* Potential plant growth and yield are usually not achieved due to constraints imposed by the environment. The model estimates stresses caused by water, nutrients and temperature.

### 2.1.4 Erosion
Erosion and sediment yield are estimated for each HRU with the Modified Universal Soil Loss Equation (MUSLE) (Williams, 1975). While the USLE uses rainfall as an indicator of erosive energy, MUSLE uses the amount of runoff to simulate erosion and sediment yield. The substitution results in a number of benefits: the prediction accuracy of the model is increased, the need for a delivery ratio is eliminated, and single storm estimates of sediment yields can be calculated. The hydrology model supplies estimates of runoff volume and peak runoff rate which, with the subbasin area, are used to calculate the runoff erosive energy variable. The crop management factor is recalculated every day that runoff occurs. It is a function of aboveground biomass, residue on the soil surface, and the minimum C factor for the plant. Other factors of the erosion equation are evaluated as described by Wischmeier and Smith (1978).

### 2.1.5 Nutrients
SWAT tracks the movement and transformation of several forms of nitrogen and phosphorus in the watershed. In the soil, transformation of nitrogen from one form to another is governed by the nitrogen cycle as depicted in Figure 6. The transformation of phosphorus in the soil is controlled by the phosphorus cycle shown in Figure 7. Nutrients may be introduced to the main channel and transported downstream through surface runoff and lateral subsurface flow.

*Nitrogen.* The different processes modeled by SWAT in the HRUs and the various pools of nitrogen in the soil are depicted in Figure 6. Plant use of nitrogen is estimated using the supply and demand approach described in the section on plant growth. In addition to plant use, nitrate and organic N may be removed from the soil via mass flow of water. Amounts of $NO_3$-N contained in runoff, lateral flow and percolation are estimated as products of the volume of water and the average

16

## NITROGEN

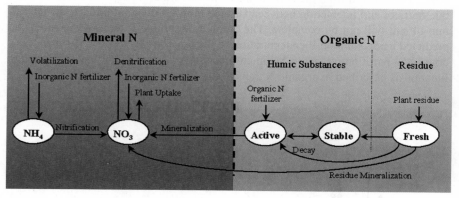

**Figure 6.** Partitioning of ntrogen in SWAT.

## PHOSPHORUS

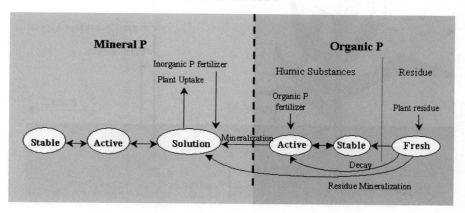

**Figure 7.** Partitioning of phosphorus in SWAT.

concentration of nitrate in the layer. Organic N transport with sediment is calculated with a loading function developed by McElroy et al. (1976) and modified by Williams and Hann (1978) for application to individual runoff events. The loading function estimates the daily organic N runoff loss based on the concentration of organic N in the top soil layer, the sediment yield, and the enrichment ratio. The enrichment ratio is the concentration of organic N in the sediment divided by that in the soil.

*Phosphorus.* The different processes modeled by SWAT in the HRUs and the various pools of phosphorus in the soil are depicted in Figure 7. Plant use of phosphorus is estimated using the supply and demand approach described in the

17

section on plant growth. In addition to plant use, soluble phosphorus and organic P may be removed from the soil via mass flow of water. Phosphorus is not a mobile nutrient and interaction between surface runoff with solution P in the top 10 mm of soil will not be complete. The amount of soluble P removed in runoff is predicted using solution P concentration in the top 10 mm of soil, the runoff volume and a partitioning factor. Sediment transport of P is simulated with a loading function as described in organic N transport.

# PESTICIDES

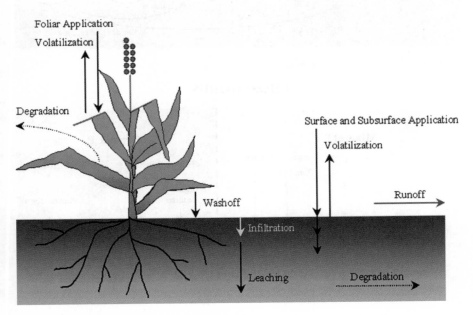

**Figure 8.** Pesticide fate and transport in SWAT.

## 2.1.6 Pesticides

Although SWAT does not simulate stress on the growth of a plant due to the presence of weeds, damaging insects, and other pests, pesticides may be applied to an HRU to study the movement of the chemical in the watershed. SWAT simulates pesticide movement into the stream network via surface runoff (in solution and sorbed to sediment transported by the runoff), and into the soil profile and aquifer by percolation (in solution). The equations used to model the movement of pesticide in the land phase of the hydrologic cycle were adopted from GLEAMS (Leonard et al., 1987). The movement of the pesticide is controlled by its solubility, degradation half-life, and soil organic carbon adsorption coefficient. Pesticide

18

on plant foliage and in the soil degrade exponentially according to the appropriate half-life. Pesticide transport by water and sediment is calculated for each runoff event and pesticide leaching is estimated for each soil layer when percolation occurs.

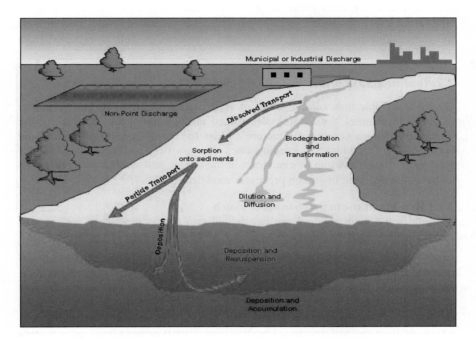

**Figure 9.** In-stream processes modeled by SWAT.

### 2.1.7 Management

SWAT allows the user to define management practices taking place in every HRU. The user may define the beginning and the ending of the growing season, specify timing and amounts of fertilizer, pesticide and irrigation applications as well as timing of tillage operations. At the end of the growing season, the bio-mass may be removed from the HRU as yield or placed on the surface as residue.

In addition to these basic management practices, operations such as grazing, automated fertilizer and water applications, and incorporation of every conceivable management option for water use are available. The latest improvement to land management is the incorporation of routines to calculate sediment and nutrient loadings from urban areas.

***Rotations.*** The dictionary defines a rotation as the growing of different crops in succession in one field, usually in a regular sequence. A rotation in SWAT refers to a change in management practices from one year to the next. There is no limit to the number of years of different management operations specified in a rotation.

SWAT also does not limit the number of land cover/crops grown within one year in the HRU. However, only one land cover can be growing at any one time.

*Water use.* The two most typical uses of water are for application to agricultural lands or use as a town's water supply. SWAT allows water to be applied on an HRU from any water source within or outside the watershed. Water may also be transferred between reservoirs, reaches and subbasins as well as exported from the watershed.

## 2.2 Routing phase of the hydrologic cycle

Once SWAT determines the loadings of water, sediment, nutrients and pesticides to the main channel, the loadings are routed through the stream network of the watershed using a command structure similar to that of HYMO (Williams and Hann, 1972). In addition to keeping track of mass flow in the channel, SWAT models the transformation of chemicals in the stream and streambed. Figure 9 illustrates the different in-stream processes modeled by SWAT.

### 2.2.1 Routing in the main channel or reach

Routing in the main channel can be divided into four components: water, sediment, nutrients and organic chemicals.

*Flood routing.* As water flows downstream, a portion may be lost due to evaporation and transmission through the bed of the channel. Another potential loss is removal of water from the channel for agricultural or human use. Flow may be supplemented by the fall of rain directly on the channel and/or addition of water from point source discharges. Flow is routed through the channel using a variable storage coefficient method developed by Williams (1969) or the Muskingum routing method.

*Sediment routing.* The transport of sediment in the channel is controlled by the simultaneous operation of two processes, deposition and degradation. Previous versions of SWAT used stream power to estimate deposition/degradation in the channels (Arnold et al., 1995). Bagnold (1977) defined stream power as the product of water density, flow rate and water surface slope. Williams (1980) used Bagnold's definition of stream power to develop a method for determining degradation as a function of channel slope and velocity. In this version of SWAT, the equations have been simplified and the maximum amount of sediment that can be transported from a reach segment is a function of the peak channel velocity. Available stream power is used to re-entrain loose and deposited material until all of the material is removed. Excess stream power causes bed degradation. Bed degradation is adjusted for stream bed erodibility and cover.

*Nutrient routing.* Nutrient transformations in the stream are controlled by the instream water quality component of the model. The in-stream kinetics used in SWAT for nutrient routing are adapted from QUAL2E (Brown and Barnwell, 1987). The model tracks nutrients dissolved in the stream and nutrients adsorbed to the sediment. Dissolved nutrients are transported with the water while those sorbed to sediments are allowed to be deposited with the sediment on the bed of the channel.

*Channel pesticide routing.* While an unlimited number of pesticides may be applied to the HRUs, only one pesticide may be routed through the channel network of the watershed due to the complexity of the processes simulated. As with the nutrients, the total pesticide load in the channel is partitioned into dissolved and sediment-attached components. While the dissolved pesticide is transported with water, the pesticide attached to sediment is affected by sediment transport and deposition processes. Pesticide transformations in the dissolved and sorbed phases are governed by first-order decay relationships. The major in-stream processes simulated by the model are settling, burial, re-suspension, volatilization, diffusion and transformation.

## 2.2.2 Routing in the reservoir
The water balance for reservoirs includes inflow, outflow, rainfall on the surface, evaporation, seepage from the reservoir bottom and diversions.

*Reservoir outflow.* The model offers three alternatives for estimating outflow from the reservoir. The first option allows the user to input measured outflow. The second option, designed for small, uncontrolled reservoirs, requires the users to specify a water release rate. When the reservoir volume exceeds the principal storage, the extra water is released at the specified rate. Volume exceeding the emergency spillway is released within one day. The third option, designed for larger, managed reservoirs, has the user specify monthly target volumes for the reservoir.

*Sediment routing.* Sediment inflow may originate from transport through the upstream reaches or from surface runoff within the subbasin. The concentration of sediment in the reservoir is estimated using a simple continuity equation based on volume and concentration of inflow, outflow, and water retained in the reservoir. Settling of sediment in the reservoir is governed by an equilibrium sediment concentration and the median sediment particle size. The amount of sediment in the reservoir outflow is the product of the volume of water flowing out of the reservoir and the suspended sediment concentration in the reservoir at the time of release.

*Reservoir nutrients.* A simple model for nitrogen and phosphorus mass balance was taken from Chapra (1997). The model assumes: 1) the lake is completely mixed; 2) phosphorus is the limiting nutrient; and, 3) total phosphorus is a measure of the lake trophic status. The first assumption ignores lake stratification and intensification of phytoplankton in the epilimnon. The second assumption is generally valid when non-point sources dominate and the third assumption implies that a relationship exists between total phosphorus and biomass. The phosphorus mass balance equation includes the concentration in the lake, inflow, outflow and overall loss rate.

*Reservoir pesticides.* The lake pesticide balance model is taken from Chapra (1997) and assumes well mixed conditions. The system is partitioned into a well mixed surface water layer underlain by a well mixed sediment layer. The pesticide is partitioned into dissolved and particulate phases in both the water and sediment layers. The major processes simulated by the model are loading, outflow, transformation, volatilization, settling, diffusion, re-suspension and burial.

# References

Arnold, J.G., J.R. Williams, A.D. Nicks, and N.B. Sammons. 1990. SWRRB: A basin scale simulation model for soil and water resources management. Texas A&M Univ. Press, College Station, TX.

Arnold, J.G., P.M. Allen, and G. Bernhardt. 1993. A comprehensive surface-groundwater flow model. J. Hydrol. 142:47-69.

Arnold, J.G., J.R. Williams and D.R. Maidment. 1995. Continuous-time water and sediment-routing model for large basins. Journal of Hydraulic Engineering 121(2):171-183.

Bagnold, R.A. 1977. Bedload transport in natural rivers. Water Resources Res. 13(2):303-312.

Brown, L.C. and T.O. Barnwell, Jr. 1987. The enhanced water quality models QUAL2E and QUAL2E-UNCAS documentation and user manual. EPA document EPA/600/3-87/007. USEPA, Athens, GA.

Chapra, S.C. 1997. Surface water-quality modeling. McGraw-Hill, Boston.

Green, W.H. and G.A. Ampt. 1911. Studies on soil physics, 1. The flow of air and water through soils. Journal of Agricultural Sciences 4:11-24.

Hargreaves, G.L., G.H. Hargreaves, and J.P. Riley. 1985. Agricultural benefits for Senegal River Basin. J. Irrig. and Drain. Engr. 111(2):113-124.

Jones, C.A. 1983. A survey of the variability in tissue nitrogen and phosphorus concentrations in maize and grain sorghum. Field Crops Res. 6:133-147.

Knisel, W.G. 1980. CREAMS, a field scale model for chemicals, runoff and erosion from agricultural management systems. USDA Conservation Research Rept. No. 26.

Leonard, R.A. and R.D. Wauchope. 1980. Chapter 5: The pesticide submodel. p. 88-112. *In* Knisel, W.G. (ed). CREAMS: A field-scale model for chemicals, runoff, and erosion from agricultural management systems. U.S. Department of Agriculture, Conservation research report no. 26.

Leonard, R.A., W.G. Knisel, and D.A. Still. 1987. GLEAMS: Groundwater loading effects on agricultural management systems. Trans. ASAE 30(5):1403-1428.

McElroy, A.D., S.Y. Chiu, J.W. Nebgen, A. Aleti, and F.W. Bennett. 1976. Loading functions for assessment of water pollution from nonpoint sources. EPA document EPA 600/2-76-151. USEPA, Athens, GA.

Monteith, J.L. 1965. Evaporation and the environment. p. 205-234. *In* The state and movement of water in living organisms. 19th Symposia of the Society for Experimental Biology. Cambridge Univ. Press, London, U.K.

Nicks, A.D. 1974. Stochastic generation of the occurrence, pattern and location of maximum amount of daily rainfall. p. 154-171. *In* Proc. Symp. Statistical Hydrology, Tucson, AZ. Aug.-Sept. 1971. USDA Misc. Publ. 1275. U.S. Gov. Print. Office, Washington, DC.

Priestley, C.H.B. and R.J. Taylor. 1972. On the assessment of surface heat flux and evaporation using large-scale parameters. Mon. Weather Rev. 100:81-92.

**Ritchie, J.T. 1972.** A model for predicting evaporation from a row crop with incomplete cover. Water Resour. Res. 8:1204-1213.

**USDA Soil Conservation Service. 1972.** National Engineering Handbook Section 4 Hydrology, Chapters 4-10.

**USDA Soil Conservation Service. 1983.** National Engineering Handbook Section 4 Hydrology, Chapter 19.

**Williams, J.R. 1969.** Flood routing with variable travel time or variable storage coefficients. Trans. ASAE 12(1):100-103.

**Williams, J.R. 1980.** SPNM, a model for predicting sediment, phosphorus, and nitrogen yields from agricultural basins. Water Resour. Bull. 16(5):843-848.

Williams, J.R. 1975. Sediment routing for agricultural watersheds. Water Resour. Bull. 11 (5):965-974.

**Williams, J.R. and R.W. Hann. 1978.** Optimal operation of large agricultural watersheds with water quality constraints. Texas Water Resources Institute, Texas A&M Univ., Tech. Rept. No. 96.

**Williams, J.R. and R.W. Hann. 1972.** HYMO, a problem-oriented computer language for building hydrologic models. Water Resour. Res. 8(1):79-85.

**Williams, J.R., C.A. Jones and P.T. Dyke. 1984.** A modeling approach to determining the relationship between erosion and soil productivity. Trans. ASAE 27(1):129-144.

**Williams, J.R., A.D. Nicks, and J.G. Arnold. 1985.** Simulator for water resources in rural basins. Journal of Hydraulic Engineering 111(6): 970-986.

**Wischmeier, W.H., and D.D. Smith. 1978.** Predicting rainfall losses: A guide to conservation planning. USDA Agricultural Handbook No. 537. U.S. Gov. Print. Office, Washington, D.C.

# 1.2 The Soil and Water Assessment Tool: Historical Development, Applications, and Future Research Directions

## Philip W. Gassman[1], Manuel R. Reyes[2], Colleen H. Green[3] and Jeffrey G. Arnold[4]

### Abstract

The Soil and Water Assessment Tool (SWAT) model is a continuation of nearly 30 years of modeling efforts conducted by the USDA Agricultural Research Service (ARS). SWAT has gained international acceptance as a robust interdisciplinary watershed modeling tool as evidenced by international SWAT conferences, hundreds of SWAT-related papers presented at numerous other scientific meetings, and dozens of articles published in peer-reviewed journals. The model has also been adopted as part of the U.S. Environmental Protection Agency (USEPA) Better Assessment Science Integrating Point and Nonpoint Sources (BASINS) software package and is being used by many U.S. federal and state agencies, including the USDA within the Conservation Effects Assessment Project (CEAP). At present, over 250 peer-reviewed published articles have been identified that report SWAT applications, reviews of SWAT components, or other research that includes SWAT. Many of these peer-reviewed articles are summarized here according to relevant application categories such as streamflow calibration and related hydrologic analyses, climate change impacts on hydrology, pollutant load assessments, comparisons with other models, and sensitivity analyses and calibration techniques. Strengths and weaknesses of the model are presented, and recommended research needs for SWAT are also provided.

**Keywords:** Developmental history, flow analysis, modeling, SWAT, water quality

---

[1] 2009 World Association of Soil and Water Conservation, *Soil and Water Assessment Tool (SWAT): Global Applications,* eds. Jeff Arnold, Raghavan Srinivasan, Susan Neitsch, Chris George, Karim Abbaspour, Philip Gassman, Fang Hua Hao, Ann van Griensven, Ashvin Gosain, Patrick Debels, Nam Won Kim, Hiroaki Somura, Victor Ella, Attachai Jintrawet, Manuel Reyes, and Samran Sombatpanit, pp. 25-93. The article has been reprinted from the original paper that appeared in the TRANSACTIONS of the American Society of Agricultural and Biological Engineers (ASABE) 50(4):1211-1250 (2007), and has been reproduced by permission of the ASABE. WASWC is grateful for the permission granted.

[1]Environmental Scientist, Center for Agricultural and Rural Development, Department of Economics, 560A Heady Hall, Iowa State University, Ames, IA 50011-1070, U.S.A.; phone: 515-294-1183; fax: 515-294-6336; pwgassma@iastate.edu
[2]Professor, Biological Engineering Program, Department of Natural Resources and Environmental Design, School of Agriculture and Environmental Sciences, North Carolina A&T State University, Greensboro, North Carolina, U.S.A. mannyreyes@nc.rr.com
[3]Soil Scientist, USDA-ARS Grassland, Soil and Water Research Laboratory, Temple, Texas, U.S.A. chgreen@spa.ars.usda.gov
[4]Agricultural Engineer, USDA-ARS Grassland, Soil and Water Research Laboratory, Temple, Texas, U.S.A. jgarnold@spa.ars.usda.gov

# 1. Introduction

The Soil and Water Assessment Tool (SWAT) model (Arnold et al., 1998; Arnold and Fohrer, 2005) has proven to be an effective tool for assessing water resource and nonpoint-source pollution problems for a wide range of scales and environmental conditions across the globe. In the U.S., SWAT is increasingly being used to support Total Maximum Daily Load (TMDL) analyses (Borah et al., 2006), research the effectiveness of conservation practices within the USDA Conservation Effects Assessment Program (CEAP, 2007) initiative (Mausbach and Dedrick, 2004), perform 'macro-scale assessments' for large regions such as the upper Mississippi River basin and the entire U.S. (e.g. Arnold et al., 1999a; Jha et al., 2006), and a wide range of other water use and water quality applications. Similar SWAT application trends have also emerged in Europe and other regions, as shown by the variety of studies presented in four previous European international SWAT conferences, which are reported for the first conference in a special issue of *Hydrological Processes* (volume 19, issue 3) and proceedings for the second (TWRI, 2003), third (EAWAG, 2005), and fourth (UNESCO-IHE, 2007) conferences.

Reviews of SWAT applications and/or components have been previously reported, sometimes in conjunction with comparisons with other models (e.g. Arnold and Fohrer, 2005; Borah and Bera, 2003, 2004; Shepherd et al., 1999). However, these previous reviews do not provide a comprehensive overview of the complete body of SWAT applications that have been reported in the peer-reviewed literature. There is a need to fill this gap by providing a review of the full range of studies that have been conducted with SWAT and to highlight emerging application trends. Thus, the specific objectives of this study are to: (1) provide an overview of SWAT development history, including the development of GIS interface tools and examples of modified SWAT models; (2) summarize research findings or methods for many of the more than 250 peer-reviewed articles that have been identified in the literature, as a function of different application categories; and (3) describe key strengths and weaknesses of the model and list a summary of future research needs.

# 2. SWAT Developmental History and Overview

The development of SWAT is a continuation of USDA Agricultural Research Service (ARS) modeling experience that spans a period of roughly 30 years. Early origins of SWAT can be traced to previously developed USDA-ARS models (Fig. 1) including the Chemicals, Runoff, and Erosion from Agricultural Management Systems (CREAMS) model (Knisel, 1980), the Groundwater Loading Effects on Agricultural Management Systems (GLEAMS) model (Leonard et al., 1987), and the Environmental Impact Policy Climate (EPIC) model (Izaurralde et al., 2006), which was originally called the Erosion Productivity Impact Calculator (Williams, 1990). The current SWAT model is a direct descendant of the Simulator for Water Resources in Rural Basins (SWRRB) model (Arnold and Williams,

1987), which was designed to simulate management impacts on water and sediment movement for ungaged rural basins across the U.S.

Development of SWRRB began in the early 1980s with modification of the daily rainfall hydrology model from CREAMS. A major enhancement was the expansion of surface runoff and other computations for up to ten subbasins, as opposed to a single field, to predict basin water yield. Other enhancements included an improved peak runoff rate method, calculation of transmission losses, and the addition of several new components: groundwater return flow (Arnold and Allen, 1993), reservoir storage, the EPIC crop growth submodel, a weather generator, and sediment transport. Further modifications of SWRRB in the late 1980s included the incorporation of the GLEAMS pesticide fate component, optional USDA-SCS technology for estimating peak runoff rates, and newly developed sediment yield equations. These modifications extended the model's capability to deal with a wide variety of watershed water quality management problems.

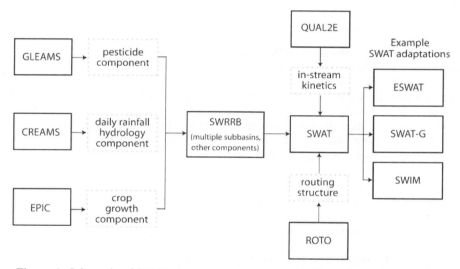

**Figure 1.** Schematic of SWAT developmental history, including selected SWAT adaptations.

Arnold et al. (1995b) developed the Routing Outputs to Outlet (ROTO) model in the early 1990s in order to support an assessment of the downstream impact of water management within Indian reservation lands in Arizona and New Mexico that covered several thousand square kilometers, as requested by the U.S. Bureau of Indian Affairs. The analysis was performed by linking output from multiple SWRRB runs and then routing the flows through channels and reservoirs in ROTO via a reach routing approach. This methodology overcame the SWRRB limitation of allowing only ten subbasins; however, the input and output of multiple SWRRB files was cumbersome and required considerable computer storage. To overcome the awkwardness of this arrangement, SWRRB and ROTO were merged into the single SWAT model (Fig. 1). SWAT retained all the features that made SWRRB such a valuable simulation model, while allowing simulations of very extensive areas.

SWAT has undergone continued review and expansion of capabilities since it was created in the early 1990s. Key enhancements for previous versions of the model (SWAT94.2, 96.2, 98.1, 99.2, and 2000) are described by Arnold and Fohrer (2005) and Neitsch et al. (2005a), including the incorporation of in-stream kinetic routines from the QUAL2E model (Brown and Barnwell, 1987), as shown in Figure 1. Documentation for some previous versions of the model is available at the SWAT web site (SWAT, 2007d). Detailed theoretical documentation and a user⬚s manual for the latest version of the model (SWAT2005) are given by Neitsch et al. (2005a, 2005b). The current version of the model is briefly described here to provide an overview of the model structure and execution approach.

## 2.1 SWAT Overview

SWAT is a basin-scale, continuous-time model that operates on a daily time step and is designed to predict the impact of management on water, sediment, and agricultural chemical yields in ungaged watersheds. The model is physically based, computationally efficient, and capable of continuous simulation over long-time periods. Major model components include weather, hydrology, soil temperature and properties, plant growth, nutrients, pesticides, bacteria and pathogens, and land management. In SWAT, a watershed is divided into multiple sub-watersheds, which are then further subdivided into hydrologic response units (HRUs) that consist of homogeneous land use, management, and soil characteristics. The HRUs represent percentages of the sub-watershed area and are not identified spatially within a SWAT simulation. Alternatively, a watershed can be subdivided into only sub-watersheds that are characterized by dominant land use, soil type, and management.

### 2.1.1 Climatic Inputs and HRU Hydrologic Balance

Climatic inputs used in SWAT include daily precipitation, maximum and minimum temperature, solar radiation data, relative humidity, and wind speed data, which can be input from measured records and/or generated. Relative humidity is required if the Penman-Monteith (Monteith, 1965) or Priestly-Taylor (Priestly and Taylor, 1972) evapotranspiration (ET) routines are used; wind speed is only necessary if the Penman-Monteith method is used. Measured or generated sub-daily precipitation inputs are required if the Green-Ampt infiltration method (Green and Ampt, 1911) is selected. The average air temperature is used to determine if precipitation should be simulated as snowfall. The maximum and minimum temperature inputs are used in the calculation of daily soil and water temperatures. Generated weather inputs are calculated from tables consisting of 13 monthly climatic variables, which are derived from long-term measured weather records. Customized climatic input data options include: (1) simulation of up to ten elevation bands to account for orographic precipitation and/or for snowmelt calculations, (2) adjustments to climate inputs to simulate climate change, and (3) forecasting of future weather patterns, which is a new feature in SWAT2005.

The overall hydrologic balance is simulated for each HRU, including canopy interception of precipitation, partitioning of precipitation, snowmelt water, and irrigation water between surface runoff and infiltration, redistribution of water within the soil profile, evapotranspiration, lateral subsurface flow from the soil profile, and return flow from shallow aquifers. Estimation of areal snow coverage, snowpack temperature, and snowmelt water is based on the approach described by Fontaine et al. (2002). Three options exist in SWAT for estimating surface runoff from HRUs, which are combinations of daily or sub-hourly rainfall and the USDA Natural Resources Conservation Service (NRCS) curve number (CN) method (USDA-NRCS, 2004) or the Green-Ampt method. Canopy interception is implicit in the CN method, while explicit canopy interception is simulated for the Green-Ampt method.

A storage routing technique is used to calculate redistribution of water between layers in the soil profile. Bypass flow can be simulated, as described by Arnold et al. (2005), for soils characterized by cracking, such as Vertisols. SWAT2005 also provides a new option to simulate perched water tables in HRUs that have seasonal high water tables. Three methods for estimating potential ET are provided: Penman-Monteith, Priestly-Taylor, and Hargreaves (Hargreaves et al., 1985). ET values estimated external to SWAT can also be input for a simulation run. The Penman-Monteith option must be used for climate change scenarios that account for changing atmospheric $CO_2$ levels. Recharge below the soil profile is partitioned between shallow and deep aquifers. Return flow to the stream system and evapotranspiration from deep-rooted plants (termed 'revap') can occur from the shallow aquifer. Water that recharges the deep aquifer is assumed lost from the system.

## 2.1.2 Cropping, Management Inputs, and HRU-Level Pollutant Losses

Crop yields and/or biomass output can be estimated for a wide range of crop rotations, grassland/pasture systems, and trees with the crop growth submodel. New routines in SWAT2005 allow for simulation of forest growth from seedling to mature stand. Planting, harvesting, tillage passes, nutrient applications, and pesticide applications can be simulated for each cropping system with specific dates or with a heat unit scheduling approach. Residue and biological mixing are simulated in response to each tillage operation. Nitrogen and phosphorus applications can be simulated in the form of inorganic fertilizer and/or manure inputs. An alternative automatic fertilizer routine can be used to simulate fertilizer applications, as a function of nitrogen stress. Biomass removal and manure deposition can be simulated for grazing operations. SWAT2005 also features a new continuous manure application option to reflect conditions representative of confined animal feeding operations, which automatically simulates a specific frequency and quantity of manure to be applied to a given HRU. The type, rate, timing, application efficiency, and percentage application to foliage versus soil can be accounted for simulations of pesticide applications.

Selected conservation and water management practices can also be simulated in SWAT. Conservation practices that can be accounted for include terraces, strip cropping, contouring, grassed waterways, filter strips, and conservation tillage. Simulation of irrigation water on cropland can be simulated on the basis of five alternative sources: stream reach, reservoir, shallow aquifer, deep aquifer, or a water body source external to the watershed. The irrigation applications can be simulated for specific dates or with an auto-irrigation routine, which triggers irrigation events according to a water stress threshold. Subsurface tile drainage is simulated in SWAT2005 with improved routines that are based on the work performed by Du et al. (2005) and Green et al. (2006); the simulated tile drains can also be linked to new routines that simulate the effects of depressional areas (potholes). Water transfer can also be simulated between different water bodies, as well as "consumptive water use" in which removal of water from a watershed system is assumed.

HRU-level and in-stream pollutant losses can be estimated with SWAT for sediment, nitrogen, phosphorus, pesticides, and bacteria. Sediment yield is calculated with the Modified Universal Soil Loss Equation (MUSLE) developed by Williams and Berndt (1977); USLE estimates are output for comparative purposes only. The transformation and movement of nitrogen and phosphorus within an HRU are simulated in SWAT as a function of nutrient cycles consisting of several inorganic and organic pools. Losses of both N and P from the soil system in SWAT occur by crop uptake and in surface runoff in both the solution phase and on eroded sediment. Simulated losses of N can also occur in percolation below the root zone, in lateral subsurface flow including tile drains, and by volatilization to the atmosphere. Accounting of pesticide fate and transport includes degradation and losses by volatilization, leaching, on eroded sediment, and in the solution phase of surface runoff and later subsurface flow. Bacteria surface runoff losses are simulated in both the solution and eroded phases with improved routines in SWAT2005.

### 2.1.3 Flow and Pollutant Loss Routing, and Auto-Calibration and Uncertainty Analysis

Flows are summed from all HRUs to the sub-watershed level, and then routed through the stream system using either the variable-rate storage method (Williams, 1969) or the Muskingum method (Neitsch et al., 2005a), which are both variations of the kinematic wave approach. Sediment, nutrient, pesticide, and bacteria loadings or concentrations from each HRU are also summed at the sub-watershed level, and the resulting losses are routed through channels, ponds, wetlands, depressional areas, and/or reservoirs to the watershed outlet. Contributions from point sources and urban areas are also accounted for in the total flows and pollutant losses exported from each sub-watershed. Sediment transport is simulated as a function of peak channel velocity in SWAT2005, which is a simplified approach relative to the stream power methodology used in previous SWAT versions. Simulation of channel erosion is accounted for with a channel erodibility factor. In-stream transformations and kinetics of algae growth, nitrogen and phosphorus cycling, carbonaceous biological oxygen demand, and dissolved oxygen are performed on the basis of routines developed for the QUAL2E model. Degradation, volatilization, and other in-stream processes are simulated for pesticides, as well as decay of bacteria. Routing of heavy metals can be simulated; however, no transformation or decay processes are simulated for these pollutants.

A final feature in SWAT2005 is a new automated sensitivity, calibration, and uncertainty analysis component that is based on approaches described by van Griensven and Meixner (2006) and van Griensven et al. (2006b). Further discussion of these tools is provided in the Sensitivity, Calibration, and Uncertainty Analyses Section.

## 2.2 SWAT Adaptations

A key trend that is interwoven with the ongoing development of SWAT is the emergence of modified SWAT models that have been adapted to provide improved simulation of specific processes, which in some cases have been focused on specific regions. Notable examples (Fig. 1) include SWAT-G, Extended SWAT (ESWAT), and the Soil and Water Integrated Model (SWIM). The initial SWAT-G model was developed by modifying the SWAT99.2 percolation, hydraulic conductivity, and interflow functions to provide improved flow predictions for typical conditions in low mountain ranges in Germany (Lenhart et al., 2002). Further SWAT-G enhancements include an improved method of estimating erosion loss (Lenhart et al., 2005) and a more detailed accounting of $CO_2$ effects on leaf area index and stomatal conductance (Eckhardt and Ulbrich, 2003). The ESWAT model (van Griensven and Bauwens, 2003, 2005) features several modifications relative to the original SWAT model including: (1) sub-hourly precipitation inputs and infiltration, runoff, and erosion loss estimates based on a user-defined fraction of an hour; (2) a river routing module that is updated on an hourly time step and is interfaced with a water quality component that features in-stream kinetics based partially on functions used in QUAL2E as well as additional enhancements; and (3) multi-objective (multi-site and/or multi-variable) calibration and autocalibration modules (similar components are now incorporated in SWAT2005). The SWIM model is based primarily on hydrologic components from SWAT and nutrient cycling components from the MATSALU model (Krysanova et al., 1998, 2005) and is designed to simulate ⊏mesoscale⊐ (100 to 100,000 $km^2$) watersheds. Recent improvements to SWIM include incorporation of a groundwater dynamics submodel (Hatterman et al., 2004), enhanced capability to simulate forest systems (Wattenbach et al., 2005), and development of routines to more realistically simulate wetlands and riparian zones (Hatterman et al., 2006).

## 2.3 Geographic Information System Interfaces and Other Tools

A second trend that has paralleled the historical development of SWAT is the creation of various Geographic Information System (GIS) and other interface tools to support the input of topographic, land use, soil, and other digital data into SWAT. The first GIS interface program developed for SWAT was SWAT/ GRASS, which was built within the GRASS raster-based GIS (Srinivasan and Arnold, 1994). Haverkamp et al. (2005) have adopted SWAT/GRASS within the InputOutputSWAT (IOSWAT) software package, which incorporates the Topographic Parameterization Tool (TOPAZ) and other tools to generate inputs and provide output mapping support for both SWAT and SWAT-G.

The ArcView-SWAT (AVSWAT) interface tool (Di Luzio et al., 2004a, 2004b) is designed to generate model inputs from ArcView 3.x GIS data layers and execute SWAT2000 within the same framework. AVSWAT was incorporated within the U.S. Environmental Protection Agency (USEPA) Better Assessment Science Integrating point and Nonpoint Sources (BASINS) software package version 3.0 (USEPA, 2006a), which provides GIS utilities that support automatic data input for SWAT2000 using ArcView (Di Luzio et al., 2002). The most recent version of the interface is denoted AVSWAT-X, which provides additional input generation functionality, including soil data input from both the USDA-NRCS State Soils Geographic (STATSGO) and Soil Survey Geographic (SSURGO) databases (USDA-NRCS, 2007a, 2007b) for applications of SWAT2005 (Di Luzio et al., 2005; SWAT, 2007b). Automatic sensitivity, calibration, and uncertainty analysis can also be initiated with AVSWAT-X for SWAT2005. The Automated Geospatial Watershed Assessment (AGWA) interface tool (Miller et al., 2007) is an alternative ArcView-based interface tool that supports data input generation for both SWAT2000 and the KINEROS2 model, including options for soil inputs from the SSURGO, STATSGO, or United Nations Food and Agriculture Organization (FAO) global soil maps. Both AGWA and AVSWAT have been incorporated as interface approaches for generating SWAT2000 inputs within BASINS version 3.1 (Wells, 2006).

A SWAT interface compatible with ArcGIS version 9.1 (ArcSWAT) has recently been developed that uses a geodatabase approach and a programming structure consistent with Component Object Model (COM) protocol (Olivera et al., 2006; SWAT, 2007a). An ArcGIS 9.x version of AGWA (AGWA2) is also being developed and is expected to be released near mid-2007 (USDA-ARS, 2007).

A variety of other tools have been developed to support executions of SWAT simulations, including: (1) the interactive SWAT (i_SWAT) software (CARD, 2007), which supports SWAT simulations using a Windows interface with an Access database; (2) the Conservation Reserve Program (CRP) Decision Support System (CRP-DSS) developed by Rao et al. (2006); (3) the AUTORUN system used by Kannan et al. (2007b), which facilitates repeated SWAT simulations with variations in selected parameters; and (4) a generic interface (iSWAT) program

(Abbaspour et al., 2007), which automates parameter selection and aggregation for iterative SWAT calibration simulations.

## 2.4 SWAT Applications

Applications of SWAT have expanded worldwide over the past decade. Many of the applications have been driven by the needs of various government agencies, particularly in the U.S. and the European Union, that require direct assessments of anthropogenic, climate change, and other influences on a wide range of water resources or exploratory assessments of model capabilities for potential future applications.

**Figure 2.** Distribution of the 2,149 8-digit watersheds within the 18 Major Water Resource Regions (MWRRs) that comprise the conterminous U.S.

One of the first major applications performed with SWAT was within the Hydrologic Unit Model of the U.S. (HUMUS) modeling system (Arnold et al., 1999a), which was implemented to support USDA analyses of the U.S. Resources Conservation Act Assessment of 1997 for the conterminous U.S. The system was used to simulate the hydrologic and/or pollutant loss impacts of agricultural and municipal water use, tillage and cropping system trends, and other scenarios within each of the 2,149 U.S. Geological Survey (USGS) 8-digit Hydrologic Cataloging Unit (HCU) watersheds (Seaber et al., 1987), referred to hereafter as "8-digit watersheds". Figure 2 shows the distribution of the 8-digit watersheds within the 18 Major Water Resource Regions (MWRRs) that comprise the conterminous U.S.

SWAT is also being used to support the USDA Conservation Effects Assessment Project, which is designed to quantify the environmental benefits of conservation practices at both the national and watershed scales (Mausbach and Dedrick, 2004). SWAT is being applied at the national level within a modified HUMUS framework to assess the benefits of different conservation practices at that scale. The model is also being used to evaluate conservation practices for watersheds of varying sizes that are representative of different regional conditions and mixes of conservation practices.

SWAT is increasingly being used to perform TMDL analyses, which must be performed for impaired waters by the different states as mandated by the 1972 U.S. Clean Water Act (USEPA, 2006b). Roughly 37% of the nearly 39,000 currently listed impaired waterways still require TMDLs (USEPA, 2007); SWAT, BASINS, and a variety of other modeling tools will be used to help determine the pollutant sources and potential solutions for many of these forthcoming TMDLs. Extensive discussion of applying SWAT and other models for TMDLs is presented in Borah et al. (2006), Benham et al. (2006), and Shirmohammadi et al. (2006).

SWAT has also been used extensively in Europe, including projects supported by various European Commission (EC) agencies. Several models including SWAT were used to quantify the impacts of climate change for five different watersheds in Europe within the Climate Hydrochemistry and Economics of Surface-water Systems (CHESS) project, which was sponsored by the EC Environment and Climate Research Programme (CHESS, 2001). A suite of nine models including SWAT were tested in 17 different European watersheds as part of the EUROHARP project, which was sponsored by the EC Energy, Environment and Sustainable Development (EESD) Programme (EUROHARP, 2006). The goal of the research was to assess the ability of the models to estimate nonpoint-source nitrogen and phosphorus losses to both freshwater streams and coastal waters. The EESD-sponsored TempQsim project focused on testing the ability of SWAT and five other models to simulate intermittent stream conditions that exist in southern Europe (TempQsim, 2006). Volk et al. (2007) and van Griensven et al. (2006a) further describe SWAT application approaches within the context of the European Union (EU) Water Framework Directive.

The following application discussion focuses on the wide range of specific SWAT applications that have been reported in the literature. Some descriptions of modified SWAT model applications are interspersed within the descriptions of studies that used the standard SWAT model.

## 3. Specific SWAT Applications

SWAT applications reported in the literature can be categorized in several ways. For this study, most of the peer-reviewed articles could be grouped into the nine subcategories listed in Table 1, and then further broadly defined as hydrologic only, hydrologic and pollutant loss, or pollutant loss only. Reviews are not provided for all of the articles included in the Table 1 summary; a complete list of the SWAT peer-reviewed articles is provided at the SWAT web site (SWAT, 2007c), which is updated on an ongoing basis.

**Table 1.** Overview of major application categories of SWAT studies reported in the literature.[a]

| Primary Application Category | Hydrologic Only | Hydrologic and Pollutant Loss | Pollutant Loss Only |
|---|---|---|---|
| Calibration and/or sensitivity analysis | 15 | 20 | 2 |
| Climate change impacts | 22 | 8 | -- |
| GIS interface descriptions | 3 | 3 | 2 |
| Hydrologic assessments | 42 | -- | -- |
| Variation in configuration or data input effects | 21 | 15 | -- |
| Comparisons with other models or techniques | 5 | 7 | 1 |
| Interfaces with other models | 13 | 15 | 6 |
| Pollutant assessments | -- | 57 | 6 |

[a] Includes studies describing applications of ESWAT, SWAT-G, SWIM, and other modified SWAT models.

## 3.1 Hydrologic Assessments

Simulation of the hydrologic balance is foundational for all SWAT watershed applications and is usually described in some form regardless of the focus of the analysis. The majority of SWAT applications also report some type of graphical and/or statistical hydrologic calibration, especially for streamflow, and many of the studies also report validation results. A wide range of statistics has been used to evaluate SWAT hydrologic predictions. By far the most widely used statistics reported for hydrologic calibration and validation are the regression correlation coefficient ($R^2$) and the Nash-Sutcliffe model efficiency (NSE) coefficient (Nash and Sutcliffe, 1970). The $R^2$ value measures how well the simulated versus observed regression line approaches an ideal match and ranges from 0 to 1, with a value of 0 indicating no correlation and a value of 1 representing that the predicted dispersion equals the measured dispersion (Krause et al., 2005). The regression slope and intercept also equal 1 and 0, respectively, for a perfect fit; the slope and intercept are often not reported. The NSE ranges from $-\infty$ to 1 and measures how well the simulated versus observed data match the 1:1 line (regression line with slope equal to 1). An NSE value of 1 again reflects a perfect fit between the simulated and measured data. A value of 0 or less than 0 indicates that the mean of the observed data is a better predictor than the model output. See Krause et al. (2005) for further discussion regarding the $R^2$, NSE, and other efficiency criteria measures.

An extensive list of $R^2$ and NSE statistics is presented in Table 2 for 115 SWAT hydrologic calibration and/or validation results reported in the literature. These statistics provide valuable insight regarding the hydrologic performance of

35

the model across a wide spectrum of conditions. To date, no absolute criteria for judging model performance have been firmly established in the literature. However, Moriasi et al. (2007) proposed that NSE values should exceed 0.5 in order for model results to be judged as satisfactory for hydrologic and pollutant loss evaluations performed on a monthly time step (and that appropriate relaxing and tightening of the standard be performed for daily and annual time step evaluations, respectively). Assuming this criterion for both the NSE and $r^2$ values at all time steps, the majority of statistics listed in Table 2 would be judged as adequately replicating observed streamflows and other hydrologic indicators. However, it is clear that poor results resulted for parts or all of some studies. The poorest results generally occurred for daily predictions, although this was not universal (e.g. Grizzetti et al., 2005). Some of the weaker results can be attributed in part to inadequate representation of rainfall inputs, due to either a lack of adequate rain gauges in the simulated watershed or sub-watershed configurations that were too coarse to capture the spatial detail of rainfall inputs (e.g. Cao et al., 2006; Conan et al., 2003b; Bouraoui et al., 2002; Bouraoui et al., 2005). Other factors that may adversely affect SWAT hydrologic predictions include a lack of model calibration (Bosch et al., 2004), inaccuracies in measured streamflow data (Harmel et al., 2006), and relatively short calibration and validation periods (Muleta and Nicklow, 2005b).

### 3.1.1 Example Calibration/Validation Studies

The SWAT hydrologic subcomponents have been refined and validated at a variety of scales (Table 2). For example, Arnold and Allen (1996) used measured data from three Illinois watersheds, ranging in size from 122 to 246 km$^2$, to successfully validate surface runoff, groundwater flow, groundwater ET, ET in the soil profile, groundwater recharge, and groundwater height parameters. Santhi et al. (2001a, 2006) performed extensive streamflow validations for two Texas watersheds that cover over 4,000 km$^2$. Arnold et al. (1999b) evaluated streamflow and sediment yield data in the Texas Gulf basin with drainage areas ranging from 2,253 to 304,260 km$^2$. Streamflow data from approximately 1,000 stream monitoring gages from 1960 to 1989 were used to calibrate and validate the model. Predicted average monthly streamflows for three major river basins (20,593 to 108,788 km$^2$) were 5% higher than measured flows, with standard deviations between measured and predicted within 2%. Annual runoff and ET were validated across the entire continental U.S. as part of the Hydrologic Unit Model for the U.S. (HUMUS) modeling system. Rosenthal et al. (1995) linked GIS to SWAT and simulated 10 years of monthly streamflow without calibration. SWAT underestimated the extreme events but produced overall accurate streamflows (Table 2). Bingner (1996) simulated runoff for 10 years for a watershed in northern Mississippi. The SWAT model produced reasonable results in the simulation of runoff on a daily and annual basis from multiple subbasins (Table 2), with the exception of a wooded subbasin. Rosenthal and Hoffman (1999) successfully used SWAT and a spatial database to simulate flows, sediment, and nutrient loadings on a 9,000 km$^2$ watershed in central Texas to locate potential water quality monitoring sites. SWAT was also successfully validated for streamflow (Table

36

2) for the Mill Creek watershed in Texas for 1965-1968 and 1968-1975 (Srinivasan et al., 1998). Monthly streamflow rates were well predicted, but the model overestimated streamflows in a few years during the spring/summer months. The overestimation may be accounted for by variable rainfall during those months.

**Table 2.** Summary of reported SWAT hydrologic calibration and validation coefficient of determination ($R^2$) and Nash-Sutcliffe model efficiency (NSE) statistics.

| Reference | Watershed | Drainage Area (km²)[a] | Indicator | Time Period (C = calib., V = valid.) | Calibration Daily R² | Calibration Daily NSE | Calibration Monthly R² | Calibration Monthly NSE | Calibration Annual R² | Calibration Annual NSE | Validation Daily R² | Validation Daily NSE | Validation Monthly R² | Validation Monthly NSE | Validation Annual R² | Validation Annual NSE |
|---|---|---|---|---|---|---|---|---|---|---|---|---|---|---|---|---|
| Afinowicz et al. (2005) | North Fork of the Upper Guadalupe River (Texas) | 60 | Stream flow | C: 1992-1996 V: 1997 to Sept. 2003 | 0.4 | | | 0.29 | | | 0.09 | | | 0.5 | | |
| Arabi et al. (2006b)[b] | Dreisbach and Smith Fry (Indiana) | 6.2 and 7.3 | Stream flow | C: 1975 to May 1977 V: June 1977 to 1978 | | | 0.92 and 0.86 | 0.84 and 0.73 | | | | | 0.87 and 0.81 | 0.73 and 0.63 | | |
| | | | Surface runoff | | | | 0.91 and 0.84 | 0.80 and 0.62 | | | | | 0.88 and 0.84 | 0.75 and 0.63 | | |
| Arnold and Allen (1996) | Goose Creek, Hadley Creek, and Panther Creek (Illinois) | 122 to 246 | Surface runoff | Varying periods | | | | | | | | | 0.79 to 0.94 | | | |
| | | | Ground water flow | | | | | | | | | | 0.38 to 0.51 | | | |
| | | | Total stream flow | | | | | | | | | | 0.63 to 0.95 | | | |
| Arnold et al. (2000) | Upper Mississippi River (north central U.S.) | 491,700 | Stream flow | C: 1961-1980 V: 1981-1985 | | | 0.63 | | | | | | 0.65 | | | |
| Arnold et al. (2005) | USDA-ARS Y-2 (Texas) | 0.53 | Crack flow | 1998-1999 | | | | | | | 0.84 | | | | | |
| | | | Surface runoff | 1998-1999 | | | | | | | 0.87 | | | | | |
| Arnold et al. (1999a)[c] | Conterminous U.S. (fig. 2) | -- | Runoff (by state) | 20-year period | | | | | | | | | | | 0.78 | |
| | | | (by soils) | | | | | | | | | | | | 0.66 | |
| Arnold et al. (1999b) | 35 8-digit watersheds (Texas) | 2,253 to 304,620 | Stream flow | 1965-1989 | | | | | | | | | 0.23 to 0.96 | -1.1 to 0.87 | | |
| | Three 6-digit watersheds[c] (Texas) | -- | Stream flow | 1965-1989 | | | | | | | | | 0.57 to 0.87 | 0.53 to 0.86 | | |
| Bärlund et al. (2007)[d,14] | Lake Pyhäjärvi (Finland) | -- | Stream flow | 1990-1994 | 0.48 | | | | | | | | | | | |
| Behera and Panda (2006) | Kapgari (India) | 9.73 | Surface runoff | C: 2002 V: 2003 (rainy season) | 0.94 | 0.88 | | | | | 0.91 | 0.85 | | | | |
| Benaman et al. (2005) | Cannonsville Reservoir (New York); C: four gauges, V: two gauges | 37 to 913 | Stream flow | C: 1994 to July 1999 V: 1990-1993 | | | 0.72 to 0.80 | 0.63 to 0.78 | | | | | 0.73 and 0.80 | 0.62 and 0.76 | | |
| Benham et al. (2006) | Shoal Creek (Missouri); upstream gauge | 367 | Stream flow | C: May 1999 to June 2000 V: June 2001 to Sept. 2002 | 0.40 | 0.21 | 0.70 | 0.63 | | | 0.61 | 0.54 | 0.61 | 0.66 | | |
| Binger (1996)[e] | Goodwin Creek (Mississippi); 14 gauges | 0.05 to 21.3 | Stream flow | V: 1982-1991 (140 r² statistics) | | | | | | | | | | | 93 ≥ 0.90 | |
| Bosch et al. (2004)[f,g] | Subwatershed J, Little River (Georgia, U.S.) | 22.1 | Stream flow | 1997-2002 | | | | | | | | -0.24 to -0.03 | | 0.55 to 0.80 | | |
| Bouraoui et al. (2005)[h] | Medjerda River (Algeria and Tunisia); three gauges | 163 to 16,000 | Stream flow | Sept. 1988 to March 1999 | | | | | | | 0.44 to 0.69 | 0.23 to 0.41 | 0.62 to 0.84 | 0.53 to 0.84 | | |
| Bouraoui et al. (2002) | Ouse River (U.K.); three gauges | 980 to 3,500 | Stream flow | 1986-1990 | 0.39 to 0.77 | | | | | | | | | | | |

**Table 2** (cont'd). Summary of reported SWAT hydrologic calibration and validation coefficient of determination ($R^2$) and Nash-Sutcliffe model efficiency (NSE) statistics.

| Reference | Watershed | Drainage Area (km²)[a] | Indicator | Time Period (C = calib., V = valid.) | Cal. Daily $R^2$ | Cal. Daily NSE | Cal. Monthly $R^2$ | Cal. Monthly NSE | Cal. Annual $R^2$ | Cal. Annual NSE | Val. Daily $R^2$ | Val. Daily NSE | Val. Monthly $R^2$ | Val. Monthly NSE | Val. Annual $R^2$ | Val. Annual NSE |
|---|---|---|---|---|---|---|---|---|---|---|---|---|---|---|---|---|
| Bouraoui et al. (2004) | Vantaanjoki (Finland) | 1,682 | Stream flow | 1965-1984 | | | | | | | | | 0.87 | | | |
| | Subwatershed | 295 | | 1982-1984 | | | | 0.81 | | | | | | | | |
| Cao et al. (2006) | Motueka River (New Zealand); seven gauges | 47.9 to 1,756.6 | Stream flow | C: 1990-1994 V: 1995-2000 | 0.52 to 0.82 | 0.36 to 0.78 | | | 0.64 to 0.95 | | 0.41 to 0.75 | 0.35 to 0.72 | | | | |
| Cerucci and Conrad (2003) | Townbrook (New York) | 36.8 | Stream flow | Oct. 1998 to Sept. 2000 | | | 0.72 | | | | | | | | | |
| Chanasyk et al. (2003) | Three watersheds (Saskatchewan) | 0.015 to 0.023 | Surface runoff | 1999-1900 | | -35.7 to -0.005 | | | | | | | | | | |
| Chaplot et al. (2004) | Walnut Creek (Iowa) | 51.3 | Stream flow | 1991-1998 | | | 0.73 | | | | | | | | | |
| Cheng et al. (2006) | Heihe River (China) | 7,241 | Stream flow | C: 1992-1997 V: 1998-1999 | | | 0.80 | 0.78 | | | | | 0.78 | 0.76 | | |
| Chu and Shirmohammadi (2004)[i] | Warner Creek (Maryland) | 3.46 | Stream flow | C: 1994-1995 V: 1996-1999 | | | 0.66 | 0.52 | | | | | 0.69 | 0.63 | | |
| | | | Surface runoff | | | | 0.43 | 0.35 | | | | | 0.88 | 0.77 | | |
| | | | Sub-surface runoff | | | | 0.56 | 0.27 | | | | | 0.47 | 0.42 | | |
| Coffey et al. (2004)[r] | University of Kentucky ARC (Kentucky) | 5.5 | Stream flow | 1995 and 1996 | 0.26 and 0.40 | 0.09 and 0.15 | 0.70 and 0.88 | 0.41 and 0.61 | | | | | | | | |
| Conan et al. (2003a)[i][j] | Coët-Dan (France) | 12 | Stream flow | C: 1995-1996 V: 1997-1999 | | | 0.79 | | | | 0.42 | | 0.87 | | | |
| | Subwatershed | | Stream flow | V: 1994 to Feb. 1999 | | | | | | | | | 0.83 | | | |
| Conan et al. (2003b) | Upper Guadiana River (Spain) | 18,100 | Stream flow | 1975-1991 | | | | | | | 0.45 | | | | | |
| Cotter et al. (2003) | Moores Creek (Arkansas) | 18.9 | Stream flow | 1997-1998 | 0.76 | | | | | | | | | | | |
| Di Luzio et al. (2005) | Goodwin Creek (Mississippi) | 21.3 | Surface runoff | 1982-1993 | | | | | | | | | 0.90 to 0.95 | 0.81 to 0.97 | | |
| Di Luzio and Arnold (2004)[i] | Blue River (Oklahoma) | 1,233 | Stream flow | 1994-2000 (auto. calib.) | 0.24 to 0.99 | 0.15 to 0.99 | | | | | | | | | | |
| | | | | (manual calib.) | 0.01 to 0.98 | -102 to 0.80 | | | | | | | | | | |
| Di Luzio et al. (2002) | Upper North Bosque River (Texas) | 932.5 | Stream flow | 1993 to July 1998 | | | | | | | | | 0.82 | | | |
| Du et al. (2005)[c] | Walnut Creek (Iowa); Subwatershed (site 310) and watershed outlet | 51.3 | Stream flow | C: 1992-1995 V: 1996-1999 (SWAT2000) | | | 0.39 and 0.47 | | 0.36 and 0.72 | | | | 0.35 and 0.32 | | 0.13 and 0.56 | |
| | Subwatershed (site 210) | -- | Tile flow | (SWAT2000) | | | -0.15 | | -0.33 | | | | -0.16 | | -0.42 | |
| | Subwatershed (site 310) and watershed outlet | 51.3 | Stream flow | (SWAT-M)[i] | | | 0.55 and 0.51 | | 0.84 and 0.88 | | | | -0.11 and 0.49 | | 0.72 and 0.82 | |
| | Subwatershed (site 210) | -- | Tile flow | (SWAT-M)[i] | | | -0.23 | | 0.67 | | | | -0.12 | | 0.70 | |
| Eckhardt et al. (2002) | Dietzhölze (Germany) | 81 | Stream flow | 1991-1993 (SWAT99.2) | | | -0.17 | | | | | | | | | |
| | | | | (SWAT-G)[b] | | | 0.76 | | | | | | | | | |
| El-Nasr et al. (2005) | Jeker (Belgium) | 465 | Stream flow | C: June 1986 to April 1989 V: June 1989 to April 1992 | 0.45 | 0.39 | | | | | 0.55 | 0.60 | | | | |

**Table 2** (cont'd). Summary of reported SWAT hydrologic calibration and validation coefficient of determination ($R^2$) and Nash-Sutcliffe model efficiency (NSE) statistics.

| Reference | Watershed | Drainage Area (km²)[a] | Indicator | Time Period (C = calib., V = valid.) | Cal. Daily $R^2$ | Cal. Daily NSE | Cal. Monthly $R^2$ | Cal. Monthly NSE | Cal. Annual $R^2$ | Cal. Annual NSE | Val. Daily $R^2$ | Val. Daily NSE | Val. Monthly $R^2$ | Val. Monthly NSE | Val. Annual $R^2$ | Val. Annual NSE |
|---|---|---|---|---|---|---|---|---|---|---|---|---|---|---|---|---|
| Fontaine et al. (2002) | Wind River (Wyoming) | 4,999 | Stream flow | 1991-1996 (new snowmelt routine) | | | | | | | | | | | | 0.86 |
| | | | | 1991-1996 (old routine) | | | | | | | | | | | | -0.70 |
| Fontaine et al. (2001) | Spring Creek (South Dakota) | 427 | Stream flow | 1987-1995 | | | 0.62 | | 0.94 | | | | | | | |
| Francos et al. (2001)[k] | Kerava River (Finland) | 400 | Stream flow | 1985-1994 | | | | | | | | | | 0.65 | | |
| Geza and McCray (2007) | Turkey Creek (Colorado) | 126 | Stream flow | 1998-2001 (SSURGO soils) | | | | 0.70 | | | | | | | | |
| | | | | (STATSGO soils) | | | | 0.61 | | | | | | | | |
| Gikas et al. (2005)[c,d] | Vistonis Lagoon (Greece); nine gauges | 1,349 | Stream flow | C: May 1998 to June 1999 | 0.71 | | | | | | 0.72 | | | | | |
| | | | | V: Nov. 1999 to Jan. 2000 | 0.89 | | | | | | 0.91 | | | | | |
| Gitau et al. (2004) | Town Brook (New York) | 36.8[l] | Stream flow | 1992-2002 | | | 0.76 | 0.44 | 0.99 | 0.84 | | | | | | |
| Gosain et al. (2005)[c,b] | Palleru River (India) | -- | Stream flow | 1972-1994 | | | | | | | | | 0.61 | 0.87 | | |
| Govender and Everson (2005) | Cathedral Park Research C VI (South Africa) | 0.68 | Stream flow | C: 1991 V: 1990-1995 (auto. calib.) | 0.86 | | | | | | 0.65 | | | | | |
| | | | | V: 1990-1995 (manual calib.) | | | | | | | 0.68 | | | | | |
| Green et al. (2006) | South Fork of the Iowa River (Iowa) | 580.5 | Stream flow | C: 1995-1998 V: 1999-2004 (scenario 1) | 0.7 | 0.7 | 0.9 | 0.9 | 1.0 | 0.7 | 0.5 | 0.4 | 0.6 | 0.5 | 0.7 | 0.6 |
| | | | | C: 1995-2000 V: 2001-2004 (scenario 2) | 0.7 | 0.7 | 0.9 | 0.8 | 0.9 | 0.9 | 0.3 | 0.2 | 0.6 | 0.5 | 0.7 | -0.8 |
| Grizzetti et al. (2005)[c] | Parts of four watersheds (U.K.); C: one gauge, V: two gauges, annual: 50 gauges | 8,900 | Stream flow | C and V: 1995-1999 | | 0.75 | | 0.86 | | | | | | | | 0.66 |
| Grizzetti et al. (2003)[c] | Vantaanjoki (Finland); C: one gauge, V: three gauges | 295 and 1,682 | Stream flow | Varying periods | | 0.81 | | | | | 0.57 to 0.66 | 0.75 to 0.81 | | | | |
| Hanratty and Stefan (1998) | Cottonwood (Minnesota) | 3,400 | Stream flow | 1967-1991 | | | | 0.78 | | | | | | | | |
| Hao et al. (2004) | Lushi (China) | 4,623 | Stream Flow | C: 1992-1997 V: 1998-1999 | 0.87 | 0.87 | | | | | 0.84 | 0.81 | | | | |
| Hernandez et al. (2000) | Watershed 11, Walnut Gulch (Arizona) | 8.2 | Stream flow | 1966-1974 (1 vs. 10 rain gauges) | | | | | | 0.33 and 0.57 | | | | | | |
| Heuvelmans et al. (2006)[i] | 25 watersheds (Schelde River basin, Belgium) | 2.2 to 209.9 | Stream flow | C: 1990-1995 V: 1996-2001 | | 0.70 to 0.95 | | | | | | 0.67 to 0.92 | | | | |
| Holvoet et al. (2005) | Nil (Belgium) | 32 | Stream flow | Nov. 1998 to Nov. 2001 | | 0.53 | | | | | | | | | | |
| Jha et al. (2004a)[c] | Maquoketa River (Iowa) | 4,776 | Stream flow | 1981-1990 | | | | | | | 0.68 | | 0.76 | | 0.65 | |
| Jha et al. (2004b) | Upper Mississippi River (north central U.S.) | 447,500 | Stream flow | C: 1989-1997 V: 1980-1988 | | | 0.75 | 0.67 | 0.91 | 0.91 | | | 0.70 | 0.59 | 0.89 | 0.86 |
| Jha et al. (2006) | Upper Mississippi River (north central U.S.) | 447,500 | Stream flow | C: 1968-1987 V: 1988-1997 | 0.67 | 0.58 | 0.74 | 0.69 | 0.82 | 0.75 | 0.75 | 0.65 | 0.82 | 0.81 | 0.91 | 0.90 |
| Jha et al. (2007)[m] | Raccoon River (Iowa); Van Meter gauge | 8,930 | Stream flow | C: 1981-1992 V: 1993-2003 | 0.87 | 0.87 | | | 0.97 | 0.97 | | | 0.89 | 0.88 | 0.94 | 0.94 |

**Table 2** (cont'd). Summary of reported SWAT hydrologic calibration and validation coefficient of determination ($R^2$) and Nash-Sutcliffe model efficiency (NSE) statistics.

| Reference | Watershed | Drainage Area ($km^2$) | Indicator | Time Period (C = calib., V = valid.) | Calibration Daily $R^2$ | NSE | Monthly $R^2$ | NSE | Annual $R^2$ | NSE | Validation Daily $R^2$ | NSE | Monthly $R^2$ | NSE | Annual $R^2$ | NSE |
|---|---|---|---|---|---|---|---|---|---|---|---|---|---|---|---|---|
| Narasimhan et al. (2005)[c] | Six watersheds (Texas); 24 gauges | 10,320 to 29,664 | Stream flow | Varying periods (overall annual average) | | | | | 0.75 | 0.75 | | | | | 0.70 | 0.70 |
| | | | | (range across 24 gauges) | | | | | 0.54 to 0.99 | 0.52 to 0.99 | | | | | 0.63 to 1.00 | 0.55 to 0.97 |
| Nasr et al. (2007)[d] | Clarianna, Dripsey, and Oona Water (Ireland) | 15 to 96 | Stream flow | Varying periods | 0.72 to 0.91 | | | | | | | | | | | |
| Olivera et al. (2006) | Upper Seco Creek (Texas) | 116 | Stream flow | C: 1991-1992 V: 1993 to June 1994 | 0.67 | | 0.88 | | | | 0.33 | | 0.90 | | | |
| Perkins and Sophocleous (1999)[h] | Lower Republican River (Kansas) | 2,569 | Stream flow | 1977-1994 | | | 0.85 | | | | | | | | | |
| Peterson and Hamlet (1998)[i] | Ariel Creek (Pennsylvania) | 39.4 | Stream flow | May 1992 to July 1994 | 0.04 | | 0.14 | | | | | | | | | |
| | | | | May 1992 to July 1994 (no snowmelt events) | 0.2 | | 0.55 | | | | | | | | | |
| Plus et al. (2006)[h] | Thau Lagoon (France); two gauges | 280 | Stream flow | Sept. 1993 to July 1996 | 0.68 and 0.45 | | | | | | | | | | | |
| Qi and Grunwald (2005) | Sandusky River (Ohio); five gauges | 90.3 to 3,240 | Surface water | C: 1998-1999 V: 2000-2001 | | | 0.31 to 0.65 | | | | | | -0.04 to 0.75 | | | |
| | | | Ground water | | | | -9.1 to 0.60 | | | | | | -0.57 to 0.22 | | | |
| | | | Total flow | | | | 0.31 to 0.81 | | | | | | 0.40 to 0.73 | | | |
| Rosenberg et al. (2003)[d] | Conterminous U.S. | | Water yield | 1961-1990 (overall mean) | | | | | | | | | | | 0.92 | |
| | (18 MWRRs; fig. 2) | | | 1961-1990 (8-digit means by MWRR) | | | | | | | | | | | 0.03 to 0.90 | |
| Rosenthal and Hoffman (1999) | Leon River (Texas) | 7,000 | Stream flow | 1972-1974 | | | | | | | | | 0.57 | | | |
| Rosenthal et al. (1995)[d,f,g] | Lower Colorado River (Texas); Bay City gauge | 8,927 | Stream flow | 1980-1989 | | | | | | | | | 0.75 | 0.69 | | |
| | Upstream gauges | | | | | | | | | | | | 0.69 to 0.90 | | | |
| Saleh et al. (2000)[g] | Upper North Bosque River (Texas); C: one gauge, V: 11 gauges | 932.5 | Stream flow | Oct. 1993 to Aug. 1995 | | | 0.56 | | | | | | 0.99 | | | |
| Saleh and Du (2004) | Upper North Bosque River (Texas) | 932.5 | Stream flow | C: 1994 to June 1995 V: July 1995 to July 1999 | 0.17 | | 0.50 | | | | 0.62 | | 0.78 | | | |
| Salvetti et al. (2006) | Lombardy Plain Region (Po River basin, Italy) | 16,000 | Stream flow | 1984-2002 | 0.50 | | >0.70 | | | | | | | | | |
| Santhi et al. (2001a)[c,d,e] | Bosque River (Texas); two gauges | 4,277 | Stream flow | Varying periods | 0.80 and 0.89 | 0.79 and 0.83 | 0.88 and 0.66 | 0.86 and 0.72 | | | | | 0.92 and 0.80 | 0.87 and 0.62 | | |
| Santhi et al. (2006)[c] | West Fork (Texas); two gauges | 4,554 | Stream flow | 1982-2001 | 0.61 and 0.81 | 0.12 and 0.72 | 0.88 and 0.86 | 0.84 and 0.78 | | | | | | | | |

**Table 2** (cont'd). Summary of reported SWAT hydrologic calibration and validation coefficient of determination (R²) and Nash-Sutcliffe model efficiency (NSE) statistics.

| Reference | Watershed | Drainage Area (km²)[d] | Indicator | Time Period (C = calib., V = valid.) | Calib. Daily R² | Calib. Daily NSE | Calib. Monthly R² | Calib. Monthly NSE | Calib. Annual R² | Calib. Annual NSE | Valid. Daily R² | Valid. Daily NSE | Valid. Monthly R² | Valid. Monthly NSE | Valid. Annual R² | Valid. Annual NSE |
|---|---|---|---|---|---|---|---|---|---|---|---|---|---|---|---|---|
| Schomberg et al. (2005)[c] | Three watersheds (Minnesota); two watersheds (Michigan) | 829 to 3,697 | Stream flow | Varying periods | 0.10 to 0.28 | -1.3 to 0.25 | 0.35 to 0.58 | -1.4 to 0.49 | | | | | | | | |
| Secchi et al. (2007)[c] | 13 watersheds (Iowa) | 2,051 to 37,496 | Stream flow | Varying periods (composite statistics) | | | | | | | | | 0.76 | 0.75 | 0.91 | 0.90 |
| Singh et al. (2005) | Iroquois River (Illinois and Indiana) | 5,568 | Stream flow | C: 1987-1995 V: 1972-1986 | 0.79 | | 0.88 | | | | 0.74 | | 0.84 | | | |
| Spruill et al. (2000) | University of Kentucky ARC (Kentucky) | 5.5 | Stream flow | C: 1996 V: 1995 | | 0.19 | | 0.89 | | | | -0.04 | | 0.58 | | |
| Srinivasan et al. (2005)[b] | Watershed FD-36 (Pennsylvania) | 0.395 | Stream flow | 1997-2000 | 0.62 | | | | | | | | | | | |
| Srinivasan and Arnold (1994) | Upper Seco Creek (Texas) | 114 | Stream flow | Jan. 1991 to Aug. 1992 | | | 0.82 | | | | | | | | | |
| Srinivasan et al. (1998)[d] | Richland-Chambers Reservoir (Texas); two gauges | 5,000 | Stream flow | C: 1965-1969 V: 1970-1984 | | | 0.87 and 0.84 | 0.77 and 0.84 | | | | | 0.65 and 0.82 | 0.52 and 0.82 | | |
| Srivastava et al. (2006)[f] | West Fork Brandywine Creek (Pennsylvania) | 47.6 | Base flow | C: July 1994 to Dec. 1997 V: Jan. 1999 to May 2001 | | | 0.51 | -0.16 | | | | | 0.29 | -1.2 | | |
| | | | Surface flow | | | | 0.38 | 0.20 | | | | | 0.39 | -0.35 | | |
| | | | Total flow | | | | 0.57 | 0.54 | | | | | 0.34 | -0.17 | | |
| Stewart et al. (2006) | Upper North Bosque River (Texas) | 932.5 | Stream flow | C: 1994-1999 V: 2001-1902 | | | 0.87 | 0.76 | | | | | 0.92 | 0.80 | | |
| Stonefelt et al. (2000) | Wind River (Wyoming) | 5,000 | Stream flow | 1990-1997 | | | 0.91 | | | | | | | | | |
| Thomson et al. (2003)[d,g] | Conterminous U.S. (18 MWRRs; fig. 2) | -- | Water yield | 1960-1989 (overall mean) | | | | | | | | | | | 0.96 | |
| | | | | 1960-1989 (8-digit means by MWRR) | | | | | | | | | | | 0.05 to 0.94 | |
| Tolson and Shoemaker (2007)[d,h] | Cannonsville Reservoir (New York); six gauges | 37 to 913[d] | Stream flow | Varying periods | 0.64 to 0.80 | 0.59 to 0.80 | | | | | 0.69 to 0.88 | 0.43 to 0.88 | 0.88 to 0.97 | 0.88 to 0.97 | | |
| Tripathi et al. (2003) | Nagwan (India) | 92.5 | Surface runoff | 1997 (daily) 1992-1998 (monthly) (June - Oct.) | | | | | | | 0.91 | 0.87 | 0.97 | 0.98 | | |
| Tripathi et al. (2006)[d] | Nagwan (India) | 90.3 | Surface runoff | 1995-1998 | | | | | | | | | 0.86 to 0.90 | | | |
| Vaché et al. (2002) | Buck Creek and Walnut Creek (Iowa) | 88.2 and 51.3 | Stream flow | Varying periods | | | 0.64 and 0.67 | | | | | | | | | |
| Van Liew et al. (2003a)[i] | Little Washita River (Oklahoma); C: two gauges, V: six gauges | 2.9 to 610 | Stream flow | Varying periods | | 0.56 and 0.58 | | 0.66 and 0.79 | | | | -0.35 to 0.72 | | -1.1 to 0.89 | | |
| Van Liew and Garbrecht (2003) | Little Washita River (Oklahoma); C: two gauges, V: three gauges | 160 to 610 | Stream flow | Varying periods | | 0.60 and 0.40 | | 0.75 and 0.71 | | | | -0.06 to 0.71 | | 0.45 to 0.86 | | |
| Van Liew et al. (2003b)[d] | Little Washita River (Oklahoma); two gauges | 160 | Stream flow | Oct. 1992 to Sept. 2000 | | 0.55 and 0.59 | | 0.78 and 0.77 | | | | | | | | |

**Table 2** (cont'd). Summary of reported SWAT hydrologic calibration and validation coefficient of determination ($R^2$) and Nash-Sutcliffe model efficiency (NSE) statistics.

| Reference | Watershed | Drainage Area (km²)[a] | Indicator | Time Period (C = calib., V = valid.) | Calibration Daily R² | NSE | Monthly R² | NSE | Annual R² | NSE | Validation Daily R² | NSE | Monthly R² | NSE | Annual R² | NSE |
|---|---|---|---|---|---|---|---|---|---|---|---|---|---|---|---|---|
| Van Liew et al. (2007)[f] | Little River (Georgia, U.S.); two gauges | 114 and 330 | Stream flow | C: 1997-2002 V: 1972-1996 | | | 0.64 and 0.71 | 0.83 and 0.90 | | | | | 0.66 and 0.68 | 0.88 and 0.89 | | |
| | Little Washita River (Oklahoma); three gauges | 160 to 600 | Stream flow | C: 1993-1999 V: varying periods | | | 0.54 and 0.63 | 0.68 and 0.76 | | | | | 0.13 to 0.56 | -0.36 to 0.60 | | |
| | Mahantango Creek (Pennsylvania); two gauges | 0.4 and 7 | Stream flow | C: 1997-2000 V: varying periods | | | 0.46 and 0.69 | 0.84 and 0.88 | | | | | 0.35 to 0.54 | 0.46 to 0.75 | | |
| | Reynolds Creek (Idaho); three gauges | 36 to 239 | Stream flow | C: 1968-1972 V: varying periods | | | 0.51 to 0.73 | 0.52 to 0.79 | | | | | -0.17 to 0.62 | 0.21 to 0.74 | | |
| | Walnut Gulch (Arizona); three gauges | 24 to 149 | Stream flow | C: 1968-1972 V: 1973-1982 | | | 0.30 to 0.76 | 0.48 to 0.86 | | | | | -1.0 to -1.8 | -0.62 to -2.5 | | |
| Varanou et al. (2002) | Ali Efenti (Greece) | 2,796 | Stream flow | 1977-1993 | | | 0.62 | 0.81 | | | | | | | | |
| Vazquez-Amabile and Engel (2005)[c] | Muscatatuck River (Indiana); three gauges | 2,952 | Stream flow | C: 1980-1994 V: 1995-2002 | | | -0.23 to 0.28 | 0.59 to 0.80 | | | | | -0.35 to 0.48 | 0.49 to 0.81 | | |
| | | | Ground water table depth | | | | -0.12 to 0.28 | 0.36 to 0.61 | | | | | -0.74 to 0.33 | -0.51 to 0.38 | | |
| Vazquez-Amábile et al. (2006) | St. Joseph River (Indiana, Michigan, and Ohio); C: three gauges, V: four gauges | 2,800 | Stream flow | C: 1989-1998 V: 1999-2002 | | | 0.46 to 0.65 | 0.64 to 0.74 | | | 0.50 to 0.66 | 0.33 to 0.60 | 0.73 to 0.76 | 0.64 to 0.74 | | |
| Veith et al. (2005) | Watershed FD-36 (Pennsylvania) | 0.395 | Stream flow | 1997-2000 (April to Oct.) | | | 0.63 | 0.75 | | | | | | | | |
| Von Stackelberg et al. (2007)[b] | Research watersheds D1 and D2 (Uruguay) | 0.69 and 1.08 | Stream flow | July 2000 to June 2004 (reduced ET scenario) | 0.92 and 0.93 | 0.77 and 0.71 | | | | | | | | | | |
| | | | | (added groundwater scenario) | 0.93 and 0.94 | 0.78 and 0.72 | | | | | | | | | | |
| Wang and Melesse (2005)[i] | Wild Rice River (Minnesota); two gauges | 2,419 and 4,040.3 | Stream flow | Varying periods | 0.73 and 0.68 | 0.64 and 0.67 | 0.89 and 0.86 | 0.86 and 0.86 | 0.82 and 0.73 | 0.80 and 0.72 | 0.69 and 0.52 | 0.62 and 0.50 | 0.93 and 0.83 | 0.90 and 0.83 | 0.93 and 0.82 | 0.90 and 0.68 |
| Wang and Melesse (2006)[i] | Elm River (North Dakota); subwatershed | 515.4 | Stream flow | C: Dec. 1984 to Nov. 1986 V: Dec. 1981 to Nov. 1984 (STATSGO soils) | 0.53 | 0.51 | 0.89 | 0.88 | | | 0.55 | 0.31 | 0.53 | 0.50 | | |
| | | | | (SSURGO soils) | 0.51 | 0.49 | 0.92 | 0.92 | | | 0.55 | 0.26 | 0.53 | 0.49 | | |
| Wang et al. (2006)[d,i] | Wild Rice River (Minnesota); two gauges | 2,419 and 4,040.3 | Stream flow | Varying periods | 0.68 to 0.76 | 0.64 to 0.70 | 0.86 to 0.92 | 0.86 to 0.90 | 0.73 to 0.91 | 0.72 to 0.90 | 0.52 to 0.69 | 0.46 to 0.64 | 0.83 to 0.93 | 0.80 to 0.91 | 0.82 to 0.93 | 0.68 to 0.91 |
| Watson et al. (2005)[k] | Woady Yaloak River (Australia) | 306 | Stream flow | C: 1978-1989 V: 1990-2001 | | | 0.54 | 0.77 | | 0.77 | | | 0.47 | 0.79 | | 0.91 |
| Weber et al. (2001) | Aar (Germany) | 59.8 | Stream flow | 1986-1987 (daily), 1983-1987 (monthly) | | | 0.63 | 0.74 | | | | | | | | |
| White and Chaubey (2005)[c,i,j] | Beaver Reservoir (Arkansas); three gauges | 362 to 1,020 | Stream flow | C: 1999 and 2000 V: 2001 and 2002 | | | 0.41 to 0.91 | 0.50 to 0.89 | | | | | 0.77 to 0.91 | 0.72 to 0.87 | | |

Van Liew and Garbrecht (2003) evaluated SWAT''s ability to predict streamflow under varying climatic conditions for three nested sub-watersheds in the 610 km² Little Washita River experimental watershed in southwestern Oklahoma. They found that SWAT could adequately simulate runoff for dry, average, and wet climatic conditions in one sub-watershed, following calibration for relatively wet years in two of the sub-watersheds. Govender and Everson (2005) report rela-

**Table 2** (cont'd). Summary of reported SWAT hydrologic calibration and validation coefficient of determination (R²) and Nash-Sutcliffe model efficiency (NSE) statistics.

| Reference | Watershed | Drainage Area (km²)[a] | Indicator | Time Period (C = calib., V = valid.) | Calibration Daily R² | NSE | Monthly R² | NSE | Annual R² | NSE | Validation Daily R² | NSE | Monthly R² | NSE | Annual R² | NSE |
|---|---|---|---|---|---|---|---|---|---|---|---|---|---|---|---|---|
| Wu and Johnston (2007) | South Branch Ontonagon River (Michigan) | 901 | Stream flow | C: 1948-1949 V: 1950-1965 (drought years for calib.) | | | | 0.8 | | | | | | 0.8 | | |
| | | | | C: 1969-1970 V: 1950-1965 (average years for calib.) | | | | 0.9 | | | | | | 0.4 | | |
| Wu and Xu (2006)[c] | Amite, Tangipahoa, and Tickfaw Rivers (Louisiana) | 662.2 to 3434.9 | Stream flow | C: 1975-1977 V: 1979-1999 | 0.83 to 0.93 | | 0.94 to 0.96 | | | | 0.69 to 0.78 | | 0.81 to 0.87 | | | |
| Zhang et al. (2007) | Luohe River (China) | 5,239 | Stream flow | C: 1992-1996 V: 1997-2000 | 0.82 | 0.65 | 0.82 | 0.64 | | | 0.74 | 0.54 | 0.86 | 0.82 | | |

[a] Based on drainage areas to the gauge(s) rather than total watershed area where reported (see footnote [c] for further information).
[b] The same statistics were also reported by Bracmort et al. (2006); the validation time period was not reported and thus was inferred from graphical results reported by Bracmort et al. (2006).
[c] Explicit or estimated drainage areas were not reported for some or all of the gauge sites; the total watershed area is listed for those studies that reported it.
[d] The exact time scale of comparison was not explicitly stated and thus was inferred from other information provided.
[e] These statistics were computed on the basis of comparisons between simulated and measured data within specific years, rather than across multiple years.
[f] The SWAT simulations were not calibrated.
[g] These statistics represent ranges for different input data configurations for either: (1) different combinations of land use, DEM, and/or soil resolution inputs; (2) different subwatershed/HRU configurations; or (3) different ET equation options.
[h] Specific calibration and/or validation time periods were reported, but the statistics were based on the overall simulated time period (calibration plus validation time periods).
[i] Other statistics were reported for different time periods, conditions, gauge combinations, and/or variations in selected in input data.
[j] The comparisons were performed on an hourly basis for this study, for 24 different runoff events, because the Green and Ampt infiltration method was used.
[k] A modified SWAT model was used.
[l] As reported in Cerucci and Conrad (2003).
[m] A similar set of Raccoon River watershed statistics were reported for slightly different time periods by Secchi et al. (2007).
[n] The APEX model (Williams and Izaurralde, 2006) was interfaced with SWAT for this study. The calibration statistic was based on a comparison between simulated and measured flows at the watershed outlet, while the validation statistic was based on a comparison between simulated and measured flows averaged across 11 different gauges including the watershed outlet.
[o] The calibration and validation statistics were also reported by Santhi et al. (2001b).
[p] Similar statistics for the same time periods were reported by Thomsen et al. (2005).
[q] As reported by Benaman et al. (2005).
[r] Previous NSE statistics were reported by Van Liew et al. (2005) for the same Little River and Little Washita River subwatersheds and time periods for four different sets of simulations (one set was based on a manual calibration approach, while the other three sets were based on an automatic calibration approach with different objective functions and/or selected calibration input parameters).
[s] The statistics for the War Eagle Creek gauge were also reported by Migliaccio et al. (2007).

tively strong streamflow simulation results (Table 2) for a small (0.68 km²) research watershed in South Africa. However, they also found that SWAT performed better in drier years than in a wet year, and that the model was unable to adequately simulate the growth of Mexican Weeping Pine due to inaccurate accounting of observed increased ET rates in mature plantations.

Qi and Grunwald (2005) point out that, in most studies, SWAT has usually been calibrated and validated at the drainage outlet of a watershed. In their study, they calibrated and validated SWAT for four sub-watersheds and at the drainage outlet (Table 2). They found that spatially distributed calibration and validation accounted for hydrologic patterns in the sub-watersheds. Other studies that report the use of multiple gages to perform hydrologic calibration and validation with SWAT include Cao et al. (2006), White and Chaubey (2005), Vazquez-Amb̄ile and Engel (2005), and Santhi et al. (2001a).

### 3.1.2 Applications Accounting for Base Flow and/or for Karst-Influenced Systems

Arnold et al. (1995a) and Arnold and Allen (1999) describe a digital filter technique that can be used for determining separation of base and groundwater flow from overall streamflow, which has been used to estimate base flow and/or groundwater flow in several SWAT studies (e.g. Arnold et al., 2000; Santhi et al., 2001a; Hao et al., 2004; Cheng et al., 2006; Kalin and Hantush, 2006; Jha et al., 2007). Arnold et al. (2000) found that SWAT groundwater recharge and discharge (base flow) estimates for specific 8-digit watersheds compared well with filtered estimates for the 491,700 km$^2$ upper Mississippi River basin. Jha et al. (2007) report accurate estimates of streamflow (Table 2) for the 9,400 km$^2$ Raccoon River watershed in west central Iowa, and that their predicted base flow was similar to both the filtered estimate and a previous base flow estimate. Kalin and Hantush (2006) report accurate surface runoff and streamflow results for the 120 km$^2$ Pocono Creek watershed in eastern Pennsylvania (Table 2); their base flow estimates were weaker, but they state those estimates were not a performance criteria. Base flow and other flow components estimated with SWAT by Srivastava et al. (2006) for the 47.6 km$^2$ West Branch Brandywine Creek watershed in southwest Pennsylvania were found to be generally poor (Table 2). Peterson and Hamlett (1998) also found that SWAT was not able to simulate base flows for the 39.4 km$^2$ Ariel Creek watershed in northeast Pennsylvania, due to the presence of soil fragipans. Chu and Shirmohammadi (2004) found that SWAT was unable to simulate an extremely wet year for a 3.46 km$^2$ watershed in Maryland. After removing the wet year, the surface runoff, base flow, and streamflow results were within acceptable accuracy on a monthly basis. Subsurface flow results also improved when the base flow was corrected.

Spruill et al. (2000) calibrated and validated SWAT with 1 year of data each for a small experimental watershed in Kentucky. The 1995 and 1996 daily NSE values reflected poor peak flow values and recession rates, but the monthly flows were more accurate (Table 2). Their analysis confirmed the results of a dye trace study in a central Kentucky karst watershed, indicating that a much larger area contributed to streamflow than was described by topographic boundaries. Coffey et al. (2004) report similar statistical results for the same Kentucky watershed (Table 2). Benham et al. (2006) report that SWAT streamflow results (Table 2) did not meet calibration criteria for the karst-influenced 367 km$^2$ Shoal Creek watershed in southwest Missouri, but that visual inspection of the simulated and observed hydrographs indicated that the system was satisfactorily modeled. They suggest that SWAT was not able to capture the conditions of a very dry year in combination with flows sustained by the karst features.

Afinowicz et al. (2005) modified SWAT in order to more realistically simulate rapid subsurface water movement through karst terrain in the 360 km$^2$ Guadalupe River watershed in southwest Texas. They report that simulated base flows matched measured streamflows after the modification, and that the predicted daily and monthly and daily results (Table 2) fell within the range of published model efficiencies for similar systems. Eckhardt et al. (2002) also found that their modifications for SWAT-G resulted in greatly improved simulation of subsurface interflow in German low mountain conditions (Table 2).

### 3.1.3 Soil Water, Recharge, Tile Flow, and Related Studies

Mapfumo et al. (2004) tested the model's ability to simulate soil water patterns in small watersheds under three grazing intensities in Alberta, Canada. They observed that SWAT had a tendency to overpredict soil water in dry soil conditions and to underpredict in wet soil conditions. Overall, the model was adequate in simulating soil water patterns for all three watersheds with a daily time step. SWAT was used by Deliberty and Legates (2003) to document 30-year (1962-1991) long-term average soil moisture conditions and variability, and topsoil variability, for Oklahoma. The model was judged to be able to accurately estimate the relative magnitude and variability of soil moisture in the study region. Soil moisture was simulated with SWAT by Narasimhan et al. (2005) for six large river basins in Texas at a spatial resolution of 16 $km^2$ and a temporal resolution of one week. The simulated soil moisture was evaluated on the basis of vegetation response, by using 16 years of normalized difference vegetation index (NDVI) data derived from NOAA-AVHRR satellite data. The predicted soil moistures were well correlated with agriculture and pasture NDVI values. Narasimhan and Srinivasan (2005) describe further applications of a soil moisture deficit index and an evapotranspiration deficit index.

Arnold et al. (2005) validated a crack flow model for SWAT, which simulates soil moisture conditions with depth to account for flow conditions in dry weather. Simulated crack volumes were in agreement with seasonal trends, and the predicted daily surface runoff levels also were consistent with measured runoff data (Table 2). Sun and Cornish (2005) simulated 30 years of bore data for a 437 $km^2$ watershed. They used SWAT to estimate recharge in the headwaters of the Liverpool Plains in New South Wales, Australia. These authors determined that SWAT could estimate recharge and incorporate land use and land management at the watershed scale. A code modification was performed by Vazquez-Ambi le and Engel (2005) that allowed reporting of soil moisture for each soil layer. The soil moisture values were then converted into groundwater table levels based on the approach used in DRAINMOD (Skaggs, 1982). It was concluded that predictions of groundwater table levels would be useful to include in SWAT.

Modifications were performed by Du et al. (2006) to SWAT2000 to improve the original SWAT tile drainage function. The modified model was referred to as SWAT-M and resulted in clearly improved tile drainage and streamflow predictions for the relatively flat and intensively cropped 51.3 $km^2$ Walnut Creek watershed in central Iowa (Table 2). Green et al. (2006) report a further application of the revised tile drainage routine using SWAT2005 for a large tile-drained watershed in north central Iowa, which resulted in a greatly improved estimate of the overall water balance for the watershed (Table 2). This study also presented the importance of ensuring that representative runoff events are present in both the calibration and validation in order to improve the model's effectiveness.

### 3.1.4 Snowmelt-related Applications

Fontaine et al. (2002) modified the original SWAT snow accumulation and snowmelt routines by incorporating improved accounting of snowpack temperature and accumulation, snowmelt, and areal snow coverage, and an option to input precipitation and temperature as a function of elevation bands. These enhancements resulted in greatly improved streamflow estimates for the mountainous 5,000 km$^2$ upper Wind River basin in Wyoming (Table 2). Abbaspour et al. (2007) calibrated several snow-related parameters and used four elevation bands in their SWAT simulation of the 1,700 km$^2$ Thur watershed in Switzerland that is characterized by a pre-alpine/alpine climate. They report excellent SWAT discharge estimates.

Other studies have reported mixed SWAT snowmelt simulation results, including three that reported poor results for watersheds (0.395 to 47.6 km$^2$) in eastern Pennsylvania. Peterson and Hamlett (1998) found that SWAT was unable to account for unusually large snowmelt events, and Srinivasan et al. (2005) found that SWAT underpredicted winter streamflows; both studies used SWAT versions that predated the modifications performed by Fontaine et al. (2002). Srivastava et al. (2006) also found that SWAT did not adequately predict winter flows. Qi and Grunwald found that SWAT did not predict winter season precipitation-runoff events well for the 3,240 km$^2$ Sandusky River watershed. Chanasyk et al. (2003) found that SWAT was not able to replicate snowmelt-dominated runoff (Table 2) for three small grassland watersheds in Alberta that were managed with different grazing intensities. Wang and Melesse (2005) report that SWAT accurately simulated the monthly and annual (and seasonal) discharges for the Wild Rice River watershed in Minnesota, in addition to the spring daily streamflows, which were predominantly from melted snow. Accurate snowmelt-dominated streamflow predictions were also found by Wang and Melesse (2006) for the Elm River in North Dakota. Wu and Johnston (2007) found that the snow melt parameters used in SWAT are altered by drought conditions and that streamflow predictions for the 901 km$^2$ South Branch Ontonagon River in Michigan improved when calibration was based on a drought period (vs. average climatic conditions), which more accurately reflected the drought conditions that characterized the validation period. Statistical results for all these studies are listed in Table 2.

Benaman et al. (2005) found that SWAT2000 reasonably replicated streamflows for the 1,200 km$^2$ Cannonsville Reservoir watershed in New York (Table 2), but that the model underestimated snowmelt-driven winter and spring streamflows. Improved simulation of cumulative winter streamflows and spring base flows were obtained by Tolston and Shoemaker (2007) for the same watershed (Table 2) by modifying SWAT2000 so that lateral subsurface flow could occur in frozen soils. Francos et al. (2001) also modified SWAT to obtain improved streamflow results for the Kerava River watershed in Finland (Table 2) by using a different snowmelt submodel that was based on degree-days and that could account for variations in land use by sub-watershed. Incorporating modifications such as those described in these two studies may improve the accuracy of snowmelt-related processes in future SWAT versions.

### 3.1.5 Irrigation and Brush Removal Scenarios

Gosain et al. (2005) assessed SWAT's ability to simulate return flow after the introduction of canal irrigation in a basin in Andra Pradesh, India. SWAT provided the assistance water managers needed in planning and managing their water resources under various scenarios. Santhi et al. (2005) describe a new canal irrigation routine that was used in SWAT. Cumulative irrigation withdrawal was estimated for each district for each of three different conservation scenarios (relative to a reference scenario). The percentage of water that was saved was also calculated. SWAT was used by Afinowicz et al. (2005) to evaluate the influence of woody plants on water budgets of semi-arid rangeland in southwest Texas. Baseline brush cover and four brush removal scenarios were evaluated. Removal of heavy brush resulted in the greatest changes in ET (approx. 32 mm year$^{-1}$ over the entire basin), surface runoff, base flow, and deep recharge. Lemberg et al. (2002) also describe brush removal scenarios.

### 3.1.6 Applications Incorporating Wetlands, Reservoirs, and Other Impoundments

Arnold et al. (2001) simulated a wetland with SWAT that was proposed to be sited next to Walker Creek in the Fort Worth, Texas area. They found that the wetland needed to be above 85% capacity for 60% of a 14-year simulation period, in order to continuously function over the entire study period. Conan et al. (2003b) found that SWAT adequately simulated conversion of wetlands to dry land for the upper Guadiana River basin in Spain but was unable to represent all of the discharge details impacted by land use alterations. Wu and Johnston (2007) accounted for wetlands and lakes in their SWAT simulation of a Michigan watershed, which covered over 23% of the watershed. The impact of flood-retarding structures on streamflow for dry, average, and wet climatic conditions in Oklahoma was investigated with SWAT by Van Liew et al. (2003b). The flood-retarding structures were found to reduce average annual streamflow by about 3% and to effectively reduce annual daily peak runoff events. Reductions of low streamflows were also predicted, especially during dry conditions. Mishra et al. (2007) report that SWAT accurately accounted for the impact of three checkdams on both daily and monthly streamflows for the 17 km$^2$ Banha watershed in northeast India (Table 2). Hotchkiss et al. (2000) modified SWAT based on U.S. Army Corp of Engineers reservoir rules for major Missouri River reservoirs, which resulted in greatly improved simulation of reservoir dynamics over a 25-year period. Kang et al. (2006) incorporated a modified impoundment routine into SWAT, which allowed more accurate simulation of the impacts of rice paddy fields within a South Korean watershed (Table 2).

### 3.1.7 Green-Ampt Applications

Very few SWAT applications in the literature report the use of the Green-Ampt infiltration option. Di Luzio and Arnold (2004) report sub-hourly results for two different calibration methods using the Green-Ampt method (Table 2). King et al. (1999) found that the Green-Ampt option did not provide any significant advantage as compared to the curve number approach for uncalibrated SWAT simulations for the 21.3 km² Goodwin Creek watershed in Mississippi (Table 2). Kannan et al. (2007b) report that SWAT streamflow results were more accurate using the curve number approach as compared to the Green-Ampt method for a small watershed in the U.K. (Table 2). However, they point out that several assumptions were not optimal for the Green-Ampt approach.

## 3.2 Pollutant Loss Studies

Nearly 50% of the reviewed SWAT studies (Table 1) report simulation results of one or more pollutant loss indicator. Many of these studies describe some form of verifying pollutant prediction accuracy, although the extent of such reporting is less than what has been published for hydrologic assessments. Table 3 lists $R^2$ and NSE statistics for 37 SWAT pollutant loss studies, which again are used here as key indicators of model performance. The majority of the $R^2$ and NSE values reported in Table 3 exceed 0.5, indicating that the model was able to replicate a wide range of observed in-stream pollutant levels. However, poor results were again reported for some studies, especially for daily comparisons. Similar to the points raised for the hydrologic results, some of the weaker results were due in part to inadequate characterization of input data (Bouraoui et al., 2002), uncalibrated simulations of pollutant movement (Bärlund et al., 2007), and uncertainties in observed pollutant levels (Harmel et al., 2006).

**Table 3.** Summary of reported SWAT environmental indicator calibration and validation coefficient of determination ($R^2$) and Nash-Sutcliffe model efficiency (NSE) statistics.

| Reference | Watershed | Drainage Area (km²)[a] | Indicator[b] | Time Period (C = calib., V = valid.) | Calibration Daily $R^2$ | NSE | Calibration Monthly $R^2$ | NSE | Calibration Annual $R^2$ | NSE | Validation Daily $R^2$ | NSE | Validation Monthly $R^2$ | NSE | Validation Annual $R^2$ | NSE |
|---|---|---|---|---|---|---|---|---|---|---|---|---|---|---|---|---|
| Arabi et al. (2006b)[c] | Dreisbach and Smith Fry (Indiana) | 6.2 and 7.3 | Suspended solids | C: 1974-1975 V: 1976 to May 1977 | | | 0.97 and 0.94 | 0.92 and 0.86 | | | | | 0.86 and 0.85 | 0.75 and 0.68 | | |
| | | | Total P | | | | 0.93 and 0.64 | 0.78 and 0.51 | | | | | 0.90 and 0.73 | 0.79 and 0.37 | | |
| | | | Total N | | | | 0.76 and 0.61 | 0.54 and 0.50 | | | | | 0.75 and 0.52 | 0.85 and 0.72 | | |
| Bärlund et al. (2007)[d],[e] | Lake Pyhäjärvi (Finland) | -- | Sediment | 1990-1994 | | 0.01 | | | | | | | | | | |
| Behera and Panda (2006) | Kapgari (India) | 9.73 | Sediment | C: 2002 V: 2003 (rainy season) | 0.93 | 0.84 | | | | | 0.89 | 0.86 | | | | |
| | | | Nitrate | | 0.93 | 0.92 | | | | | 0.87 | 0.83 | | | | |
| | | | Total P | | 0.92 | 0.83 | | | | | 0.94 | 0.89 | | | | |
| Bouraoui et al. (2002) | Ouse River (Yorkshire, U.K.) | 3,500 | Nitrate | 1986-1990 | | | | 0.64 | | | | | | | | |
| | | | Ortho P | | | | | 0.02 | | | | | | | | |
| Bouraoui et al. (2004) | Vantaanjoki (Finland); subwatershed | 295 | Susp. solids | 1982-1984 | | | 0.49 | | | | | | | | | |
| | | | Total N | | | | 0.61 | | | | | | | | | |
| | | | Total P | | | | 0.74 | | | | | | | | | |
| | Entire watershed | 1,682 | Nitrate | 1974-1998 | | | | | | | | | 0.34 | | | |
| | | | Total P | | | | | | | | | | 0.62 | | | |
| Bracmort et al. (2006)[c] | Dreisbach and Smith Fry (Indiana) | 6.2 and 7.3 | Mineral P | C: 1974-1975 V: 1976 to May 1977 | | | 0.92 and 0.90 | 0.84 and 0.78 | | | | | 0.86 and 0.73 | 0.74 and 0.51 | | |
| Cerucci and Conrad (2003)[e],[f] | Townbrook (New York) | 36.8 | Sediment | Oct. 1999- Sept. 2000 | | | 0.70 | | | | | | | | | |
| | | | Dissolved P | | | | 0.91 | | | | | | | | | |
| | | | Particulate P | | | | 0.40 | | | | | | | | | |
| Chaplot et al. (2004) | Walnut Creek | 51.3 | Nitrate | 1991-1998 | | | 0.56 | | | | | | | | | |
| Cheng et al. (2006) | Heihe River (China) | 7,241 | Sediment | C: 1992-1997 V: 1998-1999 | | | 0.70 | 0.74 | | | | | 0.78 | 0.76 | | |
| | | | Ammonia | C: 1992-1997 V: 1998-1999 | | | 0.75 | 0.76 | | | | | 0.74 | 0.72 | | |
| Chu et al. (2004)[g] | Warner Creek | 3.46 | Sediment | Varying periods | 0.10 | 0.05 | | | | | 0.19 | 0.11 | | | 0.91 | 0.90 |
| | | | Nitrate | | 0.27 | 0.16 | | | | | 0.38 | 0.36 | | | 0.96 | 0.90 |
| | | | Ammonium | | | | | | | | 0.38 | -0.05 | | | 0.80 | 0.19 |
| | | | Total Kjeldahl N | | | | | | | | 0.40 | 0.15 | | | 0.66 | -0.56 |
| | | | Soluble P | | 0.39 | -0.08 | | | | | 0.65 | 0.64 | | | 0.87 | 0.80 |
| | | | Total P | | | | | | | | 0.38 | 0.08 | | | 0.83 | 0.19 |
| Cotter et al. (2003) | Moores Creek (Arkansas) | 18.9 | Sediment | 1997-1998 | | | 0.48 | | | | | | | | | |
| | | | Nitrate | | | | 0.44 | | | | | | | | | |
| | | | Total P | | | | 0.66 | | | | | | | | | |
| Di Luzio et al. (2002) | Upper North Bosque River (Texas) | 932.5 | Sediment | Jan. 1993 to July 1998 | | | | | | | | | 0.78 | | | |
| | | | Organic N | | | | | | | | | | 0.60 | | | |
| | | | Nitrate | | | | | | | | | | 0.60 | | | |
| | | | Organic P | | | | | | | | | | 0.70 | | | |
| | | | Ortho P | | | | | | | | | | 0.58 | | | |

**Table 3** (cont'd). Summary of reported SWAT environmental indicator calibration and validation coefficient of determination ($R^2$) and Nash-Sutcliffe model efficiency (NSE) statistics.

| Reference | Watershed | Drainage Area (km²)[a] | Indicator[b] | Time Period (C = calib., V = valid.) | Calib. Daily R² | Calib. Daily NSE | Calib. Monthly R² | Calib. Monthly NSE | Calib. Annual R² | Calib. Annual NSE | Valid. Daily R² | Valid. Daily NSE | Valid. Monthly R² | Valid. Monthly NSE | Valid. Annual R² | Valid. Annual NSE |
|---|---|---|---|---|---|---|---|---|---|---|---|---|---|---|---|---|
| Du et al. (2006)[a],[b],[d] | Walnut Creek (Iowa); subwatershed (site 310) and watershed outlet | 51.3 | Nitrate (stream flow) | C: 1992-1995 V: 1996-2001 (SWAT2000) | | -0.37 and -0.41 | | -0.21 and -0.26 | | | | -0.14 and -0.18 | | -0.21 and -0.22 | | |
| | Subwatershed (site 210) | -- | Nitrate (tile flow) | (SWAT2000) | | -0.60 | | -0.08 | | | | -0.16 | | -0.31 | | |
| | Subwatershed (site 310) and watershed outlet | 51.3 | Nitrate (stream flow) | (SWAT-M)[c] | | 0.61 and 0.53 | | 0.91 and 0.85 | | | | 0.41 and 0.26 | | 0.80 and 0.67 | | |
| | Subwatershed (site 210) | -- | Nitrate (tile flow) | (SWAT-M) | | 0.25 | | 0.73 | | | | 0.42 | | 0.71 | | |
| | Subwatershed (site 310) and watershed outlet | 51.3 | Atrazine (stream flow) | (SWAT2000) | | -0.05 and -0.12 | | -0.01 and -0.02 | | | | -0.02 and -0.39 | | -0.04 and 0.06 | | |
| | Subwatershed (site 210) | -- | Atrazine (tile flow) | (SWAT2000) | | -0.47 | | -0.04 | | | | -0.46 | | -0.06 | | |
| | Subwatershed (site 310) and watershed outlet | 51.3 | Atrazine (stream flow) | (SWAT-M) | | 0.21 and 0.47 | | 0.50 and 0.73 | | | | 0.12 and -0.41 | | 0.53 and 0.58 | | |
| | Subwatershed (site 210) | -- | Atrazine (tile flow) | (SWAT-M) | | 0.51 | | 0.92 | | | | 0.09 | | 0.31 | | |
| Gikas et al. (2005)[a],[b] | Vistonis Lagoon (Greece); nine gauges | 1,349 | Sediment | C: May 1998 to June 1999 V: Nov. 1999 to Jan. 2000 | | | | 0.40 to 0.98 | | | | | | 0.34 to 0.98 | | |
| | | | Nitrate | | | | | 0.51 to 0.87 | | | | | | 0.57 to 0.89 | | |
| | | | Total P | | | | | 0.50 to 0.82 | | | | | | 0.43 to 0.97 | | |
| Grizzetti et al. (2005)[a] | Parts of four watersheds (U.K.); C: one gauge, V: two gauges, annual: 50 gauges | 1,380 to 8,900 | Nitrate and nitrite | 1995-1999 | 0.24 | | 0.32 | | | | 0.004 and 0.28 | | -0.66 and 0.38 | | 0.68 | |
| Grizzetti et al. (2003) | Vantaanjoki (Finland); three gauges | 295 to 1,682 | Total N | Varying periods | 0.59 | | | | | | 0.43 and 0.51 | | 0.10 and 0.30 | | | |
| | | | Total P | | 0.74 | | | | | | 0.54 and 0.44 | | 0.63 and 0.64 | | | |
| Grunwald and Qi (2006) | Sandusky (Ohio); three gauges | 90.3 to 3,240 | Suspended sediment | C: 1998-1999 V: 2000-2001 | | | | -5.1 to 0.2 | | | | | | -1.0 to 0.02 | | |
| | | | Total P | | | | | -0.89 to 0.07 | | | | | | 0.08 to 0.45 | | |
| | | | Nitrite | | | | | -4.6 to 0.19 | | | | | | -0.16 to 0.48 | | |
| | | | Nitrate | | | | | -0.12 to 0.29 | | | | | | -0.1 to 0.57 | | |
| | | | Ammonia | | | | | -0.44 to -0.24 | | | | | | -0.44 to -0.21 | | |

Table 3 (cont'd). Summary of reported SWAT environmental indicator calibration and validation coefficient of determination ($R^2$) and Nash-Sutcliffe model efficiency (NSE) statistics.

| Reference | Watershed | Drainage Area (km²)[a] | Indicator[b] | Time Period (C = calib., V = valid.) | Cal. Daily R² | Cal. Daily NSE | Cal. Monthly R² | Cal. Monthly NSE | Cal. Annual R² | Cal. Annual NSE | Val. Daily R² | Val. Daily NSE | Val. Monthly R² | Val. Monthly NSE | Val. Annual R² | Val. Annual NSE |
|---|---|---|---|---|---|---|---|---|---|---|---|---|---|---|---|---|
| Hanratty and Stefan (1998) | Cottonwood (Minnesota) | 3,400 | Suspended sediment | 1967-1991 | | | 0.59 | | | | | | | | | |
| | | | Nitrate and nitrite | | | | 0.68 | | | | | | | | | |
| | | | Total P | | | | 0.54 | | | | | | | | | |
| | | | Organic N and ammonia | | | | 0.57 | | | | | | | | | |
| Hao et al. (2004) | Lushi (China) | 4,623 | Sediment | C: 1992-1997 V: 1998-1999 | | | 0.72 | 0.72 | | | | | 0.98 | 0.94 | | |
| Jha et al. (2007)[j] | Raccoon River (Iowa) | 8,930 | Sediment | C: 1981-1992 V: 1993-2003 | | | 0.55 | 0.53 | 0.97 | 0.93 | | | 0.80 | 0.78 | 0.89 | 0.79 |
| | | | Nitrate | | | | 0.76 | 0.73 | 0.83 | 0.78 | | | 0.79 | 0.78 | 0.91 | 0.84 |
| Kang et al. (2006)[k] | Baran (South Korea) | 29.8 | Suspended solids | C: 1996-1997 V: 1999-2000 | 0.77 | 0.70 | | | | | 0.89 | 0.89 | | | | |
| | | | Total N | | 0.84 | 0.73 | | | | | 0.85 | 0.65 | | | | |
| | | | Total P | | 0.81 | 0.42 | | | | | 0.85 | 0.19 | | | | |
| Kaur et al. (2004) | Nagwan (India) | 9.58 | Sediment | C: 1984 and 1992 V: 1981-1983, 1985-1989, and 1991 | 0.54 | -0.67 | | | | | 0.65 | 0.70 | | | | |
| Kirsch et al. (2002) | Rock River (Wisconsin); Windsor gauge | 190 | Sediment | 1991-1995 | | | | | 0.82 | 0.75 | | | | | | |
| | | | Total P | | | | | | 0.95 | 0.07 | | | | | | |
| Mishra et al. (2007) | Banha (India) | 17 | Sediment | C: 1996 V: 1997-2001 | 0.82 | 0.82 | 0.99 | 0.98 | | | 0.77 | 0.58 | 0.89 | 0.63 | | |
| Muleta and Nicklow (2005a) | Big Creek (Illinois) | 86.5 | Sediment | 1999-2001 | 0.42 | | | | | | | | | | | |
| Muleta and Nicklow (2005b) | Big Creek (Illinois); separate gauges for C and V | 23.9 and 86.5 | Sediment | C: June 1999 to Aug. 2001 V: Apr. 2000 to Aug. 2001 | 0.46 | | | | | | -0.005 | | | | | |
| Nasr et al. (2007)[c] | Clarianna, Dripsey, and Oona Water (Ireland) | 15 to 96 | Total P | Varying periods | 0.44 to 0.59 | | | | | | | | | | | |
| Plus et al. (2006)[d,m] | Thau Lagoon (France); two gauges | 280 | Nitrate | 1993-1999 | | | | | | | 0.44 and 0.27 | | | | | |
| | | | Ammonia | | | | | | | | 0.31 and 0.15 | | | | | |
| | | | Organic N | | | | | | | | 0.66 and 0.20 | | | | | |
| Saleh et al. (2000)[n] | Upper North Bosque River (Texas); C: one gauge, V: 11 gauges | 932.5 | Sediment | Oct. 1993 to Aug. 1995 | | | 0.81 | | | | | | 0.94 | | | |
| | | | Nitrate | | | | 0.27 | | | | | | 0.65 | | | |
| | | | Organic N | | | | 0.78 | | | | | | 0.82 | | | |
| | | | Total N | | | | 0.86 | | | | | | 0.97 | | | |
| | | | Ortho P | | | | 0.94 | | | | | | 0.92 | | | |
| | | | Particulate P | | | | 0.54 | | | | | | 0.89 | | | |
| | | | Total P | | | | 0.83 | | | | | | 0.93 | | | |

## 3.2.1 Sediment Studies

Several studies showed the robustness of SWAT in predicting sediment loads at different watershed scales. Saleh et al. (2000) conducted a comprehensive SWAT evaluation for the 932.5 km² upper North Bosque River watershed in north-central Texas, and found that predicted monthly sediment losses matched measured data well but that SWAT daily output was poor (Table 3). Srinivasan et al. (1998) concluded that SWAT sediment accumulation predictions were satisfactory for the 279 km² Mill Creek watershed, again located in north-central Texas. Santhi et al. (2001a) found that SWAT-simulated sediment loads matched measured sediment loads well (Table 3) for two Bosque River (4,277 km²) sub-watersheds, except in March. Arnold et al. (1999b) used SWAT to simulate average annual sedi-

**Table 3** (cont'd). Summary of reported SWAT environmental indicator calibration and validation coefficient of determination ($R^2$) and Nash-Sutcliffe model efficiency (NSE) statistics.

| Reference | Watershed | Drainage Area (km²)[a] | Indicator[b] | Time Period (C = calib., V = valid.) | Calibration Daily $R^2$ | Calibration Daily NSE | Calibration Monthly $R^2$ | Calibration Monthly NSE | Calibration Annual $R^2$ | Calibration Annual NSE | Validation Daily $R^2$ | Validation Daily NSE | Validation Monthly $R^2$ | Validation Monthly NSE | Validation Annual $R^2$ | Validation Annual NSE |
|---|---|---|---|---|---|---|---|---|---|---|---|---|---|---|---|---|
| Saleh and Du (2004) | Upper North Bosque River (Texas) | 932.5 | Total suspended solids | C: Jan. 1994 to June 1995 V: July 1995 to July 1999 | | -2.5 | | 0.83 | | | | -3.5 | | 0.59 | | |
| | | | Nitrate and nitrite | | | 0.04 | | 0.29 | | | | 0.50 | | 0.50 | | |
| | | | Organic N | | | -0.07 | | 0.87 | | | | 0.69 | | 0.77 | | |
| | | | Total N | | | 0.01 | | 0.81 | | | | 0.68 | | 0.75 | | |
| | | | Ortho P | | | 0.08 | | 0.76 | | | | 0.45 | | 0.40 | | |
| | | | Particulate P | | | -0.74 | | 0.59 | | | | 0.59 | | 0.73 | | |
| | | | Total P | | | -0.08 | | 0.77 | | | | 0.63 | | 0.71 | | |
| Santhi et al. (2001a)[d],[e] | Bosque River (Texas); two gauges | 4,277 | Sediment | C: 1993-1997 V: 1998 | | | 0.81 and 0.87 | 0.80 and 0.69 | | | | | 0.98 and 0.95 | 0.70 and 0.23 | | |
| | | | Mineral N | | | | 0.64 and 0.72 | 0.59 and -0.08 | | | | | 0.89 and 0.72 | 0.75 and 0.64 | | |
| | | | Organic N | | | | 0.61 and 0.60 | 0.58 and 0.57 | | | | | 0.92 and 0.71 | 0.73 and 0.43 | | |
| | | | Mineral P | | | | 0.60 and 0.66 | 0.59 and 0.53 | | | | | 0.83 and 0.93 | 0.53 and 0.81 | | |
| | | | Organic P | | | | 0.71 and 0.61 | 0.70 and 0.59 | | | | | 0.95 and 0.80 | 0.72 and 0.39 | | |
| Stewart et al. (2006) | Upper North Bosque River (Texas) | 932.5 | Sediment | C: 1994-1999 V: 2001-2002 | | | 0.94 | 0.80 | | | | | 0.82 | 0.63 | | |
| | | | Mineral N | | | | 0.80 | 0.60 | | | | | 0.57 | -0.04 | | |
| | | | Organic N | | | | 0.87 | 0.71 | | | | | 0.89 | 0.73 | | |
| | | | Mineral P | | | | 0.88 | 0.75 | | | | | 0.82 | 0.37 | | |
| | | | Organic P | | | | 0.85 | 0.69 | | | | | 0.89 | 0.58 | | |
| Tolson and Shoemaker (2007)[d],[e] | Cannonsville (New York) | 37 to 913[c] | Total suspended solids | Varying periods | | | 0.70 (0.47) | 0.67 (0.24) | | | 0.42 and 0.83 | 0.33 and 0.83 | 0.72 and 0.83 | 0.52 and 0.76 | | |
| | | | Total dissolved P | | | | 0.79 (0.84) | 0.78 (0.84) | | | 0.62 and 0.71 | 0.61 and -5.3 | 0.93 and 0.89 | 0.89 and -6.5 | | |
| | | | Particulate P | | | | 0.67 (0.50) | 0.61 (0.26) | | | 0.37 and 0.85 | 0.32 and 0.85 | 0.63 and 0.88 | 0.48 and 0.79 | | |
| | | | Total P | | | | 0.73 (0.58) | 0.78 (0.37) | | | 0.43 and 0.87 | 0.40 and 0.78 | 0.75 and 0.92 | 0.63 and 0.92 | | |
| Tripathi et al. (2003) | Nagwan (India) | 92.5 | Sediment | June-Oct. 1997 | | | | | | | 0.89 | 0.89 | 0.89 | 0.79 | | |
| | | | Nitrate | | | | | | | | 0.89 | | | | | |
| | | | Organic N | | | | | | | | 0.82 | | | | | |
| | | | Soluble P | | | | | | | | 0.82 | | | | | |
| | | | Organic P | | | | | | | | 0.86 | | | | | |
| Vazquez-Amabile et al. (2006)[i] | St. Joseph River (Indiana, Michigan, and Ohio); ten sampling sites | 628.2 to 1620 | Atrazine | 1996-1999 | | | 0.14 | 0.42 | | | | | | | | |
| | Main outlet at Fort Wayne, Indiana | 2,620 | Atrazine | 2000-2004 | | | | | | | 0.27 | -0.31 | 0.59 | 0.28 | | |

ment loads for five major Texas river basins (20,593 to 569,000 km²) and concluded that the SWAT-predicted sediment yields compared reasonably well with estimated sediment yields obtained from rating curves.

Besides Texas, the SWAT sediment yield component has also been tested in several Midwest and northeast U.S. states. Chu et al. (2004) evaluated SWAT sediment prediction for the Warner Creek watershed located in the Piedmont physiographic region of Maryland. Evaluation results indicated strong agreement between yearly measured and SWAT-simulated sediment load, but simulation of monthly sediment loading was poor (Table 3). Tolston and Shoemaker (2007)

**Table 3** (cont'd). Summary of reported SWAT environmental indicator calibration and validation coefficient of determination ($R^2$) and Nash-Sutcliffe model efficiency (NSE) statistics.

| Reference | Watershed | Drainage Area (km²)[a] | Indicator[b] | Time Period (C = calib., V = valid.) | Calibration Daily R² | NSE | Calibration Monthly R² | NSE | Calibration Annual R² | NSE | Validation Daily R² | NSE | Validation Monthly R² | NSE | Validation Annual R² | NSE |
|---|---|---|---|---|---|---|---|---|---|---|---|---|---|---|---|---|
| Veith et al. (2005) | Watershed FD-36 (Pennsylvania) | 0.395 | Sediment | 1997-2000 | | | 0.04 | -0.75 | | | | | | | | |
| White and Chaubey (2005)[i][l][k] | Beaver Reservoir (Arkansas); three gauges | 362 to 1,020 | Sediment | C: 2000 or 2001 V: 2001 or 2002 | | | 0.45 to 0.85 | 0.23 to 0.76 | | | | | 0.69 to 0.82 | 0.32 to 0.85 | | |
| | | | Nitrate and nitrite | | | | 0.01 to 0.84 | -2.36 to 0.29 | | | | | 0.59 and 0.71 | 0.13 and 0.49 | | |
| | | | Total P | | | | 0.50 to 0.82 | 0.40 to 0.67 | | | | | 0.58 and 0.76 | -0.29 and 0.67 | | |

[a] Based on drainage areas to the gauge(s)/sampling site(s) rather than total watershed area where reported (see footnote [d] for further information).

[b] The reported indicators are listed here as reported in each respective study; the standard SWAT variables for relevant in-stream constituents are: sediment, organic nitrogen (N), organic phosphorus (P), nitrate ($NO_3$-N), ammonium ($NH_4$-N), nitrite ($NO_2$-N), and mineral P (Neitsch et al., 2005b).

[c] Arabi et al. (2006b) and Bracmort et al. (2006) reported the same set of $r^2$ and NSE statistics for sediment and total P; the calibration time periods were reported by Arabi et al. (2006b), and the validation time periods were inferred from graphical results reported by Bracmort et al. (2006).

[d] Explicit or estimated drainage areas were not reported for some or all of the gauge sites; the total watershed area is listed for those studies that reported it.

[e] The exact time scale of comparison was not explicitly stated and thus was inferred from other information provided.

[f] The statistics reported for sediment and organic P excluded the months of February and March 2000; large underestimations of both constituents occurred in those two months.

[g] The nutrient statistics were based on adjusted flows that accounted for subsurface flows that originated from outside the watershed as reported by Chu and Shirmohammadi (2004); the annual sediment, nitrate, and soluble P statistics were based on the combined calibration and validation periods.

[h] The daily and monthly statistics were reported based only on the days that sampling occurred.

[i] Other statistics were reported for different time periods, conditions, gauge combinations, and/or variations in selected in input data.

[j] A modified SWAT model was used.

[k] The exact time scale of comparison was not explicitly stated and thus was inferred from other information provided.

[l] A similar set of Raccoon River watershed statistics were reported for slightly different time periods by Secchi et al. (2007).

[m] Specific calibration and/or validation time periods were reported, but the statistics were based on the overall simulated time period (calibration plus validation time periods).

[n] The APEX model (Williams and Izaurralde, 2006) was interfaced with SWAT for this study. The calibration statistics were based on a comparison between simulated and measured flows at the watershed outlet, while the validation statistics were based on a comparison between simulated and measured flows averaged across 11 different gauges.

[o] The calibration and validation statistics were also reported by Santhi et al. (2001b).

[p] The calibration statistics in parentheses include January 1996; an unusually large runoff and erosion event occurred during that month.

[q] As reported by Benamen et al. (2005).

[r] These statistics were computed on the basis of comparisons between simulated and measured data within specific years, rather than across multiple years.

[s] The statistics for the War Eagle Creek subwatershed gauge were also reported by Migliaccio et al. (2007).

modified the SWAT2000 sediment yield equation to account for both the effects of snow cover and snow runoff depth (the latter is not accounted for in the standard SWAT model) to overcome snowmelt-induced prediction problems identified by Benaman et al. (2005) for the Cannonsville Reservoir watershed in New York. They also reported improved sediment loss predictions (Table 3). Jha et al. (2007) found that the sediment loads predicted by SWAT were consistent with sediment loads measured for the Raccoon River watershed in Iowa (Table 3). Arabi et al. (2006b) report satisfactory SWAT sediment simulation results for two small watersheds in Indiana (Table 3). White and Chaubey (2005) report that SWAT sediment predictions for the Beaver Reservoir watershed in northeast Arkansas (Table 3) were satisfactory. Sediment results are also reported by Cotter et al. (2003) for another Arkansas watershed (Table 3). Hanratty and Stefan (1998) calibrated SWAT using water quality and quantity data measured in the Cottonwood River in Minnesota (Table 3). In Wisconsin, Kirsch et al. (2002) calibrated SWAT annual predictions for two sub-watersheds located in the Rock River basin (Table 3), which lies within the glaciated portion of south-central and eastern Wisconsin. Muleta and Nicklow (2005a) calibrated daily SWAT sediment yield with observed sediment yield data from the Big Creek watershed in southern Illinois and concluded that sediment fit seems reasonable (Table 3). However, validation was not conducted due to lack of data.

SWAT sediment simulations have also been evaluated in Asia, Europe, and North Africa. Behera and Panda (2006) concluded that SWAT simulated sediment yield satisfactorily throughout the entire rainy season based on comparisons with daily observed data (Table 3) for an agricultural watershed located in eastern India. Kaur et al. (2004) concluded that SWAT predicted annual sediment yields reasonably well for a test watershed (Table 3) in Damodar-Barakar, India, the second most seriously eroded area in the world. Tripathi et al. (2003) found that SWAT sediment predictions agreed closely with observed daily sediment yield for the same watershed (Table 3). Mishra et al. (2007) found that SWAT accurately replicated the effects of three checkdams on sediment transport (Table 3) within the Banha watershed in northeast India. Hao et al. (2004) state that SWAT was the first physically based watershed model validated in China's Yellow River basin. They found that the predicted sediment loading accurately matched loads measured for the 4,623 km$^2$ Lushi sub-watershed (Table 3). Cheng et al. (2006) successfully tested SWAT (Table 3) using sediment data collected from the 7,241 km$^2$ Heihe River, another tributary of the Yellow River. In Finland, Bärlund et al. (2007) report poor results for uncalibrated simulations performed within the Lake Pyhäjärvi watershed (Table 3). Gikas et al. (2005) conducted an extensive evaluation of SWAT for the Vistonis Lagoon watershed, a mountainous agricultural watershed in northern Greece, and concluded that agreement between observed and SWAT-predicted sediment loads were acceptable (Table 3). Bouraoui et al. (2005) evaluated SWAT for the Medjerda River basin in northern Tunisia and reported that the predicted concentrations of suspended sediments were within an order of magnitude of corresponding measured values.

### 3.2.2 Nitrogen and Phosphorus Studies
Several published studies from the U.S. showed the robustness of SWAT in predicting nutrient losses. Saleh et al. (2000), Saleh and Du (2004), Santhi et al. (2001a), Stewart et al. (2006), and Di Luzio et al. (2002) evaluated SWAT by comparing SWAT nitrogen prediction with measured nitrogen losses in the upper North Bosque River or Bosque River watersheds in Texas. They all concluded that SWAT reasonably predicted nitrogen loss, with most of the average monthly validation NSE values greater than or equal to 0.60 (Table 3). Phosphorus losses were also satisfactorily simulated with SWAT in these four studies, with validation NSE values ranging from 0.39 to 0.93 (Table 3). Chu et al. (2004) applied SWAT to the Warner Creek watershed in Maryland and reported satisfactory annual but poor monthly nitrogen and phosphorus predictions (Table 3). Hanratty and Stefan (1998) calibrated SWAT nitrogen predictions using measured data collected for the Cottonwood River, Minnesota, and concluded that if properly calibrated, SWAT is an appropriate model to use for simulating the effect of climate change on water quality; they also reported satisfactory SWAT phosphorus results (Table 3).

In Iowa, Chaplot et al. (2004) calibrated SWAT using 9 years of data for the

Walnut Creek watershed and concluded that SWAT gave accurate predictions of nitrate load (Table 3). Du et al. (2006) showed that the modified tile drainage functions in SWAT-M resulted in far superior nitrate loss predictions for Walnut Creek (Table 3), as compared to the previous approach used in SWAT2000. However, Jha et al. (2007) report accurate nitrate loss predictions (Table 3) for the Raccoon River watershed in Iowa using SWAT2000. In Arkansas, Cotter et al. (2003) calibrated SWAT with measured nitrate data for the Moores Creek watershed and reported an NSE of 0.44. They state that SWAT's response was similar to that of other published reports.

Bracmort et al. (2006) and Arabi et al. (2006b) found that SWAT could account for the effects of best management practices (BMPs) on phosphorus and nitrogen losses for two small watersheds in Indiana, with monthly validation NSE statistics ranging from 0.37 to 0.79 (Table 3). SWAT tended to underpredict both mineral and total phosphorus yields for the months with high measured phosphorus losses, but overpredicted the phosphorus yields for months with low measured losses. Cerucci and Conrad (2003) calibrated SWAT soluble phosphorus predictions using measured data obtained for the Townbrook watershed in New York. They reported monthly NSE values of 0.91 and 0.40, if the measured data from February and March were excluded. Kirsch et al. (2002) reported that SWAT phosphorus loads were considerably higher than corresponding measured loads for the Rock River watershed in Wisconsin. Veith et al. (2005) found that SWAT-predicted losses were similar in magnitude to measured watershed exports of dissolved and total phosphorus during a 7-month sampling period from a Pennsylvania watershed.

SWAT nutrient predictions have also been evaluated in several other countries. In India, SWAT N and P predictions were tested using measured data within the Midnapore (Behera and Panda, 2006) and Hazaribagh (Tripathi et al., 2003) districts of eastern India (Table 3). Both studies concluded that the SWAT model could be successfully used to satisfactorily simulate nutrient losses. SWAT-predicted ammonia was close to the observed value (Table 3) for the Heihe River study in China (Cheng et al., 2006). Three studies conducted in Finland for the Vantaanjoki River (Grizzetti et al., 2003; Bouraoui et al., 2004) and Kerava River (Francos et al., 2001) watersheds reported that SWAT N and P simulations were generally satisfactory. Plus et al. (2006) evaluated SWAT from data on two rivers in the Thau Lagoon watershed, which drains part of the French Mediterranean coast. The best correlations were found for nitrate loads, and the worst for ammonia loads (Table 3). Gikas et al. (2005) evaluated SWAT using nine gages within the Vistonis Lagoon watershed in Greece and found that the monthly validation statistics generally indicated good model performance for nitrate and total P (Table 3). SWAT nitrate and total phosphorus predictions were found to be excellent and good, respectively, by Abbaspour et al. (2007) for the 1,700 km$^2$ Thur River basin in Switzerland. Bouraoui et al. (2005) applied SWAT to a part of the Medjerda River basin, the largest surface water reservoir in Tunisia, and reported that SWAT was able to predict the range of nitrate concentrations in surface water, but lack of data prevented in-depth evaluation.

### 3.2.3 Pesticide and Surfactant Studies

Simulations of isoaxflutole (and its metabolite RPA 202248) were performed by Ramanarayanan et al. (2005) with SWAT for four watersheds in Iowa, Nebraska, and Missouri that ranged in size from 0.49 to 1,434.6 $km^2$. Satisfactory validation results were obtained based on comparisons with measured data. Long-term simulations indicated that accumulation would not be a problem for either compound in semistatic water bodies. Kannan et al. (2006) report that SWAT accurately simulated movement of four pesticides for the Colworth watershed in the U.K. The results of different application timing and split application scenarios are also described. Two scenarios of surfactant movement are described by Kannan et al. (2007a) for the same watershed. Prediction of atrazine greatly improved using SWAT-M as reported by Du et al. (2006) for the Walnut Creek watershed in Iowa (Table 3), which is a heavily tile-drained watershed. Vazquez-Amabile et al. (2006) found that SWAT was very sensitive to the estimated timing of atrazine applications in the 2,800 $km^2$ St. Joseph River watershed in northeast Indiana. The predicted atrazine mass at the watershed outlet was in close agreement with measured loads for the period of September through April during 2000-2003. Graphical and statistical analyses indicated that the model replicated atrazine movement trends well, but the NSE statistics (e.g. Table 3) were generally weak.

### 3.2.4 Scenarios of BMP and Land Use Impacts on Pollutant Losses

Simulation of hypothetical scenarios in SWAT has proven to be an effective method of evaluating alternative land use, BMP, and other factors on pollutant losses. SWAT studies in India include identification of critical or priority areas for soil and water management in a watershed (Kaur et al., 2004; Tripathi et al., 2003). Santhi et al. (2006) report the impacts of manure and nutrient related BMPs, forage harvest management, and other BMPs on water quality in the West Fork watershed in Texas. The effects of BMPs related to dairy manure management and municipal wastewater treatment plant effluent were evaluated by Santhi et al. (2001b) with SWAT for the Bosque River watershed in Texas. Stewart et al. (2006) describe modifications of SWAT for incorporation of a turfgrass harvest routine, in order to simulate manure and soil P export that occurs during harvest of turfgrass sod within the upper North Bosque River watershed in north-central Texas. Kirsch et al. (2002) describe SWAT results showing that improved tillage practices could result in reduced sediment yields of almost 20% in the Rock River in Wisconsin. Chaplot et al. (2004) found that adoption of no-tillage, changes in nitrogen application rates, and land use changes could greatly impact nitrogen losses in the Walnut Creek watershed in central Iowa. Analysis of BMPs by Vaché et al. (2002) for the Walnut Creek and Buck Creek watersheds in Iowa indicated that large sediment reductions could be obtained, depending on BMP choice. Bracmort et al. (2006) present the results of three 25-year SWAT scenario simulations for two small watersheds in Indiana in which the impacts of no BMPs, BMPs in good condition, and BMPs in varying condition are reported for streamflow, sediment, and total P. Nelson et al. (2005) report that large nutrient and sediment loss reductions occurred in response to simulated shifts of cropland into switchgrass production within the 3,000 km$^2$ Delaware River basin in northeast Kansas. Benham et al. (2006) describe a TMDL SWAT application for a watershed in southwest Missouri. Frequency curves comparing simulated and measured bacteria concentrations were used to calibrate SWAT. The model was then used to simulate the contributions of different bacteria sources to the stream system, and to assess the impact of different BMPs that could potentially be used to mitigate bacteria losses in the watershed.

## 3.3 Climate Change Impact Studies

Climate change impacts can be simulated directly in SWAT by accounting for: (1) the effects of increased atmospheric $CO_2$ concentrations on plant development and transpiration, and (2) changes in climatic inputs. Several SWAT studies provide useful insights regarding the effects of arbitrary $CO_2$ fertilization changes and/or other climatic input shifts on plant growth, streamflow, and other responses, including Stonefelt et al. (2000), Fontaine et al. (2001), and Jha et al. (2006). The SWAT results reported below focus on approaches that relied on downscaling of climate change projections generated by general circulation models (GCMs) or GCMs coupled with regional climate models (RCMs).

### 3.3.1 SWAT Studies Reporting Climate Change Impacts on Hydrology
Muttiah and Wurbs (2002) used SWAT to simulate the impacts of historical climate trends versus a 2040-2059 climate change projection for the 7,300 km$^2$ San Jacinto River basin in Texas. They report that the climate change scenario resulted in a higher mean streamflow due to greater flooding and other high flow increases, but that normal and low streamflows decreased. Gosain et al. (2006) simulated the impacts of a 2041-2060 climate change scenario on the streamflows of 12 major river basins in India, ranging in size from 1,668 to 87,180 km$^2$. Surface runoff was found to generally decrease, and the severity of both floods and droughts increased, in response to the climate change projection.

Rosenberg et al. (2003) simulated the effect of downscaled HadCM2 GCM (Johns et al., 1997) climate projections on the hydrology of the 18 MWRRs (Fig. 2) with SWAT within the HUMUS framework. Water yields were predicted to change from -11% to 153% and from 28% to 342% across the MWRRs in 2030 and 2095, respectively, relative to baseline conditions. Thomson et al. (2003) used the same HadCM2-HUMUS (SWAT) approach and found that three El Niō /Southern Oscillation (ENSO) scenarios resulted in MWRR water yield impacts ranging from -210% to 77% relative to baseline levels, depending on seasonal and dominant weather patterns. An analysis of the impacts of 12 climate change scenarios on the water resources of the 18 MWRRs was performed by Thomson et al. (2005) using the HUMUS approach, as part of a broader study that comprised the entire issue of volume 69 (number 1) of *Climatic Change*. Water yield shifts exceeding □50% were predicted for portions of Midwest and

Southwest U.S., relative to present water yield levels. Rosenberg et al. (1999) found that driving SWAT with a different set of 12 climate projections generally resulted in Ogallala Aquifer recharge decreases (of up to 77%) within the Missouri and Arkansas-White-Red MWRRs (Fig. 2).

Stone et al. (2001) predicted climate change impacts on Missouri River basin (Fig. 2) water yields by inputting downscaled climate projections into SWAT, which were generated by nesting the RegCM RCM (Giorgi et al., 1998) within the CISRO GCM (Watterson et al., 1997) into the previously described version of SWAT that was modified by Hotchkiss et al. (2000). A structure similar to the HUMUS approach was used, in which 310 8-digit watersheds were used to define the sub-watersheds. Water yields declined at the basin outlet by 10% to 20% during the spring and summer months, but increased during the rest of the year. Further research revealed that significant shifts in Missouri River basin water yield impacts were found when SWAT was driven by downscaled CISRO GCM projections only versus the nested RegCM-CISRO GCM approach (Stone et al., 2003).

Jha et al. (2004b), Takle et al. (2005), and Jha et al. (2006) all report performing GCM-driven studies for the 447,500 km$^2$ upper Mississippi River basin (Fig. 2), with an assumed outlet at Grafton, Illinois, using a framework consisting of 119 8-digit sub-watersheds and land use, soil, and topography data that was obtained from BASINS. Jha et al. (2004b) found that streamflows in the upper Mississippi River basin increased by 50% for the period 2040-2049, when climate projections generated by a nested RegCM2-HadCM2 approach were used to drive SWAT. Jha et al. (2006) report that annual average shifts in upper Mississippi River basin streamflows, relative to the baseline, ranged from -6% to 38% for five 2061-2090 GCM projections and increased by 51% for a RegCM-CISRO projection reported by Giorgi et al. (1998). An analysis of driving SWAT with precipitation output generated with nine GCM models indicated that GCM multimodel results may be used to depict 20th century annual streamflows in the upper Mississippi River basin, and that the interface between the single high-resolution GCM used in the study and SWAT resulted in the best replication of observed streamflows (Takle et al., 2005).

Krysanova et al. (2005) report the impacts of 12 different climate scenarios on the hydrologic balance and crop yields of a 30,000 km$^2$ watershed in the state of Brandenburg in Germany using the SWIM model. Further uncertainty analysis of climate change was performed by Krysanova et al. (2007) for the 100,000 km$^2$ Elbe River basin in eastern Germany, based on an interface between a downscaled GCM scenario and SWIM. Eckhardt and Ulbrich (2003) found that the spring snowmelt peak would decline, winter flooding would likely increase, and groundwater recharge and streamflow would decrease by as much as 50% in response to two climate change scenarios simulated in SWAT-G. Their approach featured variable stomatal conductance and leaf area responses by incorporating different stomatal conductance decline factors and leaf area index (LAI) values as a function of five main vegetation types; these refinements have not been adopted in the standard SWAT model.

### 3.3.2 SWAT Studies Reporting Climate Change Impacts on Pollutant Loss

Several studies report climate change impacts on both hydrology and pollutant losses using SWAT, including four that were partially or completely supported by the EU CHESS project (Varanou et al., 2002; Bouraoui et al., 2002; Boorman, 2003; Bouraoui et al., 2004). Nearing et al. (2005) compared runoff and erosion estimates from SWAT versus six other models, in response to six climate change scenarios that were simulated for the 150 $km^2$ Lucky Hills watershed in southeastern Arizona. The responses of all seven models were similar across the six scenarios for both watersheds, and it was concluded that climate change could potentially result in significant soil erosion increases if necessary conservation efforts are not implemented. Hanratty and Stefan (1998) found that streamflows and P, organic N, nitrate, and sediment yields generally decreased for the 3,400 $km^2$ Cottonwood River watershed in southwest Minnesota in response to a downscaled $2 \times CO_2$ GCM climate change scenario. Varanou et al. (2002) also found that average streamflows, sediment yields, organic N losses, and nitrate losses decreased in most months in response to nine different climate change scenarios downscaled from three GCMs for the 2,796 $km^2$ Pinios watershed in Greece. Bouraoui et al. (2002) reported that six different climate change scenarios resulted in increased total nitrogen and phosphorus loads of 6% to 27% and 5% to 34%, respectively, for the 3,500 $km^2$ Ouse River watershed located in the Yorkshire region of the U.K. Bouraoui et al. (2004) further found for the Vantaanjoki River watershed, which covers 1,682 $km^2$ in southern Finland, that snow cover decreased, winter runoff increased, and slight increases in annual nutrient losses occurred in response to a 34-year scenario representative of observed climatic changes in the region. Boorman (2003) evaluated the impacts of climate change for five different watersheds located in Italy, France, Finland, and the U.K., including the three watersheds analyzed in the Varanou et al. (2002), Bouraoui et al. (2002), and Bouraoui et al. (2004) studies.

## *3.4 Sensitivity, Calibration, and Uncertainty Analyses*

Sensitivity, calibration, and uncertainty analyses are vital and interwoven aspects of applying SWAT and other models. Numerous sensitivity analyses have been reported in the SWAT literature, which provide valuable insights regarding which input parameters have the greatest impact on SWAT output. As previously discussed, the vast majority of SWAT applications report some type of calibration effort. SWAT input parameters are physically based and are allowed to vary within a realistic uncertainty range during calibration. Sensitivity analysis and calibration techniques are generally referred to as either manual or automated, and can be evaluated with a wide range of graphical and/or statistical procedures.

Uncertainty is defined by Shirmohammadi et al. (2006) as "the estimated amount by which an observed or calculated value may depart from the true value." They discuss sources of uncertainty in depth and list model algorithms, model calibration and validation data, input variability, and scale as key sources of uncertainty. Several automated uncertainty analyses approaches have been developed, which incorporate various sensitivity and/or calibration techniques, which are briefly reviewed here along with specific sensitivity analysis and calibration studies.

### 3.4.1 Sensitivity Analyses

Spruill et al. (2000) performed a manual sensitivity/calibration analysis of 15 SWAT input parameters for a 5.5 $km^2$ watershed with karst characteristics in Kentucky, which showed that saturated hydraulic conductivity, alpha base flow factor, drainage area, channel length, and channel width were the most sensitive parameters that affected streamflow. Arnold et al. (2000) show surface runoff, base flow, recharge, and soil ET sensitivity curves in response to manual variations in the curve number, soil available water capacity, and soil evaporation coefficient (ESCO) input parameters for three different 8-digit watersheds within their upper Mississippi River basin SWAT study. Lenhart et al. (2002) report on the effects of two different sensitivity analysis schemes using SWAT-G for an artificial watershed, in which an alternative approach of varying 44 parameter values within a fixed percentage of the valid parameter range was compared with the more usual method of varying each initial parameter by the same fixed percentage. Both approaches resulted in similar rankings of parameter sensitivity and thus could be considered equivalent.

A two-step sensitivity analysis approach is described by Francos et al. (2003), which consists of: (1) a 'Morris' screening procedure that is based on the one factor at a time (OAT) design, and (2) the use of a Fourier amplitude sensitivity test (FAST) method. The screening procedure is used to determine the qualitative ranking of an entire input parameter set for different model outputs at low computational cost, while the FAST method provides an assessment of the most relevant input parameters for a specific set of model output. The approach is demonstrated with SWAT for the 3,500 $km^2$ Ouse watershed in the U.K. using 82 input and 22 output parameters. Holvoet et al. (2005) present the use of a Latin hypercube (LH) OAT sampling method, in which initial LH samples serve as the points for the OAT design. The method was used for determining which of 27 SWAT hydrologic-related input parameters were the most sensitive regarding streamflow and atrazine outputs for 32 $km^2$ Nil watershed in central Belgium. The LH-OAT method was also used by van Griensven et al. (2006b) for an assessment of the sensitivity of 41 input parameters on SWAT flow, sediment, total N, and total P estimates for both the UNBRW and the 3,240 $km^2$ Sandusky River watershed in Ohio. The results show that some parameters, such as the curve number (CN2), were important in both watersheds, but that there were distinct differences in the influences of other parameters between the two watersheds. The LH-OAT method has been incorporated as part of the automatic sensitivity/calibration package included in SWAT2005.

### 3.4.2 Calibration Approaches

The manual calibration approach requires the user to compare measured and simulated values, and then to use expert judgment to determine which variables to adjust, how much to adjust them, and ultimately assess when reasonable results have been obtained. Coffey et al. (2004) present nearly 20 different statistical tests that can be used for evaluating SWAT streamflow output during a manual calibration process. They recommended using the NSE and $R^2$ coefficients for analyzing monthly output and median objective functions, sign test, autocorrelation, and cross-correlation for assessing daily output, based on comparisons of SWAT streamflow results with measured streamflows (Table 2) for the same watershed studied by Spruill et al. (2000). Cao et al. (2006) present a flowchart of their manual calibration approach that was used to calibrate SWAT based on five hydrologic outputs and multiple gage sites within the 2,075 km² Motueka River basin on the South Island of New Zealand. The calibration and validation results were stronger for the overall basin as compared to results obtained for six sub-watersheds (Table 2). Santhi et al. (2001a) successfully calibrated and validated SWAT for streamflow and pollutant loss simulations (Tables 2 and 3) for the 4,277 km² Bosque River in Texas. They present a general procedure, including a flowchart, for manual calibration that identifies sensitive input parameters (15 were used), realistic uncertainty ranges, and reasonable regression results (i.e. satisfactory $r^2$ and NSE values). A combined sensitivity and calibration approach is described by White and Chaubey (2005) for SWAT streamflow and pollutant loss estimates (Tables 2 and 3) for the 3,100 km² Bear Reservoir watershed, and three sub-watersheds, in northwest Arkansas. They also review calibration approaches, including calibrated input parameters, for previous SWAT studies.

Automated techniques involve the use of Monte Carlo or other parameter estimation schemes that determine automatically what the best choice of values are for a suite of parameters, usually on the basis of a large set of simulations, for a calibration process. Govender and Everson (2005) used the automatic Parameter Estimation (PEST) program (Doherty, 2004) and identified soil moisture variables, initial groundwater variables, and runoff curve numbers to be some of the sensitive parameters in SWAT applications for two small South African watersheds. They also report that manual calibration resulted in more accurate predictions than the PEST approach (Table 2). Wang and Melesse (2005) also used PEST to perform an automatic SWAT calibration of three snowmelt-related and eight hydrologic-related parameters for the 4,335 km² Wild Rice River watershed in northwest Minnesota, which included daily and monthly statistical evaluation (Table 2).

Applications of an automatic shuffled complex evolution (SCE) optimization scheme are described by van Griensven and Bauwens (2003, 2005) for ESWAT simulations, primarily for the Dender River in Belgium. Calibration parameters and ranges along with measured daily flow and pollutant data are input for each application. The automated calibration scheme executes up to several thousand model runs to find the optimum input data set. Similar automatic calibration studies were performed with a SCE algorithm and SWAT-G by Eckhardt and Arnold (2001) and Eckhardt et al. (2005) for watersheds in Germany. Di Luzio and Arnold (2004) described the background, formulation and results (Table 2) of an hourly SCE input-output calibration approach used for a SWAT application in Oklahoma. Van Liew et al. (2005) describe an initial test of the SCE automatic approach that has been incorporated into SWAT2005, for streamflow predictions for the Little River watershed in Georgia and the Little Washita River watershed in Oklahoma. Van Liew et al. (2007) further evaluated the SCE algorithm for five watersheds with widely varying climatic characteristics (Table 2), including the same two in Georgia and Oklahoma and three others located in Arizona, Idaho, and Pennsylvania.

### 3.4.3 Uncertainty Analyses

Shirmohammadi et al. (2006) state that Monte Carlo simulation and first-order error or approximation (FOE or FOA) analyses are the two most common approaches for performing uncertainty analyses, and that other methods have been used, including the mean value first-order reliability method, LH simulation with constrained Monte Carlo simulations, and generalized likelihood uncertainty estimation (GLUE). They present three case studies of uncertainty analyses using SWAT, which were based on the Monte Carlo, LH-Monte Carlo, and GLUE approaches, respectively, within the context of TMDL assessments. They report that uncertainty is a major issue for TMDL assessments, and that it should be taken into account during both the TMDL assessment and implementation phases. They also make recommendations to improve the quantification of uncertainty in the TMDL process.

Benaman and Shoemaker (2004) developed a six-step method that includes using Monte Carlo runs and an interval-spaced sensitivity approach to reduce uncertain parameter ranges. After parameter range reduction, their method reduced the model output range by an order of magnitude, resulting in reduced uncertainty and the amount of calibration required for SWAT. However, significant uncertainty remained with the SWAT sediment routine. Lin and Radcliffe (2006) performed an initial two-stage automatic calibration streamflow prediction process with SWAT for the 1,580 km$^2$ Etowah River watershed in Georgia in which an SCE algorithm was used for automatic calibration of lumped SWAT input parameters, followed by calibration of heterogeneous inputs with a variant of the Marquardt-Levenberg method in which 'regularization' was used to prevent parameters taking on unrealistic values. They then performed a nonlinear calibration and uncertainty analysis using PEST, in which confidence intervals were generated for annual and 7-day streamflow estimates. Their resulting calibrated statistics are shown in Table 2. Muleta and Nicklow (2005b) describe a study for the Big Creek watershed that involved three phases: (1) parameter sensitivity analysis for 35 input parameters, in which LH samples were used to reduce the number of Monte Carlo simulations needed to conduct the analysis; (2) automatic calibration using a genetic algorithm, which systematically determined the best set of input parameters using a sum of the square of differences criterion; and (3) a Monte Carlo-based GLUE approach for the uncertainty analysis, in which LH sampling is again used to generate input samples and reduce the computation requirements. Uncertainty bounds corresponding to the 95% confidence limit are reported for both streamflow and sediment loss, as well as final calibrated statistics (Tables 2 and 3). Arabi et al. (2007b) used a three-step procedure that included OAT and interval-spaced sensitivity analyses, and a GLUE analysis to assess uncertainty of SWAT water quality predictions of BMP placement in the Dreisbach and Smith Fry watersheds in Indiana. Their results point to the need for site-specific calibration of some SWAT inputs, and that BMP effectiveness could be evaluated with enough confidence to justify using the model for TMDL and similar assessments.

Additional uncertainty analysis insights are provided by Vanderberghe et al. (2007) for an ESWAT-based study and by Huisman et al. (2004) and Eckhardt et al. (2003), who assessed the uncertainty of soil and/or land use parameter variations on SWAT-G output using Monte Carlo-based approaches. Van Greinsven and Meixner (2006) describe several uncertainty analysis tools that have been incorporated into SWAT2005, including a modified SCE algorithm called 'parameter solutions' (ParaSol), the Sources of Uncertainty Global Assessment using Split Samples (SUNGLASSES), and the Confidence Analysis of Physical Inputs (CANOPI), which evaluates uncertainty associated with climatic data and other inputs.

## 3.5 Effects of HRU and Sub-watershed Delineation and Other Inputs on SWAT Output

Several studies have been performed that analyzed impacts on SWAT output as a function of: (1) variation in HRU and/or sub-watershed delineations, (2) different resolutions in topographic, soil, and/or land use data, (3) effects of spatial and temporal transfers of inputs, (4) actual and/or hypothetical shifts in land use, and (5) variations in precipitation inputs or ET estimates. These studies serve as further SWAT sensitivity analyses and provide insight into how the model responds to variations in key inputs.

### 3.5.1 HRU and Sub-watershed Delineation Effects

Bingner et al. (1997), Manguerra and Engel (1998), FitzHugh and Mackay (2000), Jha et al. (2004a), Chen and Mackay (2004), Tripathi et al. (2006), and Muleta et al. (2007) found that SWAT streamflow predictions were generally insensitive to variations in HRU and/or sub-watershed delineations for watersheds ranging in size from 21.3 to 17,941 $km^2$. Tripathi et al. (2006) and Muleta et al. (2007) further discuss HRU and sub-watershed delineation impacts on other hydrologic components. Haverkamp et al. (2002) report that streamflow accuracy was much greater when using multiple HRUs to characterize each sub-watershed, as opposed to using just a single dominant soil type and land use within a sub-watershed, for two watersheds in Germany and one in Texas. However, the gap in accuracy between the two approaches decreased with increasing numbers of sub-watersheds.

Bingner et al. (1997) report that the number of simulated sub-watersheds affected predicted sediment yield and suggest that sensitivity analyses should be performed to determine the appropriate level of sub-watersheds. Jha et al. (2004a) found that SWAT sediment and nitrate predictions were sensitive to variations in both HRUs and sub-watersheds, but mineral P estimates were not. The effects of BMPS on SWAT sediment, total P, and total N estimates was also found by Arabi et al. (2006b) to be very sensitive to watershed subdivision level. Jha et al. (2004a) suggest setting sub-watershed areas ranging from 2% to 5% of the overall watershed area, depending on the output indicator of interest, to ensure accuracy of estimates. Arabi et al. (2006b) found that an average sub-watershed equal to about 4% of the overall watershed area was required to accurately account for the impacts of BMPs in the model.

FitzHugh and Mackay (2000, 2001) and Chen and Mackay (2004) found that sediment losses predicted with SWAT did not vary at the outlet of the 47.3 km$^2$ Pheasant Branch watershed in south-central Wisconsin as a function of increasing numbers of HRUs and sub-watersheds due to the transport-limited nature of the watershed. However, sediment generation at the HRU level dropped 44% from the coarsest to the finest resolutions (FitzHugh and Mackay, 2000), and sediment yields varied at the watershed outlet for hypothetical source-limited versus transport-limited scenarios (FitzHugh and Mackay, 2001) in response to eight different HRU/sub-watershed combinations used in both studies. Chen and Mackay (2004) further found that SWAT's structure influences sediment predictions in tandem with spatial data aggregation effects. They suggest that errors in MUSLE sediment estimates can be avoided by using only sub-watersheds, instead of using HRUs, within sub-watersheds.

In contrast, Muleta et al. (2007) found that sediment generated at the HRU level and exported from the outlet of the 133 km$^2$ Big Creek watershed in Illinois decreased with increasing spatial coarseness, and that sediment yield varied significantly at the watershed outlet across a range of HRU and sub-watershed delineations, even when the channel properties remained virtually constant.

### 3.5.2 DEM, Soil, and Land Use Resolution Effects

Bosch et al. (2004) found that SWAT streamflow estimates for a 22.1 km$^2$ sub-watershed of the Little River watershed in Georgia were more accurate using high-resolution topographic, land use, and soil data versus low-resolution data obtained from BASINS. Cotter et al. (2003) report that DEM resolution was the most critical input for a SWAT simulation of the 18.9 km$^2$ Moores Creek watershed in Arkansas, and provide minimum DEM, land use, and soil resolution recommendations to obtain accurate flow, sediment, nitrate, and total P estimates. Di Luzio et al. (2005) also found that DEM resolution was the most critical for SWAT simulations of the 21.3 km$^2$ Goodwin Creek watershed in Mississippi; land use resolution effects were also significant, but the resolution of soil inputs was not. Chaplot (2005) found that SWAT surface runoff estimates were sensitive to DEM mesh size, and that nitrate and sediment predictions were sensitive to both the choice of DEM and soil map resolution, for the Walnut Creek watershed in central Iowa. The most accurate results did not occur for the finest DEM mesh sizes, contrary to expectations. Di Luzio et al. (2004b) and Wang and Melesse (2006) present additional results describing the impacts of STATSGO versus SSURGO soil data inputs on SWAT output.

### 3.5.3 Effects of Different Spatial and Temporal Transfers of Inputs

Heuvelmans et al. (2004a) evaluated the effects of transferring seven calibrated SWAT hydrologic input parameters, which were selected on the basis of a sensitivity analysis, in both time and space for three watersheds ranging in size from 51 to 204 $km^2$ in northern Belgium. Spatial transfers resulted in the greatest loss of streamflow efficiency, especially between watersheds. Heuvelmans et al. (2004b) further evaluated the effect of four parameterization schemes on SWAT streamflow predictions, for the same set of seven hydrologic inputs, for 25 watersheds that covered 2.2 to 210 $km^2$ within the 20,000 $km^2$ Scheldt River basin in northern Belgium. The highest model efficiencies were achieved when optimal parameters for each individual watershed were used; optimal parameters selected on the basis of regional zones with similar characteristics proved superior to parameters that were averaged across all 25 watersheds.

### 3.5.4 Historical and Hypothetical Land Use Effects

Miller et al. (2002) describe simulated streamflow impacts with SWAT in response to historical land use shifts in the 3,150 $km^2$ San Pedro watershed in southern Arizona and the Cannonsville watershed in south-central New York. Streamflows were predicted to increase in the San Pedro watershed due to increased urban and agricultural land use, while a shift from agricultural to forest land use was predicted to result in a 4% streamflow decrease in the Cannonsville watershed. Hernandez et al. (2000) further found that SWAT could accurately predict the relative impacts of hypothetical land use change in an 8.2 $km^2$ experimental sub-watershed within the San Pedro watershed. Heuvelmans et al. (2005) report that SWAT produced reasonable streamflow and erosion estimates for hypothetical land use shifts, which were performed as part of a life cycle assessment (LCA) of $CO_2$ emission reduction scenarios for the 29.2 $km^2$ Meerdaal watershed and the 12.1 $km^2$ Latem watersheds in northern Belgium. However, they state that an expansion of the SWAT vegetation parameter dataset is needed in order to fully support LCA analyses. Increased streamflow was predicted with SWAT for the 59.8 $km^2$ Aar watershed in the German state of Hessen, in response to a grassland incentive scenario in which the grassland area increased from 20% to 41% while the extent of forest coverage decreased by about 70% (Weber et al., 2001). The impacts of hypothetical forest and other land use changes on total runoff using SWAT are presented by Lorz et al. (2007) in the context of comparisons with three other models. The impacts of other hypothetical land use studies for various German watersheds have been reported on hydrologic impacts with SWAT-G (e.g. Fohrer et al., 2002, 2005) and SWIM (Krysanova et al., 2005) and on nutrient and sediment loss predictions with SWAT-G (Lenhart et al., 2003).

### 3.5.5 Climate Data Effects

Chaplot et al. (2005) analyzed the effects of rain gage distribution on SWAT output by simulating the impacts of climatic inputs for a range of 1 to 15 rain gages in both the Walnut Creek watershed in central Iowa and the upper North Bosque River watershed in Texas. Sediment predictions improved significantly when the densest rain gage networks were used; only slight improvements occurred for the corresponding surface runoff and nitrogen predictions. However, Hernandez et al. (2000) found that increasing the number of simulated rain gages from 1 to 10 resulted in clear estimated streamflow improvements (Table 2). Moon et al. (2004) found that SWAT's streamflow estimates improved when Next-Generation Weather Radar (NEXRAD) precipitation input was used instead of rain gage inputs (Table 2). Kalin and Hantush (2006) report that NEXRAD and rain gage inputs resulted in similar streamflow estimates at the outlet of the Pocono Creek watershed in Pennsylvania (Table 2), and that NEXRAD data appear to be a promising source of alternative precipitation data. A weather generator developed by Schuol and Abbaspour (2007) that uses climatic data available at $0.5°$ intervals was found to result in better streamflow estimates than rain gage data for a region covering about 4 million $km^2$ in Western Africa that includes the Niger, Volta, and Senegal river basins. Sensitivity of precipitation inputs on SWAT hydrologic output are reported for comparisons of different weather generators by Harmel et al. (2000) and Watson et al. (2005). The effects of different ET options available in SWAT on streamflow estimates are further described by Wang et al. (2006) and Kannan et al. (2007b).

## 3.6 Comparisons of SWAT with Other Models

Borah and Bera (2003, 2004) compared SWAT with several other watershed-scale models. In the 2003 study, they report that the Dynamic Watershed Simulation Model (DWSM) (Borah et al., 2004), Hydrologic Simulation Program - Fortran (HSPF) model (Bicknell et al., 1997), SWAT, and other models have hydrology, sediment, and chemical routines applicable to watershed-scale catchments and concluded that SWAT is a promising model for continuous simulations in predominantly agricultural watersheds. In the 2004 study, they found that SWAT and HSPF could predict yearly flow volumes and pollutant losses, were adequate for monthly predictions except for months having extreme storm events and hydrologic conditions, and were poor in simulating daily extreme flow events. In contrast, DWSM reasonably predicted distributed flow hydrographs and concentration or discharge graphs of sediment and chemicals at small time intervals. Shepherd et al. (1999) evaluated 14 models and found SWAT to be the most suitable for estimating phosphorus loss from a lowland watershed in the U.K.

Van Liew et al. (2003a) compared the streamflow predictions of SWAT and HSPF on eight nested agricultural watersheds within the Little Washita River basin in southwestern Oklahoma. They concluded that SWAT was more consistent than HSPF in estimating streamflow for different climatic conditions and may thus be better suited for investigating the long-term impacts of climate variability on surface water resources. Saleh and Du (2004) found that the average daily flow, sediment loads, and nutrient loads simulated by SWAT were closer than HSPF to measured values collected at five sites during both the calibration and verification periods for the upper North Bosque River watershed in Texas. Singh et al. (2005) found that SWAT flow predictions were slightly better than corresponding HSPF estimates for the 5,568 $km^2$ Iroquois River watershed in eastern Illinois and western Indiana, primarily due to better simulation of low flows by SWAT. Nasr et al. (2007) found that HSPF predicted mean daily discharge most accurately, while SWAT simulated daily total phosphorus loads the best, in a comparison of three models for three Irish watersheds that ranged in size from 15 to 96 $km^2$. El-Nasr et al. (2005) found that both SWAT and the MIKE-SHE model (Refsgaard and Storm, 1995) simulated the hydrology of Belgium's Jeker River basin in an acceptable way. However, MIKE-SHE predicted the overall variation of river flow slightly better.

Srinivasan et al. (2005) found that SWAT estimated flow more accurately than the Soil Moisture Distribution and Routing (SMDR) model (Cornell, 2003) for 39.5 ha FD-36 experimental watershed in east-central Pennsylvania, and that SWAT was also more accurate on a seasonal basis. SWAT estimates were also found to be similar to measured dissolved and total P for the same watershed, and 73% of the 22 fields in the watershed were categorized similarly on the basis of the SWAT analysis as compared to the Pennsylvania P index (Veith et al., 2005). Grizzetti et al. (2005) reported that both SWAT and a statistical approach based on the SPARROW model (Smith et al., 1997) resulted in similar total oxidized nitrogen loads for two monitoring sites within the 1,380 $km^2$ Great Ouse watershed in the U.K. They also state that the statistical reliability of the two approaches was similar, and that the statistical model should be viewed primarily as a screening tool while SWAT is more useful for scenarios. Srivastava et al. (2006) found that an artificial neural network (ANN) model was more accurate than SWAT for streamflow simulations of a small watershed in southeast Pennsylvania.

## 3.7 Interfaces of SWAT with Other Models

Innovative applications have been performed by interfacing SWAT with other environmental and/or economic models. These interfaces have expanded the range of scenarios that can be analyzed and allowed for more in-depth assessments of questions that cannot be considered with SWAT by itself, such as groundwater withdrawal impacts or the costs incurred from different choices of management practices.

### 3.7.1 SWAT with MODFLOW and/or Surface Water Models

Sophocleus et al. (1999) describe an interface between SWAT and the MODFLOW groundwater model (McDonald and Harbaugh, 1988) called SWATMOD, which they used to evaluate water rights and withdrawal rate management scenarios on stream and aquifer responses for the Rattlesnake Creek watershed in south-central Kansas. The system was used by Sophocleus and Perkins (2000) to investigate irrigation effects on streamflow and groundwater levels in the lower Republican River watershed in north-central Kansas and on streamflow and groundwater declines within the Rattlesnake Creek watershed. Perkins and Sophocleous (1999) describe drought impact analyses with the same system. SWAT was coupled with MODFLOW to study the 12 $km^2$ Cot-Dan watershed in Brittany, France (Conan et al., 2003a). Accurate results were reported, with respective monthly NSE values for streamflow and nitrate of 0.88 and 0.87.

Menking et al. (2003) interfaced SWAT with both MODFLOW and the MODFLOW LAK2 lake modeling package to assess how current climate conditions would impact water levels in ancient Lake Estancia (central New Mexico), which existed during the late Pleistocene era. The results indicated that current net inflow from the 5,000 $km^2$ drainage basin would have to increase by about a factor of 15 to maintain typical Late Pleistocene lake levels. Additional analyses of Lake Estancia were performed by Menking et al. (2004) for the Last Glacial Maximum period. SWAT was interfaced with a 3-D lagoon model by Plus et al. (2006) to determine nitrogen loads from a 280 $km^2$ drainage area into the Thau Lagoon, which lies along the south coast of France. The main annual nitrogen load was estimated with SWAT to be 117 t $year^{-1}$; chlorophyll a concentrations, phytoplankton production, and related analyses were performed with the lagoon model. Galbiati et al. (2006) interfaced SWAT with QUAL2E, MODFLOW, and another model to create the Integrated Surface and Subsurface model (ISSm). They found that the system accurately predicted water and nutrient interactions between the stream system and aquifer, groundwater dynamics, and surface water and nutrient fluxes at the watershed outlet for the 20 $km^2$ Bonello coastal watershed in northern Italy.

### 3.7.2 SWAT with Environmental Models or Genetic Algorithms for BMP Analyses

Renschler and Lee (2005) linked SWAT with the Water Erosion Prediction Project (WEPP) model (Ascough et al., 1997) to evaluate both short- and long-term assessments, for pre- and post-implementation, of grassed waterways and field borders for three experimental watersheds ranging in size from 0.66 to 5.11 ha. SWAT was linked directly to the Geospatial Interface for WEPP (GeoWEPP), which facilitated injection of WEPP output as point sources into SWAT. The long-term assessment results were similar to SWAT-only evaluations, but the short-term results were not. Cerucci and Conrad (2003) determined the optimal riparian buffer configurations for 31 sub-watersheds in the 37 $km^2$ Town Brook watershed in south-central New York, by using a binary optimization approach and interfacing SWAT with the Riparian Ecosystem Model (REMM) (Lowrance et al., 2000). They determined the marginal utility of buffer widths and the most affordable parcels in which to establish riparian buffers. Pohlert et al. (2006) describe SWAT-N, which was created by extending the original SWAT2000 nitrogen cycling routine primarily with algorithms from the Denitrification-Decomposition (DNDC) model (Li et al., 1992). They state that SWAT-N was able to replicate nitrogen cycling and loss processes more accurately than SWAT.

Muleta and Nicklow (2005a) interfaced SWAT with a genetic algorithm and a multi-objective evolutionary algorithm to perform both single and multi-objective evaluations for the 130 km$^2$ Big Creek watershed in southern Illinois. They found that conversion of 10% of the HRUs into conservation programs (cropping system/tillage practice BMPs), within a maximum of 50 genetic algorithm generations, would result in reduced sediment yield of 19%. Gitau et al. (2004) interfaced baseline P estimates from SWAT with a genetic algorithm and a BMP tool containing site-specific BMP effectiveness estimates to determine the optimal on-farm placement of BMPs so that P losses and costs were both minimized. The two most efficient scenarios met the target of reducing dissolved P loss by at least 60%, with corresponding farm-level cost increases of $1,430 and $1,683, respectively, relative to the baseline. SWAT was interfaced with an economic model, a BMP tool, and a genetic algorithm by Arabi et al. (2006a) to determine optimal placement for the Dreisbach and Smith Fry watersheds in Indiana. The optimization approach was found to be three times more cost-effective as compared to environmental targeting strategies.

### 3.7.3 SWAT with Economic and/or Environmental Models

A farm economic model was interfaced with the Agricultural Policy Extender (APEX) model (Williams and Izaurralde, 2006) and SWAT to simulated the economic and environmental impacts of manure management scenarios and other BMPs for the 932.5 km$^2$ upper North Bosque River and 1,279 km$^2$ Lake Fork Reservoir watersheds in Texas and the 162.2 km$^2$ upper Maquoketa River watershed in Iowa (Gassman et al., 2002). The economic and environmental impacts of several manure application rate scenarios are described for each watershed, as well as for manure haul-off, intensive rotational grazing, and reduced fertilizer scenarios that were simulated for the upper North Bosque River watershed, Lake Fork Reservoir watershed, and upper Maquoketa River watershed, respectively. Osei et al. (2003) report additional stocking density scenario results for pasture-based dairy productions in the Lake Fork Reservoir watershed. They concluded that appropriate pasture nutrient management, including stocking density adjustments and more efficient application of commercial fertilizer, could lead to significant reductions in nutrient losses in the Lake Fork Reservoir watershed. Gassman et al. (2006) further assessed the impacts of seven individual BMPs and four BMP combinations for upper Maquoketa River watershed. Terraces were predicted to be very effective in reducing sediment and organic nutrient losses but were also the most expensive practice, while no-till or contouring in combination with reduced fertilizer rates were predicted to result in reductions of all pollutant indictors and also positive net returns.

Lemberg et al. (2002) evaluated the economic impacts of brush control in the Frio River basin in south-central Texas using SWAT, the Phytomass Growth Simulator (PHYGROW) model (Rowan, 1995), and two economic models. It was determined that subsidies on brush control would not be worthwhile. Economic evaluations of riparian buffer benefits in regards to reducing atrazine concentration and other factors were performed by Qiu and Prato (1998) using SWAT, a budget generator, and an economic model for the 77.4 km$^2$ Goodwater Creek watershed in north-central Missouri (riparian buffers were not directly simulated). The implementation of riparian buffers was found to result in substantial net economic return and savings in government costs, due to reduced CRP rental payments. Qiu (2005) used a similar approach for the same watershed to evaluate the economic and environmental impacts of five different alternative scenarios. SWAT was interfaced with a data envelope analysis linear programming model by Whittaker et al. (2003) to determine which of two policies would be most effective in reducing N losses to streams in the 259,000 km$^2$ Columbia Plateau region in the northwest U.S. The analysis indicated that a 300% tax on N fertilizer would be more efficient than a mandated 25% reduction in N use. Evaluation of different policies were demonstrated by Attwood et al. (2000) by showing economic and environmental impacts at the U.S. national scale and for Texas by linking SWAT with an agricultural sector model. Volk et al. (2007) and Turpin et al. (2005) describe respective modeling systems that include interfaces between SWAT, an economic model, and other models and data to simulate different watershed scales and conditions in European watersheds.

### 3.7.4 SWAT with Ecological and Other Models
Weber et al. (2001) interfaced SWAT with the ecological model ELLA and the Proland economic model to investigate the streamflow and habitat impacts of a "grassland incentive scenario" that resulted in grassland area increasing from 21% to 40%, and forest area declining by almost 70%, within the 59.8 km$^2$ Aar watershed in Germany. SWAT-predicted streamflow increased while Skylark bird habitat decreased in response to the scenario. Fohrer et al. (2002) used SWAT-G, the YELL ecological model, and the Proland to assess the effects of land use changes and associated hydrologic impacts on habitat suitability for the Yellowhammer bird species. The authors report effects of four average field size scenarios (0.5, 0.75, 1.0, and 2.0 ha) on land use, bird nest distribution and habitat, labor and agricultural value, and hydrological response. SWAT is also being used to simulate crop growth, hydrologic balance, soil erosion, and other environmental responses by Christiansen and Altaweel (2006) within the ENKIMDU modeling framework (named after the ancient Sumerian god of agriculture and irrigation), which is being used to study the natural and societal aspects of Bronze Age Mesopotamian cultures.

## 4. SWAT Strengths, Weaknesses, and Research Needs

The worldwide application of SWAT reveals that it is a versatile model that can be used to integrate multiple environmental processes, which support more effective watershed management and the development of better-informed policy decisions. The model will continue to evolve as users determine needed improvements that: (1) will enable more accurate simulation of currently supported processes, (2) incorporate advancements in scientific knowledge, or (3) provide new functionality that will expand the SWAT simulation domain. This process is aided by the open-source status of the SWAT code and ongoing encouragement of collaborating scientists to pursue needed model development, as demonstrated by a forthcoming set of papers in *Hydrological Sciences Journal* describing various SWAT research needs that were identified at the 2006 Model Developer's Workshop held in Potsdam, Germany. The model has also been included in the Collaborative Software Development Laboratory that facilitates development by multiple scientists (CoLab, 2006).

The foundational strength of SWAT is the combination of upland and channel processes that are incorporated into one simulation package. However, every one of these processes is a simplification of reality and thus subject to the need for improvement. To some degree, the strengths that facilitate widespread use of SWAT also represent weaknesses that need further refinement, such as simplified representations of HRUs. There are also problems in depicting some processes accurately due to a lack of sufficient monitoring data, inadequate data needed to characterize input parameters, or insufficient scientific understanding. The strengths and weaknesses of five components are discussed here in more detail, including possible courses of action for improving current routines in the model. The discussion is framed to some degree from the perspective of emerging applications, e.g. bacteria die-off and transport. Additional research needs are also briefly listed for other components, again in the context of emerging application trends where applicable.

### 4.1 Hydrologic Interface

The use of the NRCS curve number method in SWAT has provided a relatively easy way of adapting the model to a wide variety of hydrologic conditions. The technique has proved successful for many applications, as evidenced by the results reported in this study. However, the embrace of the method in SWAT and similar models has proved controversial due to the empirical nature of the approach, lack of complete historical documentation, poor results obtained for some conditions, inadequate representation of "critical source areas" that generate pollutant loss (which can occur even after satisfactory hydrologic calibration of the model), and other factors (e.g. Ponce and Hawkins, 1996; Agnew et al., 2006; Bryant et al., 2006; Garen and Moore, 2005).

The Green-Ampt method provides an alternative option in SWAT, which was found by Rawls and Brakenseik (1986) to be more accurate than the curve number method and also to account for the effects of management practices on soil properties in a more rational manner. However, the previously discussed King et al. (1999) and Kannan et al. (2007b) SWAT applications did not find any advantage to using the Green-Ampt approach, as compared to the curve number method. These results lend support to the viewpoint expressed by Ponce and Hawkins (1996) that alternative point infiltration techniques, including the Green-Ampt method, have not shown a clear superiority to the curve number method.

71

Improved SWAT hydrologic predictions could potentially be obtained through modifications in the curve number methodology and/or incorporation of more complex routines. Borah et al. (2007) propose inserting a combined curve number-kinematic wave methodology used in DWSM into SWAT, which was found to result in improved simulation of daily runoff volumes for the 8,400 km² Little Wabash River watershed in Illinois. Bryant et al. (2006) propose modifications of the curve number initial abstraction term, as a function of soil physical characteristics and management practices, that could result in more accurate simulation of extreme (low and high) runoff events. Model and/or data input modifications would be needed to address phenomena such as variable source area (VSA) saturated excess runoff, which dominants runoff in some regions including the northeast U.S., where downslope VSA saturated discharge often occurs due to subsurface interflow over relatively impermeable material (Agnew et al., 2006; Walter et al., 2000). Steenhuis (2007) has developed a method of reclassifying soil types and associated curve numbers that provides a more accurate accounting of VSA-driven runoff and pollutant loss for a small watershed in New York. The modified SWAT model described by Watson et al. (2005) may also provide useful insights, as it accounts for VSA-dominated hydrology in southwest Victoria, Australia, by incorporating a saturated excess runoff routine in SWAT.

## 4.2 Hydrologic Response Units (HRUs)

The incorporation of nonspatial HRUs in SWAT has supported adaptation of the model to virtually any watershed, ranging in size from field plots to entire river basins. The fact that the HRUs are not landscape dependent has kept the model simple while allowing soil and land use heterogeneity to be accounted for within each sub-watershed. At the same time, the nonspatial aspect of the HRUs is a key weakness of the model. This approach ignores flow and pollutant routing within a sub-watershed, thus treating the impact of pollutant losses identically from all landscape positions within a sub-watershed. Thus, potential pollutant attenuation between the source area and a stream is also ignored, as discussed by Bryant et al. (2006) for phosphorus movement. Explicit spatial representation of riparian buffer zones, wetlands, and other BMPs is also not possible with the current SWAT HRU approach, as well as the ability to account for targeted placement of grassland or other land use within a given sub-watershed. Incorporation of greater spatial detail into SWAT is being explored with the initial focus on developing routing capabilities between distinct spatially defined landscapes (Volk et al., 2005), which could be further subdivided into HRUs.

## 4.3 Simulation of BMPs

A key strength of SWAT is a flexible framework that allows the simulation of a wide variety of conservation practices and other BMPs, such as fertilizer and manure application rate and timing, cover crops (perennial grasses), filter strips, conservation tillage, irrigation management, flood-prevention structures, grassed waterways, and wetlands. The majority of conservation practices can be simulated in

SWAT with straightforward parameter changes. Arabi et al. (2007a) have proposed standardized approaches for simulating specific conservation practices in the model, including adjustment of the parameters listed in Table 4. Filter strips and field borders can be simulated at the HRU level, based on empirical functions that account for filter strip trapping effects of bacteria or sediment, nutrients, and pesticides (which are invoked when the filter strip width parameter is set input to the model). However, assessments of targeted filter strip placements within a watershed are limited, due to the lack of HRU spatial definition in SWAT. There are also further limitations in simulating grassed waterways, due to the fact that channel routing is not simulated at the HRU level. Arabi et al. (2007a) proposed simulating grassed waterways by modifying sub-watershed channel parameters, as shown in Table 4. However, this approach is usually only viable for relatively small watersheds, such as the example they present in their study.

Wetlands can be simulated in SWAT on the basis of one wetland per sub-watershed, which is assumed to capture discharge and pollutant loads from a user-specified percentage of the overall sub-watershed. The ability to site wetlands with more spatial accuracy within a sub-watershed would clearly provide improvements over the current SWAT wetland simulation approach, although this can potentially be overcome for some applications by subdividing a watershed into smaller sub-watersheds.

The lack of spatial detail in SWAT also hinders simulation of riparian buffer zones and other conservation buffers, which again need to be spatially defined at the landscape or HRU level in order to correctly account for upslope pollutant source areas and the pollutant mitigation impacts of the buffers. The riparian and

**Table 4.** Proposed key parameters to adjust for accounting of different conservation practice effects in SWAT (source: Arabi et al., 2007a).

| Conservation Practice | Channel Depth | Channel Width | Channel Erodibility Factor | Channel Cover Factor | Channel Manning Roughness Coeff. | Channel Slope Segment | Filter Strip Width[a] | Hillside Slope Length | Manning N for Overland Flow | SCS Runoff Curve Number | USLE C Factor | USLE P Factor |
|---|---|---|---|---|---|---|---|---|---|---|---|---|
| Contouring | | | | | | | | | | X | | X |
| Field border | | | | | | | | | X | | | |
| Filter strips | | | | | | | X | | | | | |
| Grade stabilization structures | | | X | | | X | | | | | | |
| Grassed waterways | X | X | | X | X | | | | | | | |
| Lined waterways | X | X | X | | X | | | | | | | |
| Parallel terraces | | | | | | | | X | | X | | X |
| Residue management[b] | | | | | | | | | X | X | X | |
| Stream channel stabilization | X | X | X | | X | | | | | | | |
| Strip cropping | | | | | | | | | X | X | X | X |

[a] Setting a filter strip width triggers one of two filter strip trapping efficiency functions (one for bacteria and the other for sediment, pesticides, and nutrients) that account for the effect of filter strip removal of pollutants.
[b] Soil incorporation of residue by tillage implements is also a key aspect of simulated residue management in SWAT.

wetland processes recently incorporated into the SWIM model (Hatterman et al., 2006) may prove useful for improving current approaches used in SWAT.

## 4.4 Bacteria Life Cycle and Transport

Benham et al. (2006) state that SWAT is one of two primary models used for watershed-scale bacteria fate and transport assessments in the U.S. The strengths of the SWAT bacteria component include: (1) simultaneous assessment of fecal coliform (as an indicator pathogen) and a more persistent second pathogen that possesses different growth/die-off characteristics, (2) different rate constants that can be set for soluble versus sediment-bound bacteria, and (3) the ability to account for multiple point and/or nonpoint bacteria sources such as land-applied livestock and poultry manure, wildlife contributions, and human sources such as septic tanks. Jamieson et al. (2004) further point out that SWAT is the only model that currently simulates partitioning of bacteria between adsorbed and non-adsorbed fractions; however, they also state that reliable partitioning data is currently not available. Bacteria die-off is simulated in SWAT on the basis of a first-order kinetic function (Neitsch et al., 2005a), as a function of time and temperature. However, Benham et al. (2006), Jamieson et al. (2004), and Pachepsky et al. (2006) all cite several studies that show that other factors such as moisture content, pH, nutrients, and soil type can influence die-off rates. Leaching of bacteria is also simulated in SWAT, although all leached bacteria are ultimately assumed to die off. This conflicts with some actual observations in which pathogen movement has been observed in subsurface flow (Pachepsky et al., 2006; Benham et al., 2006), which is especially prevalent in tile-drained areas (Jamieson et al., 2004). Benham et al. (2006), Jamieson et al. (2004), and Pachepsky et al. (2006) list a number of research needs and modeling improvements needed to perform more accurate bacteria transport simulations with SWAT and other models including: (1) more accurate characterization of bacteria sources, (2) development of bacteria life cycle equations that account for different phases of die-off and the influence of multiple factors on bacteria die-off rates, (3) accounting of subsurface flow bacteria movement including transport via tile drains, and (4) depiction of bacteria deposition and resuspension as function of sediment particles rather than just discharge.

## 4.5 In-Stream Kinetic Functions

The ability to simulate in-stream water quality dynamics is a definite strength of SWAT. However, Horn et al. (2004) point out that very few SWAT-related studies discuss whether the QUAL2E-based in-stream kinetic functions were used or not. Santhi et al. (2001a) opted to not use the in-stream functions for their SWAT analysis of the Bosque River in central Texas because the functions do not account for periphyton (attached algae), which dominates phosphorus-limited systems including the Bosque River. This is a common limitation of most water quality models with in-stream components, which focus instead on just suspended algae. Migliaccio et al. (2007) performed parallel SWAT analyses of total P and nitrate (including nitrite) movement for the 60 km$^2$ War Eagle Creek watershed in northwest Arkansas by: (1) loosely coupling SWAT with QUAL2E (with the SWAT in-stream component turned off), and (2) executing SWAT by itself with and without the in-stream functions activated. They found no statistical difference in the results generated between the SWAT-QUAL2E interface approach versus the standalone SWAT approach, or between the two standalone SWAT simulations. They concluded that further testing and refinement of the SWAT in-stream algorithms are warranted, which is similar to the views expressed by Horn et al. (2004). Further investigation is also needed to determine if the QUAL2E modifications made in ESWAT should be ported to SWAT, which are described by Van Griensven and Bauwens (2003, 2005).

## 4.6 Additional Research Needs

- Development of concentrated animal feeding operation and related manure application routines, that support simulation of surface and integrated manure application techniques and their influence on nutrient fractionation, distribution in runoff and soil, and sediment loads. Current development is focused on a manure cover layer.

- All aspects of stream routing need further testing and refinement, including the QUAL2E routines as discussed above.

- Improved stream channel degradation and sediment deposition routines are needed to better describe sediment transport, and to account for nutrient loads associated with sediment movement, as discussed by Jha et al. (2004a). Channel sediment routing could be improved by accounting for sediment size effects, with separate algorithms for the wash and bed loads. Improved flood plain deposition algorithms are needed, and a stream bank erosion routine should be incorporated.

- SWAT currently assumes that soil carbon contents are static. This approach will be replaced by an updated carbon cycling submodel that provides more realistic accounting of carbon cycling processes.

- Improvements to the nitrogen cycling routines should be investigated based on the suggestions given by Borah et al. (2006). Other aspects of the nitrogen cycling process should also be reviewed and updated if needed, including current assumptions of plant nitrogen uptake. Soil phosphorus cycling improvements have been initiated and will continue. The ability to simulate leaching of soil phosphorus through the soil profile, and in lateral, groundwater, and tile flows, has recently been incorporated into the model.

- Expansion of the plant parameter database is needed, as pointed out by Heuvelmans et al. (2005), to support a greater range of vegetation scenarios that can be simulated in the model. In general, more extensive testing of the crop growth component is needed, including revisions to the crop parameters where needed.

- Modifications have been initiated by McKeown et al. (2005) in a version of the model called SWAT2000-C to more accurately simulate the hydrologic balance and other aspects of Canadian boreal forest systems including: (1) incorporation of a surface litter layer into the soil profile, (2) accounting of water storage and release by wetlands, and (3) improved simulation of spring thaw generated runoff. These improvements will ultimately be grafted into SWAT2005.

- Advancements have been made in simulating subsurface tile flows and nitrate losses (Du et al., 2005, 2006). Current research is focused on incorporating a second option, based on the DRAINMOD (Skaggs, 1982) approach, that includes the effects of tile drain spacing and shallow water table depth. Future research should also be focused on controlled drainage BMPs.

- Routines for automated sensitivity, calibration, and input uncertainty analysis have been added to SWAT (van Griensven and Bauwens, 2003). These routines are currently being tested on several watersheds, including accounting of uncertainty encountered in measured water quality data, as discussed by Harmel et al. (2006).

- The effects of atmospheric $CO_2$ on plant growth need to be revised to account for varying stomatal conductance and leaf area responses as a function of plant species, similar to the procedure developed for SWAT-G by Eckhardt et al. (2003).

## 5. Conclusions

The wide range of SWAT applications that have been described here underscores that the model is a very flexible and robust tool that can be used to simulate a variety of watershed problems. The process of configuring SWAT for a given watershed has also been greatly facilitated by the development of GIS-based interfaces, which provide a straightforward means of translating digital land use, topographic, and soil data into model inputs. It can be expected that additional support tools will be created in the future to facilitate various applications of SWAT. The ability of SWAT to replicate hydrologic and/or pollutant loads at a variety of spatial scales on an annual or monthly basis has been confirmed in numerous studies. However, the model performance has been inadequate in some studies, especially when comparisons of predicted output were made with time series of measured daily flow and/or pollutant loss data. These weaker results underscore the need for continued testing of the model, including more thorough uncertainty analyses, and ongoing improvement of model routines. Some users have addressed weaknesses in SWAT by component modifications, which support more accurate simulation of specific processes or regions, or by interfacing SWAT with other models. Both of these trends are expected to continue. The SWAT model will continue to evolve in response to the needs of the ever-increasing worldwide user community and to provide improved simulation accuracy of key processes. A major challenge of the ongoing evolution of the model will be meeting the desire for additional spatial complexity while maintaining ease of model use. This goal will be kept in focus as the model continues to develop in the future.

# Acknowledgments

Partial support for this study was provided by the U.S. EPA Office of Policy, Economics, and Innovation and Office of Wastewater Management under cooperating agreement number CR 820374-02-7 and the Cooperative State Research, Education, and Extension Service of the USDA, Project No. NCX-186-5-04-130-1, in the Agricultural Research Program, North Carolina Agricultural and Technical State University. The opinions expressed in this document remain the sole responsibility of the authors and do not necessarily express the position of the U.S. EPA or the USDA.

# References

**Abbaspour, K.C., J. Yang, I. Maximov, R. Siber, K. Bogner, J. Mieleitner, J. Zobrist, and R. Srinivasan. 2007.** Modelling hydrology and water quality in the pre-alpine/alpine Thur watershed using SWAT. *J. Hydrol.* 333(2-4): 413-430.

**Afinowicz, J. D., C.L. Munster, and B.P. Wilcox. 2005.** Modeling effects of brush management on the rangeland water budget: Edwards Plateau, Texas. *J. American Water Resour. Assoc.* 41(1): 181-193.

**Agnew, L.J., S. Lyon, P. Gérard-Marchant, V.B. Collins, A.J. Lembo, T.S. Steenhuis, and M.T. Walter. 2006.** Identifying hydrologically sensitive areas: Bridging the gap between science and application. *J. Environ. Mgmt.* 78(1): 63-76.

**Arabi, M., R.S. Govindaraju, and M.M. Hantush. 2006a.** Cost-effective allocation of watershed management practices using a genetic algorithm. *Water Resour. Res.* 42.W10429, doi:10,1029/2006WR004931.

**Arabi, M., J. Frankenberger, B. Engel, and J. Arnold. 2007a.** Representation of agricultural management practices with SWAT. *Hydrol. Process.* (submitted).

**Arabi, M., R.S. Govindaraju, and M.M. Hantush. 2007b.** A probabilistic approach for analysis of uncertainty in evaluation of watershed management practices. *J. Hydrol.* 333(2-4): 459-471.

**Arabi, M., R.S. Govindaraju, M.M. Hantush, and B.A. Engel. 2006b.** Role of watershed subdivision on modeling the effectiveness of best management practices with SWAT. *J. American Water Resour. Assoc.* 42(2): 513-528.

**Arnold, J.G., and J.R. Williams. 1987.** Validation of SWRRB: Simulator for water resources in rural basins. *J. Water Resour. Plan. Manage.* ASCE 113(2): 243-256.

**Arnold, J.G., and P.M. Allen. 1993.** A comprehensive surface-ground water flow model. *J. Hydrol.* 142(1-4): 47-69.

**Arnold, J.G., and P.M. Allen. 1996.** Estimating hydrologic budgets for three Illinois watersheds. *J. Hydrol.* 176(1-4): 57-77.

**Arnold, J.G., and P.M. Allen. 1999.** Automated methods for estimating baseflow and groundwater recharge from streamflow records. *J. American Water Resour. Assoc.* 35(2): 411-424.

**Arnold, J.G., and N. Fohrer. 2005.** SWAT2000: Current capabilities and research opportunities in applied watershed modeling. *Hydrol. Process.* 19(3): 563-572.

**Arnold, J.G., P.M. Allen, R.S. Muttiah, and G. Bernhardt. 1995a.** Automated base flow separation and recession analysis techniques. *Groundwater* 33(6): 1010-1018.

**Arnold, J.G., J.R. Williams, and D.R. Maidment. 1995b.** Continuous-time water and sediment-routing model for large basins. *J. Hydrol. Eng.* ASCE 121(2): 171-183.

**Arnold, J.G., R. Srinivasan, R.S. Muttiah, and J.R. Williams. 1998.** Large-area hydrologic modeling and assessment: Part I. Model development. *J. American Water Resour. Assoc.* 34(1): 73-89.

**Arnold, J.G., R. Srinivasan, R.S. Muttiah, P.M. Allen, and C. Walker. 1999a.** Continental-scale simulation of the hydrologic balance. *J. American Water Resour. Assoc.* 35 (5): 1037-1052.

**Arnold, J.G., R. Srinivasan, T.S. Ramanarayanan, and M. Di Luzio. 1999b.** Water resources of the Texas gulf basin. *Water Sci. Tech.* 39(3): 121-133.

**Arnold, J.G., R.S. Muttiah, R. Srinivasan, and P.M. Allen. 2000.** Regional estimation of base flow and groundwater recharge in the upper Mississippi basin. *J. Hydrol.* 227(1-4): 21-40.

**Arnold, J.G., P.M. Allen, and D. Morgan. 2001.** Hydrologic model for design of constructed wetlands. *Wetlands* 21(2): 167-178.

**Arnold, J.G., K.N. Potter, K.W. King, and P.M. Allen. 2005.** Estimation of soil cracking and the effect on surface runoff in a Texas Blackland Prairie watershed. *Hydrol. Process.* 19(3): 589-603.

**Ascough II, J.C., C. Baffaut, M.A. Nearing, and B.Y. Liu. 1997.** The WEPP watershed model: I. Hydrology and erosion. *Trans. ASAE* 40(4): 921-933.

**Attwood, J.D., B. McCarl, C.C. Chen, B.R. Eddleman, B. Nayda, and R. Srinivasan. 2000.** Assessing regional impacts of change: Linking economic and environmental models. *Agric. Syst.* 63(3): 147-159.

**Bärlund, I., T. Kirkkala, O. Malve, and J. Kämäri. 2007.** Assessing the SWAT model performance in the evaluation of management actions for the implementation of the Water Framework Directive in a Finnish catchment. *Environ. Model. Soft.* 22(5): 719-724.

**Behera, S., and R.K. Panda. 2006.** Evaluation of management alternatives for an agricultural watershed in a sub-humid subtropical region using a physical process model. *Agric. Ecosys. Environ.* 113(1-4): 62-72.

**Benaman, J., and C.A. Shoemaker. 2004.** Methodology for analyzing ranges of uncertain model parameters and their impact on total maximum daily load processes. *J. Environ. Eng.* 130(6): 648-656.

**Benaman, J., C.A. Shoemaker, and D.A. Haith. 2005.** Calibration and validation of Soil and Water Assessment Tool on an agricultural watershed in upstate New York. *J. Hydrol. Eng.* 10(5): 363-374.

**Benham, B.L., C. Baffaut, R.W. Zeckoski, K.R. Mankin, Y.A. Pachepsky, A.M. Sadeghi, K. M. Brannan, M.L. Soupir, and M.J. Habersack. 2006.** Modeling bacteria fate and transport in watershed models to support TMDLs. *Trans. ASABE* 49(4): 987-1002.

**Bicknell, B.R., J.C. Imhoff, A.S. Donigian, and R.C. Johanson. 1997.** Hydrological simulation program - FORTRAN (HSPF): User's manual for release 11. EPA-600/R-97/080. Athens, Ga.: U.S. Environmental Protection Agency.

**Bingner, R.L. 1996.** Runoff simulated from Goodwin Creek watershed using SWAT. *Trans. ASAE* 39(1): 85-90.

**Bingner, R.L., J. Garbrecht, J.G. Arnold, and R. Srinivasan. 1997.** Effect of watershed subdivision on simulated runoff and fine sediment yield. *Trans. ASAE* 40(5): 1329-1335.

**Boorman, D.B. 2003.** Climate, Hydrochemistry, and Economics of Surface-water Systems (CHESS): Adding a European dimension to the catchment modelling experience developed under LOIS. *Sci. Total Environ.* 314-316: 411-437.

**Borah, D.K., and M. Bera. 2003.** Watershed-scale hydrologic and nonpoint-source pollution models: Review of mathematical bases. *Trans. ASAE* 46(6): 1553-1566.

**Borah, D.K., and M. Bera. 2004.** Watershed-scale hydrologic and nonpoint-source pollution models: Review of applications. *Trans. ASAE* 47(3): 789-803.

**Borah, D.K., M. Bera, M. and R. Xia. 2004.** Storm event flow and sediment simulations in agricultural watersheds using DWSM. *Trans. ASAE* 47(5): 1539-1559.

**Borah, D.K., G. Yagow, A. Saleh, P.L. Barnes, W. Rosenthal, E.C. Krug, and L.M. Hauck. 2006.** Sediment and nutrient modeling for TMDL development and implementation. *Trans. ASABE* 49(4): 967-986.

**Borah, D.K., J. G. Arnold, M. Bera, E.C. Krug, and X.Z. Liang. 2007.** Storm event and continuous hydrologic modeling for comprehensive and efficient watershed simulations. *J. Hydrol. Eng. (in press).*

**Bosch, D.D., J.M. Sheridan, H.L. Batten, and J.G. Arnold. 2004.** Evaluation of the SWAT model on a coastal plain agricultural watershed. *Trans. ASAE* 47(5): 1493-1506.

**Bouraoui, F., L. Galbiati, and G. Bidoglio. 2002.** Climate change impacts on nutrient loads in the Yorkshire Ouse catchment (UK). *Hydrol. Earth System Sci.* 6(2): 197-209.

**Bouraoui, F., B. Grizzetti, K. Granlund, S. Rekolainen, and G. Bidoglio. 2004.** Impact of climate change on the water cycled and nutrient losses in a Finnish catchment. *Clim. Change* 66(1-2): 109-126.

**Bouraoui, F., S. Benabdallah, A. Jrad, and G. Bidoglio. 2005.** Application of the SWAT model on the Medjerda River basin (Tunisia). *Phys. Chem. Earth* 30(8-10): 497-507.

**Bracmort, K.S., M. Arabi, J.R. Frankenberger, B.A. Engel, and J.G. Arnold. 2006.** Modeling long-term water quality impact of structural BMPs. *Trans. ASABE* 49(2): 367-374.

**Brown, L.C., and T.O. Barnwell, Jr. 1987.** The enhanced water quality models QUAL2E and QUAL2E-UNCAS: Documentation and user manual. EPA document EPA/600/3-87/007. Athens, Ga.: USEPA.

**Bryant, R.B., W.J. Gburek, T.L. Veith, and W.D. Hively. 2006.** Perspectives on the potential for hydropedology to improve watershed modeling of phosphorus loss. *Geoderma* 131(3-4): 299-307.

**CARD. 2007.** CARD interactive software programs. Ames, Iowa: Iowa State University, Center for Agricultural and Rural Development. Available at: www.card.iastate.edu/ environment/interactive_programs.aspx. Accessed 12 February 2007.

**Cao, W., W.B. Bowden, T. Davie, and A. Fenemor. 2006.** Multi-variable and multi-site calibration and validation of SWAT in a large mountainous catchment with high spatial variability. *Hydrol. Proc.* 20(5): 1057-1073.

**Cerucci, M., and J.M. Conrad. 2003.** The use of binary optimization and hydrologic models to form riparian buffers. *J. American Water Resour. Assoc.* 39(5): 1167-1180.

**Chanasyk, D.S., E. Mapfumo, and W. Willms. 2003.** Quantification and simulation of surface runoff from fescue grassland watersheds. *Agric. Water Mgmt.* 59(2): 137-153.

**Chaplot, V. 2005.** Impact of DEM mesh size and soil map scale on SWAT runoff, sediment, and $NO_3$-N loads predictions. *J. Hydrol.* 312(1-4): 207-222.

**Chaplot, V., A. Saleh, D.B. Jaynes, and J. Arnold. 2004.** Predicting water, sediment, and $NO_3$-N loads under scenarios of land-use and management practices in a flat watershed *Water Air Soil Pollut.* 154(1-4): 271-293.

**Chaplot, V., A. Saleh, and D.B. Jaynes. 2005.** Effect of the accuracy of spatial rainfall information on the modeling of water, sediment, and $NO_3$-N loads at the watershed level. *J. Hydrol.* 312(1-4): 223-234.

**CEAP. 2007.** Conservation Effects Assessment Project. Washington, D.C.: USDA Natural Resources Conservation Service. Available at: www.nrcs.usda.gov/technical/NRI/ceap/. Accessed 14 February 2007.

**Chen, E., and D.S. Mackay. 2004.** Effects of distribution-based parameter aggregation on a spatially distributed agricultural nonpoint-source pollution model. *J. Hydrol.* 295(1-4): 211-224.

**Cheng, H., W. Ouyang, F. Hao, X. Ren, and S. Yang. 2006.** The nonpoint-source pollution in livestock-breeding areas of the Heihe River basin in Yellow River. *Stoch. Environ. Res. Risk Assess.* doi:10.1007/s00477-006-0057-2.

**CHESS. 2001.** Climate, hydrochemistry, and economics of surface-water systems. Available at: www.nwl.ac.uk/ih/www/research/images/chessreport.pdf. Accessed 25 August 2006.

**Christiansen, J.H., and M. Altaweel. 2006.** Simulation of natural and social process interactions: An example from Bronze Age Mesopotamia. *Soc. Sci. Comp. Rev.* 24(2): 209-226.

**Chu, T.W., and A. Shirmohammadi. 2004.** Evaluation of the SWAT model's hydrology component in the Piedmont physiographic region of Maryland. *Trans. ASAE* 47(4): 1057-1073.

**Chu, T.W., A. Shirmohammadi, H. Montas, and A. Sadeghi. 2004.** Evaluation of the SWAT model's sediment and nutrient components in the Piedmont physiographic region of Maryland. *Trans. ASAE* 47(5): 1523-1538.

**Coffey, M.E., S.R. Workman, J.L. Taraba, and A.W. Fogle. 2004.** Statistical procedures for evaluating daily and monthly hydrologic model predictions. *Trans. ASAE* 47(1): 59-68.

**CoLab. 2006.** CoLab: Project Integration - Change Control - Life Cycle Management. Washington, D.C.: USDA Collaborative Software Development Laboratory. Available at: colab.sc.egov.usda.gov/cb/sharedProjectsBrowser.do. Accessed 30 October 2006.

**Conan, C., F. Bouraoui, N. Turpin, G. de Marsily, and G. Bidoglio. 2003a.** Modeling flow and nitrate fate at catchment scale in Brittany (France). *J. Environ. ūa l.* 32(6): 2026-2032.

**Conan, C., G. de Marsily, F. Bouraoui, and G. Bidoglio. 2003b.** A long-term hydrological modelling of the upper Guadiana river basin (Spain). *Phys. Chem. Earth* 28(4-5): 193-200.

**Cornell. 2003.** SMDR: The soil moisture distribution and routing model. Documentation version 2.0. Ithaca, N.Y.: Cornell University Department of Biological and Environmental Engineering, Soil and Water Laboratory. Available at: soilandwater.bee.cornell.edu/Research/smdr/downloads/SMDR-manual-v200301.pdf. Accessed 11 February 2007.

**Cotter, A.S., I. Chaubey, T.A. Costello, T.S. Soerens, and M.A. Nelson. 2003.** Water quality model output uncertainty as affected by spatial resolution of input data. *J. American Water Res. Assoc.* 39(4): 977-986.

**Deliberty, T.L., and D.R. Legates. 2003.** Interannual and seasonal variability of modelled soil moisture in Oklahoma. *Intl. J. Climatol.* 23(9): 1057-1086.

**Di Luzio, M., and J.G. Arnold. 2004.** Formulation of a hybrid calibration approach for a physically based distributed model with NEXRAD data input. *J. Hydrol.* 298(1-4): 136-154.

**Di Luzio, M., R. Srinivasan, and J.G. Arnold. 2002.** Integration of watershed tools and SWAT model into BASINS. *J. American Water Resour. Assoc.* 38(4): 1127-1141.

**Di Luzio, M., R. Srinivasan, and J.G. Arnold. 2004a.** A GIS-coupled hydrological model system for the watershed assessment of agricultural nonpoint and point sources of pollution. *Trans. GIS* 8(1): 113-136.

**Di Luzio, M., J.G. Arnold, and R. Srinivasan 2004b.** Integration of SSURGO maps and soil parameters within a geographic information system and nonpoint-source pollution model system. *J. Soil Water Cons.* 59(4): 123-133.

**Di Luzio, M., J.G. Arnold, and R. Srinivasan. 2005.** Effect of GIS data quality on small watershed streamflow and sediment simulations. *Hydrol. Process.* 19(3): 629-650.

**Doherty, J. 2004.** *PEST: Model-Independent Parameter Estimation User Manual.* 5th ed. Brisbane, Australia: Watermark Numerical Computing. Available at: www.simulistics.com/documents/pestman.pdf. Accessed 18 February 2007.

**Du, B., J.G. Arnold, A. Saleh, and D.B. Jaynes. 2005.** Development and application of SWAT to landscapes with tiles and potholes. *Trans. ASAE* 48(3): 1121-1133.

**Du, B., A. Saleh, D.B. Jaynes, and J.G. Arnold. 2006.** Evaluation of SWAT in simulating nitrate nitrogen and atrazine fates in a watershed with tiles and potholes. *Trans. ASABE* 49(4): 949-959.

**EAWAG. 2005.** *Proc. 3rd International SWAT Conference.* Zurich, Switzerland: Swiss Federal Institute for Environmental Science and Technology. Available at: www.brc.tamus.edu/swat/3rdswatconf/SWAT%20Book%203rd%20Conference.pdf. Accessed 14 February 2007.

**Eckhardt, K., and J.G. Arnold. 2001.** Automatic calibration of a distributed catchment model. *J. Hydrol.* 251(1-2): 103-109.

**Eckhardt, K., and U. Ulbrich. 2003.** Potential impacts of climate change on groundwater recharge and streamflow in a central European low mountain range. *J. Hydrol.* 284(1-4): 244-252.

**Eckhardt, K., S. Haverkamp, N. Fohrer, and H.-G. Frede. 2002.** SWAT-G, a version of SWAT99.2 modified for application to low mountain range catchments. *Phys. Chem. Earth* 27(9-10): 641-644.

**Eckhardt, K., L. Breuer, and H.-G. Frede. 2003.** Parameter uncertainty and the significance of simulated land use change effects. *J. Hydrol.* 273(1-4): 164-176.

**Eckhardt, K., N. Fohrer, and H.-G. Frede. 2005.** Automatic model calibration. *Hydrol. Process.* 19(3): 651-658.

**El-Nasr, A. J.G. Arnold, J. Feyen, and J. Berlamont. 2005.** Modelling the hydrology of a catchment using a distributed and a semi-distributed model. *Hydrol. Process.* 19(3): 573-587.

**EUROHARP. 2006.** Towards European harmonised procedures for quantification of nutrient losses from diffuse sources. Available at: euroharp.org/pd/pd/index.htm5 Accessed 25 August 2006.

**FitzHugh, T.W., and D.S. Mackay. 2000.** Impacts of input parameter spatial aggregation on an agricultural nonpoint-source pollution model. *J. Hydrol.* 236(1-2): 35-53.

**FitzHugh, T.W., and D.S. Mackay. 2001.** Impact of subwatershed partitioning on modeled source- and transport-limited sediment yields in an agricultural nonpoint-source pollution model. *J. Soil Water Cons.* 56(2): 137-143.

**Fohrer, N., D. Müller, and N. Steiner. 2002.** An interdisciplinary modelling approach to evaluate the effects of land use change. *Phys. Chem. Earth* 27(9-10): 655-662.

**Fohrer, N., S. Haverkamp, and H.-G. Frede. 2005.** Assessment of the effects of land use patterns on hydrologic landscape functions: Development of sustainable land use concepts for low mountain range areas. *Hydrol. Process.* 19(3): 659-672.

**Fontaine, T.A., J.F. Klassen, T.S. Cruickshank, and R.H. Hotchkiss. 2001.** Hydrological response to climate change in the Black Hills of South Dakota, USA. *Hydrol. Sci. J.* 46 (1): 27-40.

**Fontaine, T.A., T.S. Cruickshank, J.G. Arnold, and R.H. Hotchkiss. 2002.** Development of a snowfall-snowmelt routine for mountainous terrain for the Soil and Water Assessment Tool (SWAT). *J. Hydrol.* 262(1-4): 209-223.

Francos, A., G. Bidoglio, L. Galbiati, F. Bouraoui, F.J. Elorza, S. Rekolainen, K. Manni, and K. Granlund. 2001. Hydrological and water quality modelling in a medium-sized coastal basin. *Phys. Chem. Earth (B)* 26(1): 47-52.

Francos, A., F.J. Elorza, F. Bouraoui, G. Bidoglio, and L. Galbiati. 2003. Sensitivity analysis of distributed environmental simulation models: Understanding the model behaviour in hydrological studies at the catchment scale. *Real. Eng. Syst. Safe.* 79(2): 205-218.

Galbiati, L., F. Bouraoui, F.J. Elorza, and G. Bidoglio. 2006. Modeling diffuse pollution loading into a Mediterranean lagoon: Development and application of an integrated surface-subsurface model tool. *Ecol. Model.* 193(1-2): 4-18.

Garen, D.C., and D.S. Moore. 2005. Curve number hydrology in water quality modeling: Uses, abuses, and future directions. *J. American Water Resour. Assoc.* 41(2): 377-388.

Gassman, P.W., E. Osei, A. Saleh, and L.M. Hauck. 2002. Application of an environmental and economic modeling system for watershed assessments. *J. American Water Resour. Assoc.* 38(2): 423-438.

Gassman, P.W., E. Osei, A. Saleh, J. Rodecap, S. Norvell, and J. Williams. 2006. Alternative practices for sediment and nutrient loss control on livestock farms in northeast Iowa. *Agric. Ecosys. Environ.* 117(2-3): 135-144.

Geza, M., and J.E. McCray. 2007. Effects of soil data resolution on SWAT model stream flow and water quality predictions. *J. Environ. Mgmt.* (in press).

Gikas, G.D., T. Yiannakopoulou, and V.A. Tsihrintzis. 2005. Modeling of nonpoint-source pollution in a Mediterranean drainage basin. *Environ. Model. Assess.* 11(3): 219-233

Gitau, M.W., T.L. Veith, and W.J. Gburek. 2004. Farm-level optimization of BMP placement for cost-effective pollution reduction. *Trans. ASAE* 47(6): 1923-1931.

Giorgi, F., L.O. Mearns, C. Shields, and L. McDaniel. 1998. Regional nested model simulations of present day and $2 \times CO_2$ climate over the central plains of the U.S. *Clim. Change* 40(3-4): 457-493.

Gosain, A.K., S. Rao, R. Srinivasan, and N. Gopal Reddy. 2005. Return-flow assessment for irrigation command in the Palleru River basin using SWAT model. *Hydrol. Process.* 19(3): 673-682.

Gosain, A.K., S. Rao, and D. Basuray. 2006. Climate change impact assessment on hydrology of Indian river basins. *Current Sci.* 90(3): 346-353.

Govender, M., and C.S. Everson. 2005. Modelling streamflow from two small South African experimental catchments using the SWAT model. *Hydrol. Process.* 19(3): 683-692.

Green, W.H., and G.A. Ampt. 1911. Studies on soil physics: 1. The flow of air and water through soils. *J. Agric. Sci.* 4: 11-24.

Green, C.H., M.D. Tomer, M. Di Luzio, and J.G. Arnold. 2006. Hydrologic evaluation of the Soil and Water Assessment Tool for a large tile-drained watershed in Iowa. *Trans. ASABE* 49(2): 413-422.

Grizzetti, B., F. Bouraoui, K. Granlund, S. Rekolainen, and G. Bidoglio. 2003. Modelling diffuse emission and retention of nutrients in the Vantaanjoki watershed (Finland) using the SWAT model. *Ecol. Model.* 169(1): 25-38.

Grizzetti, B., F. Bouraoui, and G. De Marsily. 2005. Modelling nitrogen pressure in river basins: A comparison between a statistical approach and the physically-based SWAT model. *Physics and Chemistry of the Earth* 30(8-10): 508-517.

Grunwald, S., and C. Qi. 2006. GIS-based water quality modeling in the Sandusky watershed, Ohio, USA. *J. American Water Resour. Assoc.* 42(4): 957-973.

Hao, F.H., X.S. Zhang, and Z.F. Yang. 2004. A distributed nonpoint-source pollution model: Calibration and validation in the Yellow River basin. *J. Environ. Sci.* 16(4): 646-650.

Hanratty, M.P., and H.G. Stefan. 1998. Simulating climate change effects in a Minnesota agricultural watershed. *J. Environ. Qual.* 27(6): 1524-1532.

Hargreaves, G.L., G.H. Hargreaves, and J.P. Riley. 1985. Agricultural benefits for Senegal River basin. *J. Irrig. Drain. Eng.* 108(3): 225-230.

Harmel, R.D., C.W. Richardson, and K.W. King. 2000. Hydrologic response of a small watershed model to generated precipitation. *Trans. ASAE* 43(6): 1483-1488.

Harmel, R.D., R.J. Cooper, R.M. Slade, R.L. Haney, and J.G. Arnold. 2006. Cumulative uncertainty in measured streamflow and water quality data for small watersheds. *Trans. ASABE* 49(3): 689-701.

Hatterman, F., V. Krysanova, F. Wechsung, and M. Wattenbach. 2004. Integrating groundwater dynamics in regional hydrological modelling. *Environ. Model. Soft.* 19(11): 1039-1051.

Hatterman, F.F., V. Krysanova, A. Habeck, and A. Bronstert. 2006. Integrating wetlands and riparian zones in river basin modeling. *Ecol. Model.* 199(4): 379-392.

Haverkamp, S., R. Srinivasan, H.-G. Frede, and C. Santhi. 2002. Subwatershed spatial analysis tool: Discretization of a distributed hydrologic model by statistical criteria. *J. American Water Resour. Assoc.* 38(6): 1723-1733.

Haverkamp, S., N. Fohrer, and H.-G. Frede. 2005. Assessment of the effect of land use patterns on hydrologic landscape functions: A comprehensive GIS-based tool to minimize model uncertainty resulting from spatial aggregation. *Hydrol. Process.* 19(3): 715-727.

Hernandez, M., S.C. Miller, D.C. Goodrich, B.F. Goff, W.G. Kepner, C.M. Edmonds, and K.B. Jones. 2000. Modeling runoff response to land cover and rainfall spatial variability in semi-arid watersheds. *Environ. Monitoring Assess.* 64(1): 285-298.

Heuvelmans, G., B. Muys, and J. Feyen. 2004a. Analysis of the spatial variation in the parameters of the SWAT model with application in Flanders, northern Belgium. *Hydrol. Earth Syst. Sci.* 8(5): 931-939.

Heuvelmans, G., B. Muys, and J. Feyen. 2004b. Evaluation of hydrological model parameter transferability for simulating the impact of land use on catchment hydrology. *Phys. Chem. Earth* 29(11-12): 739-747.

Heuvelmans, G., J. F. Garcio-Qujano, B. Muys, J. Feyen, and P. Coppin. 2005. Modelling the water balance with SWAT as part of the land use impact evaluation in a life cycle study of $CO_2$ emission reduction scenarios. *Hydrol. Process.* 19(3): 729-748.

Heuvelmans, G., B. Muys, and J. Feyen. 2006. Regionalisation of the parameters of a hydrological model: Comparison of linear regression models with artificial neural nets. *J. Hydrol.* 319(1-4): 245-265.

Holvoet, K., A. van Griensven, P. Seuntjens, and P.A. Vanrolleghem. 2005. Sensitivity analysis for hydrology and pesticide supply towards the river in SWAT. *Phys. Chem. Earth* 30(8-10): 518-526.

Horn, A.L., F.J. Rueda, G. Hörmann, and N. Fohrer. 2004. Implementing river water quality modelling issues in mesoscale watersheds for water policy demands: An overview on current concepts, deficits, and future tasks. *Phys. Chem. Earth* 29(11-12): 725-737.

Hotchkiss, R.H., S.F. Jorgensen, M.C. Stone, and T.A. Fontaine. 2000. Regulated river modeling for climate change impact assessment: The Missouri River. *J. American Water Res. Assoc.* 36(2): 375-386.

Huisman, J.A., L. Breuer, and H.G. Frede. 2004. Sensitivity of simulated hydrological fluxes towards changes in soil properties in response to land use change. *Phys. Chem. Earth* 29(11-12): 749-758.

Izaurralde, R.C., J.R. Williams, W.B. McGill, N.J. Rosenberg, and M.C. Quiroga Jakas. 2006. Simulating soil C dynamics with EPIC: Model description and testing against long-term data. *Ecol. Model.* 192(3-4): 362-384.

**Jamieson, R., R. Gordon, D. Joy, and H. Lee. 2004.** Assessing microbial pollution of rural surface waters: A review of current watershed-scale modeling approaches. *Agric. Water Mgmt.* 70(1): 1-17.

**Jha, M., P.W. Gassman, S. Secchi, R. Gu, and J. Arnold. 2004a.** Effect of watershed subdivision on SWAT flow, sediment, and nutrient predictions. *J. American Water Resour. Assoc.* 40(3): 811-825.

**Jha, M., Z. Pan, E.S. Takle, and R. Gu. 2004b.** Impacts of climate change on streamflow in the upper Mississippi River basin: A regional climate model perspective. *J. Geophys. Res.* 109: D09105, doi:10.1029/2003JD003686.

**Jha, M., J.G. Arnold, P.W. Gassman, F. Giorgi, and R. Gu. 2006.** Climate change sensitivity assessment on upper Mississippi river basin steamflows using SWAT. *J. American Water Resour. Assoc.* 42(4): 997-1015.

**Jha, M., P.W. Gassman, and J.G. Arnold. 2007.** Water quality modeling for the Raccoon River watershed using SWAT2000. *Trans. ASABE* 50(2): 479-493.

**Johns, T.C., R.E. Carnell, J.F. Crossley, J.M. Gregory, J.F.B. Mitchell, C.A. Senior, S.F.B. Tett, and R.A. Wood. 1997.** The second Hadley Centre coupled ocean-atmosphere GCM: Mode description, spinup, and validation. *Clim. Dynam.* 13(2): 103-134.

**Kalin, L., and M.H. Hantush. 2006.** Hydrologic modeling of an eastern Pennsylvania watershed with NEXRAD and rain gauge data. *J. Hydrol. Eng.* 11(6): 555-569.

**Kang, M.S., S.W. Park, J.J. Lee, and K.H. Yoo. 2006.** Applying SWAT for TMDL programs to a small watershed containing rice paddy fields. *Agric. Water Mgmt.* 79(1): 72-92.

**Kannan, N., S.M. White, F. Worrall, and M.J. Whelan. 2006.** Pesticide modeling for a small catchment using SWAT-2000. *J. Environ. Sci. Health, Part B* 41(7): 1049-1070.

**Kannan, N., S.M. White, and M.J. Whelan. 2007a.** Predicting diffuse-source transfers of surfactants to surface waters using SWAT. *Chemosphere* 66(7): 1336-1345

**Kannan, N., S.M. White, F. Worrall, and M.J. Whelan. 2007b.** Sensitivity analysis and identification of the best evapotranspiration and runoff options for hydrological modeling in SWAT-2000. *J. Hydrol.* 332(3-4): 456-466.

**Kaur, R., O. Singh, R. Srinivasan, S.N. Das, and K. Mishra. 2004.** Comparison of a subjective and a physical approach for identification of priority areas for soil and water management in a watershed: A case study of Nagwan watershed in Hazaribagh District of Jharkhand, India. *Environ. Model. Assess.* 9(2): 115-127.

**King, K.W., J.G. Arnold, and R.L. Bingner. 1999.** Comparison of Green-Ampt and curve number methods on Goodwin Creek watershed using SWAT. *Trans. ASAE* 42(4): 919-925.

**Kirsch, K., A. Kirsch, and J.G. Arnold. 2002.** Predicting sediment and phosphorus loads in the Rock River basin using SWAT. *Trans. ASAE* 45(6): 1757-1769.

**Knisel, W.G. 1980.** CREAMS, a field-scale model for chemicals, runoff, and erosion from agricultural management systems. USDA Conservation Research Report No. 26. Washington, D.C.: USDA.

**Krause, P., D.P. Boyle, and F. Bäse. 2005.** Comparison of different efficiency criteria for hydrological model assessment. *Adv. Geosci.* 5: 89-97.

**Krysanova, V., D.-I.Müller-Wohlfeil, and A. Becker. 1998.** Development and test of a spatially distributed hydrological/water quality model for mesoscale watersheds. *Ecol. Model.* 106(2-3): 261-289.

**Krysanova, V., F. Hatterman, and F. Wechsung. 2005.** Development of the ecohydrological model SWIM for regional impact studies and vulnerability assessment. *Hydrol. Process.* 19(3): 763-783.

Krysanova, V., F. Hatterman, and F. Wechsung. 2007. Implications of complexity and uncertainty for integrated modelling and impact assessment in river basins. *Environ. Model. Soft.* 22(5): 701-709.

Lemberg, B., J.W. Mjelde, J.R. Conner, R.C. Griffin, W.D. Rosenthal, and J.W. Stuth. 2002. An interdisciplinary approach to valuing water from brush control. *J. American Water Resour. Assoc.* 38(2): 409-422.

Lenhart, T., K. Eckhardt, N. Fohrer, and H.-G. Frede. 2002. Comparison of two different approaches of sensitivity analysis. *Phys. Chem. Earth* 27(9-10): 645-654.

Lenhart, T., N. Fohrer, and H.-G. Frede. 2003. Effects of land use changes on the nutrient balance in mesoscale catchments. *Phys. Chem. Earth* 28(33-36): 1301-1309.

Lenhart, T., A. Van Rompaey, A. Steegen, N. Fohrer, H.-G. Frede, and G. Govers. 2005. Considering spatial distribution and deposition of sediment in lumped and semi-distributed models. *Hydrol. Process.* 19(3): 785-794.

Leonard, R.A., W.G. Knisel, and D.A. Still. 1987. GLEAMS: Groundwater loading effects of agricultural management systems. *Trans. ASAE* 30(5): 1403-1418.

Li, C., J. Aber, F. Stange, K. Butterbach-Bahl, and H. Papen. 1992. A model of nitrous oxide evolution driven from soil driven by rainfall events: 1. Model structure and sensitivity. *J. Geophys. Res.* 97(D9): 9759-9776.

Limaye, A.S., T.M. Boyington, J.F. Cruise, A. Bulus, and E. Brown. 2001. Macroscale hydrologic modeling for regional climate assessment studies in the southeastern United States. *J. American Water Resour. Assoc.* 37(3): 709-722.

Lin, Z., and D.E. Radcliffe. 2006. Automatic calibration and predictive uncertainty analysis of a semidistributed watershed model. *Vadose Zone J.* 5(1): 248-260.

Lorz, C., M. Volk, and G. Schmidt. 2007. Considering spatial distribution and functionality of forests in a modeling framework for river basin management. *For. Ecol. Mgmt.* 248(1-2): 17-25.

Lowrance, R., L.S. Altier, R.G. Williams, S.P. Inamdar, J.M. Sheridan, D.D. Bosch, R.K. Hubbard, and D.L. Thomas. 2000. REMM: The riparian ecosystem management model. *J. Soil Water Cons.* 55(1): 27-34.

Manguerra, H.B., and B.A. Engel. 1998. Hydrologic parameterization of watersheds for runoff prediction using SWAT. *J. American Water Res. Assoc.* 34(5): 1149-1162.

Mapfumo, E., D.S. Chanasyk, and W.D. Willms. 2004. Simulating daily soil water under foothills fescue grazing with the Soil and Water Assessment Tool model (Alberta, Canada). *Hydrol. Process.* 18(3): 2787-2800.

Mausbach, M.J., and A.R. Dedrick. 2004. The length we go: Measuring environmental benefits of conservation practices. *J. Soil Water Cons.* 59(5): 96A-103A.

McDonald, M.G., and A.W. Harbaugh. 1988. A modular three-dimensional finite-differences ground-water flow model. In *Techniques of Water-Resources Investigations*. Reston, Va.: U.S. Geological Survey.

McKeown, R., G. Putz, J. Arnold, and M. Di Luzio. 2005. Modifications of the Soil and Water Assessment Tool (SWAT-C) for streamflow modeling in a small, forested watershed on the Canadian boreal plain. In *Proc. 3rd International SWAT Conf.*, 189-199. R. Srinivasan, J. Jacobs, D. Day, and K. Abbaspour, eds. Zurich, Switzerland: Swiss Federal Institute for Environmental Science and Technology (EAWAG). Available at: ww.brc.tamus.edu/swat/3rdswatconf/. Accessed 30 October 2006.

Menking, K.M., K.H. Syed, R.Y. Anderson, N.G. Shafike, and J.G. Arnold. 2003. Model estimates of runoff in the closed, semiarid Estancia basin, central New Mexico, USA. *Hydrol. Sci. J.* 48(6): 953-970.

Menking, K.M., R.Y, Anderson, N.G. Shafike, K.H. Syed, and B.D. Allen. 2004. Wetter or colder during the last glacial maximum? Revisiting the pluvial lake question in southwestern North America. *ūart. Res.* 62(3): 280-288.

Migliaccio, K.W., I. Chaubey, and B.E. Haggard. 2007. Evaluation of landscape and instream modeling to predict watershed nutrient yields. *Environ. Model. Soft.* 22(7): 987-999.

Miller, S.N., W.G. Kepner, M.H. Mehaffey, M. Hernandez, R.C. Miller, D.C. Goodrich, K.K. Devonald, D.T. Heggem, and W.P. Miller. 2002. Integrating landscape assessment and hydrologic modeling for land cover change analysis. *J. American Water Res. Assoc.* 38(4): 915-929.

Miller, S.N., D.J. Semmens, D.C. Goodrich, M. Hernandez, R.C. Miller, W.G. Kepner, and D. P. Guertin. 2007. The automated geospatial watershed assessment tool. *Environ. Model. Soft.* 22(3): 365-377.

Mishra, A., J. Froebrich, and P.W. Gassman. 2007. Evaluation of the SWAT model for assessing sediment control structures in a small watershed in India. *Trans. ASABE* 50(2): 469-478.

Monteith, J.L. 1965. Evaporation and the environment. In *The State and Movement of Water in īving Organisms, Proc. 19th Symp.* Swansea, U.K.: Society of Experimental Biology, Cambridge University Press.

Moon, J., R. Srinivasan, and J.H. Jacobs. 2004. Stream flow estimation using spatially distributed rainfall in the Trinity River basin, Texas. *Trans. ASAE* 47(5): 1445-1451.

Moriasi, D.N., J.G. Arnold, M.W. Van Liew, R.L. Binger, R.D. Harmel, and T. Veith. 2007. Model evaluation guidelines for systematic quantification of accuracy in watershed simulations. *Trans. ASABE* 50(3): 885-900.

Muleta, M.K., and J.W. Nicklow. 2005a. Decision support for watershed management using evolutionary algorithms. *J. Water Resour. Plan. Mgmt.* 131(1): 35-44.

Muleta, M.K., and J.W. Nicklow. 2005b. Sensitivity and uncertainty analysis coupled with automatic calibration for a distributed watershed model. *J. Hydrol.* 306(1-4): 127-145.

Muleta, M.K., J.W. Nicklow, and E.G. Bekele. 2007. Sensitivity of a distributed watershed simulation model to spatial scale. *J. Hydrol. Eng.* 12(2): 163-172.

Muttiah, R.S., and R.A. Wurbs. 2002. Modeling the impacts of climate change on water supply reliabilities. *Water Intl., Intl. Water Resources Assoc.* 27(3): 407-419.

Narasimhan, B., and R. Srinivasan. 2005. Development and evaluation of soil moisture deficit index (SMDI) and evapotranspiration deficit index (ETDI) for agricultural drought monitoring. *Agric. For. Meteor.* 133(1-4): 69-88.

Narasimhan, B., R. Srinivasan, J.G. Arnold, and M. Di Luzio. 2005. Estimation of long-term soil moisture using a distributed parameter hydrologic model and verification using remotely sensed data. *Trans. ASABE* 48(3): 1101-1113.

Nash, J.E., and J.V. Sutcliffe. 1970. River flow forecasting through conceptual models: Part I. A discussion of principles. *J. Hydrol.* 10(3): 282-290.

Nasr, A., M. Bruen, P. Jordan, R. Moles, G. Kiely, and P. Byrne. 2007. A comparison of SWAT, HSPF, and SHETRAN/GOPC for modeling phosphorus export from three catchments in Ireland. *Water Res.* 41(5): 1065-1073.

Nearing, M.A., V. Jetten, C. Baffaut, O. Cerdan, A. Couturier, M. Hernandez, Y. Le Bissonnais, M.H. Nichols, J.P. Nunes, C.S. Renschler, V. Souchłre, and K. van Ost. 2005. Modeling response of soil erosion and runoff to changes in precipitation and cover. *Catena* 61(2-3): 131-154.

Neitsch, S.L., J.G. Arnold, J.R. Kiniry, and J.R. Williams. 2005a. Soil and Water Assessment Tool Theoretical Documentation, Version 2005. Temple, Tex.: USDA-ARS

Grassland, Soil and Water Research Laboratory. Available at: www.brc.tamus.edu/swat/doc.html. Accessed 1 November 2006.

**Neitsch, S.L., J.G. Arnold, J.R. Kiniry, R. Srinivasan, and J.R. Williams. 2005b.** Soil and Water Assessment Tool Input/Output File Documentation, Version 2005. Temple, Tex.: USDA-ARS Grassland, Soil and Water Research Laboratory. Available at: www.brc.tamus.edu/swat/doc.html. Accessed 1 November 2006.

**Nelson, R.G., J.C. Ascough II, and M.R. Langemeier. 2005.** Environmental and economic analysis of switchgrass production for water quality improvement in northeast Kansas. *J. Environ. Mgmt.* 79(4): 336-347.

**Olivera, F., M. Valenzuela, R. Srinivasan, J. Choi, H. Cho, S. Koka, and A. Agrawal. 2006.** ArcGIS-SWAT: A geodata model and GIS interface for SWAT. *J. American Water Resour. Assoc.* 42(2): 295-309.

**Osei, E., P.W. Gassman, L.M. Hauck, S. Neitsch, R.D. Jones, J. Mcnitt, and H. Jones. 2003.** Using nutrient management to control nutrient losses from dairy pastures. *J. Range Mgmt.* 56(3): 218-226.

**Pachepsky, Y.A., A.M. Sadeghi, S.A. Bradford, D.R. Shelton, A.K. Gruber, and T. Dao. 2006.** Transport and fate of manure-borne pathogens: Modeling perspective. *Agric. Water Mgmt.* 86(1-2): 81-92.

**Perkins, S.P., and M. Sophocleous. 1999.** Development of a comprehensive watershed model applied to study stream yield under drought conditions. *Groundwater* 37(3): 418-426.

**Peterson, J.R., and J.M. Hamlet. 1998.** Hydrologic calibration of the SWAT model in a watershed containing fragipan soils. *J. American Water Resour. Assoc.* 34(3): 531-544.

**Pohlert, T., J.A. Huisman, L. Breuer, and H.-G. Freude. 2007.** Integration of a detailed biogeochemical model into SWAT for improved nitrogen predictions: Model development, sensitivity, and GLUE analysis. *Ecol. Model.* 203(3-4): 215-228.

**Ponce, V.M., and R.H. Hawkins. 1996.** Runoff curve number: Has it reached maturity? *J. Hydrol. Eng.* 1(1): 11-19.

**Plus, M., I. La Jeunesse, F. Bouraoui, J.-M. Zaldívar, A. Chapelle, and P. Lazure. 2006.** Modelling water discharges and nitrogen inputs into a Mediterranean lagoon: Impact on the primary production. *Ecol. Model.* 193(1-2): 69-89.

**Priestly, C.H.B., and R.J. Taylor. 1972.** On the assessment of surface heat flux and evaporation using large-scale parameters. *Monthly Weather Rev.* 100(2): 81-92.

**Qi, C., and S. Grunwald. 2005.** GIS-based hydrologic modeling in the Sandusky watershed using SWAT. *Trans. ASABE* 48(1): 169-180.

**Qiu, Z. 2005.** Using multi-criteria decision models to assess the economic and environmental impacts of farming decisions in an agricultural watershed. *Rev. Agric. Econ.* 27(2): 229-244.

**Qiu, Z., and T. Prato. 1998.** Economic evaluation of riparian buffers in an agricultural watershed. *J. American Water Resour. Assoc.* 34(4): 877-890.

**Rao, M., G. Fan, J. Thomas, G. Cherian, V. Chudiwale, and M. Awawdeh. 2006.** A web-based GIS decision support system for managing and planning USDA's Conservation Reserve Program (CRP). *Environ. Model. Soft.* 22(9): 1270-1280.

**Ramanarayanan, T., B. Narasimhan, and R. Srinivasan. 2005.** Characterization of fate and transport of isoxaflutole, a soil-applied corn herbicide, in surface water using a watershed model. *J. Agric. Food Chem.* 53(22): 8848-8858.

**Rawls, W.J., and D.L. Brakensiek. 1986.** Comparison between Green-Ampt and curve number runoff predictions. *Trans. ASAE* 29(6): 1597-1599.

Refsgaard, J.C., and B. Storm. 1995. MIKE-SHE. In *Computer Models in Watershed Hydrology*, 809-846. V. J. Singh, ed. Highland Ranch, Colo.: Water Resources Publications.

Renschler, C.S., and T. Lee. 2005. Spatially distributed assessment of short- and long-term impacts of multiple best management practices in agricultural watersheds. *J. Soil Water Cons.* 60(6): 446-455.

Rosenberg, N.J., D.L. Epstein, D. Wang, L. Vail, R. Srinivasan, and J.G. Arnold. 1999. Possible impacts of global warming on the hydrology of the Ogallala aquifer region. *Clim. Change* 42(4): 677-692.

Rosenberg, N.J., R.A. Brown, R.C. Izaurralde, and A.M. Thomson. 2003. Integrated assessment of Hadley Centre (HadCM2) climate change projections in agricultural productivity and irrigation water supply in the conterminous United States: I. Climate change scenarios and impacts on irrigation water supply simulated with the HUMUS model. *Agric. For. Meteor.* 117(1-2): 73-96.

Rosenthal, W.D., and D.W. Hoffman. 1999. Hydrologic modeling/GIS as an aid in locating monitoring sites. *Trans. ASAE* 42(6): 1591-1598.

Rosenthal, W.D., R. Srinivasan, and J.G. Arnold. 1995. Alternative river management using a linked GIS-hydrology model. *Trans. ASAE* 38(3): 783-790.

Rowan, R.C. 1995. PHYGROW model documentation, version 2.0. College Station, Tex.: Texas A&M University, Department of Rangeland Ecology and Management, Ranching Systems Group.

Saleh, A., and B. Du. 2004. Evaluation of SWAT and HSPF within BASINS program for the upper North Bosque River watershed in central Texas. *Trans. ASAE* 47(4): 1039-1049.

Saleh, A., J.G. Arnold, P.W. Gassman, L.W. Hauck, W.D. Rosenthal, J.R. Williams, and A.M.S. McFarland. 2000. Application of SWAT for the upper North Bosque River watershed. *Trans. ASAE* 43(5): 1077-1087.

Salvetti, R., A. Azzellino, and R. Vismara. 2006. Diffuse source apportionment of the Po River eutrophying load to the Adriatic Sea: Assessment of Lombardy contribution to Po River nutrient load apportionment by means of an integrated modelling approach. *Chemosphere* 65(11): 2168-2177.

Santhi, C., J.G. Arnold, J.R. Williams, W.A. Dugas, R. Srinivasan, and L.M. Hauck. 2001a. Validation of the SWAT model on a large river basin with point and nonpoint sources. *J. American Water Resour. Assoc.* 37(5): 1169-1188.

Santhi, C., J.G. Arnold, J.R. Williams, L.M. Hauck, and W.A. Dugas. 2001b. Application of a watershed model to evaluate management effects on point and nonpoint source pollution. *Trans. ASAE* 44(6): 1559-1570.

Santhi, C., R.S. Muttiah, J.G. Arnold, and R. Srinivasan. 2005. A GIS-based regional planning tool for irrigation demand assessment and savings using SWAT. *Trans. ASABE* 48(1): 137-147.

Santhi, C., R. Srinivasan, J.G. Arnold, and J.R. Williams. 2006. A modeling approach to evaluate the impacts of water quality management plans implemented in a watershed in Texas. *Environ. Model. Soft.* 21(8): 1141-1157.

Schomberg, J.D., G. Host, L.B. Johnson, and C. Richards. 2005. Evaluating the influence of landform, surficial geology, and land use on streams using hydrologic simulation modeling. *Aqua. Sci.* 67(4): 528-540.

Schuol, J., and K.C. Abbaspour. 2007. Using monthly weather statistics to generate daily data in a SWAT model application to west Africa. *Ecol. Model.* 201(3-4): 301-311.

Seaber, P.R., F.P. Kapinos, and G.L. Knapp. 1987. Hydrologic units maps. USGS Water-Supply Paper No. 2294. Reston, Va.: U.S. Geological Survey.

**Secchi, S., P.W. Gassman, M. Jha, L. Kurkalova, H.H. Feng, T. Campbell, and C. Kling. 2007.** The cost of cleaner water: Assessing agricultural pollution reduction at the watershed scale. *J. Soil Water Cons.* 62(1): 10-21.

**Shepherd, B., D. Harper, and A. Millington. 1999.** Modelling catchment-scale nutrient transport to watercourses in the U.K. *Hydrobiologia* 395-396: 227-237.

**Shirmohammadi, A., I. Chaubey, R.D. Harmel, D.D. Bosch, R. Muñoz-Carpena, C. Dharmasri, A. Sexton, M. Arabi, M.L. Wolfe, J. Frankenberger, C. Graff, and T.M. Sohrabi. 2006.** Uncertainty in TMDL models. *Trans. ASABE* 49(4): 1033-1049.

**Singh, J., H.V. Knapp, J.G. Arnold, and M. Demissie. 2005.** Hydrological modeling of the Iroquois River watershed using HSPF and SWAT. *J. American Water Resour. Assoc.* 41(2): 343-360.

**Skaggs, R. W. 1982.** Field evaluation of a water management simulation model. *Trans. ASAE* 25(3): 666-674.

**Smith, R.A., G.E. Schwarz, and R.A. Alexander. 1997.** Regional interpretation of water-quality monitoring data. *Water Resour. Res.* 33(12): 2781-2798.

**Sophocleous, M., and S.P. Perkins 2000.** Methodology and application of combined watershed and ground-water models in Kansas. *J. Hydrol.* 236 (3-4): 185-201.

**Sophocleous, M.A., J.K. Koelliker, R.S. Govindaraju, T. Birdie, S.R. Ramireddygari, and S.P. Perkins. 1999.** Integrated numerical modeling for basin-wide water management: The case of the Rattlesnake Creek basin in south-central Kansas. *J. Hydrol.* 214(1-4): 179-196.

**Spruill, C.A., S.R. Workman, and J.L. Taraba. 2000.** Simulation of daily and monthly stream discharge from small watersheds using the SWAT model. *Trans. ASAE* 43(6): 1431-1439.

**Srinivasan, R., and J.G. Arnold. 1994.** Integration of a basin-scale water quality model with GIS. *Water Resour. Bull.* (30)3: 453-462.

**Srinivasan, R., T.S. Ramanarayanan, J.G. Arnold, and S.T. Bednarz. 1998.** Large-area hydrologic modeling and assessment: Part II. Model application. *J. American Water Resour. Assoc.* 34(1): 91-101.

**Srinivasan, M.S., P. Gerald-Marchant, T.L. Veith, W.J. Gburek, and T.S. Steenhuis. 2005.** Watershed-scale modeling of critical source areas of runoff generation and phosphorus transport. *J. American Water Resour. Assoc.* 41(2): 361-375.

**Srivastava, P., J.N. McNair, and T.E. Johnson. 2006.** Comparison of process-based and artificial neural network approaches for streamflow modeling in an agricultural watershed. *J. American Water Resour. Assoc.* 42(2): 545-563.

**Steenhuis, T.S. 2007.** Personal communication. Ithaca, N.Y.: Cornell University, Department of Biological and Agricultural Engineering.

**Stewart, G.R., C.L. Munster, D.M. Vietor, J.G. Arnold, A.M.S. McFarland, R. White, and T. Provin. 2006.** Simulating water quality improvements in the upper North Bosque River watershed due to phosphorus export through turfgrass sod. *Trans. ASABE* 49(2): 357-366.

**Stone, M.C., R.H. Hotchkiss, C.M. Hubbard, T.A. Fontaine, L.O. Mearns, and J.G. Arnold. 2001.** Impacts of climate change on Missouri river basin water yield. *J. American Water Resour. Assoc.* 37(5): 1119-1130.

**Stone, M.C., R.C. Hotchkiss, and L.O. Mearnes. 2003.** Water yield responses to high and low spatial resolution climate change scenarios in the Missouri River basin. *Geophys. Res. Letters* 30(4): 35.1-35.4.

**Stonefelt, M.D., T.A. Fontaine, and R.H. Hotchkiss. 2000.** Impacts of climate change on water yield in the upper Wind River basin. *J. American Water Resour. Assoc.* 36(2): 321-336.

**Sun, H., and P.S. Cornish. 2005.** Estimating shallow groundwater recharge in the headwaters of the Liverpool Plains using SWAT. *Hydrol. Process.* 19(3): 795-807.

**SWAT. 2007a.** Soil and Water Assessment Tool: ArcSWAT. College Station, Tex.: Texas A&M University. Available at: www.brc.tamus.edu/swat/arcswat.html. Accessed 20 February 2007.

**SWAT. 2007b.** Soil and Water Assessment Tool: AVSWAT. College Station, Tex.: Texas A&M University. Available at: www.brc.tamus.edu/swat/avswat.html. Accessed 13 February 2007.

**SWAT. 2007c.** Soil and Water Assessment Tool: Peer-reviewed literature. College Station, Tex.: Texas A&M University. Available at: www.brc.tamus.edu/swat/ pubs_peerreview.html. Accessed 17 February 2007.

**SWAT. 2007d.** Soil and Water Assessment Tool: SWAT model. College Station, Texas: Tex. A&M University. Available at: www.brc.tamus.edu/swat/soft_model.html. Accessed 21 February 2007.

**Takle, E.S., M. Jha, and C.J. Anderson. 2005.** Hydrological cycle in the upper Mississippi River basin: 20th century simulations by multiple GCMs. *Geophys. Res. Letters* 32 (18): L18407.1-L18407.5.

**TempQsim. 2006.** Evaluation and improvement of water quality models for application to temporary waters in southern European catchments (TempQsim). Available at: www.tempqsim.net/. Accessed 25 August 2006.

**Thomson, A.M., R.A. Brown, N.J. Rosenberg, R.C. Izaurralde, D.M. Legler, and R. Srinivasan. 2003.** Simulated impacts of El Nino/southern oscillation on United States water resources. *J. American Water Resour. Assoc.* 39(1): 137-148.

**Thomson, A.M., R.A. Brown, N.J. Rosenberg, R. Srinivasan, and R.C. Izaurralde. 2005.** Climate change impacts for the conterminous USA: An integrated assessment: Part 4. Water resources. *Clim. Change* 69(1): 67-88.

**Tolson, B.A., and C.A. Shoemaker. 2007.** Cannonsville reservoir watershed SWAT2000 model development, calibration, and validation. *J. Hydrol.* 337(1-2): 68-86.

**Tripathi, M.P., R.K. Panda, and N.S. Raghuwanshi. 2003.** Identification and prioritisation of critical sub-watersheds for soil conservation management using the SWAT model. *Biosys. Eng.* 85(3): 365-379.

**Tripathi, M.P., N.S. Raghuwanshi, and G. P. Rao. 2006.** Effect of watershed subdivision on simulation of water balance components. *Hydrol. Process.* 20(5): 1137-1156.

**Turpin, N., P. Bontems, G. Rotillon, I. Bärlund, M. Kaljonen, S. Tattari, F. Feichtinger, P. Strauss, R. Haverkamp, M. Garnier, A. Lo Porto, G. Benigni, A. Leone, M. Nicoletta Ripa, O.M. Eklo, E. Romstad, T. Bioteau, F. Birgand, P. Bordenave, R. Laplana, J.M. Lescot, L. Piet, and F. Zahm. 2005.** AgriBMPWater: Systems approach to environmentally acceptable farming. *Environ. Model. Soft.* 20(2): 187-196.

**TWRI. 2003.** *SWAT2003: Proc. 2nd Intl. SWAT Conference.* TWRI Technical Report No. 266. College Station, Tex.: Texas Water Resources Institute, Texas A&M University. Available at: www.brc.tamus.edu/swat/pubs_2ndconf.html. Accessed 4 February 2007.

**UNESCO-IHE. 2007.** *4$^{TH}$ International SWAT conference: Book of abstracts.* Delft, Netherlands: United Nations Educational, Scientific and Cultural Organization, Institute for Water Education. Available at: www.brc.tamus.edu/swat/4thswatconf/docs/BOOK% 20OF%20ABSTRACTS%20final.pdf. Accessed 5 August 2007.

**USDA-ARS. 2007.** The Automated Geospatial Watershed Assessment tool (AGWA). Tucson, Ariz.: USDA Agricultural Research Service. Available at: www.tucson.ars.ag.gov/agwa/. Accessed 23 March 2007.

**USDA-NRCS. 2004.** Part 630: Hydrology. Chapter 10: Estimation of direct runoff from storm rainfall: Hydraulics and hydrology: Technical references. In *NRCS National Engi-*

*neering Handbook*. Washington, D.C.: USDA National Resources Conservation Service. Available at: www.wcc.nrcs.usda.gov/hydro/hydro-techref-neh-630.html. Accessed 14 February 2007.

**USDA-NRCS. 2007a.** Soil Survey Geographic (SSURGO) database. Washington, D.C.: USDA National Resources Conservation Service. Available at: www.ncgc.nrcs.usda.gov/products/datasets/ssurgo/. Accessed 23 march 2007.

**USDA-NRCS. 2007b.** U.S. general soil map (STATSGO). Washington, D.C.: USDA National Resources Conservation Service. Available at: www.ncgc.nrcs.usda.gov/products/datasets/statsgo/. Accessed 23 march 2007.

**USEPA. 2006a.** Better Assessment Science Integrating Point and Nonpoint Sources. Washington, D.C.: U.S. Environmental Protection Agency. Available at: www.epa.gov/waterscience/BASINS/. Accessed 23 August 2006.

**USEPA. 2006b.** Overview of current total maximum daily load - TMDL - Program and regulations. Washington, D.C.: U.S. Environmental Protection Agency. Available at: www.epa.gov/owow/tmdl/overviewfs.html. Accessed 25 August 2006.

**USEPA. 2007.** Total maximum daily loads: National section 303(d) list fact sheet. Washington, D.C.: U.S. Environmental Protection Agency. Available at: oaspub.epa.gov/waters/national_rept.control. Accessed 22 March 2007.

**Vaché, K.B., J.M. Eilers, and M.V. Santelman. 2002.** Water quality modeling of alternative agricultural scenarios in the U.S. Corn Belt. *J. American Water Resour. Assoc.* 38(2): 773-787.

**Vandenberghe, V., W. Bauwens, and P.A. Vanrolleghem. 2007.** Evaluation of uncertainty propagation into river water quality predictions to guide future monitoring campaigns. *Environ. Model. Soft.* 22(5): 725-732.

**Van Griensven, A., and W. Bauwens. 2003.** Multiobjective autocalibration for semidistributed water quality models. *Water Resour. Res.* 39(12): SWC 9.1- SWC 9.9.

**Van Griensven, A., and W. Bauwens. 2005.** Application and evaluation of ESWAT on the Dender basin and Wister Lake basin. *Hydrol. Process.* 19(3): 827-838.

**Van Griensven A., and T. Meixner. 2006.** Methods to quantify and identify the sources of uncertainty for river basin water quality models. *Water Sci. Tech.* 53(1): 51-59.

**Van Griensven, A., L. Breuer, M. Di Luzio, V. Vandenberghe, P. Goethals, T. Meixner, J. Arnold, and R. Srinivasan. 2006a.** Environmental and ecological hydroinformatics to support the implementation of the European Water Framework Directive for river basin management. *J. Hydroinformatics* 8(4): 239-252.

**Van Griensven, A., T. Meixner, S. Grunwald, T. Bishop, M. Diluzio, and R. Srinivasan. 2006b.** A global sensitivity analysis tool for the parameters of multi-variable catchment models. *J. Hydrol.* 324(1-4): 10-23.

**Van Liew, M.W., and J. Garbrecht. 2003.** Hydrologic simulation of the Little Washita River experimental watershed using SWAT. *J. American Water Resour. Assoc.* 39(2): 413-426.

**Van Liew, M.W., J.G. Arnold, and J.D. Garbrecht. 2003a.** Hydrologic simulation on agricultural watersheds: choosing between two models. *Trans. ASAE* 46(6): 1539-1551.

**Van Liew, M.W., J.D. Garbrecht, and J.G. Arnold. 2003b.** Simulation of the impacts of flood retarding structures on streamflow for a watershed in southwestern Oklahoma under dry, average, and wet climatic conditions. *J. Soil Water Cons.* 58(6): 340-348.

**Van Liew, M.W., J.G. Arnold, and D.D. Bosch. 2005.** Problems and potential of autocalibrating a hydrologic model. *Trans. ASABE* 48(3): 1025-1040.

**Van Liew, M.W., T.L. Veith, D.D. Bosch, and J.G. Arnold. 2007.** Suitability of SWAT for the Conservation Effects Assessment Project: A comparison on USDA-ARS watersheds. *J. Hydrol. Eng.* 12(2): 173-189.

Varanou, E, E. Gkouvatsou, E. Baltas, and M. Mimikou. 2002. Quantity and quality integrated catchment modelling under climatic change with use of Soil and Water Assessment Tool model. *J. Hydrol. Eng.* 7(3): 228-244.

Vazquez-Amabile, G.G., and B.A. Engel. 2005. Use of SWAT to compute groundwater table depth and streamflow in the Muscatatuck River watershed. *Trans. ASABE* 48(3): 991-1003.

Vazquez-Amabile, G.G., B.A. Engel, and D.C. Flanagan. 2006. Modeling and risk analysis of nonpoint-source pollution caused by atrazine using SWAT. *Trans. ASABE* 49 (3): 667-678.

Veith, T.L., A.N. Sharpley, J.L. Weld, and W.J. Gburek. 2005. Comparison of measured and simulated phosphorus losses with indexed site vulnerability. *Trans. ASAE* 48(2): 557-565.

Volk, M., P.M. Allen, J.G. Arnold, and P.Y. Chen. 2005. Towards a process-oriented HRU-concept in SWAT: Catchment-related control on baseflow and storage of landscape units in medium to large river basins. In *Proc. 3rd Intl. SWAT Conf.*, 159-168. R. Srinivasan, J. Jacobs, D. Day, and K. Abbaspour, eds. Zurich, Switzerland: Swiss Federal Institute for Environmental Science and Technology (EAWAG). Available at: www.brc.tamus.edu/swat/3rdswatconf/. Accessed 30 October 2006.

Volk, M., J. Hirschfeld, G. Schmidt, C. Bohn, A. Dehnhardt, S. Liersch, and L. Lymburner. 2007. A SDSS-based ecological-economic modeling approach for integrated river basin management on different scale levels: The project FLUMAGIS. *Water Resour. Mgmt.* (in press).

Von Stackelberg, N.O., G.M. Chescheir, R.W. Skaggs, and D.K. Amatya. 2007. Simulation of the hydrologic effects of afforestation in the Tacuarembó River basin, Uruguay. *Trans. ASABE* 50(2): 455-468.

Walter, M.T., M.F. Walter, E.S. Brooks, T.S. Steenhuis, J. Boll, and K. Weiler. 2000. Hydrologically sensitive areas: Variable source area hydrology implications for water quality risk assessment. *J. Soil Water Cons.* 55(3): 277-284.

Wang, X., and A.M. Melesse. 2005. Evaluation of the SWAT model's snowmelt hydrology in a northwestern Minnesota watershed. *Trans. ASABE* 48(4): 1359-1376.

Wang, X., and A.M. Melesse. 2006. Effects of STATSGO and SSURGO as inputs on SWAT model's snowmelt simulation. *J. American Water Resour. Assoc.* 42(5): 1217-1236.

Wang, X., A.M. Melesse, and W. Yang. 2006. Influences of potential evapotranspiration estimation methods on SWAT's hydrologic simulation in a northwestern Minnesota watershed. *Trans. ASABE* 49(6): 1755-1771.

Watson, B.M., R. Srikanthan, S. Selvalingam, and M. Ghafouri. 2005. Evaluation of three daily rainfall generation models for SWAT. *Trans. ASABE* 48(5): 1697-1711.

Wattenbach, M., F. Hatterman, R. Weng, F. Wechsung, V. Krysanova, and F. Badeck. 2005. A simplified approach to implement forest eco-hydrological properties in regional hydrological modelling. *Ecol. Model.* 187(1): 49-50.

Watterson, J.G., S.P. O'Farrell, and M.R. Dix. 1997. Energy and water transport in climates simulated by a general circulation model that includes dynamic sea ice. *J. Geophys. Res.* 11(D10): 11027-11037.

Weber, A., N. Fohrer, and D. Moller. 2001. Long-term land use changes in a mesocale watershed due to socio-economic factors: Effects on landscape structures and functions. *Ecol. Model.* 140(1-2): 125-140.

Wells, D. 2006. Personal communication. Washington, D.C.: U.S. Environmental Protection Agency.

**White, K.L., and I. Chaubey. 2005.** Sensitivity analysis, calibration, and validations for a multisite and multivariable SWAT model. *J. American Water Resour. Assoc.* 41(5): 1077-1089.

**Whittaker, G., R. Fare, R. Srinivasan, and D.W. Scott. 2003.** Spatial evaluation of alternative nonpoint nutrient regulatory instruments. *Water Resour. Res.* 39(4): WES 1.1 - WES 1.9.

**Williams, J.R. 1969.** Flood routing with variable travel time or variable storage coefficients. *Trans. ASAE* 12(1): 100-103.

**Williams, J.R. 1990.** The erosion productivity impact calculator (EPIC) model: A case history. *Phil. Trans. R. Soc. London* 329(1255): 421-428.

**Williams, J.R., and H.D. Berndt. 1977.** Sediment yield prediction based on watershed hydrology. *Trans. ASAE* 20(6): 1100-4.

**Williams, J.R., and R.C. Izaurralde. 2006.** The APEX model. In *Watershed Models*, 437-482. V. P. Singh and D. K. Frevert, eds. Boca Raton, Fla.: CRC Press.

**Wu, K., and Y.J. Xu. 2006.** Evaluation of the applicability of the SWAT model for coastal watersheds in southeastern Louisiana. *J. American Water Resour. Assoc.* 42(5): 1247-1260.

**Wu, K., and C. Johnston. 2007.** Hydrologic response to climatic variability in a Great Lakes watershed: A case study with the SWAT model. *J. Hydrol.* 337(1-2): 187-199.

**Zhang, X., R. Srinivasan, and F. Hao. 2007.** Predicting hydrologic response to climate change in the Luohe River basin using the SWAT model. *Trans. ASABE* 50(3): 901-910.

# Part 2

# Worldwide Applications of SWAT

# 2.1 Modeling Blue and Green Water Availability in Africa

## Jürgen Schuol[1], Karim C. Abbaspour[1], Hong Yang[1], Raghavan Srinivasan[2] and Alexander J.B. Zehnder[3]

## Abstract

Despite the general awareness that in Africa many people and large areas are suffering from insufficient water supply, spatially and temporally detailed information on freshwater availability and water scarcity is so far rather limited. By applying a semidistributed hydrological model SWAT (Soil and Water Assessment Tool), the freshwater components blue water flow (i.e. water yield plus deep aquifer recharge), green water flow (i.e. actual evapotranspiration), and green water storage (i.e. soil water) were estimated at a subbasin level with monthly resolution for the whole of Africa. Using the program SUFI-2 (Sequential Uncertainty Fitting Algorithm), the model was calibrated and validated at 207 discharge stations, and prediction uncertainties were quantified. The presented model and its results could be used in various advanced studies on climate change, water and food security, and virtual water trade, among others. The model results are generally good albeit with large prediction uncertainties in some cases. These uncertainties, however, disclose the actual knowledge about the modeled processes. The effect of considering these model-based uncertainties in advanced studies is shown for the computation of water scarcity indicators.

**Keywords:** SWAT, SUFI-2, soil water, prediction uncertainty, water scarcity, water balance components

## 1. Introduction

On a continental and annual basis Africa has abundant water resources but the problem is their high spatial and temporal variability within and between countries and river basins (UN-Water/Africa, 2006). Considering this variability, the continent can be seen as dry with pressing water problems (Falkenmark, 1989;

---

© 2009 World Association of Soil and Water Conservation, *Soil and Water Assessment Tool (SWAT): Global Applications,* eds. Jeff Arnold, Raghavan Srinivasan, Susan Neitsch, Chris George, Karim Abbaspour, Philip Gassman, Fang Hua Hao, Ann van Griensven, Ashvin Gosain, Patrick Debels, Nam Won Kim, Hiroaki Somura, Victor Ella, Attachai Jintrawet, Manuel Reyes, and Samran Sombatpanit, pp. 97-124. This paper has been published by the American Geophysical Union (2008), and is reproduced by permission of the American Geophysical Union. WASWC is grateful for the permission granted.
[1]Swiss Federal Institute of Aquatic Science and Technology (Eawag), P.O. Box 611, 8600 Dübendorf, Switzerland, and Swiss Federal Institute of Technology, 8092 Zürich, Switzerland. Juergen.Schuol@eawag.ch, abbaspour@eawag.ch
[2]Texas A&M University, Texas Agricultural Experimental Station, Spatial Science Lab, 1500 Research Plaza, College Station, TX 77845, USA. r-srinivasan@tamu.edu
[3]Board of the Swiss Federal Institutes of Technology, ETH-Zentrum, 8092 Zürich, Switzerland

Vörösmarty et al., 2005). Though of critical importance, detailed information on water resources and water scarcity is still limited in Africa (Wallace and Gregory, 2002).

Freshwater availability is a prerequisite for food security, public health, ecosystem protection, etc. Thus freshwater is important and relevant for achieving all development goals contained in the United Nations Millennium Declaration (http://www.un.org/millennium/declaration/ares552e.pdf). Two important targets of the Declaration are to halve, by the year 2015, the proportion of people without sustainable access to safe drinking water and to halve the proportion of people who suffer from hunger. These two targets are closely related to freshwater availability.

Up to now, studies of freshwater availability have predominantly focused on the quantification of the 'blue water', while ignoring the 'green water' as part of the water resource and its great importance especially for rainfed agriculture (e.g. in sub-Saharan Africa more than 95% is rainfed (Rockström et al., 2007)). Two of the few studies dealing with green water are Rockström and Gordon (2001) and Gerten et al. (2005). Blue water flow, or the internal renewable water resource (IRWR), is traditionally quantified as the sum of the water yield and the deep aquifer recharge. Green water, on the other hand, originates from the naturally infiltrated water, which is more and more being thought of as a manageable water resource. Falkenmark and Rockström (2006) differentiate between two components of the green water: green water resource (or storage), which equals the moisture in the soil, and green water flow, which equals the sum of the actual evaporation (the non-productive part) and the actual transpiration (the productive part). In some references only the transpiration is regarded as the green water component (e.g. Savenije, 2004). As evaporation and transpiration are closely interlinked processes and evaporated water has the potential to be partly used as productive flow for food production, we prefer to consider the total actual evapotranspiration as the green water flow.

Spatially and temporally detailed assessments of the different components of freshwater availability are essential for locating critical regions, and thus, the basis for rational decision-making in water resources planning and management. There exist already a few global freshwater assessments based on (1) data generalization (e.g. Shiklomanov, 2000; Shiklomanov and Rodda, 2003), (2) general circulation models (GCMs) (e.g. TRIP, Oki et al., 2001; Oki and Kanae, 2006), and (3) hydrological models (e.g. WBM, Vörösmarty et al., 1998, 2000; Fekete et al., 1999; Macro-PDM, Arnell, 1999; WGHM (WaterGAP 2), Alcamo et al., 2003; Döll et al., 2003; LPJ, Gerten et al., 2004; WASMOD-M, Widén-Nilsson et al., 2007). GCMs with their strength on the atmospheric model component perform poorly on the soil water processes (Döll et al., 2003). All the above mentioned hydrological models are raster models with a spatial resolution of $0.5°$ but show different degrees of complexities. These models either have not been calibrated (e.g. WBM) or only one (e.g. WGHM) or few parameters (e.g. WAS-

MOD-M) have been checked and adjusted against long-term average runoffs. In WGHM, for some basins one or two correction factors have been additionally applied in order to guarantee a maximum of 1% error of the simulated long-term annual average runoff (Döll et al., 2003). Intra-annual runoff differences, which are of key importance in many regions have been included in some studies (e.g. Widén-Nilsson et al., 2007) but not used for calibration.

The existing global and continental freshwater assessment models have been used for climate and socioeconomic change scenarios (Alcamo et al., 2007), water stress computation (Vörösmarty et al., 2005), analysis of seasonal and interannual continental water storage variations (Güntner et al., 2007), global water scarcity analysis taking into account environmental water requirements (Smakhtin et al., 2004), and virtual water trading (Islam et al., 2007) among others. Hence it is important that these models pass through a careful calibration, validation, and uncertainty analysis. Particularly in large-scale (hydrological) models, the expected uncertainties are rather large. For this task, several different procedures have been developed: e.g. Generalized Likelihood Uncertainty Estimation (GLUE) (Beven and Binley, 1992), Bayesian inference based on Markov Chain Monte Carlo (MCMC) (Vrugt et al., 2003), Parameter Solution (ParaSol) (van Griensven and Meixner, 2006), and Sequential Uncertainty Fitting (SUFI-2) (Abbaspour et al., 2007).

In this study, we modeled the monthly subcountry-based freshwater availability for Africa and explicitly differentiated between the different freshwater components: blue water flow, green water storage and green water flow. The model of choice was "Soil and Water Assessment Tool" (SWAT) (Arnold et al., 1998) because of two reasons. *First,* SWAT has been already successfully applied for water quantity and quality issues for a wide range of scales and environmental conditions around the globe. A comprehensive SWAT review paper summarizing the findings of more than 250 peer-reviewed articles is written by Gassman et al. (2007). The suitability of SWAT for very large scale applications has been shown in the "Hydrologic Unit Model for the United States" (HUMUS) project (Arnold et al., 1999; Srinivasan et al., 1998). SWAT was also recently applied in the national and watershed assessments of the U.S. Department of Agriculture (USDA) Conservation Effects Assessment Program (CEAP, http://www.nrcs.usda.gov/Technical/nri/ceap/index.html). The *second* reason for choosing SWAT for this exclusive water quantity study was its ability to perform plant growth and water quality modeling, a topic we plan to study in the future. An advantage of SWAT is its modular implementation where processes can be selected or not. As processes are represented by parameters in the model, in data scarce regions SWAT can run with a minimum number of parameters. As more is known about a region, more processes can be invoked for by updating and running the model again.

The African model was calibrated and validated at 207 discharge stations across the continent. Uncertainties were quantified using SUFI-2 program

(Abbaspour et al., 2007). Yang et al. (2008) compared different uncertainty analysis techniques in connection to SWAT and found that SUFI-2 needed the smallest number of model runs to achieve a similarly good solution and prediction uncertainty. This efficiency issue is of great importance when dealing with computationally intensive, complex, and large-scale models. In addition, SUFI-2 is linked to SWAT (in the SWAT-CUP software) (Abbaspour et al., 2008) through an interface that includes also the programs GLUE, ParaSol, and MCMC.

## 2. Materials and Methods

### 2.1 SWAT2005 model and ArcSWAT interface

To simulate the water resources availability in Africa, the latest version of the semiphysically based, semidistributed, basin-scale model SWAT (Arnold et al., 1998) was selected (SWAT2005) (Neitsch et al., 2005). SWAT is a continuous time model and operates on a daily time step. Only the hydrologic component of the model was used in this study. In SWAT the modeled area is divided into multiple subbasins by overlaying elevation, land cover, soil, and slope classes. In this study the subbasins were characterized by dominant land use, soil, and slope classes. This choice was essential for keeping the size of the model at a practical limit. For each of the subunits, water balance was simulated for four storage volumes: snow, soil profile, shallow aquifer, and deep aquifer. In our case, potential evapotranspiration was computed using the Hargreaves method which requires the climatic input of daily precipitation, and minimum and maximum temperature. Surface runoff was simulated using a modification of the SCS Curve Number (CN) method. Despite the empirical nature, this approach has been proven to be successful for many applications and a wide variety of hydrologic conditions (Gassman et al., 2007). The runoff from each subbasin was routed through the river network to the main basin outlet using, in our case, the variable storage method. Further technical model details are given by Arnold et al. (1998) and Neitsch et al. (2005).

The preprocessing of the SWAT model input (e.g. watershed delineation, manipulation of the spatial and tabular data) was performed within ESRI ArcGIS 9.1 using the ArcSWAT interface (Winchell et al., 2007). In comparison to the Arc-View GIS interface AVSWAT2000 (Di Luzio et al., 2001), ArcSWAT has no apparent limitation concerning the size and complexity of the simulated area as it was able to model the entire African continent.

### 2.2 The calibration and uncertainty analysis procedure-SUFI-2

The program SUFI-2 (Abbaspour et al., 2007) was used for a combined calibration and uncertainty analysis. In any (hydrological) modeling work there are uncertainties in input (e.g. rainfall), in conceptual model (e.g. by process simplification or by ignoring important processes), in model parameters (non-uniqueness) and in the measured data (e.g. discharge used for calibration). SUFI-2 maps the aggregated uncertainties to the parameters and aims to obtain the smallest pa-

100

rameter uncertainty (ranges). The parameter uncertainty leads to uncertainty in the output which is quantified by the 95% prediction uncertainty (95PPU) calculated at the 2.5% (L95PPU) and the 97.5% (U95PPU) levels of the cumulative distribution obtained through Latin hypercube sampling. Starting with large but physically meaningful parameter ranges that bracket 'most' of the measured data within the 95PPU, SUFI-2 decreases the parameter uncertainties iteratively. After each iteration, new and narrower parameter uncertainties are calculated (see Abbaspour et al., 2007) where the more sensitive parameters find a larger uncertainty reduction than the less sensitive parameters. In deterministic simulations, output (i.e. river discharge) is a signal and can be compared to a measured signal using indices such as R2, root mean square error, or Nash-Sutcliffe. In stochastic simulations where predicted output is given by a prediction uncertainty band instead of a signal, we devised two different indices to compare measurement to simulation: the P-factor and the R-factor (Abbaspour et al., 2007). These indices were used to gauge the strength of calibration and uncertainty measures. The P-factor is the percentage of measured data bracketed by the 95PPU. As all correct processes and model inputs are reflected in the observations, the degree to which they are bracketed in the 95PPU indicates the degree to which the model uncertainties are being accounted for. The maximum value for the P-factor is 100%, and ideally we would like to bracket all measured data, except the outliers, in the 95PPU band. The R-factor is calculated as the ratio between the average thickness of the 95PPU band and the standard deviation of the measured data. It represents the width of the uncertainty interval and should be as small as possible. R-factor indicates the strength of the calibration and should be close to or smaller than a practical value of 1. As a larger P-factor can be found at the expense of a larger R-factor, often a trade off between the two must be sought.

## 2.3 Database

The model for the continent of Africa was constructed using in most cases freely available global information. The collection of the data was followed by an accurate compilation and analysis of the quality and integrity. The basic input maps included the digital elevation model (DEM) GTOPO30, the digital stream network HYDRO1k (http://edc.usgs.gov/products/elevation/gtopo30/hydro/index.html), and the land cover map Global Land Cover Characterization (GLCC) (http://edcsns17.cr.usgs.gov/glcc/) both at a resolution of 1 km from U.S. Geological Survey (USGS). The soil map was produced by the Food and Agriculture Organization of the United Nations (FAO, 1995) at a resolution of 10 km, including almost 5,000 soil types and two soil layers. Because of the few and unevenly distributed weather stations in Africa with often only short and erroneous time series, the daily weather input (precipitation, minimum and maximum temperature) was generated for each subbasin based on the 0.5_ grids monthly statistics from Climatic Research Unit (CRU TS 1.0 and 2.0, http://www.cru.uea.ac.uk/cru/data/hrg.htm). We developed a semiautomated weather generator, dGen, for this purpose (Schuol and Abbaspour, 2007). Information on lakes, wetlands and reservoirs was extracted from the Global Lakes and Wetlands Database (GLWD) (Lehner and Döll, 2004). River discharge data, which is essential for calibration and validation, were obtained from the Global Runoff Data Centre (GRDC, http://grdc.bafg.de). More details on the databases are discussed by Schuol et al. (2008).

## 2.4 Model setup

The ArcSWAT interface was used for the setup and parameterization of the model. On the basis of the DEM and the stream network, a minimum drainage area of 10,000 km$^2$ was chosen to discretize the continent into 1,496 subbasins. The geomorphology, stream parameterization, and overlay of soil and land cover were automatically done within the interface. To mitigate the effect of land cover change over time, and to decrease the computational time of the very large-scale model, the dominant soil and land cover were used in each subbasin. The simulation period was from 1968 to 1995 and for these years we provided daily generated weather input. The first 3 years were used as warm-up period to mitigate the unknown initial conditions and were excluded from the analysis. Lakes, wetlands, and reservoirs, which affect the river discharge to a great extent, were also included in the model. As detail information was lacking, only 64 reservoirs with storage volumes larger than 1 km$^3$ were included (Fig. 1). In this study, wetlands on the main channel networks as well as lakes were treated as reservoirs. The parameterization was mostly based on information from GLWD-1 (Lehner and Döll, 2004).

## 2.5 Model calibration procedures

Model calibration and validation is a necessary, challenging but also to a certain degree subjective step in the development of any complex hydrological model. The African model was calibrated using monthly river discharges from 207 stations. These stations were unevenly distributed throughout the continent (Fig. 1) and covered, in most cases, only parts of the whole analysis period from 1971 to 1995. For this reason it was inevitable to include different time lengths (minimum of 3 years) and time periods at the different stations in the calibration procedure. Consistently at all stations, using a split-sample procedure, the more recent half of the discharge data were used for calibration and the prior half were used for validation. In order to compare the monthly measured and simulated discharges, , a weighted version of the coefficient of determination (slightly modified; Krause et al., 2005) was selected as efficiency criteria:

$$\Phi = \begin{cases} |b| \, R^2 & \text{if } |b| \leq 1 \\ |b|^{-1} \, R^2 & \text{if } |b| > 1 \end{cases}$$

(1)

where the coefficient of determination $R^2$ represents the discharge dynamics, and $b$ is the slope of the regression line between the monthly observed and simulated runoff. Including $b$ guarantees that runoff under- or over-predictions are also reflected.

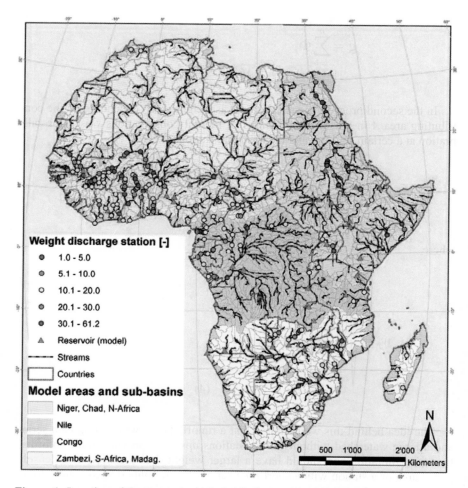

**Figure 1.** Location of the reservoirs included in the model and the four model areas used in the third calibration procedure. Also shown are the discharge stations and their associated weights in the calibration.

A major advantage of this efficiency criterion is that it ranges from 0 to 1, which compared to Nash-Sutcliff coefficient with a range of -∞ to 1, ensures that in a multisite calibration the objective function is not governed by a single or a few badly simulated stations.

In order to obtain some knowledge of the uncertainty associated with the selected calibration method, three independent calibrations were performed, each having a different objective function. In the first procedure the objective function was formulated as the *n*-station-sum of Φ:

$$g = \sum_{i=1}^{n} \Phi_i$$

(2)

In the second procedure, each station was weighted ($w$) depending on the contributing area $A$ in km$^2$ and the number of monthly observations $s$ used for calibration at a certain station $i$ and the upstream stations $j$:

$$g = \sum_{i=1}^{n} (w_i \cdot \Phi_i)$$

(3)

where

$$w_i = \sqrt{\frac{\left(A_i - \sum_{j=1}^{n} A_j\right) \cdot s_i}{s_i + \sum_{j=1}^{n} s_j}}$$

(4)

The idea behind this weighting is that a runoff station with a long data series and a large watershed without further stations upstream provides more information for calibration and should have a larger weight than a station in a densely gaged area or a station with a short time series. The weights ranged from 1 to 61 for the furthest downstream station on Congo River at Kinshasa (Fig. 1).

In the third calibration procedure the region was divided into four modeling zones and each zone was calibrated independently. The four model areas basically delineated the large river basins in the continent (Fig. 1) and included: Area 1, Niger, Chad, and North Africa with an area of 11.8 million km$^2$ and 106 stations; Area 2, Nile with an area of 6.1 million km$^2$ and 27 stations; Area 3, Congo with an area of 4.8 million km$^2$ and 38 stations; and Area 4, Zambezi, South Africa, and Madagascar with an area of 5.1 million km$^2$ and 36 stations. The zoning was based on the intra-continental variations in the climate as well as the dominant land covers and soil types.

The choice of the parameters initially included in the calibration procedures was based on the experience gained in modeling West Africa (Schuol et al., 2008) for which a detailed literature-based pre-selection as well as a sensitivity analysis

104

has been performed. Some of the selected SWAT parameters (e.g. curve number) are closely related to land cover, while some others (e.g. available water capacity, bulk density) are related to soil texture. For these parameters a separate value for each land cover/soil texture was selected, which increased the number of calibrated parameters substantially. The percentage of land cover and soil texture distribution within Africa and the four sub-regions is listed in Table 1. In the course of the iterative SUFI-2 calibration, not only the parameter ranges were narrowed, but also the number of parameters was decreased by excluding those that turned out to be insensitive.

**Table 1.** Soil texture and land cover distribution within the modeled African basin and the four subareas.

| | Abbrev. | Africa [%] | Area 1 [%] | Area 2 [%] | Area 3 [%] | Area 4 [%] |
|---|---|---|---|---|---|---|
| **Land cover** | | | | | | |
| Barren or sparsely vegetated | BSVG | 32.7 | 58.6 | 35.6 | - | 0.6 |
| Dryland cropland and pasture | CRDY | 4.3 | 0.3 | 3.9 | 5.9 | 12.5 |
| Cropland/grassland mosaic | CRGR | 1.3 | - | - | - | 7.3 |
| Cropland/woodland mosaic | CRWO | 2.4 | 1.8 | 2.6 | 5.1 | 0.7 |
| Deciduous broadleaf forest | FODB | 3.2 | - | - | 11.8 | 6.2 |
| Evergreen broadleaf forest | FOEB | 8.6 | 0.9 | - | 46.7 | 0.6 |
| Mixed forest | FOMI | 0.1 | - | - | 0.9 | - |
| Grassland | GRAS | 5.9 | 6.7 | 2.1 | 0.0 | 14.0 |
| Mixed grassland/shrubland | MIGS | 0.6 | 1.3 | - | - | - |
| Savannah | SAVA | 30.0 | 26.9 | 30.2 | 27.1 | 39.5 |
| Shrubland | SHRB | 9.4 | 3.4 | 22.3 | - | 16.5 |
| Water bodies | WATB | 1.5 | - | 3.0 | 2.4 | 2.1 |
| Herbaceous wetland | WEHB | 0.0 | - | 0.2 | - | - |
| **Soil** | | | | | | |
| Clay | C | 8.7 | 0.8 | 17.5 | 20.8 | 4.7 |
| Clay-loam | CL | 11.3 | 17.8 | 10.6 | 3.4 | 4.8 |
| Loam | L | 29.9 | 42.9 | 30.0 | 9.7 | 19.0 |
| Loamy-sand | LS | 5.0 | 4.3 | 0.0 | 14.4 | 3.4 |
| Sand | S | 2.6 | 3.7 | 4.7 | - | 0.0 |
| Sandy-clay-loam | SCL | 19.0 | 11.8 | 17.1 | 32.4 | 25.0 |
| Sandy-loam | SL | 23.5 | 18.6 | 19.7 | 19.2 | 43.2 |
| Silt-loam | IL | 0.1 | - | 0.4 | - | - |
| Silty-clay | IC | 0.0 | 0.0 | - | - | - |

**Table 2.** Final statistics for the three calibration procedures.

| | Φ | | P-factor | | R-factor | |
|---|---|---|---|---|---|---|
| | Cal. | Val. | Cal. | Val. | Cal. | Val. |
| **Procedure 1** | 0.44 | 0.47 | 55.4 | 55.6 | 1.56 | 1.48 |
| **Procedure 2** | 0.44 | 0.46 | 58.9 | 58.5 | 1.65 | 1.49 |
| **Procedure 3** | 0.48 | 0.48 | 60.8 | 59.3 | 1.52 | 1.43 |

**Table 3.** The SWAT model parameters included in the final calibration procedures and their initial and final ranges.

| Parameter name | Initial range | 1st proc. final range | 2nd proc. final range | 3rd proc. final range | | | |
|---|---|---|---|---|---|---|---|
| | | | | Area 1 | Area 2 | Area 3 | Area 4 |
| CN2_BSVG* | -0.50-0.15 | -0.45-(-0.05) | -0.40-0.00 | - | -0.40-(-0.10) | - | - |
| CN2_CRDY* | -0.50-0.15 | -0.25-0.05 | -0.05-0.10 | -0.45-(-0.10) | - | -0.20-0.15 | -0.10-0.10 |
| CN2_FODB* | -0.50-0.15 | -0.45-(-0.05) | -0.35-0.00 | - | - | -0.30-0.00 | -0.45-(-0.05) |
| CN2_FOEB* | -0.50-0.15 | -0.30-0.05 | -0.20-0.10 | -0.45-0.10 | - | -0.25-0.10 | - |
| CN2_GRAS* | -0.50-0.15 | -0.40-0.00 | -0.35-(-0.05) | -0.38-0.02 | - | - | -0.40-(-0.10) |
| CN2_SAVA* | -0.50-0.15 | -0.50-(-0.20) | -0.50-(-0.30) | -0.50-(-0.35) | -0.25-0.00 | -0.45-(-0.20) | -0.10-0.15 |
| CN2_SHRB* | -0.50-0.15 | -0.45-0.05 | -0.35-(-0.10) | - | -0.45-(-0.10) | - | -0.35-0.15 |
| CN2_CRWO* | -0.50-0.15 | - | - | 0.00-0.17 | -0.45-0.05 | -0.45-0.15 | - |
| CN2_MIGS* | -0.50-0.15 | - | - | -0.40-0.10 | - | - | - |
| CN2_FOMI* | -0.50-0.15 | - | - | - | - | -0.45-0.10 | - |
| CN2_CRGR* | -0.50-0.15 | - | - | - | - | - | -0.45-0.00 |
| S_AWC_C* | -0.50-0.50 | -0.40-0.00 | -0.50-(-0.05) | - | -0.25-0.40 | -0.48-0.00 | -0.20-0.50 |
| S_AWC_CL* | -0.50-0.50 | -0.40-0.10 | -0.20-0.15 | 0.00-0.45 | -0.45-0.20 | -0.25-0.30 | -0.45-0.00 |
| S_AWC_L* | -0.50-0.50 | -0.25-0.30 | 0.15-0.50 | -0.15-0.40 | -0.30-0.15 | -0.05-0.20 | -0.30-0.10 |
| S_AWC_LS* | -0.50-0.50 | -0.50-0.20 | -0.30-0.50 | - | -0.30-0.25 | - | -0.20-0.45 |
| S_AWC_SCL* | -0.50-0.50 | -0.35-0.05 | -0.20-0.30 | -0.10-0.25 | -0.50-(0.20) | -0.40-0.25 | -0.35-0.00 |
| S_AWC_SL* | -0.50-0.50 | -0.20-0.40 | -0.20-0.50 | -0.20-0.15 | -0.15-0.30 | -0.30-0.20 | 0.00-0.45 |
| S_AWC_S* | -0.50-0.50 | - | - | -0.20-0.45 | - | - | - |
| S_BD_C* | -0.50-0.50 | -0.40-0.20 | -0.25-0.15 | - | -0.04-0.23 | -0.35-0.10 | -0.10-0.40 |
| S_BD_CL* | -0.50-0.50 | -0.25-0.40 | -0.25-0.20 | -0.30-0.30 | -0.05-0.10 | -0.25-0.45 | -0.45-0.30 |
| S_BD_L* | -0.50-0.50 | -0.05-0.35 | -0.05-0.40 | -0.10-0.40 | -0.10-0.35 | -0.45-0.25 | -0.25-0.15 |
| S_BD_LS* | -0.50-0.50 | -0.40-0.25 | -0.45-(-0.05) | - | - | -0.32-0.10 | -0.40-0.35 |
| S_BD_SCL* | -0.50-0.50 | -0.15-0.40 | -0.20-0.30 | -0.35-0.25 | -0.45-0.20 | -0.45-0.00 | -0.35-0.25 |
| S_BD_SL* | -0.50-0.50 | -0.30-0.35 | -0.20-0.25 | -0.25-0.10 | -0.20-0.40 | -0.45-0.25 | -0.10-0.45 |
| S_BD_S* | -0.50-0.50 | - | - | -0.40-0.20 | - | - | - |
| ESCO | 0.00-1.00 | 0.10-0.60 | 0.35-0.70 | 0.25-0.55 | 0.10-0.50 | 0.20-0.65 | 0.10-0.60 |
| GW_DELAY | 0-100 | 1-30 | 20-40 | 25-42 | 0-30 | 30-60 | 10-80 |
| GW_REVAP | 0.02-0.20 | 0.03-0.17 | 0.08-0.16 | 0.05-0.13 | 0.02-0.13 | 0.02-0.09 | 0.03-0.17 |
| GWQMN | 0-1000 | 20-300 | 25-300 | 175-350 | 200-750 | 125-400 | 5-100 |
| RCHRG_DP | 0.00-1.00 | 0.35-0.65 | 0.35-0.60 | 0.40-0.55 | 0.25-0.65 | 0.25-0.50 | 0.10-0.55 |
| REVAPMN | 0-500 | 225-500 | 200-500 | 275-500 | 200-400 | 225-375 | 125-350 |
| SURLAG | 0.0-10.0 | 2.0-8.0 | 2.0-4.5 | - | - | - | - |

**CN2**: SCS runoff curve number; **S_AWC**: soil available water storage capacity; **S_BD**: moist soil bulk density; **ESCO**: soil evaporation compensation factor [-]; **GW_DELAY**: groundwater delay time (lag between the time that water exits the soil profile and enters the shallow aquifer) [days]; **GW_REVAP**: groundwater 'revap' coefficient (regulates the movement of water from the shallow aquifer to the root zone [-]; **GWQMN**: Threshold depth of water in the shallow aquifer required for return flow [mm H₂O]; **RCHRG_DP**: deep aquifer percolation fraction [-]; **REVAPMN**: threshold depth of water in the shallow aquifer for 'revap' or percolation to the deep aquifer [mm H₂O]; **SURLAG**: surface runoff lag coefficient [days]

**CN2, S_AWC** and **S_BD** have different parameter values depending on the land cover or the soil texture type. For the abbreviations please refer to Table 1. Asterisk means relative change of the parameter value

To account for the uncertainty in the measured discharge data, a relative error of 10% (Butts et al., 2004) and an absolute measured discharge uncertainty of 0.1 m³ s⁻¹ were included when calculating the *P-factor*. The absolute uncertainty was included in order to capture the dry periods of the many intermittent streams.

# 3. Results and Analysis

## 3.1 Model calibration

The three calibration procedures produced more or less similar results for the whole of Africa in terms of the values of the objective function F, the *P-factor*, and the *R-factor* (Table 2). The final parameter ranges in the three procedures, although different, were clustered around the same regions of the parameter space as shown in Table 3. This is typical of a non-uniqueness problem in the calibration of hydrologic models. In other words, if there is a single model that fits the measurements there will be many of them (Abbaspour, 2005; Abbaspour et al., 2007). Yang et al. (2008) used four different calibration procedures, namely GLUE, MCMC, ParaSol, and SUFI-2, for a watershed in China. All four produced very similar final results in terms of $R^2$, Nash-Sutcliffe (*NS*), *P-factor* and *R-factor* while converging to quite different final parameter ranges. In this study also, where only SUFI-2 was used with three different objective functions, all three methods resulted in different final parameter values.

In the following, we used the results of the third approach, because dividing Africa into four different hydrologic regions accounted for more of the spatial variability and resulted in a slightly better objective function value.

In order to provide an overview of the model performance in different regions, the *P-factor* (percent data bracketed) and the *R-factor* (a measure of the thickness of the 95PPU band) at all the stations across Africa are shown for both calibration and validation in Figure 2. In addition, the efficiency criteria, F, calculated based on the observed and the 'best' simulation (i.e. simulation with the largest value of the objective function), and also the *NS* coefficient are shown at each station. Overall, in calibration (validation), at 61% (55%) of the stations over 60% of the observed data were bracketed by the 95PPU and at 69% (70%) of the stations the R-factor was below 1.5. The F value was at 38% (37%) of the stations higher than 0.6 and the *NS* was at 23% (21%) of the stations higher than 0.7. In general, the model performance criteria were quite satisfactory for such a large-scale application. Some areas of poorly simulated runoffs were the Upper Volta, the East African Lakes region, and the Zambezi and Orange basin in the South of Africa. The reasons for this might be manifold and are not always clearly attributable. Of great importance are (1) over- or under-estimation in precipitation; (2) difficulties in simulating the outflow from lakes and wetlands; (3) insufficient data on the management of the reservoirs; (4) the effect of smaller lakes, reservoirs, wetlands, and irrigation projects that were not included; (5) simplifications by using dominant soil types and land cover classes in the subbasins; and (6) various water use abstractions, which were not included.

## 3.2 Quantification of blue and green water resources and their uncertainty ranges

Using the calibrated model, the annual and monthly blue water flow (water yield plus deep aquifer recharge), green water flow (actual evapotranspiration), and green water storage (soil water) were calculated for each subbasin and summed up for different countries or regions and also the whole continent. We compared our model results with other studies for blue water flow only, as to the best of our knowledge, the green water flow and storage were not explicitly quantified in the other models.

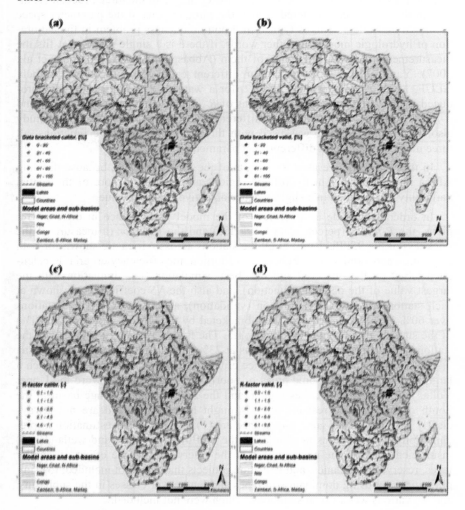

**Figure 2** (this page and next page). The *P-factor* (a,b), the *R-factor* (c,d), the weighted coefficient of determination $\Phi$ (e,f), and the Nash-Sutcliff coefficient (g,h) of the calibration (a,c,e,g) and validation (b,d,f,h) at all 207 stations.

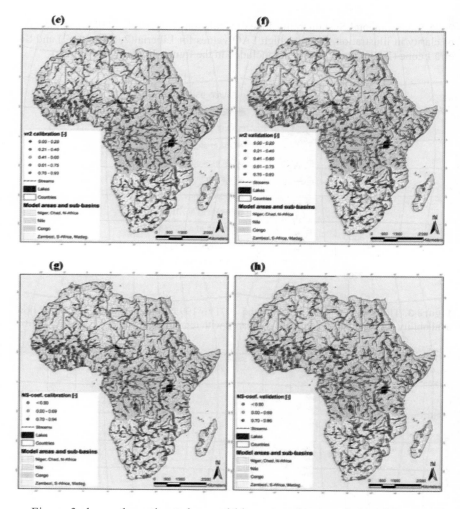

Figure 3 shows the estimated annual blue water for the whole African continent averaged over the period 1971-1995 and the results of ten other existing data-based (DB) or model-based (M) assessments. A direct one-to-one comparison of these values is not possible due to the different time periods and study-specific assumptions. The intent of this comparison is to give an overview of the differences in the existing numbers that are used in various advanced studies. The variation in different estimates indicates the uncertainty associated in such calculations, which is captured almost entirely in our prediction uncertainty as shown in Figure 3.

On the country basis, the simulated long-term annual (averaged over 1971-1995) blue water flow availability in mm a$^{-1}$ was compared with two other global assessments: the FAO estimates (FAO, 2003) and the annual (averaged over 1961-1995) simulation from WaterGAP 2.1e model (Fig. 4). The latter has been produced for the

109

2005 Environmental Sustainability Index calculation (Esty et al., 2005). For the sake of clarity in illustration, the very high FAO values for Liberia (2,077 mm a$^{-1}$) and Sierra Leone (2,206 mm a$^{-1}$) were not included in the figure (limited y axis range).

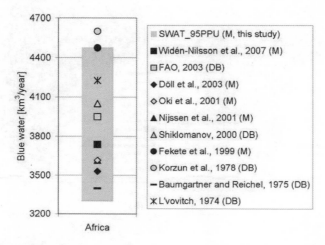

**Figure 3.** The SWAT 95PPU range of the 1971 to 1995 annual average blue water flow availability for the African continent compared with ten other existing assessments.

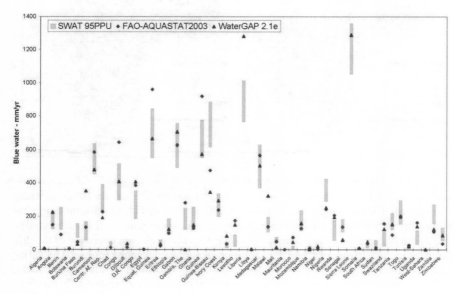

**Figure 4.** Comparison of the SWAT 95PPU ranges of the annual average (1971-1995) blue water flow availability in the African countries with the results from the FAO assessment and the WaterGAP model.

**Table 4.** The average precipitation (model input) and the 95PPU ranges for the components of freshwater availability in the African countries.

| Country | Area [10³ km²] | Precipitation [km³ year⁻¹] | Blue water flow [km³ year⁻¹] | Green water flow [km³ year⁻¹] | Green water storage [km³] |
|---|---|---|---|---|---|
| Algeria | 2321.0 | 198.6 | 2.1 - 8.8 | 181.5 - 200.1 | 9.8 - 13.8 |
| Angola | 1252.4 | 1232.3 | 150.0 - 287.3 | 893.8 - 1024.1 | 49.4 - 71.1 |
| Benin | 116.5 | 116.4 | 13.7 - 29.6 | 84.6 - 96.1 | 4.4 - 6.8 |
| Botswana | 580.0 | 226.9 | 2.4 - 11.1 | 201.5 - 234.2 | 6.9 - 13.5 |
| Burkina Faso | 273.7 | 201.3 | 19.0 - 42.5 | 153.1 - 173.1 | 6.6 - 10.0 |
| Burundi | 27.3 | 32.3 | 1.5 - 4.5 | 22.2 - 24.6 | 1.2 - 2.1 |
| Cameroon | 466.3 | 751.8 | 210.5 - 296.9 | 443.0 - 492.0 | 23.9 - 36.4 |
| Cent. Af. Rep. | 621.5 | 809.8 | 143.2 - 243.8 | 545.4 - 615.5 | 29.6 - 42.8 |
| Chad | 1168.0 | 397.3 | 26.9 - 57.6 | 325.8 - 363.2 | 16.7 - 24.0 |
| Congo | 345.4 | 554.6 | 102.1 - 178.5 | 361.0 - 411.1 | 19.3 - 30.0 |
| D.R. Congo | 2337.0 | 3526.9 | 424.8 - 825.2 | 2525.9 - 2841.9 | 160.7 - 255.9 |
| Djibouti | 21.6 | 6.1 | 0.1 - 0.8 | 4.8 - 6.3 | 0.1 - 0.2 |
| Egypt | 982.9 | 36.3 | 0.0 - 0.3 | 34.8 - 37.1 | 0.5 - 0.7 |
| Equat. Guinea | 27.1 | 52.9 | 14.9 - 22.9 | 29.4 - 33.4 | 1.5 - 2.8 |
| Eritrea | 121.9 | 38.1 | 2.3 - 7.1 | 29.1 - 33.9 | 0.6 - 1.3 |
| Ethiopia | 1132.3 | 877.5 | 99.1 - 211.9 | 627.7 - 707.2 | 19.9 - 38.4 |
| Gabon | 261.7 | 462.6 | 128.8 - 198.3 | 257.4 - 295.4 | 12.5 - 21.8 |
| Gambia, The | 10.7 | 8.2 | 1.3 - 2.7 | 5.4 – 6.3 | 0.2 - 0.4 |
| Ghana | 240.0 | 277.6 | 28.5 - 61.4 | 208.2 - 234.8 | 9.7 - 16.3 |
| Guinea | 246.1 | 398.6 | 135.7 - 190.9 | 210.6 - 234.3 | 12.8 - 18.9 |
| Guinea-Bissau | 33.6 | 50.4 | 20.7 - 29.8 | 22.0 - 25.0 | 1.4 - 2.0 |
| Ivory Coast | 322.2 | 418.5 | 63.6 - 108.5 | 301.1 - 332.7 | 16.1 - 24.2 |
| Kenya | 584.4 | 383.8 | 6.0 - 28.3 | 308.4 - 331.6 | 9.7 - 15.2 |
| Lesotho | 30.4 | 22.0 | 0.6 - 2.7 | 18.3 - 21.2 | 0.6 - 1.4 |
| Liberia | 96.3 | 213.7 | 73.4 - 97.7 | 115.9 - 125.1 | 6.3 - 9.0 |
| Libya | 1620.5 | 76.6 | 0.1 - 0.7 | 72.1 - 79.7 | 2.6 - 3.8 |
| Madagascar | 594.9 | 864.4 | 219.1 - 374.2 | 502.8 - 566.4 | 32.8 - 57.8 |
| Malawi | 119.0 | 130.9 | 12.2 - 23.5 | 51.2 - 58.0 | 1.5 - 2.6 |
| Mali | 1256.7 | 366.3 | 47.7 - 92.1 | 267.7 - 297.8 | 8.5 - 12.6 |
| Mauritania | 1041.6 | 89.9 | 2.3 - 7.2 | 78.7 - 87.4 | 1.0 - 1.7 |
| Morocco | 403.9 | 113.6 | 1.9 - 10.2 | 98.0 - 113.2 | 6.4 - 9.4 |
| Mozambique | 788.6 | 769.5 | 87.1 - 186.6 | 522.1 - 630.0 | 25.8 - 47.8 |
| Namibia | 825.6 | 237.6 | 3.0 - 19.0 | 204.5 - 243.4 | 6.3 - 13.2 |
| Niger | 1186.0 | 185.3 | 3.3 - 9.4 | 165.5 - 186.6 | 5.3 - 8.8 |
| Nigeria | 912.0 | 1004.0 | 263.1 - 387.6 | 605.2 - 677.2 | 35.2 - 49.6 |
| Rwanda | 25.2 | 30.1 | 1.3 - 4.5 | 25.0 - 27.3 | 1.4 - 2.5 |
| Senegal | 196.9 | 124.1 | 20.4 - 35.9 | 85.3 - 97.4 | 3.6 - 5.7 |
| Sierra Leone | 72.5 | 166.5 | 76.3 - 98.7 | 70.0 - 76.8 | 4.1 - 6.0 |
| Somalia | 639.1 | 190.6 | 1.2 - 7.8 | 174.5 - 190.8 | 4.6 - 7.3 |
| South Africa | 1223.1 | 578.8 | 11.3 - 37.4 | 521.7 - 568.9 | 16.6 - 29.7 |
| Sudan | 2490.4 | 1020.7 | 45.1 - 138.3 | 830.9 - 930.7 | 28.3 - 44.4 |
| Swaziland | 17.2 | 14.5 | 0.4 - 1.9 | 11.8 - 14.0 | 0.3 - 0.9 |
| Tanzania | 945.0 | 977.5 | 111.4 - 208.3 | 599.3 - 666.4 | 24.0 - 35.0 |
| Togo | 57.3 | 63.8 | 8.7 - 17.0 | 45.8 - 51.0 | 2.2 - 3.3 |
| Tunisia | 155.4 | 44.7 | 1.0 - 5.1 | 37.3 - 44.2 | 2.7 - 4.3 |
| Uganda | 243.0 | 283.6 | 7.7 - 28.0 | 206.9 - 228.1 | 6.7 - 14.1 |
| W. Sahara | 269.6 | 9.3 | 0.0 - 0.0 | 8.7 – 9.7 | 0.1 - 0.2 |
| Zambia | 754.8 | 727.5 | 115.6 - 204.9 | 479.5 - 559.8 | 25.1 - 38.8 |
| Zimbabwe | 390.8 | 256.0 | 20.7 - 51.7 | 193.9 - 234.5 | 8.4 - 16.0 |
| **Africa** | **30222** | **19865** | **3301 - 4476** | **14449 - 15348** | **785 – 996** |

Also not shown in the figure are the values for six African countries for which WaterGAP produced negative values (as it considers evaporation losses from lakes and wetlands even though they depend on inflow from other countries). In general, the large differences between FAO and WaterGAP estimates indicate the uncertainty in the country-based blue water estimates. Overall, a large number of these estimates fell within our prediction uncertainties. Although the calculated uncertainties may appear large, we maintain that the actual uncertainty may indeed be even larger because the coverage of the measured data in the 95PPU was in some areas relatively small (small *P-factor*). To decrease model uncertainty, a better description of the climate data, reservoir management, and water use would be essential.

In Table 4 the annual average water availability in each country is shown in $km^3 a^{-1}$. The subbasin-based precipitation and the 95PPU ranges for the blue water flow, green water flow, and the green water storage were aggregated to obtain country- and then continental-based values. The uncertainties (95PPU) in green water flow estimates were generally smaller than those of the blue water flow or green water storage because of its sensitivity to fewer parameters. It should be noted that the modeled green water storage was solely calibrated indirectly as there were no soil moisture observations. This study explored the possibility of using data from remote sensing satellites, but so far only found monitored surface soil moisture (top few centimeters) in areas without forest or sand dunes. The relationship between these values and that of the root zone soil moisture is still unclear (Wagner et al., 2003, 2007).

Next to the above annual continental and country-based estimates, this study also provides monthly time series of freshwater components for each subbasin with valuable information on both spatial and temporal distributions. Such information has not been available at this detail for the whole continent. In Figures 5a-5c the long-term average annual freshwater components are shown in each subbasin. These figures show the local (sub-country) differences especially in large countries with partly (semi-)arid climate. In areas like North Africa, the south of Chad (Chari basin), or the Limpopo basin in the southeast of Africa, with scarce blue water availability, there are considerable green water resources sustaining ecosystems, rainfed agriculture and ultimately people's lives.

Despite the spatial distribution, the intra- and inter-annual variability of the freshwater availability is of great importance. Figure 6 shows the coefficient of variation (CV) of the 1971-1995 annual values in each subbasin for the blue water flow, the green water flow and the green water storage. In general the CV, which is an indicator for the reliability of a freshwater source, varied noticeably within the continent and was the lowest for the green water flow, while it was the largest for the blue water flow. The reason for this is that the supply of water for evapotranspiration is limited by soil's capacity to deliver water to the roots. This capacity is within a narrow range between soil's field capacity and wilting point. The inter-annual variability of the blue water flow is especially large in the Sahel, at the Horn of Africa, and in the southern part of Africa, areas which are known for recurring severe droughts.

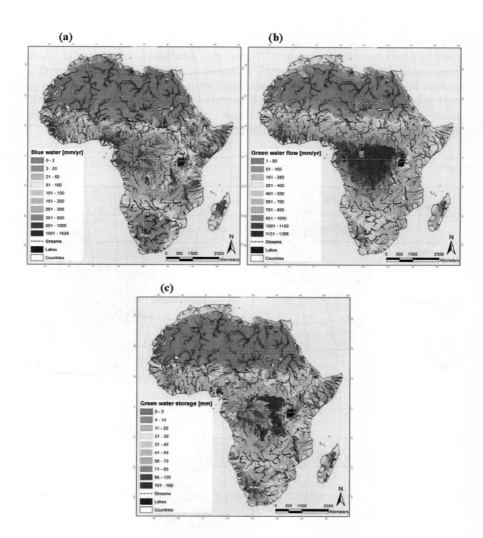

**Figure 5.** The 1971 to 1995 annual average (a) blue water flow, (b) green water flow, and (c) green water storage in all 1,496 modeled subbasins in Africa.

The intra-annual variability, presented by the 1971-1995 average monthly 95PPU bands of the blue water flow, the green water flow and the green water storage is shown in Figure 7 for three countries as an example. These countries, all with different climatic conditions, are Niger in Western Africa, Zimbabwe in the Southern Africa, and Gabon in Central Africa with an annual average precipitation of 185 mm, 256 mm, and 463 mm, respectively. In order to see the relation between the freshwater components and the water input, the figures also include the average monthly precipitation. All values are shown in mm or mm month[-1]

113

and thus can be directly compared. The trends in blue water flow in different countries become clearly apparent. Niger and Zimbabwe, in particular, show large uncertainties for the wet months. It should be noted that the reported uncertainties in the average monthly values combine both modeling uncertainties as well as natural variability. Hence the reliability of the water resources decreases as the uncertainties increase. The green water storage can potentially benefit the agriculture in months with little or without precipitation.

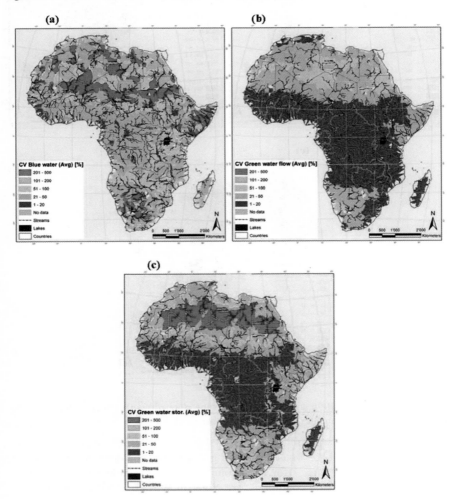

**Figure 6.** The coefficient of variation (CV) of the average of the 95PPU ranges (Avg) of the 1971 to 1995 modeled annual values of the (a) blue water flow, (b) green water flow, and (c) green water storage in each subbasin.

In Niger the soil water storage is depleted for about half of the year, while in Gabon this volume persists much longer within the (much shorter) dry period. This information is quite helpful in planning cropping season and helps to model scenarios of changing cropping seasons and patterns and its impacts on green and blue water flow and storage.

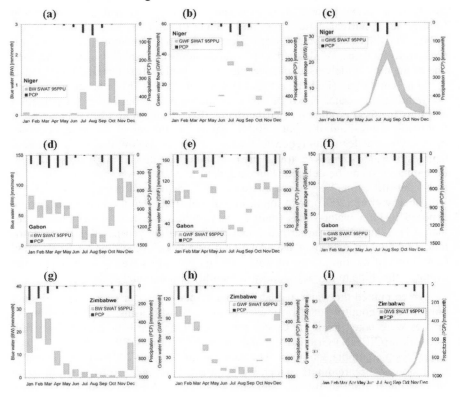

**Figure 7.** Average (1971-1995) monthly 95PPU ranges of the blue water flow (a,d,g), the green water flow (b,e,h), and the green water storage (c,f,i) in the countries Niger (a-c), Gabon (d-f), and Zimbabwe (g-i).

It should be pointed out that for large countries, variations can be substantial across subbasins. For example, in Niger the country-based annual average blue water flow availability is 3 to 8 mm a$^{-1}$ but some subbasins in the south of the country provide about 10 times more. While not shown in further detail, the model can provide monthly information of the freshwater components for each of the 1,496 subbasins in Africa and they will be published in a special report.

# 4. Implications of the Model Results

## 4.1 Blue water scarcity indicators considering uncertainty

The model results of the temporal and spatial variations of the freshwater avail-ability components and their uncertainty bands can be used in global and national water planning and management, in advanced studies concerning the water and food security, virtual water flow, and effects of land use and climate change (UNESCO, 2006). This study briefly presents the use of the model results for wa-ter scarcity analysis. While there exist a large number of water scarcity indicators, one of the most widely used and accepted is the water stress threshold, defined as $1,700 \text{ m}^3 \text{ capita}^{-1} \text{ a}^{-1}$ (Falkenmark and Widstrand, 1992). This scarcity index does not indicate that water is scarce for domestic purposes, but rather for irrigation and thus for food production (Rijsberman, 2006). Yang et al. (2003) have found that below a threshold of about $1,500 \text{ m}^3 \text{ capita}^{-1} \text{ a}^{-1}$ the cereal import in a country inversely correlates to its renewable water resources. Below this value different degrees of water stresses (extreme stress: $<500 \text{ m}^3 \text{ capita}^{-1} \text{ a}^{-1}$, high stress: $<1,000$ $\text{m}^3 \text{ capita}^{-1} \text{ a}^{-1}$) can be defined (Falkenmark et al., 1989). A value between 1,700 and $4,000 \text{ m}^3 \text{ capita}^{-1} \text{ a}^{-1}$ is considered as just adequate (Revenga et al., 2000). Vörösmarty et al. (2000) have found in a global study that the number of people exposed to high water stress (defined as withdrawal-to-availability-ratio larger than 0.4) is three times larger if the analysis is based on geospatial data at a reso-lution of 50 km instead of using national estimates. According to Rijsberman (2006) one of the limitations of water scarcity indicators are the annual, national averages that hide important scarcity at monthly and regional scales.

We computed the water availability per capita and water stress indicators not only for each country but also for each of the 1,496 subbasins. The population es-timates were taken from the Center for International Earth Science Information Network's (CIESIN) Gridded Population of the World (GPW, version 3, http://sedac.ciesin.columbia.edu/gpw). The data are for the year 2005 and has a spatial resolution of 2.5 arcminute, which we aggregated for each subbasin. In order to address uncertainty of future water stress estimates, Alcamo et al. (2007) com-puted and compared globally three different indicators of water stress (withdrawals-to availability ratio greater than 0.4, water availability per capita less than $1,000 \text{ m}^3 \text{ a}^{-1}$, and consumption to-Q90 ratio greater than 1). Although there was a large overlap in the estimated areas with severe water stress, in many regions the three indicators disagreed. Overall, using the water availability per capita indicator resulted in the lowest values of affected area and number of peo-ple with severe water stress. In this study we address uncertainty by calculating the per capita water availability by using the lower (L95PPU), the upper (U95PPU) and the average (Avg) 95PPU values of the blue water flow during the simulation time period.

Looking at the water scarcity on a country basis, the use of the L95PPU blue water flow values led to 29 countries with water stress ($<1,700 \text{ m}^3 \text{ capita}^{-1} \text{ a}^{-1}$), while the use of the U95PPU values led to merely 16 affected countries (Table 5).

Taking the average of the 95PPU range resulted in 20 vulnerable countries. In countries where both L95PPU and U95PPU result in the same conclusion, the risk situation is quite clear. However, in countries such as Burkina Faso, Ethiopia, Ghana, Sudan, and Zimbabwe where only the use of the L95PPU blue water flow values signalizes water scarcity, the situation demands more detailed studies. One can conclude that in many of these countries, and in fact in larger countries in general, it might be of great importance to analyze the water scarcity in a spatially distributed manner on a sub-country level rather than consider the country as a whole.

**Table 5.** The country-based per capita blue water flow (BW) availability considering the L95PPU and the U95PPU value of the annual average (1971-1995) BW and the population in the year 2005. Gray shaded cells indicate water stress ($< 1,700$ $m^3 cap^{-1} yr^{-1}$). The shading of the country name cells correspond to the estimated water stress based on the average 95PPU value of the blue water flow availability.

| Country | BW-L95PPU [$m^3$/cap/yr] | BW-U95PPU [$m^3$/cap/yr] | Country | BW-L95PPU [$m^3$/cap/yr] | BW-U95PPU [$m^3$/cap/yr] |
|---|---|---|---|---|---|
| Algeria | 63 | 268 | Libya | 23 | 113 |
| Angola | 9407 | 18022 | Madagascar | 11778 | 20114 |
| Benin | 1619 | 3508 | Malawi | 948 | 1823 |
| Botswana | 1336 | 6297 | Mali | 3529 | 6817 |
| Burkina Faso | 1440 | 3210 | Mauritania | 733 | 2359 |
| Burundi | 194 | 602 | Morocco | 60 | 323 |
| Cameroon | 12895 | 18189 | Mozambique | 4400 | 9429 |
| Cent. Af. Rep. | 35471 | 60388 | Namibia | 1497 | 9369 |
| Chad | 2763 | 5906 | Niger | 236 | 674 |
| Congo | 25528 | 44629 | Nigeria | 2001 | 2947 |
| D.R. Congo | 7381 | 14339 | Rwanda | 147 | 493 |
| Djibouti | 85 | 955 | Senegal | 1749 | 3076 |
| Egypt | 1 | 4 | Sierra Leone | 13815 | 17864 |
| Equat. Guinea | 29537 | 45367 | Somalia | 142 | 954 |
| Eritrea | 530 | 1614 | South Africa | 239 | 789 |
| Ethiopia | 1280 | 2737 | Sudan | 1245 | 3816 |
| Gabon | 93095 | 143289 | Swaziland | 345 | 1820 |
| Gambia, The | 833 | 1766 | Tanzania | 2907 | 5433 |
| Ghana | 1290 | 2776 | Togo | 1411 | 2770 |
| Guinea | 14438 | 20308 | Tunisia | 98 | 507 |
| Guinea-Bissau | 13052 | 18774 | Uganda | 266 | 972 |
| Ivory Coast | 3504 | 5976 | W. Sahara | 11 | 91 |
| Kenya | 176 | 825 | Zambia | 9912 | 17565 |
| Lesotho | 307 | 1507 | Zimbabwe | 1591 | 3974 |
| Liberia | 22363 | 29754 | **Africa** | **3613** | **4899** |

The computed blue water flow availability per capita in each of the 1,496 sub-basins considering the extremities of the 95PPU range is shown in Figure 8. In critical regions like the Sahel, the South and the East of Africa, the use of the L95PPU and the U95PPU, respectively, lead to quite different assessments of the water scarcity-affected regions and ultimately to the number of the affected people living there.

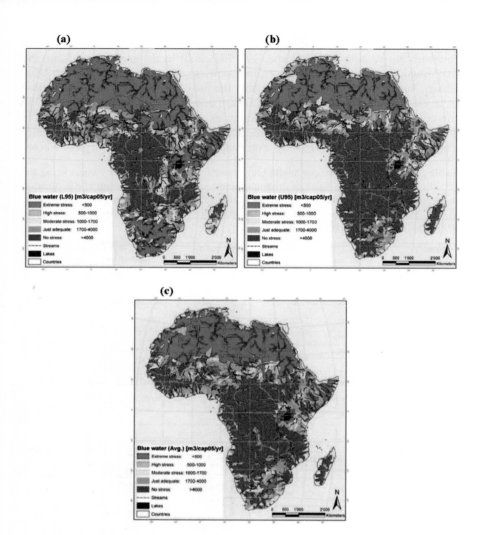

**Figure 8.** The water scarcity in each modeled African subbasin represented by the modeled 1971 to 1995 annual average blue water flow availability per capita (using population of 2005) using (a) the lower (L95), (b) the upper (U95), and (c) the average (Avg) value of the 95PPU range.

## 4.2 Model-based uncertainty and natural variation in green water storage

Irrigation, water transfer, and virtual water transfer on a regional, national, and international level are common measures to deal with regional blue water scarcity.

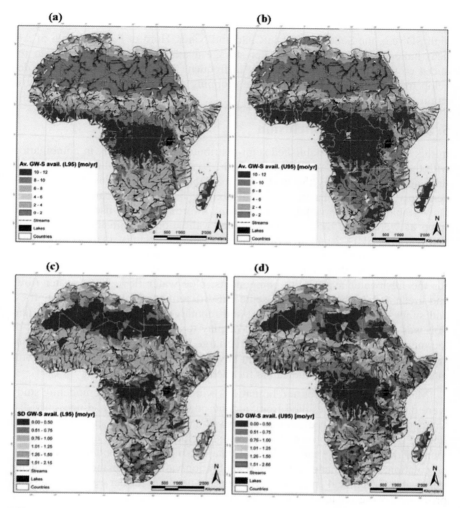

**Figure 9.** The 1971-1995 average (Avg) (a,b) and standard deviation (SD) (c,d) of the number of months per year where the green water storage (GW-S) is not depleted using the lower (L95) and the upper (U95) value of the 95PPU range.

A better use of the green water, through a more efficient rainfed production, can also partially overcome regional water short falls in countries like Nigeria or South Africa. For the rainfed agriculture, the average (1971-1995) number of months per year where soil water is available (defined as $>1$ mm m$^{-1}$) is of utmost importance. This is presented on a subbasin level in Figures 9a and 9b.

Because of the model-inherent uncertainties and natural variability, the border of the areas where rainfed agriculture can be realized can shift remarkably. The standard deviation (SD) of the months per year without depleted green water storage is shown for the 1971-1995 period in Figures 9c and 9d. The areas with a high SD (e.g. the Sahel regions in Chad and Niger, Horn of Africa, South of Africa) indicate unreliable green water storage availability that often leads to reduced crop yield and thus potentially to frequent famines. These areas must develop irrigation systems or alternative cropping practices for a sustainable agriculture.

## 5. Summary and Conclusion

In this study the well-established semi-distributed model SWAT, in combination with the GIS interface ArcSWAT and SUFI-2 calibration procedure, was successfully applied to quantify the freshwater availability for the whole African continent at a detailed subbasin level and monthly basis with uncertainty analysis. Only globally readily available data sets and information were used for the model setup as well as the model calibration and validation. Within the multisite and multivariable SUFI-2 parameter optimization and uncertainty analysis procedure, three different approaches were performed, which provided valuable insight into the effect of the calibration procedure on model results. The final model results for the freshwater availability components, blue water flow, green water flow, and green water storage were presented at different spatial (continent, countries, and subbasins) and temporal (annual and monthly) resolutions. Particular attention was paid to clearly quantify and display the 95% prediction uncertainty of the outputs, which turned out to be quite large in some cases. The effect of considering these uncertainty estimates in advanced studies was shown for the computation of water scarcity indicators for each of the 1,496 subbasins.

Many of the difficulties and limitations within this continental modeling study were data related and resulted from, among others, (1) limited and unevenly distributed rain gages and discharge stations with varying time series lengths, (2) limited globally available knowledge of the attributes and especially the management of the reservoirs, and (3) lack of data on soil moisture and/or deep aquifer percolation, which made a desirable calibration/validation of these components impossible. Technical modeling problems in need of further research and improvement were related to the inclusion of the lakes and their outflow to rivers. These resulted in poorer model results in the area of the great lakes of East Africa. This study did not include water use and especially irrigation in the model. Compared to other continents like Asia, this was thought to be of lesser importance in this study.

Some interesting further development would be to (1) make use of the model results in advanced studies on climate change, water and food security, as well as virtual water trade, which, as it has been pointed out by Yang and Zehnder (2007), are in great need of the estimates of spatially and temporally differentiated freshwater components; (2) further improve the African model as new data becomes available (e.g. remote sensing data); and (3) model the freshwater availability in the other continents, in order to finally obtain a global picture.

Overall, this study provided significant insights into continental freshwater availability on a subbasin level and with a monthly time step. This information was very useful for developing an overview of the actual water resources status and helped to spot regions where an in-depth analysis may be necessary. As shown, the inherent uncertainties need to be considered, before general conclusions are drawn.

## Acknowledgment

This work was supported by grants from the Swiss National Science Foundation (Project No: 200021-100076).

## References

**Abbaspour, K.C. 2005.** Calibration of hydrologic models: When is a model calibrated?, MODSIM 2005 International Congress on Modelling and Simulation Proceedings, 2449-2455.

**Abbaspour, K.C., J. Yang, I. Maximov, R. Siber, K. Bogner, J. Mieleitner, J. Zobrist, and R. Srinivasan. 2007a.** Modelling hydrology and water quality in the pre-alpine/alpine Thur watershed using SWAT, *J. Hydrol., 333*, 413-430.

**Abbaspour, K.C., J. Yang, M. Vejdani, and S. Haghighat. 2007b.** SWAT-CUP: calibration and uncertainty programs for SWAT, 4th International SWAT Conference Proceedings, in press.

**Alcamo, J., P. Döll, T. Henrichs, F. Kaspar, B. Lehner, T. Rosch, and S. Siebert (2003).** Development and testing of the WaterGAP 2 global model of water use and availability, *Hydrol. Sci. J.-J. Sci. Hydrol., 48*(3), 317-337.

**Alcamo, J., M. Flörke, and M. Märker. 2007.** Future long-term changes in global water resources driven by socio-economic and climatic changes, *Hydrol. Sci. J.-J. Sci. Hydrol., 52*(2), 247-275.

**Arnell, N.W. (1999).** Climate change and global water resources, *Glob. Environ. Change - Human Policy Dimens., 9*, S31-S49.

**Arnold, J.G., R. Srinivasan, R.S. Muttiah, and J.R. Williams. 1998.** Large area hydrologic modeling and assessment - Part 1: Model development, *J. Am. Water Resour. Assoc., 34*(1), 73-89.

**Arnold, J.G., R. Srinivasan, R.S. Muttiah, and P.M. Allen. 1999.** Continental scale simulation of the hydrologic balance, *J. Am. Water Resour. Assoc., 35*(5), 1037-1051.

**Baumgartner, A., and E. Reichel. 1975.** *The world water balance*, 182pp., Elsevier, Amsterdam.

**Beven, K, and A. Binley. 1992.** The future of distributed models - model calibration and uncertainty prediction, *Hydrol. Process., 6*(3), 279-298.

**Butts, M.B., J.T. Payne, M. Kristensen, and H. Madsen. 2004.** An evaluation of the impact of model structure on hydrological modelling uncertainty for streamflow simulation, *J. Hydrol., 298*(1-4), 242-266.

**Di Luzio, M., R. Srinivasan, and J.G. Arnold. 2001.** *ArcView Interface for SWAT2000 - User's Guide*, Blackland Research Center, Texas Agricultural Experiment Station and Grassland, Soil and Water Research Laboratory, USDA Agricultural Research Service, Temple, Texas.

**Döll, P., F. Kaspar, and B. Lehner. 2003.** A global hydrological model for deriving water availability indicators: Model tuning and validation, *J. Hydrol., 270*(1-2), 105-134.

Esty, D.C., M. Levy, T. Srebotnjak, and A. de Sherbinin. 2005. *2005 Environmental Sustainability Index: Benchmarking National Environmental Stewardship*, Yale Center for Environmental Law & Policy, New Haven.

Falkenmark, M. 1989. The massive water scarcity now threatening Africe - Why isn't it being addressed?, *AMBIO, 18*(2), 112-118.

Falkenmark, M., and J. Rockström. 2006. The new blue and green water paradigm: Breaking new ground for water resources planning and management, *J. Water Resour. Plan. Manage.-ASCE, 132*(3), 129-132.

Falkenmark, M., and C. Widstrand. 1992. Population and water resources: A delicate balance, *Popul. Bull., 47*(3), 1-36.

Falkenmark, M., J. Lundquist, and C. Widstrand. 1989. Macro-scale water scarcity requires micro-scale approaches: Aspects of vulnerability in semi-arid development, *Nat. Resour. Forum, 13*, 258-267.

FAO (Food and Agriculture Organization). 1995. The digital soil map of the world and derived soil properties, (CD-ROM), Version 3.5, Rome.

FAO (Food and Agriculture Organization). 2003. Review of the world water resources by country, *Water Report Nr. 23*, Rome.

Fekete, B.M., C.J. Vörösmarty, and W. Grabs. 1999. Global composite runoff fields of observed river discharge and simulated water balances, *Report No. 22*, Global Runoff Data Centre, Koblenz, Germany.

Gassman, P.W., M.R. Reyes, C.H. Green, and J.G. Arnold. 2007. The Soil and Water Assessment Tool: Historical development, applications, and future research directions, *Trans. ASABE, 50*(4), 1211-1250.

Gerten, D., S. Schaphoff, U. Haberlandt, W. Lucht, and S. Sitch. 2004. Terrestrial vegetation and water balance - hydrological evaluation of a dynamic global vegetation model, *J. Hydrol., 286*, 249-270.

Gerten, D., H. Hoff, A. Bondeau, W. Lucht, P. Smith, and S. Zaehle. 2005. Contemporary "green" water flows: Simulations with a dynamic global vegetation and water balance model, *Phys. Chem. Earth, 30*, 334-338.

Güntner A., J. Stuck, S. Werth, P. Döll, K. Verzano, and B. Merz. 2007. A global analysis of temporal and spatial variations in continental water storage, *Water Resour. Res., 43(5)*, W05416.

Islam, M.S., T. Oki, S. Kanae, N. Hanasaki, Y. Agata, and K. Yoshimura. 2007. A grid-based assessment of global water scarcity including virtual water trading, *Water Resour. Manage., 21*, 19-33.

Korzun, V.I., A.A. Sokolow, M.I. Budyko, K.P. Voskresensky, G.P. Kalinin, A.A. Konoplyanstev, E.S. Korotkevich, P.S. Kuzin, and M.I. L'vovich (Eds.). 1978. *World water balance and water resources of the earth*, UNESCO, Paris.

Krause, P., D.P. Boyle, and F. Bäse. 2005. Comparison of different efficiency criteria for hydrological model assessment, *Adv. Geosci., 5*, 89-97.

Lehner, B., and P. Döll. 2004. Development and validation of a global database of lakes, reservoirs and wetlands, *J. Hydrol., 296*(1-4), 1-22.

L'vovitch, M.I. 1974. *The water resources and their future* (in Russian), Mysl' P. H. Moscow; trans. ed. by R. Nace, American Geophysical Union, Washington, D.C., 1979.

Neitsch, S.L., J.G. Arnold, J.R. Kiniry, and J.R. Williams. 2005. *Soil and Water Assessment Tool - Theoretical Documentation - Version 2005*, Grassland, Soil and Water Research Laboratory, Agricultural Research Service and Blackland Research Center, Texas Agricultural Experiment Station, Temple, Texas.

Nijssen, B., G.M. O'Donnell, D.P. Lettenmaier, D. Lohmann, and E.F. Wood. 2001. Predicting the discharge of global rivers, *J. Clim., 14*(15), 3307-3323.

**Oki, T., and S. Kanae. 2006.** Global hydrological cycles and world water resources, *Science*, *313*, 1068-1072.

**Oki, T., Y. Agata, S. Kanae, T. Saruhashi, D.W. Yang, and K. Musiake. 2001.** Global assessment of current water resources using total runoff integrating pathways, *Hydrol. Sci. J.-J. Sci. Hydrol.*, *46*(6), 983-995.

**Revenga, C., J. Brunner, N. Henninger, K. Kassem, and R. Payne. 2000.** Pilot analysis of global ecosystems: Freshwater systems, World Resources Institute, Washington DC, USA.

**Rijsberman, F.R. 2006.** Water scarcity: Fact or fiction?, *Agricult. Water Manag.*, *80*, 5-22.

**Rockström, J., and L. Gordon. 2001.** Assessment of green water flows to sustain major biomes of the world: Implications for future ecohydrological landscape management, *Phys. Chem. Earth (B)*, *26*(11-12), 843-851.

**Rockström, J., M. Lannerstad, and M. Falkenmark. 2007.** Assessing the water challenge of a new green revolution in developing countries, *PNAS*, *104*(15), 6253-6260.

**Savenije, H.H.G. 2004.** The importance of interception and why we should delete the term evapotranspiration from our vocabulary, *Hydrol. Process.*, *18*, 1507-1511.

**Schuol, J., and K.C. Abbaspour. 2007.** Using monthly weather statistics to generate daily data in a SWAT model application to West Africa, *Ecol. Model.*, *201*, 301-311.

**Schuol, J., K.C. Abbaspour, R. Srinivasan, and H. Yang. 2007.** Estimation of freshwater availability in the West African sub-continent using the SWAT hydrologic model, *J. Hydrol.*, in press.

**Shiklomanov, I.A. (2000).** Appraisal and assessment of world water resources, *Water Int.*, *25*(1), 11-32.

**Shiklomanov, I.A., and J. Rodda (Eds.). 2003.** *World water resources at the beginning of the 21st century*, Cambridge Univ. Press, New York.

**Smakhtin, V., C. Revenga, and P. Döll. 2004.** Taking into account environmental water requirements in global-scale water resources assessments, *Comprehensive Assessment Research Report 2*, Colombo, Sri Lanka.

**Srinivasan, R., T.S. Ramanarayanan, J.G. Arnold, and S.T. Bednarz. 1998.** Large area hydrologic modeling and assessment - Part II: Model application, *J. Am. Water Resour. Assoc.*, *34*(1), 91-101.

**UNESCO. 2006.** Water a shared responsibility, *The United Nations World Water Development Report 2*, UNESCO-WWAP.

**UN-Water/Africa. 2006.** African water development report 2006, Economic Commission for Africa, Addis Ababa, Ethiopia.

**van Griensven, A., and T. Meixner. 2006.** Methods to quantify and identify the sources of uncertainty for river basin water quality models, *Water Sci. Technol.*, *53*(1), 51-59.

**Vörösmarty, C.J., C.A. Federer, and A.L. Schloss. 1998.** Evaporation functions compared on US watersheds: Possible implications for global-scale water balance and terrestrial ecosystem modeling, *J. Hydrol.*, *207*(3-4), 147-169.

**Vörösmarty, C.J., P. Green, J. Salisbury, and R.B. Lammers. 2000.** Global water resources: Vulnerability from climate change and population growth, *Science*, *289*, 284-288.

**Vörösmarty, C.J., E.M. Douglas, P.A. Green, and C. Revenga. 2005.** Geospatial indicators of emerging water stress: an application to Africa, *Ambio*, *34*(3), 230-236.

**Vrugt, J.A., H.V. Gupta, W. Bouten, and S. Sorooshian. 2003.** A Shuffled Complex Evolution Metropolis algorithm for optimization and uncertainty assessment of hydrologic model parameters, *Water Resour. Res.*, *39*(8), 1201.

**Wagner, W., K. Scipal, C. Pathe, D. Gerten, W. Lucht, and B. Rudolf. 2003.** Evaluation of the agreement between the first global remotely sensed soil moisture data with model and precipitation data, *J. Geophys. Res.*, *108*(D19), 4611.

**Wagner, W., G. Blöschl, P. Pampaloni, J.-C. Calvet, B. Bizzarri, J.-P. Wigneron, and Y. Kerr. 2007.** Operational readiness of microwave remote sensing of soil moisture for hydrologic applications, *Nord. Hydrol.*, *38*(1), 1-20.

**Wallace J.S., and P.J. Gregory. 2002.** Water resources and their use in food production systems, *Aquat. Sci.*, *64*, 363-375.

**Widén-Nilsson, E., S. Halldin, and C.-Y. Xu. 2007.** Global water-balance modelling with WASMOD-M: Parameter estimation and regionalisation, *J. Hydrol.*, *340*, 105-118.

**Winchell, M., R. Srinivasan, M. Di Luzio, and J.G. Arnold. 2007.** *ArcSWAT interface for SWAT2005 - User's Guide*, Blackland Research Center, Texas Agricultural Experiment Station and Grassland, Soil and Water Research Laboratory, USDA Agricultural Research Service, Temple, Texas.

**Yang, H., and A.J.B. Zehnder. 2007.** 'Virtual water' - an unfolding concept in integrated water resources management, *Water Resour. Res.*, *43*(12), W12301.

**Yang, H., P. Reichert, K.C. Abbaspour, and A.J.B. Zehnder. 2003.** A water resources threshold and its implications for food security, *Environ. Sci. Technol.*, *37*(14), 3048-3054.

**Yang, J., P. Reichert, K.C. Abbaspour, H. Yang, and J. Xia. 2007.** Comparing uncertainty analysis techniques for a SWAT application to the Chaohe basin in China, *J. Hydrol.*, submitted.

124

# 2.2 Environmental and Ecological Hydroinformatics to Support the European Water Framework Directive for River Basin Management

## Ann van Griensven[1], L. Breuer[2], M. Di Luzio[3], V. Vandenberghe[4], P. Goethals[5], T. Meixner[6], J. Arnold[7] and R. Srinivasan[8]

## Abstract

Research and development in hydroinformatics can play an important role in environmental assessment by integrating physically-based models, data-driven models and other Information and Communication Tools (ICT). An important illustration is given with the developments around the Soil and Water Assessment Tool (SWAT) to support the implementation of the EU Water Framework Directive. SWAT operates on the river basin scale, includes processes for the assessment of complex diffuse pollution and is open-source, which allows for site-specific modifications to the source and easy linkage to other hydroinformatics tools. A crucial step in the worldwide applicability of SWAT was the integration of the model into a GIS environment, allowing for a quick model setup using digital information on elevation, weather, land use and management and soil properties. Integration with model analysis tools assists in the tedious tasks of model calibration such as parameter optimization, sensitivity and uncertainty analysis and allows better understanding of the model to address scientific and societal questions. Finally, further linkage of SWAT to ecological assessment tools, land use prediction tools and tools for optimal experimental design shows that SWAT can play an important role in multi-disciplinary assessments.

**KEYWORDS:** Catchment modeling, eco-hydrology, environmental hydroinformatics, model integration, SWAT, water framework directive

---

© 2009 World Association of Soil and Water Conservation, *Soil and Water Assessment Tool (SWAT): Global Applications,* eds. Jeff Arnold, Raghavan Srinivasan, Susan Neitsch, Chris George, Karim Abbaspour, Philip Gassman, Fang Hua Hao, Ann van Griensven, Ashvin Gosain, Patrick Debels, Nam Won Kim, Hiroaki Somura, Victor Ella, Attachai Jintrawet, Manuel Reyes, and Samran Sombatpanit, pp. 125-144. This paper has been published by the Journal of Hydroinformatics, Vol. 8 (2006), No. 4, pp. 239-252 with permission from the copyright holders, International Water Association (IWA) Publishing. WASWC is grateful for the permission granted.

[1]UNESCO-IHE Water Education Institute, Department of Hydroifrormatics and Knowledge Management, P.O. Box 3015, 2601 DA DELFT, The Netherlands (Tel: ++31-15-2151812, Fax: ++31-15-2122921 A.vanGriensven@unesco-ihe.org) *and* Ghent University, BIOMATH: Department of Applied Mathematics, Biometrics and Process Control, Coupure Links 653, B-9000 Ghent, Belgium

[2]Justus-Liebig-University Giessen, Institute for Landscape Ecology and Resources Manament (ILR), Heinrich-Buff-Ring 26, 35392 Giessen, Germany (lutz.breuer@agrar.uni-giessen.de)

[3]Texas A&M University, Environmental Blackland Research and Extension Center, 720 E. Blackland Road,, Temple, TX7650 (diluzio@bcr.tamus.edu)

[4]Ghent University, BIOMATH: Department of Applied Mathematics, Biometrics and Process Control, Coupure Links 653, B-9000 Ghent, Belgium (Veronique.Vandenberghe@Ugent.be) *(Cont. next page)*

# 1. River Basin Modeling for the Water Framework Directive

A worldwide increase in consumption of water has led to problems such as water scarcity and water pollution. A decrease in quantity and quality threatens human health and also impacts the environment and aquatic ecology. This awareness has induced more stringent legislation such as the European Water Framework Directive (WFD) (EU, 2000). The WFD does not prescribe fixed measures or best practices, but promotes to elaborate a river basin specific planning where the different functions of water bodies, all sources of pollution and an active involvement of all stakeholders are integrated at the river basin scale with targets set to the desired ecological quality. The WFD imposes a planning process that consists of an identification of the system with an impact-effect analysis, the set-up of a program of measures and the implementation and evaluation of the latter, supported by monitoring programs for water physicochemistry and ecology. This process requires the integration, synthesis, analysis and communication of large amounts of information and knowledge on the geophysical, biological, social and economical aspects to aid in decision-making.

Although many environmental modeling methods exist, their practical application to support river management is rather limited (van Griensven and Vanrolleghem, 2006). In particular for river restoration management, there is a need for tools to guide the investments needed to meet the ecological status targeted by the European Water Framework Directive.

Recently, several practical concepts and software systems have been developed related to environmental decision support, e.g. Rizolli and Young (1997), Paggio et al. (1999), Reed et al. (1999), Young et al. (2000), Booty et al. (2001), Lam and Swayne (2001), Argent (2004), Lam et al. (2004) and Voinov et al. (2004). From a technical point of view, one can opt to build a new model for each application or to utilize existing models where possible. The first approach has the benefit of control in the models design and linkage, but requires a long model development period. The second approach saves on development time, but requires additional work to link existing models (Lam et al., 2004).

However, when suitable models are already available, it is probably the better option. The use of the linked models can also be a good start to learning what processes are of major importance for the different simulations and which can be neglected. Since watersheds form the physical borders for river basin management, catchment modeling is the most appropriate frame for integrated modeling.

[5]Ghent University, Department Applied Ecology and Environmental Biology, J. Plateaustraat 22, B-9000 Gent, Belgium (Email: Peter.Goethals@UGent.be)

[6]University of Arizona, College of Engineering, Department of Hydrology and Water Resources, 845 North Park Avenue, Tucson, AZ 85721-0158 U.S.A. (meixner@hwr.arizona.edu)

[7]Arnold,USDA-ARS, Grassland Soil and Water Research Laboratory ,808 East Blackland Road, Temple, TX76502, U.S.A. .(jgarnold@spa.ars.usda.gov)

[8]Texas A&M University, Spatial Sciences Laboratory, 1500 Research Parkway, Suite B223, College Station, TX 77845, U.S.A. (r-srinivasan@tamus.edu)

Even though there exist several catchment tools and models in today's scientific community, their application has focused on scientific and not societal questions. There is a need to simplify some of these tool sets, for example by the development of decision support systems. In addition, it is of crucial importance to improve the dissemination of these tools to decision-makers and stakeholders by education and training.

About 50 peer-reviewed papers discussed the application of SWAT on pollution loss studies for a wide range of small and large river basins (Gassman et al., 2005). Several of these studies refer to the application of SWAT with regard to the U.S. water quality legislation such as for Total Maximum Daily Load (TMDL) analysis or Best Management Practices (BMP). With the European Water Framework Directive in mind, SWAT was applied in the framework of several EU research projects on catchment modeling (Fig. 1), such as in CHESS (2001) to investigate the effect of climate change on water quality in European rivers, in TempQSim (2004) for the analysis of Mediterranean and semi-arid catchments with intermittent flow regimes, in EuroHarp (2004) for nutrient modeling studies and in BMW (2004) for the use in integrated modeling assessment. In the latter project, SWAT was successfully evaluated against the qualitative diffuse pollution benchmark criteria for the application of models for the Water Framework Directive, where it received 'good' classification for 70% of the questions asked and at no point during the assessment was it 'not recommended' for use (Dilks et al., 2003). SWAT has been applied in Europe for sediment, nitrogen or phosphorus predictions, among many others, in several watersheds in Finland (Frances et al., 2001; Grizetti et al., 2003), several watersheds in Belgium (van Griensven and Bauwens, 2005), in the U.K. (Dilks et al., 2003), for large-scale applications in Europe (Bouraoui et al., 2005) and on low mountain range catchments in central Germany within the framework of the Joint Research Project SFB299 (Fohrer et al., 2002, 2005).

This paper describes initiatives with the Soil and Water Assessment Tool (SWAT) (Arnold et al., 1998) that were done over the last decade. SWAT appears to be a proper instrument for the assessment and prediction of point and diffuse pollution in river basins (Jayakrishnan et al., 2005). Since it has an open-sources policy, SWAT has a high level of flexibility for application by allowing the users to do case-specific adaptation to the source code and for linking it to other models and modeling tools.

## 2. SWAT

SWAT is a conceptual model that operates on a daily time step. The objectives in model development were to predict the impact of management on water, sediment and agricultural chemical yields in large basins. To satisfy these objectives, the model (a) uses readily available inputs for large areas; (b) is computationally efficient to operate on large basins in a reasonable time, and (c) is continuous temporally and capable of simulating long periods for computing the effects of management changes.

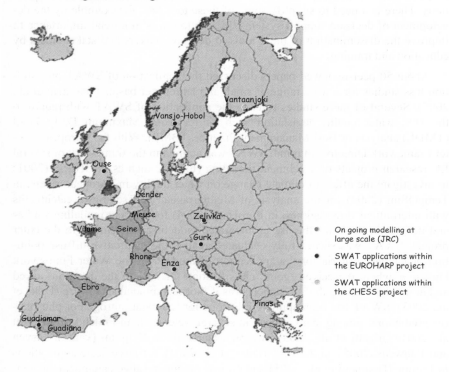

**Figure 1.** Applications of SWAT model in EU funded projects.

A command structure is used for routing runoff and chemicals through a watershed similar to the structure for routing flows through streams and reservoirs, adding flows, and inputting measured data on point sources (Fig. 2). Using the routing command language, the model can simulate a basin sub-divided into grid cells or sub-watersheds. Additional commands have been developed to allow measured and point source data to be input to the model and routed with simulated flows.

Model subbasin components can be divided as follows: hydrology, weather, sedimentation, soil temperature, crop growth, nutrients, pesticides and agricultural management. Hydrological processes simulated include surface runoff estimated using the SCS curve number or Green and Ampt infiltration equation; percolation modeled with a layered storage routing technique combined with a crack flow model; lateral subsurface flow; groundwater flow to streams from shallow aquifers, potential evapotranspiration by the Hargreaves, Priestley-Taylor or Pen-

128

man-Monteith methods; snowmelt; transmission losses from streams; and water storage and losses from ponds (Arnold et al., 1998; Arnold and Fohrer, 2005).

Channel routing is simulated using either the variable-storage method or the Muskingum method; both methods are variations of the kinematic wave model (Chow et al., 1988). The channel sediment routing equation uses a modification of Bagnold's sediment transport equation (Bagnold, 1977) that estimates the transport concentration capacity as a function of velocity. The model either deposits excess sediment or re-entrains sediment through channel erosion depending on the sediment load entering the channel.

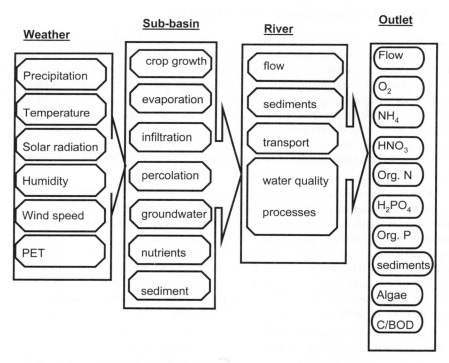

**Figure 2.** Overview of the modules in SWAT.

SWAT simulates the complete nutrient cycle for nitrogen and phosphorus. The nitrogen cycle is simulated using five different pools; two are inorganic forms (ammonium and nitrate) while the other three are organic forms: fresh, stable, and active. Similarly, SWAT monitors six different pools of phosphorus in soil; three are inorganic forms and the rest are organic forms. Mineralization, decomposition, and immobilization are important parts in both cycles. These processes are allowed to occur only if the temperature of the soil layer is above 0°C. Nitrate export with runoff, lateral flow, and percolation are estimated as products of the volume of water and the average concentration of nitrate in the soil layer.

Organic N and organic P transport with sediment is calculated with a loading function developed by McElroy et al. (1976) and modified by Williams and Hann (1978) for application to individual runoff events. The loading function estimates daily organic N and P runoff loss based on the concentrations of constituents in the top soil layer, the sediment yield, and an enrichment ratio. The amount of soluble P removed in runoff is predicted using labile P concentration in the top 10 mm of the soil, the runoff volume and a phosphorus soil partitioning coefficient. In-stream nutrient dynamics are simulated in SWAT using the kinetic routines from the QUAL2E in-stream water quality model (Brown and Barnwell, 1987).

## 3. AVSWAT: Integration of SWAT in GIS

An extension of ArcView[Ó] 3.x Geographical Information System (GIS) software was developed to support the SWAT model (Di Luzio et al., 2004a). This GIS software, named AVSWAT, provides a complete set of user-friendly and interactive input/output tools designed to help the user in performing numerous tasks, such as: delineating, segmenting and dimensioning the watershed from a digital description of the landscape (DEM, Digital Elevation Model), importing, formatting and processing the supporting data (i.e. land use and soil maps, weather station time series), formulating management scenarios and performing basic calibrations, analyzing and displaying output data from the SWAT model simulations (Fig. 3).

AVSWAT was developed using AVENUE, the ArcView 3.x's object oriented programming language. ArcView Spatial Analyst extension was used to apply fundamental spatial analysis procedures for raster data, whereas ArcView alone provides spatial analysis capabilities using vector data. ArcView's Dialog Designer extension was used to embed plug-in controls, such as menus, buttons/tools, and ultimately build several dialog interfaces to help users accomplish a number of interactive tasks. Due to the implementation of standard format data sets, the applications of AVSWAT are not limited to a particular geographic location, thereby allowing applications around the world.

The current development of the GIS software, now named AVSWATX, provides users with an additional level of customized software tools (i.e. extension of an extension) that are designed to accomplish specific tasks. One such example (Di Luzio et al., 2004b) was developed to acquire, process and utilize Soil Survey Geographic (SSURGO) (USDA, 1995) data sets, a more detailed alternative to State Soil Geographic (STATSGO) (USDA, 1994) in the U.S. While a number of additional extensions are being developed, recent fundamental additions include: (a) a 'splitting' tool that allows to disaggregate land use maps at the sub-pixel level to overcome the limitations of the readily available data sets, (b) a set of user-friendly dialogs, which expedite the input-output management required by embedded procedures for the sensitivity analysis, automatic calibration and uncertainty analysis of the model, and which are described in the next section.

## 4. Integration with Tools for Optimization and Model Analysis

Due to their complexity, water quality models require specific methods so that their structure and predictive accuracy and precision can be assessed (Fig. 4). Any computational assessment of water quality models must take into account three salient features of water quality models: the immense number of parameters, the general lack of data available for model calibration and assessment and the fact that we know our models are far from perfect and have structural problems in simulating complex natural processes. All three of these problems intersect with the further problem that water quality models are computationally intensive. For that reason, automated methods for model analysis and parameter calibration were designed for the SWAT model (e.g. van Griensven and Bauwens, 2003b; Eckhardt et al., 2003; Huisman et al., 2005). Recently, several other tools were developed directly within the SWAT model to enable execution of answers to aforementioned three problems. First a simple yet robust sensitivity analysis tool "Latin Hypercube - One Factor at a Time" (LH-OAT) (van Griensven et al., 2006) was developed for reducing the high number of model parameters by defining the most sensitive ones. The method was designed to handle a large number of parameters and parameter non-linearities. LH-OAT combines the robustness of Latin Hypercube sampling that ensures that the full range of all parameters is being sampled in a computationally efficient manner. The One Factor at a Time design assures that the changes in the model output can be unambiguously attributed to the parameter that was changed.

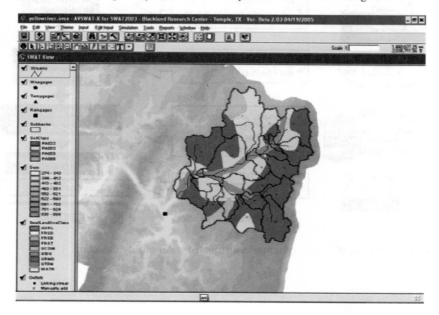

**Figure 3.** SWAT view in the AVSWAT-X interface.

Second, a parameter calibration and parameter uncertainty assessment algorithm was developed that has special equations to deal with multi-objective problems in an efficient way. The algorithm 'ParaSol' (Parameter Solutions) (van Griensven and Meixner, 2006) was developed to perform optimization and model parameter for complex models with multiple output variables such as SWAT. The ParaSol method calculates objective functions based on model outputs and observation time series. It aggregates these objective functions to a global optimization criterion. The objective function, OF, or the global optimization criterion, GOC, are minimized using the SCE-UA (citation) algorithm. Finally, ParaSol performs a statistical analysis to calculate the parameter uncertainty and corresponding uncertainy on the model results. In addition, a tool was developed to do some additional model verification using Split-Sample strategy in order to account for remaining uncertainties present in a water quality model using the model bias as a simple assessment tool (SUNGLASSES).

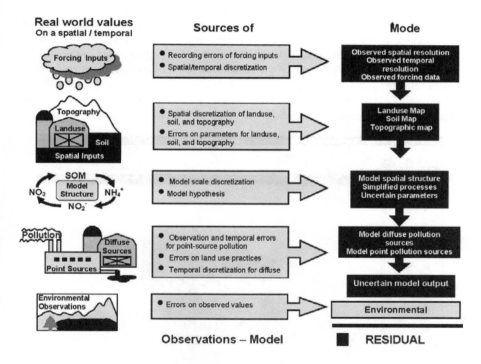

**Figure 4.** Scheme of sources of errors in distributed water quality modeling.

# 5. Multi-disciplinary Integration

## 5.1 Linkage to ecological modeling

Model integration with ecological tools is facilitated by the use of simplified and inter-tuned models. So far, mainly data driven methods (e.g. artificial neural networks and classification trees) are preferred in this context, given their time efficient development (Goethals, 2005). However knowledge based methods (e.g. fuzzy logic, Bayesian belief networks) can be of considerable importance, in particular when enough data of good quality are missing to develop data driven models (Adriaenssens et al., 2004).

A practical example of coupling SWAT results to ecological modeling is presented by Vandenberghe et al. (2005). This research was performed on the River Dender in Flanders. The River Dender is highly affected by nutrient inflow from agricultural and wastewater discharges from industries and households. Additionally, habitat modifications were established to ease flood control and guarantee boat traffic. These modifications have had a severe impact on the habitat characteristics and induced a completely different fish community compared to natural conditions. To gain a better understanding of these combined effects, water quality models of Dender River were developed in ESWAT, a SWAT2000 version that was extended with hourly hydrological and water quality processes (van Griensven and Bauwens, 2001). Pollution is estimated for the upstream boundary using daily water quality data for dissolved oxygen (DO), biological oxygen demand (BOD), nitrate ($NO_3^-$), and ammonia ($NH_4^+$). Point pollution inputs comprise wastewater treatment plants outlets, industries and untreated household effluents. Land management and agricultural processes are taken into account to calculate diffuse pollution to the river.

The outputs of the model were used for an ecological data driven models to predict presence or absence of fish species. These latter models allow predicting communities on the basis of the outcomes of the water quality model simulations and habitat data. For this purpose, classification trees were constructed on the basis of the Weka software (Witten and Frank, 2000) using an algorithm to grow a classification tree. A dataset was constructed on the basis of electrofishing data, collected in rivers of Flanders. In total, 168 measurements were used, of which in 50% of the cases pike was present. A training set of 112 instances was used for classification tree development, while 56 instances served for validation of the model. In both subsets 50% of the instances were characterized by the presence of pike. In addition to the presence/absence of pike, eight variables (river characteristics) were available that served for the prediction of pike: width, slope, depth, electrical conductivity, dissolved oxygen, pH, and water temperature.

The reliability of the model was proven by the prediction assessment in the validation dataset. About 71% of the instances was correctly predicted (CCI of 71 and Cohen's Kappa of 0.43). The tree consisted of the following rule set as shown in Figure 5.

The results of the coupled models showed that long periods in DO concentration were below critical value of pike. Pike is thus endangered based on the water quality mainly related to algae blooms, as a result of nutrient inflow. On top of this also the habitat quality is very poor in the stem river, while the tributaries are characterized by a very bad water quality. The remaining pike population is based on fish stockings, but when water quality is not improved, these activities seem to be useless. As such, the coupled models are very useful instruments to find the causes of ecosystem deterioration and also to test the potential effect of different restoration options.

WIDTH <= 2.54

    SLOPE <=0.8 : PIKE PRESENT

    SLOPE >0.8 : PIKE ABSENT

WIDTH > 2.54

    SLOPE <=0.3 : PIKE PRESENT

    SLOPE >0.3

        EC <= 419 : PIKE PRESENT

        EC > 419

            EC <= 607 : PIKE ABSENT

            EC > 607

                DO <= 7.1 : PIKE ABSENT

                DO > 7.1

                    DEPTH <= 0.5

                        SLOPE <= 2.1: PIKE PRESENT

                        SLOPE > 2.1: PIKE ABSENT

                    DEPTH > 0.5 PIKE PRESENT

Figure 5. Classification tree model for pike in Dender River.

## 5.2 Integrated modeling of landscape services

Landscapes provide a wide range of services, comprising employment, economic income, habitat, water supply, or food production amongst many others (Costanza et al., 1997). Within the framework of the collaborative research centre SFB 299 (http://www.sfb299.de), the Integrated Tool for Ecological and Economical Modeling (ITE$^2$M) has been developed to investigate landscape services for the peripheral Dill catchment (692 km$^2$) in central Germany. ITE$^2$M comprises of several models addressing agro-economy (ProLand), agricultural policy (CHOICE) and environmental services with respect to the risk of heavy metals in soil (ATOMIS), water quantity and quality (SWAT), as well as faunal and floristic diversity (ANIMO, ProF) (Fig. 6).

134

### 5.2.1 The Agro-economic model ProLand

ProLand (Prognosis of Land use) assumes that land use patterns are a function of climate, soil type, biological, economic and social conditions (Weinmann et al., 2005). Spatial distribution of these data form the basis for the allocation of land use systems, assuming land rent maximizing behavior of the land user for any parcel of land. Land rent is defined as the sum of monetary yields including all subsidies minus input costs, depreciation, taxes and opportunity costs for employed capital and labor. As a result, two different types of model outputs are derived: (i) maps of the potential spatial land use distribution and (ii) sets of aggregated key indicators to characterize the economic performance of land use.

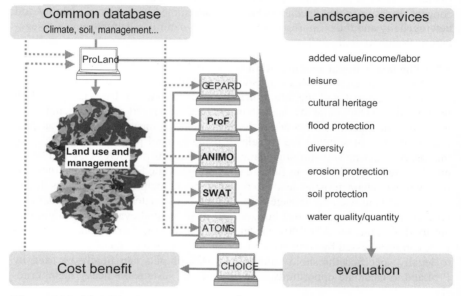

**Figure 6.** Model and database structure of ITE$^2$M.

### 5.2.2 The eco-hydrologic model SWAT-N

A modified version of SWAT is applied to predict hydrological and nitrogen fluxes on the landscape scale (SWAT-N, Pohlert et al., 2006). The hydrological components differ in the way of representing interflow by (i) simulating soil anisotropy and (ii) parameterizing the deepest soil horizon to account for the fissured rock aquifer characteristic in the Dill catchment. To improve the simulations of N turnover and export in the Dill catchment, SWAT was coupled to the mineralization and nitrification modules of the biogeochemistry model DNDC and to the denitrification module of CropSyst.

### 5.2.3 The biodiversity models ANIMO and ProF

The spatially explicit landscape model ANIMO (Steiner and Köhler, 2003), a cel-

135

lular automaton, quantifies the effect of land use change on regional diversity. The model assumes that each habitat (land use) has its own species inventory depending on environmental, regional and historical constraints. An intrinsic species pool is determined with its portions of habitat generalists and specialists. Single cells interact with neighboring cells in the way that habitat generalists disperse into surrounding cells, whereas habitat specialists remain static. The number of species in a cell (a-diversity) is affected by the species inventory surrounding the cell (habitat dissimilarity, b-diversity). The overall g-diversity of a landscape is the product of a- and b-diversity.

To assess floristic diversity the habitat model ProF (Prognosis of Floristic richness) is applied. ProF is a probabilistic GIS tool that is based on the mosaic concept. It assumes that species richness is determined by habitat variability and heterogeneity and the proportion of natural, semi-natural and anthropogenic vegetation (Waldhart et al., 2004).

### 5.2.4 The heavy metal accumulation soil model ATOMIS

The Assessment Tool for Metals in Soils (ATOMIS, Reiher et al., 2004) provides site-specific estimates of the fate of heavy metals such as Ni, Cu, Zn, Cd, and Pb in top soils. Metal input by land management is derived from ProLand data, whereas atmospheric input is taken from precipitation measurements. Metal concentrations in soil solution are calculated using general purpose Freundlich isotherms, considering soil sorption characteristics such as pH, SOC, clay and heavy metal content. ATOMIS identifies areas where geologic background in combination with site characteristics leads to potential enrichment of heavy metals due to agricultural land use and management. SWAT-N estimates on mean annual percolation rates from the top soil horizon and mean annual evapotranspiration rate are used as input for ATOMIS. Sustainability of land use and management options can be assessed by comparing the predicted future total metal concentrations to legally specified threshold values. ATOMIS outputs can finally be used by ProLand to calculate opportunity costs in terms of sustainable heavy metal criteria.

### 5.2.5 Trade-off and win-win situations

Integrating the results obtained by ITE$^2$M can assist in the definition of sustainable land use concepts. Based on the same spatial land use and management information provided by ProLand the remaining members of ITE$^2$M predict combinations of ecological landscape services such as faunal and floristic diversity, N export from rivers, groundwater recharge, or metal accumulation in soils. In combination with the economic services simulated by ProLand, trade-offs and win-win situation on land use and management can be predicted, as is shown in Figure 7 for the Aar catchment, a 60 km$^2$ subcatchment of the Dill catchment. The basis of this evaluation is an extensification of pasture management, the so-called suckler cow land management scenario. In this scenario, cows and their offspring are kept on the meadows all year round to save infrastructural farmstead costs and labor. In the present case study, the increase in economic value is accompanied by a slight increase in floristic diversity simulated by ANIMO and an almost constant groundwater recharge as predicted by SWAT (Fig. 7). The relative optima of economic and ecological services can be depicted at an added value of €3.02 Millions. This value is equivalent to a reduction in land cover of dairy pasture by -2.5% and cropland by -5.5% as well as an increase of 8% in extensive suckler cow management of the total land area as predicted by ProLand. In addition to this, ProLand not only calculates the overall changes in land management, but also provides spatially explicit information where these changes are best to realize.

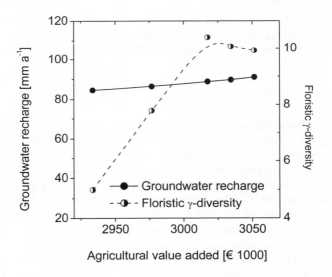

**Figure 7.** Ecological-economic trade-offs for optimized suckler cow management as predicted by the agro-economic model ProLand, the biodiversity model ANIMO and SWAT (Breuer et al. 2004). Suckler cow management presents an extensive pasture management system where cows and their offspring are kept outside all year around to save labour and infrastructural farmstead costs. Floristic γ-diversity defines overall landscape diversity. See text for additional comments on the models and the technique of trade-offs estimation.

Further case studies of the overall model framework are presented in Fohrer et al. (2005) and Weber et al. (2001). ITE$^2$M is generally an open concept that links models from several disciplines. Hence, the current estimates of landscape services are limited by the selection of ITE$^2$M model members.

## 5.3 Optimal Experimental Design

Optimal sampling design techniques aim at the identification of sampling schemes to improve different aspects of the mathematical modeling process, according to explicitly stated objectives (Dochain and Vanrolleghem, 2001; De

Pauw and Vanrolleghem, 2004).

Vandenberghe et al. (2002) developed a methodology for an Optimal Experimental Design (OED) for the water quality variables in a river with the purpose to increase the precision of the parameters for the water quality module using SWAT. Different experiments (sampling schemes) will reveal more or less information and more or less parameter reliability, e.g. schemes that lack dynamics will provide less information than schemes with more dynamics. The method used is the D-optimal experimental design (Goodwin and Payne, 1977; Walter and Pronzato, 1999), which is the most general method for minimizing the error on all estimated parameters.

In a D-optimal experimental design, the precision of the parameters is assessed by considering the determinant of the inverse of the covariance matrix of the parameter estimates ($C$) or Fisher Information Matrix (FIM) (Godfrey and Distefano, 1985).

$$C(b) = \sigma^2 \left( S^T S \right)^{-1} \qquad FIM(b) = C^{-1}(b)$$

with $b$ representing the model parameter vector, $Q$ a diagonal matrix, the elements being the squares of the observation weights and $S$ the sensitivity matrix of the outputs to the parameters in comparison to the observations. Calculation of the covariance matrix based on the Jacobian matrix instead of the Hessian is acceptable when assuming linearity and having constant standard deviations on the observations (Bard, 1974). The determinant of the FIM, Det(FIM) is inverse proportional to the volume of the confidence region. Thus, by maximizing Det(FIM), the volume of the confidence ellipsoids, and, correspondingly, the geometric average of the parameter errors is minimized. D-optimal experiments also have the advantage of being invariant with respect to any scaling of the parameters (Petersen, 2000). An extra aspect to be considered here is that for non-linear models the FIM is parameter dependent. The OED technique thus requires an initial data set to calibrate the model. Non-accurate parameter estimates may therefore lead to an inefficient experimental layout. This means that for the processes related to the non-accurate parameters better measurements could be identified. The design can only be approached by an iterative process of data collection and design refinement, known as a 'sequential design' (Casman et al., 1988). Figure 8 shows the iterative scheme that is used to find the optimal measurements starting with a model that is calibrated with the currently available data. Next the different steps are explained in more detail.

The methodology has been applied for an OED at the Dender river whereby the frequency of the sampling and the period of sampling, the data type (only DO or combined DO-$NO_3$, DO-$NO_3$-BOD or DO-$NO_3$-BOD-$NH_4$) and sample locations (4 possible combinations of 3 possible locations: upstream, halfway, downstream) are considered as parameters for the sampling layout. The best way to take samples is (a) on an hourly time basis (Fig. 9 left), (b) over nearly the whole year (8,730 samples) (Fig. 9 right), (c) in two locations (data not shown) and (d) of the four variables (data not shown). Whereas in general, low uncertainties are corresponding to a lot of samples (as expected), it can be depicted that other sampling schemes could be defined that provide a quasi similar accuracy, with fewer number of samples or at a lower frequency. The application of optimal experimental design for guiding monitoring campaigns can thus point out better monitoring strategies and will eventually make the monitoring more effective with less cost.

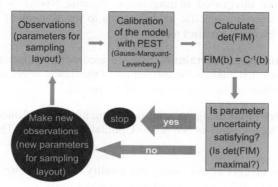

**Figure 8.** Optimal experimental design for river water quality modeling (PEST = Parameter ESTimation model; Doherty, 2000).

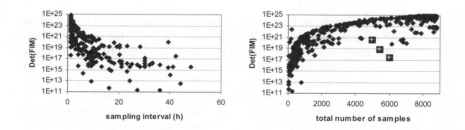

**Figure 9.** The inverse of the Det(FIM) as a function of the sampling interval (left) and the total number of samples (right) (relatively bad strategies are marked with ⊞).

## 6. Conclusions and Perspectives

SWAT has been successfully applied worldwide to address water quantity and quality issues. In general the model (along with useful GIS interfaces to process the readily available inputs) have yielded better watershed science and management. However the model and the input processing GIS interface tools alone were only the first step in the hydroinformatics for a decision-maker within the context of the WFD. In this paper, the SWAT and associated tools have been demonstrated to be the tool to support the WFD and the explanatory guidance documents:

**To do water management at the level of river basin.** SWAT operates on river basin scale, includes processes for the assessment of the complex diffuse pollution and there is hence a sound basis to use SWAT as a frame for integrated modeling.

**To promote integrated management.** Because SWAT is open-sources, it allows for site-specific modifications to the sources or easy linkage to other hydroinformatics tools.

**To account for uncertainties.** SWAT incorporates algorithms for model analysis that enables the estimation of the model uncertainties and to the evaluation of the fit-to-purpose of the model.

**To support monitoring.** A joint use of monitoring and modeling is stimulated by a linkage of SWAT to Optimal Experimental Design methodology

**To set the targets at the ecological quality.** This is illustrated with the examples of linkage to ecological assessment tools

**To support public participation.** An important development around SWAT is the integration into GIS post-processing tool AVSWAT that provides maps with results.

However, applications in Europe can also be hampered by difficulties in the data availability or the lack of regional databases. Recently, the development of some European databases has been started (Breuer et al., 2003; Breuer and Frede, 2006). Therefore, an integrated data and modeling tool, such as the 'BASINS' modeling environment for the U.S. (Di Luzio, 2002), would be of great necessity. In such a modeling environment several homogenized data on land use, soil, climate, river networks, discharge, point sources should be provided and formatted for a direct use. With respect to the European multi-national structure, the different data policies, as well as its multi-facet ways of soil and land use classification, one of the main difficulties lies in the data homogenization itself. Also, some more developments would enhance external use or consulting of the SWAT model results. Important benefit could be taken from a further integration into an internet interface to allow for simulations of the web or web-based post-processing of the model results. Finally, an open-source of not only the SWAT model but also the GIS interface would help in further integration to other tools or would offer more flexibilities for case-dependent developments in model codes.

# References

**Adriaenssens, V., De Baets, B., Goethals, P.L.M. and De Pauw, N. 2004.** Fuzzy rule-based models for decision support in ecosystem management. *The Science of the Total Environment,* **319**, 1-12.

**Argent, R.M. 2004.** An overview of model integration for environmental applications – components, frameworks and semantics. *Environmental Modelling & Software,* **19**, 219-234.

**Arnold, J.G. and Fohrer, N. 2005.** Current capabilities and research opportunities in applied watershed modeling. *Hydrological Processes,* **19**, 563-572.

**Arnold, J.G., Srinivasan, R. , Muttiah, R.S and Williams, J.R.. 1998.** Large area hydrologic modeling and assessment Part I: Model development. *Journal of the American Water Research Association,* **3**. **34**, 73-89.

**Bagnold, R.A. 1977.** Bedload transport in natural rivers. *Water Resources Research,* **13**, 303-312.

**Bard, Y. 1974.** *Nonlinear parameter estimation.* Academic press, New York and London.

BMW. 2004 Benchmark Models for the Water Framework Directive. Fifth framework program of the European Community (Contractno.EVK1-CT2001-0093).

**Booty, W.G., Lam, D.C.L., Wong, I.W.S. & Siconolfi, P. 2001.** Design and implementation of an environmental decision support system. *Environmental Modelling & Software,* **16**, 453-458.

**Bouraoui, F., Grizzetti, B., Mulligan, D. and Galbiati, L.L. 2005.** Performance of the SWAT model in an inter-comparison of nutrient loss quantification tools throughout Europe (EUROHARP project). Proc 3rd SWAT Conference, Zürich, Switzerland. http://www.brc.tamus.edu/swat/3rdswatconf/PDF/day_1/Bouraoui.pdf.

**Breuer, L., Huisman, J.A., Steiner, N., Weinmann, B. and Frede, H.-G. 2003.** Eco-Hydraulic and Economic Trade-Off functions in Watershed Management. SWAT Conference, Bari, Italy, 1-4 July, 2003.

**Breuer, L., Eckhardt, K. and Frede, H-G. 2003.** Plant parameter values for models in temperate climates. *Ecological Modelling,* **169**, 237-93.

**Breuer, L. and Frede H-G. 2006.** PlaPaDa - an online plant parameter data drill for eco-hydrological modelling approaches.http://www.unigiessen.de/~gh1461/plapada/plapada.html

**Breuer, L., Huisman, J.A., Steiner, N., Weinmann, B. and Frede, H.-G. 2004.** Eco-hydrologic and economic trade-off functions in watershed management. TWRI Technical Report 266, 255-261.

**Brown, L.C. and Barnwell, T.O. Jr. 1987.** The Enhanced Water Quality Models QUAL2E and QUAL2E-UNCAS Documentation and User Manual. EPA Document EPA/600/3-87/007. USEPA, Athens, GA.

**Casman, E.A., Naiman, D.Q. and Chamberlain, C.E., 1988.** Confronting the ironies of optimal design: nonoptimal sampling designs with desirable properties. *Water Resources Research,* **24**(3), 409-415

**CHESS. 2001.** Climate, hydrochemistry and economics of surface-water systems. EC Environment and Climate Research Programme (Contract no. ENV4-CT-97-0440) http://www.nwl.ac.uk/ih/www/research/images/chessreport.pdf

**Chow, V.T., Maidment, D.R. and Mays, L.W. 1988.** *Applied Hydrology.* New York, N.Y.: McGraw-Hill.

**Costanza, R., d´Arge, R., de Groot, R., Farber, S., Grasso, M., Hannon, B., Limburg, K., Naeem, S., O'Neill, R.V., Paruelo, J., Raskin, R.G., Sutton, P., van den Belt, M. 1997.** The value of the world's ecosystem services and natural capital. *Nature,* **387**, 253-60.

**De Pauw, D. and Vanrolleghem, P.A. 2004.** Optimal experimental design for model calibration: general procedure. In: Proceedings of the 4th PhD symposium, Ghent, Belgium.

**Dilks, C.F., Dunn, S.M. and Ferrier, R.C. 2003.** Benchmarking models for the Water Framework Directive: evaluation of SWAT for use in the Ythan catchment, UK., *SWAT Conference, Bari, Italy, 1-4 July, 2003.*

**Di Luzio, M., Srinivasan, R. and Arnold, J.G. 2002.** Integration of Watershed Tools and SWAT Model intoBASINS. *Journal of the American Water Resources Association.* **38**(4), 1127-1141.

**Di Luzio, M., Srinivasan R. and Arnold, J.G. 2004a.** A GIS-coupled hydrological model system for the watershed assessment of agricultural nonpoint and point sources of pollution. *Transactions in GIS,* 8(1), 113-136.

**Di Luzio, M., Arnold, J.G. and Srinivasan, R. 2004b.** Integration of SSURGO maps and soil parameters within a geographic information system and nonpoint source pollution model system. *Journal of Soil and Water Conservation,* **59**(4), 123-133.

**Dochain, D. and Vanrolleghem, P.A. 2001.** *Dynamical Modelling and Estimation in Wastewater Treatment Processes,* IWA publishing, London

**Eckhardt, K., Breuer, L., and Frede, H.-G. 2003.** Parameter uncertainty and the significance of simulated land use change effects. *Journal of Hydrology,* 10.1016/S0022-1694 (02)00395-5.

**EU. 2000.** Water Framework Directive. Council Directive 2000/6/EG, 22.12.2000.

**EUROHARP. 2004.** European Community (Contract no. EVK1-CT-2001-00096); http://www.euroharp.org/pd/pd/index.htm.

**Fohrer, N., Möller, D. and Steiner, N. 2002.** An interdisciplinary modelling approach to evaluate the effects of landuse change. *Physics and Chemistry of the Earth,* **27**(9/10), 655–662.

**Fohrer, N., Haverkamp, S. and Frede, H.G. 2005.** Assessment of the effects of landuse patterns on hydrologic landscape functions—development of sustainable landuse concepts for low mountain range areas *Hydrological Processes* 19, 659-672.

**Gassman, P.W., Reyes, M.R. and Arnold, J.G. 2005.** Review of peer-reviewed literature on the SWAT model. In *Proc. 3rd International SWAT Conf.,* July 13-15, 2005, Zurich, Switzerland.

**Godfrey, K.R. and Distefano, J.J. 1985.** Identifiability of model parameters. In: Identification and System Parameter Estimation. Oxford, Pergamon Press.

**Goethals, P.L.M. 2005.** *Data driven development of predictive ecological models for benthic macroinvertebrates in rivers.* PhD thesis, Ghent University, Ghent, Belgium. 400p.

**Goodwin, G.C. and Payne, R.L. 1977.** Dynamic system identification. Experiment design and data analysis, Academic Press, New York

**Grizzetti, B., Bouraoui, F., Granlund, K., Rekolainen, S. and Bidoglio, G. 2003.** Modelling diffuse emission and retention of nutrients in the Vantaanjoki watershed (Finland) using the SWAT model. *Ecological Modelling,* **169**, 25-38.

**Huisman, J.A., Pohlert, T., Breuer, L. and Frede, H.-G. 2005.** The power of multiobjective calibration: two case studies with SWAT. Proc 3rd SWAT Conference, Zürich, Switzerland. 8 pp.

**Jayakrishnan, R., Srinivasan, R., Santhi, C. and Arnold, J.G. 2005.** Advances in the application of the SWAT model for water resources management. *Hydrological Processes,* **19**, 749-62.

**Lam, D. and Swayne, D. 2001.** Issues of EIS software design: some lessons learned in the past decade. *Environmental Modelling & Software,* **16**, 419-425.

**McElroy, A.D., Chiu, S.Y. Nebgen. J.W. Aleti, A. and Bennett, F.W. 1976.** Loading functions for assessment of water pollution from nonpoint sources. Environmental Protection Technology Services, EPA 600/2-76-151.

**Paggio, R., Agre, G., Dichev, C., Umann, G., Rozman, T., Batachia, L. and Stocchero, M. 1999.** A cost-effective programmable environment for developing environmental decision support systems. *Environmental Modelling & Software*, **14**, 367-382.

**Petersen, B. 2000.** *Calibration, identifiability and optimal experimental design of activated sludge models. Ph*D thesis at Faculty of Agricultural and Applied Biological Sciences, Ghent University, Ghent Belgium.

**Pohlert, T., Breuer, L., Huisman, J.A., Frede and H.-G. 2006.** Coupling biogeochemical and hydrological models to improve predictions of land use change effects on river water quality. *Ecol Model*, submitted.

**Reed, M., Cuddy, S.M. and Rizzoli, A.E. 1999.** A framework for modeling multiple resource management issues – an open modeling approach. *Environmental Modelling & Software*, **14**, 503-509.

**Reiher, W., Düring, R.-A. and Gäth, S. 2004.** Development of Heavy Metal Contents in Soils According to Land Use and Management Systems - A Heavy Metal Balance Approach. Proceedings of the EUROSOIL 2004. http://www.bodenkunde2.uni-freiburg.de/eurosoil/abstracts/id1097_Reiher_full.pdf

**Rizzoli, A.E. and Young, W.J. 1997.** Delivering environmental decision support systems: software tools and techniques. *Environmental Modelling & Software*, **12**, 237-249.

**Steiner. N.C. and Köhler, W. 2003.** Effects of landscape patterns on species richness--a modelling approach. *Agriculture Ecosystems & Environment*, **98**, 353-61.

**TempQsim. 2004.** Fifth framework program of the European Community (Contract no. EVK1-CT2002-00112); http://www.tempqsim.net/.

**Todini, E. 1996.** The ARN Orainfall-runoff model. *Journal of Hydrology*, 175, 339–382.U.S.

**USDA, U.S. Department of Agriculture. 1994.** State soil geographic (STATSGO) Data base: data use information. Natural Resources Conservation Service Miscellaneous Publication 1492.

**USDA, U.S. Department of Agriculture. 1995.** Soil survey geographic (SSURGO) Data base: Data Use information. Natural Resources Conservation Service Miscellaneous Publication 1527.

**Vandenberghe, V., van Griensven, A. and Bauwens, W. 2002.** Detection of the most optimal measuring points for water quality variables: Application to the river water quality model of the river Dender in ESWAT. *Water Science & Technology,* **46**(3),1-7.

**Vandenberghe, V., van Griensven, A. and Bauwens, W. 2005.** Propagation of uncertainty in diffuse pollution into water quality predictions: application to the River Dender in Flanders, *Water Science & Technolology*, **51**(3-4), 347-354.

**Vandenberghe, V., van Griensven, A., Vanrolleghem, P.A., Goethals, P.L.M., Zarkami, R. and De Pauw, N. 2005.** Coupling water quality and fish habitat models for river management: simulation excercises in the Dender basin. p. 375-381. In: COST626 Network 'Proceedings from the final meeting', 19-20 May 2005, Silkeborg, Denmark. 397 pp.

**van Griensven, A. and Bauwens, W. 2001.** Integral modelling of catchments. *Water Science & Technology*, **43**(7), 321-328.

**van Griensven, A. and Bauwens, W. 2003.** Multi-objective auto-calibration for semi-distributed water quality models, *Water Resources Research*, **39**(10), 1348 doi: 10.1029/2003WR002284.

**van Griensven, A. and Bauwens, W. 2005.** Application and evaluation of ESWAT on the Dender basin and Wister Lake basin. *Hydrolological Processes* **19**(3), 827-838.

**van Griensven, A. and Meixner, T. 2006.** Methods to quantify and identify the sources of uncertainty for river basin water quality models, *Water Science & Technolology*, **53**(1), 51-59.

**van Griensven, A., Meixner, T., Grunwald S., Bishop, T., Di Luzio, M. and Srinivasan, R. 2006.** A global sensitivity analysis method for the parameters of multi-variable watershed models, *Journal of Hydrology*, in press.

**van Griensven, A. and Vanrolleghem, P. 2006.** The CatchMod Toolbox: Easy and guided access to ICT tools for Water Framework Directive implementation. *Water Science & Technolology*, 53(10), in press.

**Voinov, A., Fitz, C., Boumans, R. and Costanza, R. 2004.** Modular ecosystem modeling. *Environmental Modelling & Software*, **19**, 285-304.

**Waldhardt,R., Simmering,D. and Otte, A. 2004.** Estimation and prediction of plant species richness in a mosaic landscape. *Landscape Ecology*, **19**, 211-226.

**Walter, E. and Pronzato, L. 1999.** *Identification of parametric models from experimental data.* Springer Verlag, Heidelberg.

**Weber, A., Fohrer, N. and Möller, D. 2001.** Long-term land use changes in a mesoscale watershed due to socio-economic factors - effects on landscape and functions. *Ecological Modelling*, **140**, 125-140.

**Weinmann, B., Schroers, J.O., and Sheridian, P. 2005.** Simulating the effects of decoupled transfer payments using the land use model ProLand. *Agrarwirtschaft*, 54.

**Williams, J.R. and Hann, R.W. 1978.** Optimal operation of large agricultural watersheds with water quality constraints. Technical Report No. 96, Texas Water Resources Institute, Texas A&M University, College Station, TX.

**Witten, I.H. and Frank, E. 2000.** Data Mining: practical machine learning tools and techniques with Java implementations. Morgan Kaufmann Publishers, San Francisco. 369 pp.

**Young, W.J., Lam, D.C.L., Ressel, V. and Wong, I.W. 2000.** Development of an environmental flows decision support system. *Environmental Modelling & Software* 15, 257-265.

# 2.3 Nonpoint Source Pollution Responses Simulation for Conversion of Cropland to Forest in Mountains by SWAT in China

## Wei Ouyang[1], Fang-Hua Hao, Xue-Lei Wang and Hong-Guang Cheng

### Abstract

Several environmental protection policies have been implemented to prevent soil erosion and nonpoint source (NPS) pollution in China. After severe Yangtze River floods, the "conversion cropland to forest policy" (CCFP) was carried out throughout China, especially in the middle and upper reaches of Yangtze River. The research area of the current study is located in Bazhong City, Sichuan Province in Yangtze River watershed, where soil erosion and NPS pollution are serious concerns. Major NPS pollutants include nitrogen (N) and phosphorus (P). The objective of this study is to evaluate the long-term impact of implementation of the CCFP on streamflow, sediment yields, and the main NPS pollutant loading at watershed level. The Soil and Water Assessment Tool (SWAT) is a watershed environmental model and is applied here to simulate and quantify the impacts. Four scenarios are constructed representing different patterns of conversion from cropland to forest under various conditions set by the CCFP. Scenario A represented the baseline, i.e. the cropland and forest area conditions before the implementation of CCFP. Scenario B represents the condition under which all hillside cropland with slope larger than 25° was converted into forest. In scenarios C and D, hillside croplands with slope larger than 15° and 7.5° were substituted by forest, respectively. Under the various scenarios, the NPS pollution reduction due to CCFP implementation from 1996-2005 is estimated by SWAT. The results are presented as percentage change of water flow, sediment, organic N, and organic P at watershed level. Furthermore, a regression analysis is conducted between forest area ratio and ten years' average NPS load estimations, which confirmed the benefits of implementing CCFP in reducing nonpoint source pollution by increasing forest in mountainous areas. The reduction of organic N and organic P is significant (decrease 42.1% and 62.7%, respectively) at watershed level. In addition, this study also proves that SWAT modeling approach can be used to estimate NPS pollutants' impacts of land use conversions in large watershed.

**Keywords:** Nonpoint source pollution, conversion of cropland to forest, SWAT, simulation, China

© 2009 World Association of Soil and Water Conservation, *Soil and Water Assessment Tool (SWAT): Global Applications,* eds. Jeff Arnold, Raghavan Srinivasan, Susan Neitsch, Chris George, Karim Abbaspour, Philip Gassman, Fang Hua Hao, Ann van Griensven, Ashvin Gosain, Patrick Debels, Nam Won Kim, Hiroaki Somura, Victor Ella, Attachai Jintrawet, Manuel Reyes, and Samran Sombatpanit, pp. 145-162. This article first appeared in *Environmental Management* (2008) 41:79–89 DOI 10.1007/s00267-007-9028-8 © Springer Science and Business Media. WASWC is grateful for the permission granted. *(Continued on next page)*

# 1. Introduction

Watershed environmental issues, especially water quality and soil erosion are becoming an increasing concern in China and other parts of the world (Wang et al., 2006; Chen et al., 2006). The soil losses and nonpoint source (NPS) pollutants formations in the middle and upper reaches of Yangtze River in central China are highly vulnerable. Destruction of vegetation has led to soil erosion and NPS pollutions in the upper reaches. In the past 30 years, the forest cover has been reduced to half, while the area exposed to severe erosion doubled in size (Yin and Changan, 2001; Zhang, 2003). Soil erosion on cultivated land not only results in on-site soil degradation and NPS pollutions, but also causes off-site problems related to downstream sedimentation and water pollution (Zhang et al., 2003; Martin et al., 2006). After Yangtze River floods in 1998, there was wide agreement that agricultural production on sloping land in upper and middle reaches of Yangtze River was one of the most important causes of rapid runoff and soil erosion in the basin and a major contributor to flooding (Eckhardta and Ulbrich, 2003). Since 1999, for preventing soil erosion and water pollution, the Chinese government has carried out the so-called "Conversion Cropland to Forest Policy" (CCFP), which encourages the farmers to return hillside crop cultivation to grassland and forest with detailed compensation and subsidy schemes. From the beginning of the 21st century, 14.7 million ha of cropland have been converted to forest (Zhang et al., 2003). Despite enormous scales of CCFP, to date, there have been few assessments of the policy impact on regional sediments and NPS pollution (Wanga et al., 2006). In this article, we estimate not only the environmental effects of CCFP in preventing soil erosion and NPS pollutants, but also formulate the regression equations between forestry area ratio and envi-ronmental index. Then, the regional sediment, organic nitrogen (N), and organic phosphorus (P) can be effectively estimated with forestry ratio.

To assess the effects of CCFP, field experiments or long-term monitoring is very expensive and time consuming. During the repeated monitoring process, there are uncertainties associated with the results and is very difficult without additional resources. Watershed soil erosion and NPS pollution loading are generally a combined result of many influencing factors including climate, land cover, topography, land use and soil conditions that characterize the watershed (Tripathi et al., 2003). When implementing CCFP, it is quite difficult to assess the environ-

---

[1]W. Ouyang, F.-H. Hao, H.-G. Cheng: School of Environment, State Key Laboratory of Water Environment Simulation, Beijing Normal University, Beijing 100875, China e-mail: fanghua@bnu.edu.cn; pxhorse@sohu.com

W. Ouyang: International Institute for Geo-Information Science and Earth Observation (ITC), Enschede, Netherlands

X.-L. Wang: School of Geography, State Key Laboratory of Remote Sensing Science, Beijing Normal University, Beijing 100875, China

mental quality improvements by extensive sampling and monitoring data. Under these conditions, application models become useful and efficient. The Soil and Water Assessment Tool (SWAT) is a watershed simulation model system and can be applied to quantify environmental impacts of CCFP in watershed scale (Behera and Panda 2006). During simulation, the climate, land use, soil, topography, and geological variances are all taken into considerations (Arnold and Fohrer, 2005). SWAT has been applied by several authors to study impacts of watershed environmental policies in different perspective. Zhang and Jogensen (2005), for example, have applied the model to assess regional point and NPS pollution reductions for best management practices in Denmark. Attwood et al. (2000) have used SWAT to evaluate the impacts of natural resource policy in terms of environmental and economic implications at differing spatial scales.

For the advantages of SWAT model system, it can be used for regional environmental benefits assessment for CCFP implementations. The research motivation is to identify the reductions of NPS pollution with SWAT model, which is the foundation for conversion of cropland to forest policy decision-making. The objectives of this article, therefore, are to: (I) estimate NPS pollutant loading in this typical study area with support of SWAT model, (II) suggest approach to estimate CCFP long-term benefits for regional NPS pollution reduction at watershed level, and (III) analyze the linkage and correlation between NPS pollution load change and the various CCFP implementation levels.

## 2. Methods

### 2.2 Model description

The watershed water quality model, SWAT, was developed by the United States Department of Agriculture (USDA) (Arnold et al., 1998). The Soil and Water Assessment Tool was selected for this study because of its ability to simulate land management processes and hydrological responses in larger watershed. The Soil and Water Assessment Tool is a semi-distributed watershed model with a GIS interface that outlines the subbasins and stream networks from a digital elevation model (DEM) and can calculate daily water balances from meteorological, soil and land use data. The surface runoff is predicted at a daily step by a modification of soil conservation service (SCS) curve number method and the peak runoff rate is estimated according to rational formula. The erosion and sediment yields are estimated in each subbasin with modified universal soil loss equation (Ramanarayanan et al., 1996). SWAT applies a multilayer storage routing technique to partition drainable soil water content for each layer into components of lateral subsurface flow and percolation into the layer below.

The SWAT model is built to simulate the physical processes of pollutant in watershed as realistically as possible. Most model inputs are physically based.

However, it is important to note that SWAT is not a parametric model with a formal optimization to fit any data. In-stream nutrient dynamics have been incorporated into SWAT using kinetic routines from in-stream water quality model. The N processes, soil pools, plant supply, and demand of N can also be simulated by SWAT. The N Circle, with plant biomass, N transported with runoff, lateral flow, and percolation, can have different N formations estimated daily. The Soil and Water Assessment Tool can also model P circle and formations in similar approach to N. While predicting the amount of soluble P removed in runoff, the labile P concentration in topsoil, runoff volume, and P soil-partitioning factor are all considered. Sediment transport of P is simulated with a loading function, as is organic N transport (Santhi et al., 2006).

**Table 1.** Data type scale and data description/properties.

| Data type | Scale | Data description/properties |
|---|---|---|
| Topography | 1:200 000 | Elevation, overland and channel slopes, lengths |
| Land use | 1:1000 000 | Land use classifications, area and management information |
| Soils geographic databases | 1:400 000 | Soil physical and chemical properties. |
| Weather | 7 stations | Daily precipitation and temperature |
| Land management information | ... | Fertilizer application, planting and harvesting information |

**Table 2.** The geographical features of seven weather stations.

| ID | NAME | Lat (°) | Long (°) | Elevation(m) |
|---|---|---|---|---|
| 1 | GUANYUAN | 32.48 | 105.90 | 1939.00 |
| 2 | WANYUAN | 32.01 | 108.03 | 674.00 |
| 3 | LINZHONG | 31.51 | 105.95 | 1826.00 |
| 4 | BAZHONG | 31.90 | 106.70 | 1777.00 |
| 5 | DAXIAN | 31.20 | 107.50 | 1449.00 |
| 6 | NANCHONG | 30.70 | 106.10 | 1097.00 |
| 7 | SUINING | 30.50 | 105.55 | 355.00 |

The Soil and Water Assessment Tool was applied all over the world with diverse missions. The basic function is to estimate regional NPS pollution load. In recent years, more applications have been focused on regional managements and pollutant source identifications based on simulation results. Under assumed condition, it can assess regional NPS pollution load changes induced by, for example, climate change. Agriculture has been identified as the major contributor of NPS pollution of water resource (Cheng et al. 2007). Simulation of agricultural NPS pollutions in relation to crop patterns is one of the strong traits of SWAT.

## 2.2 Study area

The study area of Bazhong City, Sichuan Province is located in central China and in upper stream of the Yangtze River basin (Fig. 1). There are 65,959 km² cultivated land and 70% of them are cultivated sloping land. The soil erosion area in Sichuan is 199,800 km², which is 40.87% of the total soil erosion area in Yangtze River watershed. There are about 600 million tons of sediments transported from Sichuan into Yangtze River every year. In this area, the natural vegetation has been destroyed by tillage, grazing, and deforestation, which led to soil erosion and ecosystem degradation; therefore, this region is the core area to implement CCFP. Also, 34% of high to medium productivity hillside cropland has been converted to forest or grassland in the last several years.

The climate of Bazhong City is moderate, with the highest temperature at 40.2°C occurring in July and the lowest average monthly temperature is -4.7°C in January. The average annual temperature is 16.0-16.9°C and average yearly precipitation is 1120.7-1203.1 mm. The whole research area is 960,154 ha and the mean elevation is 773 m. The terrain is higher in the north and the maximum and minimum altitude is 2,464 m and 332 m, respectively. The various land uses in this watershed are: agricultural land (dry land and garden land) (48.0%), mixed forest (9.94%), range-grasses (8.12%), rice (paddy) (6.54%), honey mesquite (5.21%), sesbania (3.87%), and range-brush (0.05%). The main land use is for agricultural. The paddy is defined as a separate land use type because of its small area and lower slope distributions. Most of the soils are purple soil and lateritic red soil.

## 2.3 Model inputs

The ArcView Geographic Information System interface of AVSWAT model was used to develop input files. The 1:200,000 geographic database with topography, land use, and soils were constructed (Table 1). The watershed climate condition was simulated from 1996 through 2005 using daily historical weather information collected from seven weather stations in Sichuan Province around the study area (Table 2). The SWAT delineates watershed into sub-watersheds based on topography. The land use and soil map in this region was overlaid on subbasins. The land use was classified in seven types and codes of each land use were listed in Table 3.

In the research watershed, there are five types of soils. The dominant soil types in Bahe River watershed are purple soil and lateritic red soil. The purple soil occupies more than half of the area and lateritic red soil dominates another 41.71% in the north part of the watershed (Fig. 2). The main soil properties are listed in Table 4. The typical management practices information, such as cropping schemes, fertilizer application, and tillage operation were gathered from farmer surveys and local administrative agents.

**Table 3.** The land use type area and percentage in study area.

| LANDUSE | Area (ha) | % |
|---|---|---|
| Range-Brush (RNGB) | 522.0 | 0.05 |
| Range-Grasses (RNGE) | 77958.3 | 8.12 |
| Honey Mesquite (MESQ) | 50041.5 | 5.21 |
| Mixed Forest (FRST) | 95470.7 | 9.94 |
| Agricultural Land (AGRC) | 636190.9 | 66.26 |
| Sesbania (SESB) | 37183.2 | 3.87 |
| Rice (RICE) | 62787.8 | 6.54 |

**Table 4.** Soil properties under different soil series of Bahe River watershed.

| Soil Type | Area /ha | Area ratio/% | Depth /mm | Coarse sand/% | Fine sand/% | Silt /% | Clay /% | Organic carbon/% | TN /% | TP /% | TK /% |
|---|---|---|---|---|---|---|---|---|---|---|---|
| *Lateritic red Soil* | 401104.5 | 41.71 | 70 | 6.58 | 34.06 | 28.96 | 30.40 | 2.42 | 0.110 | 0.033 | 1.30 |
| *Yellow Soil* | 12519.4 | 1.30 | 100 | 39.11 | 11.29 | 34.80 | 14.80 | 2.78 | 0.146 | 0.024 | 1.88 |
| *Yellow brown Soil* | 9946.5 | 1.03 | 60 | 0.36 | 20.37 | 59.12 | 20.15 | 3.52 | 0.206 | 0.066 | 2.30 |
| *Carbonate purple Soil* | 52897.6 | 5.50 | 100 | 6.20 | 11.30 | 42.50 | 40.00 | 2.04 | 0.142 | 0.058 | 1.92 |
| *Purple Soil* | 485297.5 | 50.46 | 95 | 0.61 | 20.67 | 37.95 | 40.77 | 1.34 | 0.095 | 0.027 | 1.65 |

**Table 5.** The SWAT model parameters adjusted during calibration for streamflow.

| Parameter | Default value | Calibration value |
|---|---|---|
| CN2 | 0 | –7 |
| EPCO | 1.0 | 0.5 |
| ESCO | 0.95 | 0.55 |
| REVAPMN | 1.0 | 0.65 |
| GW_REVAP | 0.02 | 0.1 |
| GW_DELAY | 31 | 45 |

**Table 6.** The SWAT model parameters adjusted during calibration for stream sediment and nutrient loads.

| Parameter | Default value | Calibration value |
|---|---|---|
| SLOPE | 0.129 | 0.100 |
| SLSUBBSN | 24.390 | 7.000 |
| SOL_ORGN | 0 | 4000 |
| SOL_ORGP | 0 | 2000 |
| ERORGN | 0.0 | 4.0 |
| NPERCO | 0.20 | 0.30 |
| USLE_K1) | Various | –20% |
| SOL_Z1 | 101.6 | 65.0 |
| RSDIN | 0 | 4000 |
| RCN | 1.0 | 0.4 |
| BIOMIX | 0.92 | 0.40 |

## 2.4 Model calibration

With reference to actual historical monitoring data on streamflow and water quality, AVSWAT model was calibrated (Arnold et al., 1995). The calibration simulation period for flow and water quality was started from January to December 2004. The related SWAT model parameters were adjusted (Table 5) to correct the overestimation of average monthly streamflow. After calibration, the curve number (CN2), plant water uptake compensation factor (EPCO), the soil evaporation compensation factor (ESCO), threshold depth of water in the shallow aquifer for 'revap' or percolation to the deep aquifer to occur (REVAPMN), amount of shallow aquifer water that moved into the soil profile (GW_REVAP), and groundwater delay coefficient (GW_DELAY) were determined as listed in. As a result, the simulated water flow was acceptable.

The stream monitoring data in Bazhong watershed includes only total N and total P without distinguishing organic nutrients from mineral components. Therefore, SWAT model was calibrated with the reference to the actual monitoring data of total N and total P. The adjusted SWAT model parameters after calibration are listed in Table 6, including the average slope steepness (SLOPE), average slope length (SLSUBBSN), initial soil organic N concentration (SOL_ORGN), initial soil organic P concentration (SOL_ORGP), organic N enrichment ratio (ERORGN), N percolation coefficient (NPERCO), universal soil loss equation soil erodibility factor (USLE_K1), depth of the top layer of the Aledo soil (SOL_Z1), initial residue cover (RSDIN), N in rainfall (RCN), and biological mixing efficiency (BIOMIX).

**Table 7.** The monthly (M) simulated and monitored results after calibration at watershed outlet.

| TN density/(mg/L) | | | TP density/(mg/L) | | |
|---|---|---|---|---|---|
| M | Simulated | Monitored | M | Simulated | Monitored |
| 1 | 1.007 | 0.956 | 1 | 0.017 | 0.013 |
| 2 | 0.914 | 0.877 | 2 | 0.020 | 0.016 |
| 3 | 0.953 | 1.077 | 3 | 0.019 | 0.013 |
| 4 | 1.203 | 1.124 | 4 | 0.044 | 0.040 |
| 5 | 1.008 | 1.098 | 5 | 0.023 | 0.020 |
| 6 | 0.930 | 0.943 | 6 | 0.033 | 0.031 |
| 7 | 0.563 | 0.613 | 7 | 0.017 | 0.020 |
| 8 | 0.543 | 0.641 | 8 | 0.011 | 0.013 |
| 9 | 0.737 | 0.763 | 9 | 0.019 | 0.023 |
| 10 | 0.723 | 0.704 | 10 | 0.035 | 0.033 |
| 11 | 0.709 | 0.697 | 11 | 0.029 | 0.023 |
| 12 | 0.902 | 0.914 | 12 | 0.031 | 0.026 |

After calibration, the estimated average monthly N density at the outlet of Bazhong watershed was slightly lower than the actual average monthly N yield in the rainy season and slightly higher in the winter (Table 7). The simulated average monthly P density after calibration has similar variance trend as that of total N.

**Table 8.** Land use distributions characteristics with maximum, mean slope and their standard deviation (STD).

| TN density/(mg/L) | | | TP density/(mg/L) | | |
|---|---|---|---|---|---|
| M | Simulated | Monitored | M | Simulated | Monitored |
| 1 | 1.007 | 0.956 | 1 | 0.017 | 0.013 |
| 2 | 0.914 | 0.877 | 2 | 0.020 | 0.016 |
| 3 | 0.953 | 1.077 | 3 | 0.019 | 0.013 |
| 4 | 1.203 | 1.124 | 4 | 0.044 | 0.040 |
| 5 | 1.008 | 1.098 | 5 | 0.023 | 0.020 |
| 6 | 0.930 | 0.943 | 6 | 0.033 | 0.031 |
| 7 | 0.563 | 0.613 | 7 | 0.017 | 0.020 |
| 8 | 0.543 | 0.641 | 8 | 0.011 | 0.013 |
| 9 | 0.737 | 0.763 | 9 | 0.019 | 0.023 |
| 10 | 0.723 | 0.704 | 10 | 0.035 | 0.033 |
| 11 | 0.709 | 0.697 | 11 | 0.029 | 0.023 |
| 12 | 0.902 | 0.914 | 12 | 0.031 | 0.026 |

## 2.5 Conversion of cropland to forest scenarios analysis

In order to estimate the reductions in soil erosion and NPS pollution due to implementation of land use conversion from cropland to grassland/forest policies, four scenarios are constructed representing different conditions of implementation of CCFP in the simulated basin: baseline with (I) no conversion, (II) conversion of cropland with slope greater than 25°, (III) conversion of cropland with slope greater than 15°, and (IV) conversion of cropland with slope greater than 7.5°. Under existing conditions, the evaluation of impacts of CCFP was carried out in four scenarios. The first, Scenario A, was original land use condition, 66.26% of land use was agricultural land and 9.94% was forest. In Scenario B, agricultural land on slope greater than 25° was converted into forest and other land use did not change; therefore, agricultural land dropped to 383,429 ha and forest area climbed to 349,834 ha. In Scenario C, agricultural land on slope greater than 15° was all converted to forest, which resulted in forest area that rose to 562,971 ha and agricultural land that decreased to 170,292 ha. In the last scenario, D, agricultural land on slope greater than 7.5° was turned into forest. As the result, forest area occupied 73.43% of regional land use (706,261 ha) and agricultural land was cut down to 27,002 ha.

To substantiate the four scenarios and simulate and assess their impacts by SWAT, an analytical framework was developed (Fig. 3). Firstly, the land use distribution characteristics was analyzed according to land use type and land slope (Table 8). The average agricultural land slope is 16.49°. The study area is a highly mountainous region with limited suitable arable land resources. Consequently, much of the hillside land is also cultivated, including those with slope greater than 25°. There are 252,761 ha agricultural land with slope greater than 25°, which is about 26% of the entire study area. The details of the four scenarios are listed in Table 9.

The land use distributions of the four scenarios were also mapped in Figure 4. Based on these four kinds of land use conditions, the regional water flow, soil erosions, organic N, and organic P loading in 10 years were estimated respectively using the calibrated SWAT model.

## 3. Results and Discussion

### 3.1 Streamflow variation

The volume of surface runoff under different scenarios is simulated for the whole watershed from 1996-2005. Obviously, the overall pattern of streamflow variation is determined by the variation of precipitation (PRECIP). The highest peak runoff value (331.4 $m^3/s$) simulated by the model was in Scenario C and the lowest in Scenario B. The streamflow is very similar between Scenarios A and D despite the different land use structure. With sloping agricultural lands converted into forest from Scenario A-B, the streamflow did not decrease dramatically. However, when the agricultural land located on a slope larger than 15° was converted into forest (Scenario C), the streamflow climbed intensively, ranging from 112.0 $m^3/s$ t o 331.4 $m^3/s$, but not the highest in the first 3 years. With more lands transferred into forestry, the streamflow dropped to an original situation. The distributions of streamflow value in Scenarios A and D were plotted graphically with respect to the same line from 78.5 to 302.9 $m^3/s$.

### 3.2 Transported sediment variation

Sediment yield is the amount of overland soil loss due to water erosion in the whole study of watershed, which reflects the integrated response of sediment generation processes and stream processes at watershed scale (Fig. 6), showing the change in annual average sediment generation and precipitation of four scenarios from 1996-2005. The sediment yields exhibit similar trends with the PRECIP. Under the original land use condition, Scenario A, the sediment yields of whole watershed ranged from 1,535 x $10^3$ to 4,456 x $10^3$ t. By implementing the CCFP in scenarios B and C, the sediment yields decreased, but not intensively. However, the estimated results of these two conditions seemed to be the same as in

Figure 5. When the agricultural land on a slope greater than 7.5° was changed into forest in Scenario D, the sediment yields dropped sharply and ranged from 569 x $10^3$ to 3,037 x $10^3$ t. With the exception of four scenario analysis, the watershed sediment yield decreased as the forest area increased.

**Table 9.** Details of the four scenarios.

| Scenarios | Agriculture land(ha) | % | Forest (ha) | % | Conversion (≥25°) | Conversion (≥15°) | Conversion (≥7.5°) |
|---|---|---|---|---|---|---|---|
| A | 636190.9 | 66.26 | 95470.7 | 9.94 | – | ... | – |
| B | 383429.2 | 39.87 | 3498384.0 | 39.87 | 100% | ... | – |
| C | 170292.1 | 17.71 | 562971.5 | 58.54 | 100% | 100% | – |
| D | 27002.9 | 2.81 | 706260.7 | 73.43 | 100% | 100% | 100% |

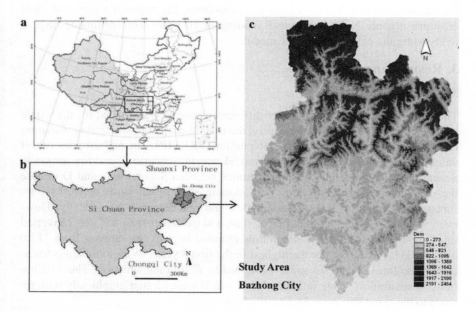

**Figure 1.** Location, topography of study area in China.

## 3.3 Organic N variation

Comparisons of the assessed organic N concentrations in the runoff water under the four scenarios and the corresponding simulated precipitation values in 10 years are shown in Figure 7. The precipitation has a similar trend with estimated results, which proved the NPS pollutants transportations were mainly controlled by the climate conditions. By the analysis of watershed organic N yields, the yield decreased with the forest area climbing, which demonstrated that the implementing of CCFP to prevent NPS pollutions was feasible. In Scenario A, the organic N yield was 67.9 x $10^4$ to 394.1 x $10^4$ kg/ha, which dropped to 63.3 x $10^4$ to

154

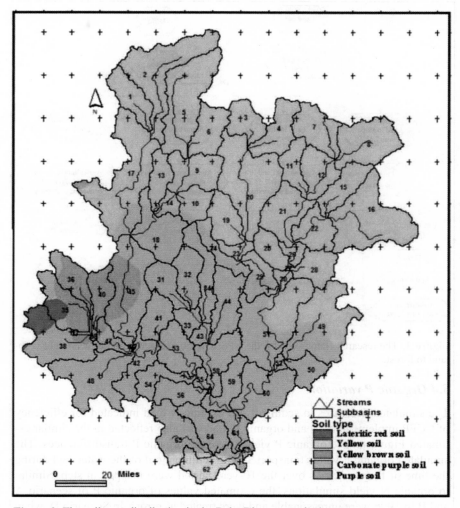

**Figure 2.** The soil type distribution in the Bahe River watershed.

251.7 x $10^4$ kg/ha in Scenario D, except the simulation error (1,284 x $10^4$ kg/ha) in 1996. The estimated value of Scenario C in 1996 was also treated as unreasonable. But the other estimations were reasonable for the reference to the local monitored values. By the simulation, the pollutant prevention benefits of different policy implementations level can be concluded clearly for the simulation differences of the four scenarios. Based on those assessments, the CCFP benefits can be estimated in advance and the environmental quality index can be forecasted, which is the guidelines for management.

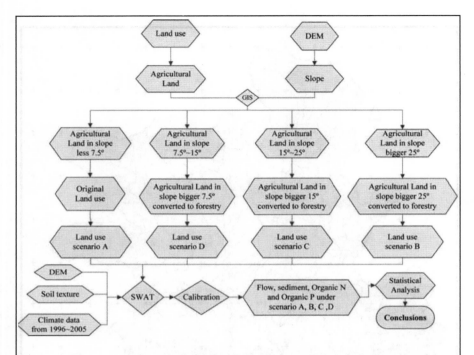

**Figure 3.** The research framework for the NPS pollution response for conversion of cropland to forest.

## 3.4 Organic P variation

The simulated decreases in sediment and organic N load indicated for efficiency of CCFP implementations and organic P load was also reflected in the similar estimated Figure 8. The organic P yields were the organic P transdifferences. The simulated organic P yields transported with sediment out of the watershed during the time of four scenarios over the 10-year period were mapped in step. Similar to organic N yield simulations, the estimated values of organic P of scenario A and B in 1996 were unreasonable and were treated as errors. In Scenario D, when the agricultural land slope was greater than 7.5% and was transferred into forest, the organic P yields dropped. The yield was between 92.3 x $10^3$ kg/ha and 758.9 x $10^3$ kg/ha. However, at the same time under the original land cover situation, the yields were ranged from 168 x $10^3$ kg/ha and 2,438 x $10^3$ kg/ha. Within the other two situations, the variations were not dramatic, but can prove the benefits of CCFP implementations. Compared to sediment variations and organic N estimations, the organic P yields difference of four scenarios over 10 years was not dramatic. One important reason is that parts of the organic N come from residue of the ground in forestry.

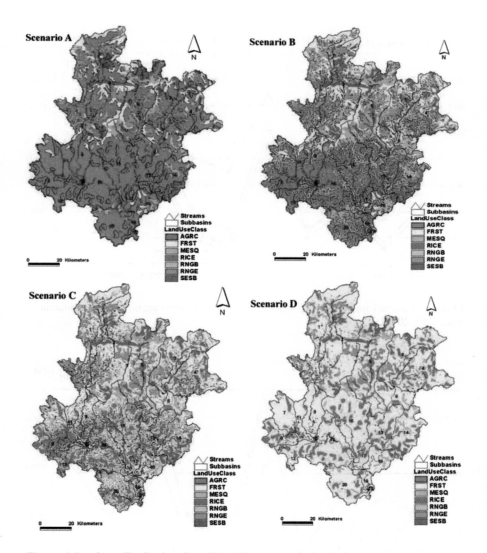

**Figure 4.** Land use distribution about Bahe River watershed with four scenarios.

## 4. Statistical Analysis

The modeling approach was applied to estimate the 10-year impacts of implementing the CCFP in Bazhong City in the Yangtze River basin. The ten years' average results (sediment, stream flow, organic N, and organic P, respectively) of

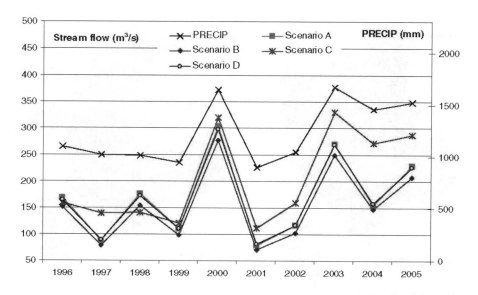

**Figure 5.** Comparison between simulated streamflow of four scenarios and precipitation from 1996-2005.

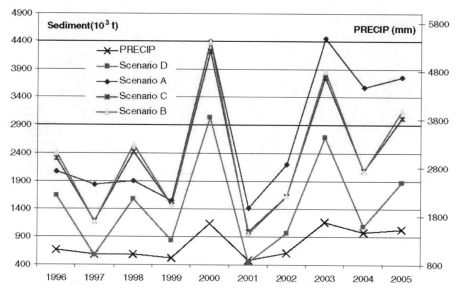

**Figure 6.** Comparison between simulated sediment yields of four scenarios and precipitations from 1996–2005.

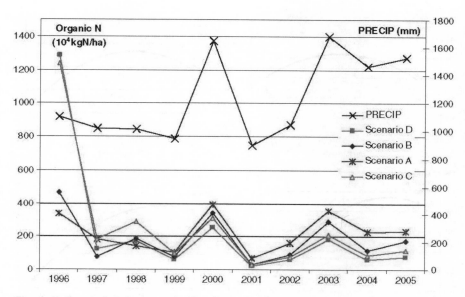

**Figure 7.** Comparison between simulated organic N value of four scenarios and precipitation from 1996–2005.

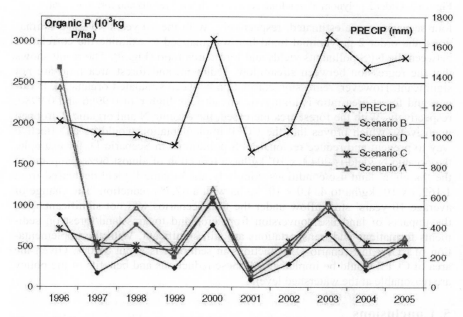

**Figure 8.** Comparison between simulated organic P of four scenarios and precipitation from 1996–2005.

159

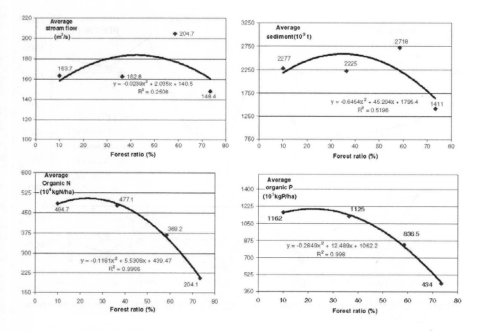

**Figure 9.** Order 2 polynomial trendline between estimated results and forest area ratio.

four scenarios were estimated, respectively. With the 10 years' average estimations, the order 2 polynomial trend-line was mapped to examine the correlation between the NPS pollutants yields and forest area ratio (Fig. 9). The result shows that the regression between streamflow, sediment, and forest area ratio are not significant. However, regression correlation between simulated organic N, P values, and forest area ratio is highly significant with high $r^2$ of 0.9966 and 0.9980, respectively. With the forest area increased, the organic N and organic P dropped intensively, which proves that the CCFP implementation would be an effective way to prevent and reduce regional NPS pollutions. In Scenario D, for example, the organic N yield is 204.1 x $10^4$ kg/ha, a reduction of almost 60% compared to the 'baseline' land use conditions. Similarly, the organic P yield decreased from 1,162.0 x $10^3$ kg/ha to 434.0 x $10^3$ kg/ha with a 62.7% reduction. The change of average 10 years' streamflow under the four scenarios was not significant. Yet, the impacts of land use conversion from cropland to grassland/forest on sediments formations and transportations are still significant. With the implementation of CCFP in Scenario D, reductions in sediment is about 38.0%. Given the area of CCFP would be implemented, these reductions and benefits of the policy are reasonable at the watershed level.

## 5. Conclusions

Land use conversion of hillside cropland to grassland/forest is one of the major

160

national policies that have been adopted by the Chinese government to curb eco-logical destruction, prevent soil erosion, and reduce NPS pollution. This study at-tempts to assess quantitatively the impacts of this policy on soil erosion and NPS pollution loading.

The need for implementing CCFP and assessing soil and forest conservation practices was climbing extensively for soil erosion and NPS pollutants manage-ment. The modeling approach was applied to estimate 10-year impacts of imple-menting CCFP in Bazhong City in the Yangtze River watershed. With GIS tech-nologies, the agricultural land at four slope grades were converted to forest, re-spectively, which indicated typical CCFP implementation levels. The 10 years' average simulation about sediment, streamflow, organic N, and organic P in the four scenarios were calculated. By SWAT modeling, the estimations demon-strated CCFP benefits about soil erosion and NPS pollution at regional scale. The results revealed that the organic N and organic P decreased 42.1% and 62.7%, re-spectively, when agricultural land with slope greater than 7.5% was transferred to forest. With regression principle between pollutant load and forest area ratio, the environmental benefits of CCFP at any level can be calculated. Quantifications of benefits of soil erosion and water quality were necessary for future planning.

The SWAT modeling approach was proved an effective tool for decision-makers to assess benefits of CCFP at watershed level. SWAT system was useful to identify effects of CCFP applied in a new watershed or to quantify long-term environmental consequences of CCFP in a watershed where they have been al-ready carried out. However, we only discussed the land use conversions in this ar-ticle. The other land management practices, which also cause better regional envi-ronmental quality, were not modeled.

## Acknowledgments

The authors gratefully acknowledge the Chinese National Nature Science Com-mittee for financial support, which enabled this research (Grant Number 40471127) to be carried out. We would also like to thank the local helpers who assisted during the field investigations and the local governments for providing data.

## References

Arnold, J.G., Allen, P.M., Muttiah, R.S., and Bernhardt, G. 1995. Automated base flow separation and recession analysis techniques. Ground Water 33(6):1010–1018

Arnold, J.G., and Fohrer, N. 2005. SWAT2000: current capabilities and research oppor-tunities in applied watershed modeling. Hydro-logic Processes 19:563–572

Arnold, J.G., Srinivasan, R., Muttiah, R.S. 1998. Large area hydrologic modeling and assessment. Part I: Model development. Journal of the American Water Resources Asso-ciation 34(1):73–89

Attwood, J.D., McCarl, B., Chi-Chung, Chen, et al. 2000. Assessing regional impacts of change: linking economic and environmental models. Agricultural Systems. 63(3):147–159

**Behera, S., and Panda, R. 2006.** Evaluation of management alternatives for an agricultural watershed in a sub-humid subtropical region using a physical process based model. Agriculture, Ecosystems and Environment 113:62–72

**Chen Ching-Ho, Liu Wei-Lin, and Leu Horng-Guang. 2006.** Sustainable Water Quality Management Framework and a Potential impacts of climate change on groundwater recharge and stream flow in a central European low mountain range. Journal of Hydrology 284:244–252

**Cheng Hong-Guang, Ouyang Wei, Hao Fang-hua. et al. 2007.** The Non-point Source Pollution in Livestock-breeding Areas of the Heihe Riverbasin in Yellow River. Journal of Stochastic Environmental Research & Risk Assessment 21(3):213–221

**Eckhardta, K., and Ulbrich, U. 2003.** Strategy Planning System for a River Basin. Environmental Management 38:952–973

**Martin Plusa, Isabelle La Jeunesseb, Faycal Bouraoui, et al. 2006.** Modelling water discharges and N inputs into a Mediterranean lagoon impact on the primary production. Ecological Modelling 193:69–89

**Ramanarayanan, T.S., Srinivasan, R., and Arnold, J.G. 1996.** Modeling Wister Lake Watershed using a GIS-linked basin scale hydrologic water quality model. In: Third International Conference on Integrating Geographic Information Systems and Environmental Modeling, January, Santa Fe, NM

**Santhi, C., Srinivasan, R., and Arnold, J.G. 2006.** A modeling approach to evaluate the impacts of water quality management plans implemented in a watershed in Texas. Environmental Modelling & Software 21:1141–1157

**Tripathi, M.P., Panda, R.K., and Raghuwanshi, N.S. 2003.** Identification and Prioritization of Critical Sub-watersheds for Soil Conservation Management using the SWAT Model. Biosystems Engineering 85(3):365–379

**Wang Qingeng, Gu Gang, and Yoshiro Higano. 2006.** Toward Integrated Environmental Management for Challenges in Water Environ-mental Protection of Lake Taihu Basin in China. Environmental Management 37(5):579–588

**Wanga, Ouyanga, and H., Maclarenc, V. 2006.** Evaluation of the economic and environmental impact of converting cropland to forest: A case study in Dunhua county, China. Journal of Environmental Management. Article in Press. Available online 22 December

**Yin Hongfu, and Li Changan. 2001.** Human impact on floods and flood disasters on the Yangtze river. Geomorphology 41(2–3):105–109

**Zhang, H. 2003.** Guidance and Practice of Converting Cropland to Forest, Chinese Press of Agricultural Science and Technology 2003:3–120

**Zhang, J., and Jogensen, S.E. 2005.** Modelling of point and non-point nutrient loadings from a watershed. Environmental Modelling and Software 20:561–574

**Zhang, Xin-bao, Zhang, Yi-yun, Wen, An-bang, et al. 2003.** Assessment of soil losses on cultivated land by using the $^{137}$Cs technique in the Upper Yangtze River Basin of China. Soil and Tillage Research. 69(1-2):99–106

# 2.4 Some of the SWAT Applications in India

## Ashvin K. Gosain[1] and Sandhya Rao[2]

### Abstract

The SWAT has evolved into a comprehensive hydrological model over the last decade. The group at the Indian Institute of Technology Delhi has been fortunate enough to be connected to the development and upgradation of SWAT since 1996. SWAT has been very extensively used by this group in India using various versions of SWAT as they kept getting released. In the present paper only some of these applications which represent different problems have been selected and presented very briefly. The intent has been to report the range of applications belonging to diversified problems and spatial scales to which SWAT has been deployed in India. It may also be mentioned that there have been many additional applications by many more researchers where they have used SWAT as well as many ongoing studies where SWAT is being used but have not been reported here.

**Keywords:** SWAT, watershed, climate change, pollution, hydrological modeling

## 1. Introduction

There have been a large number of applications involving use of SWAT model in India. It has been intended to select only those applications that represent different problems tackled by using the SWAT. Brief descriptions of these studies have been presented below

## 2. Climate Change Impact Assessment of Indian Water Resources

The project on *"Vulnerability Assessment & Adaptation for Water Sector"* is a component of the NATCOM – national project undertaken by the Ministry of Environment and Forests of India for making the India's initial National Communication to the United Nations Framework Convention on Climate Change (UNFCCC). The possible impacts of the climate change on the water resources were quantified by performing distributed hydrological modeling of the river basins of the country using SWAT (Gosain et al., 2006).

---

© 2009 World Association of Soil and Water Conservation, *Soil and Water Assessment Tool (SWAT): Global Applications,* eds. Jeff Arnold, Raghavan Srinivasan, Susan Neitsch, Chris George, Karim Abbaspour, Philip Gassman, Fang Hua Hao, Ann van Griensven, Ashvin Gosain, Patrick Debels, Nam Won Kim, Hiroaki Somura, Victor Ella, Attachai Jintrawet, Manuel Reyes, and Samran Sombatpanit, pp. 163-182.
[1]Professor, IIT Delhi, New Delhi, India gosain@civil.iitd.ac.in
[2]Executive Director, INRM Consultants Pvt. Ltd., New Delhi, India

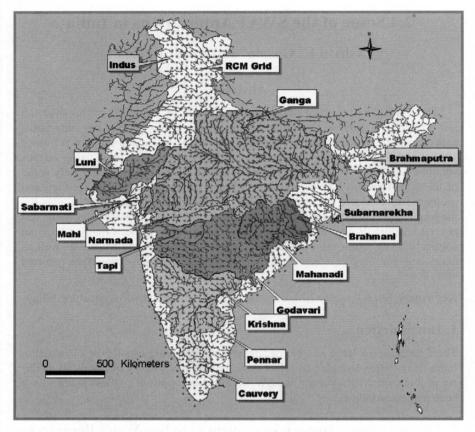

**Figure 1.** The modeled river basins along with the HadRM2 Grid Locations.

Simulation of 12 major river basins of the country as shown in Figure 1 have been conducted, with 20 years belonging to control (present) and the remaining 20 years for GHG (future) climate scenario.

The daily data generated in transient experiments by the Hadley Centre for Climate Prediction, UK, at a resolution of 0.44° x 0.44° latitude by longitude RCM (Regional Climate Model) grid points (Fig. 1) has been obtained from IITM[1] (Indian Institute of Tropical Meteorology), Pune, India. The initial analysis has revealed that the GHG scenario may deteriorate the conditions in terms of severity of droughts and intensity of floods in various parts of the country and that there is a general reduction in the quantity of the available runoff under the GHG scenario.

[1]The scenarios are generated at Indian Institute of Tropical Meteorology, Pune, using Met Office Hadley Center regional climate model PRECIS. Part of the funding for generating these scenarios is provided through the projects funded by MoEF, India and DEFRA, UK.

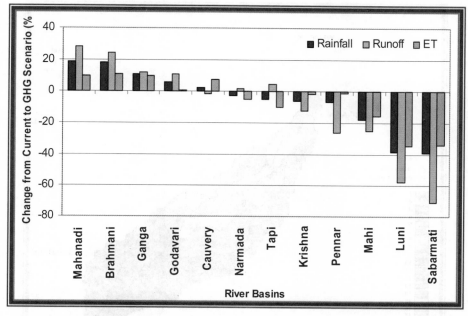

**Figure 2.** Percent change in mean annual water balance from Control to GHG Scenario.

The difference of long-term averages of some of the major water balance components from present to future for the analyses of river systems are presented in Figure 2.

The study has been carried out with the following assumptions

- The land use does not change over time

- The river systems have been assumed to be in virgin conditions, i.e. no man-made change such as reservoirs has been incorporated at this stage due to lack of data on their capacities and the operation rules (this situation is being improved upon by incorporating the baseline during the Second National Communication work on which is under progress).

## 3. Assessment of Return Flow on Account of Irrigation Project

The SWAT was used on Palleru subbasin (K-11), a subbasin of River Krishna in southern India. The length of Palleru River from its source to its outfall is about 152 km. There are seven tributaries joining the Palleru River. There is one gage and discharge site is maintained by Central Water Commission (CWC) at Palleru Bridge. There are 12 rain gage stations in and around the basin (Fig. 3). The daily rainfall data for these are available for the period from 1963 to 1994. The sub-basin experiences predominantly southwest monsoon. June to November is consi-

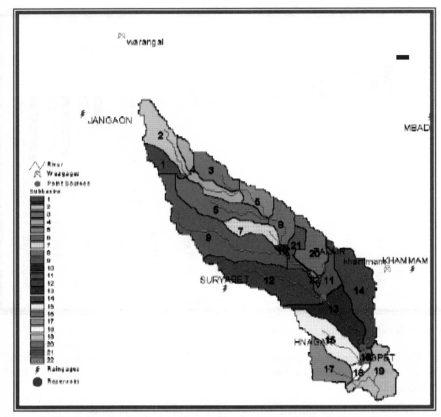

**Figure 3.** The Palleru basin along with its subbasins automatically delineated.

dered as monsoon months. Land use consists of agriculture, forest, urban, barren and rocky. Major crops grown are paddy, millet, groundnut and pulses.

The target question was to assess the return flow on account of introducing the canal irrigation in the Palleru basin. Since the return flow is dependent on many aspects such as soil characteristics, method of irrigation, etc., it is not appropriate to put a thumb rule value on such quantities. The SWAT has been deployed to assess the return flow and validated. The virgin flows from the basin, before the man-made changes of construction of reservoir and importing water for irrigation were introduced, were also computed as per the requirement of the water resources department of the State of Andhra Pradesh (Gosain et al., 2005).

The SWAT has been validated using the available flow data for the post irrigation project and the plot of monthly observed verses simulated flow has been shown in Figure 4. A value of $R^2$ of 0.84 has been achieved for the simulation.

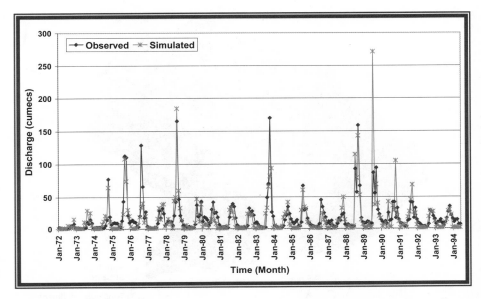

**Figure 4.** Plot showing monthly observed vs. simulated discharge at Bridge Site, Palleru River.

## 4. Modeling Non-Point Source Pollution of Nitrate with SWAT Model

Groundwater pollution from agricultural areas because of excess nutrients is causing a major concern in India. The Upper Yamuna River basin, a tributary basin of Ganges, has been used as a case for demonstration of the use of SWAT for modeling of hydrology, and hydro-chemistry (Narula and Gosain, 2007). The upper Yamuna catchment constitutes an area of 12,000 sq km, out of the total catchment area of 19,300 sq km upto Delhi.

The SWAT model has been applied on various subbasins of Upper Yamuna basin (Fig. 5). The results of the flow simulation, nitrate load simulation and comparison of simulated nitrate load with the observed load at Lakhwar have been presented in Figures 6 (a), (b) and (c), respectively.

## 5. Watershed-Scale Simulation – Karso Watershed Case

This was one of the first few applications of SWAT at the watershed scale. The Karso watershed with an area of 27 sq km (Fig. 7) was one of the very few watersheds where flow measurements were being made and were available under the Damodar Valley Project of Bihar State. The other data required for the modeling that is usually missing was available at a reasonably good scale in this watershed. For example, 5 m contours, detailed land use map, detailed soil map, a weather station were all available.

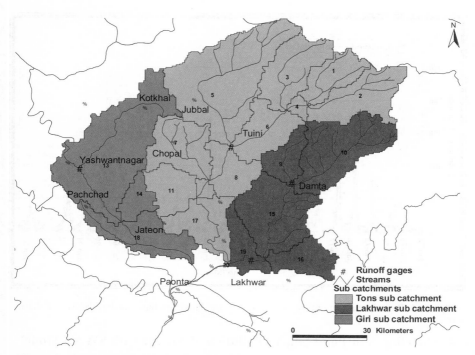

**Figure 5.** Upper Yamuna river subbasins modeled.

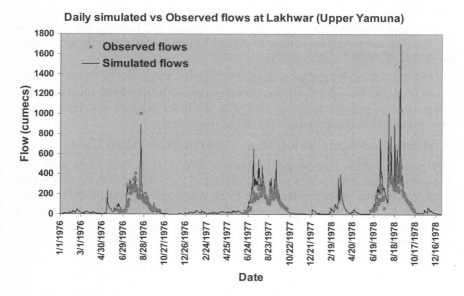

**Figure 6 (a).** Observed and simulated flow for Lakhwar subbasin.

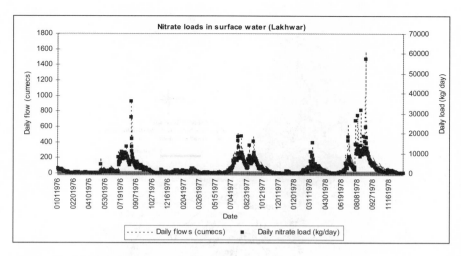

**Figure 6 (b).** Simulated nitrate load at Lakhwar.

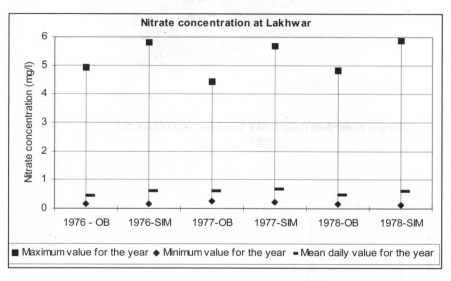

**Figure 6 (c).** Observed and simulated concentrations of nitrate at Lakhwar.

It was very encouraging to get the flow simulation to the extent shown in Figure 8 for such a small watershed and that too without much calibration (Pasricha, 1999).

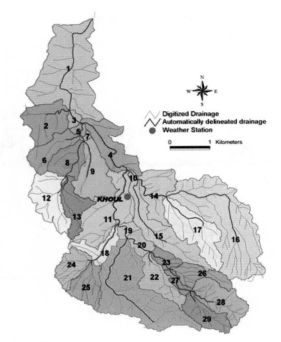

**Figure 7.** Layout of the Karso watershed.

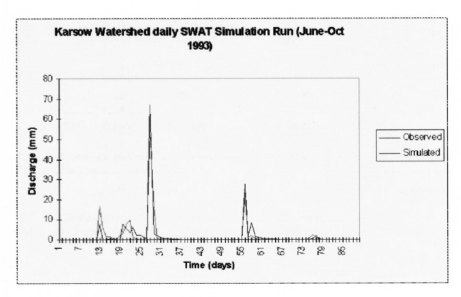

**Figure 8.** Observed and simulated flow for the Karso.

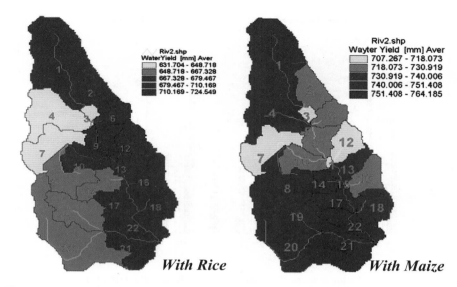

Figure 9. Impact of change in cropping pattern on water yield in Gandeshwari watershed.

## 6. Watershed-Scale Simulation – Gandeshwari Watershed Case

The intent of this study was to develop and implement new technologies in the field of watershed management. The development was undertaken through a sponsored research project titled *"Water Resources Management in Watershed Management Decision Support System (WMDSS)"* sponsored by the Department of Science and Technology, India, which was in turn a sub-segment of the UNDP project on *"GIS-based Technologies for Local Level Development Planning"*.

In India, emphasis is being placed on making the local level users to participate in the management of the natural resources at the watershed level. Therefore it is imperative that these local level organizations be strengthened by providing the integrated watershed management tools that are very user-friendly but still use all the scientific knowledge to arrive at the appropriate decisions. Invariably, they will need to assess the impact of changes made in the land use. In the agricultural area, since the common change is in the form of change in the cropping pattern, one would like to assess as to what will be the situation if one changes the cropping pattern of the area. This assessment can be with respect to the prevailing rainfall of the area if only rainfed agriculture is to be considered. However, one can also assess the requirement of supplementary irrigation in case stress levels developed with respect to a specific cropping pattern. Another concern about introduction of changed cropping pattern shall be its impact on the runoff generation. An example case has been developed in the Gandeshwari watershed with an area of 100.8 sq km to depict such scenario and is presented below.

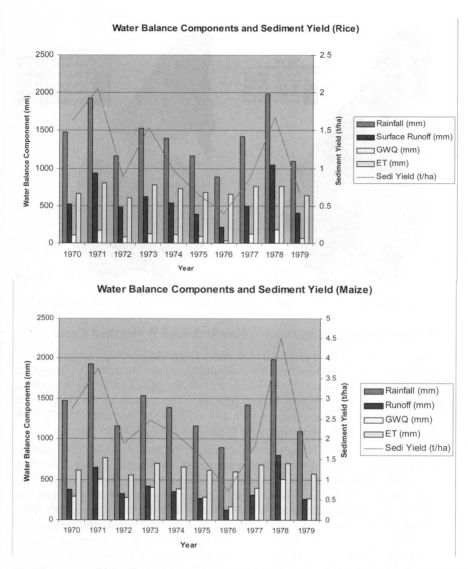

**Figure 10.** Impact of change in cropping pattern on water yield and other components of water balance in Gandeshwari watershed.

Figure 9 presents the average impact of changing the cropping pattern from rice to maize in various sub-watersheds of Gandeshwari watershed. Figure 10 depicts the average impact of such change in the cropping pattern on many components of water balance such as runoff, groundwater, and evapotranspiration besides giving the sediment yield from the Gandeshwari watershed on an annual basis (Gosain and Rao, 2004).

## 7. Watershed-Scale Simulation – Watersheds of Madhya Pradesh and Himachal Pradesh

Water resources development is a continuous process and involves interventions made at various levels and scales. One extreme of such interventions can be in the form of major water resources development projects catering hydropower and irrigation demand. The other extreme of such interventions is small-scale structures mainly for soil and water conservation, at the village level, fulfilling the requirements of a small community. While the planning is done scientifically for the big projects, it is invariably missing while incorporating the interventions at the local/ watershed level.

Therefore, it is essential to generate biophysical information that can be used to generate scenarios, which in turn can help in local level planning and management of land and water resources while keeping track of upstream-downstream connectivity. The project *'Low Base Flows and Livelihoods in India'* (LOWFLOWS, R8171) sponsored by DfID, UK, was undertaken to demonstrate the strength of hydrological modeling for monitoring and evaluation of such watershed development programs. The project had selected two watersheds, one each in the states of Himachal Pradesh and Madhya Pradesh (DfID, 2006).

In the case of Madhya Pradesh it was the twin watersheds of Dudhi and Bewas that belong to different drainage systems. The delineated watersheds along with their sub-watersheds (as per threshold value of 50 ha) are shown in Figure 11.

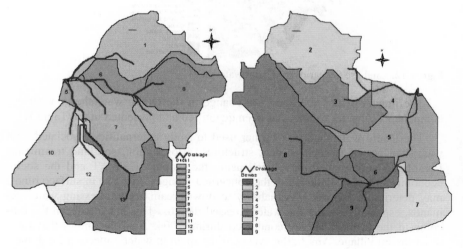

**Figure 11.** Dudhi and Bewas watersheds with their sub-watersheds.

173

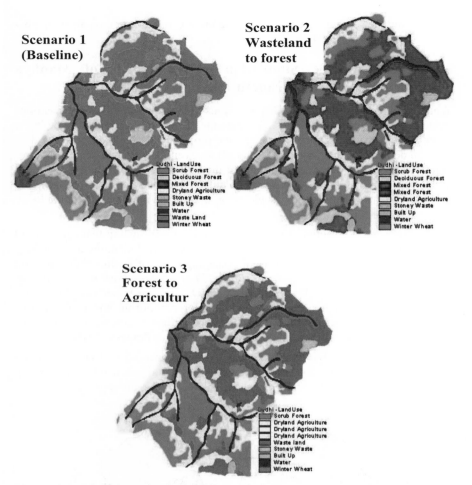

**Figure 12.** Land use Scenarios for Dudhi watershed.

The impact of possible land use change in the Dudhi watershed on various components of water balance has been quantified and presented in the Table 1.

The Dudhi watershed was further used to study externalities associated with watershed activities such as new structures, afforestation, soil/land treatments. Livelihood indices were developed using the output of SWAT and the socio-economic surveys conducted in the concerned villages. Increase in surface runoff may deteriorate the water availability to downstream areas, stressing water demands, especially during the water-stressed months. This has also been the outcome in the primary survey conducted during 2004. Analysis shows that for a downstream village, Amoli, the average time spent in water collection for domestic uses has increased by about 4% (Lodha and Gosain, 2007).

**Table 1.** Water balance components under different Land use Scenarios for Dudhi watershed.

| Average Annual over 4 | Rain (mm) | Surface Runoff | Water yield | GW Recharge - Shallow | Actual ET | Lateral Flow | PET |
|---|---|---|---|---|---|---|---|
| Scenario 1 | 1,196.0 | 263.33 | 507.97 | 235.68 | 582.4 | 8.68 | 1,486.8 |
| Scenario 2 | 1,196.0 | 186.98 | 447.12 | 253.89 | 695.4 | 6.27 | 1,485.7 |
| Scenario 3 | 1,196.0 | 272.43 | 551.69 | 270.36 | 562.80 | 8.92 | 1,485.7 |

## 8. Watershed-Scale Simulation – The Case of Western Orissa Rural Livelihood Project (WORLP)

WORLP was a Government of Orissa (GoO) initiative managed by the Orissa Watershed Development Mission (OWDM). It was funded through the Government of India by the Department for International Development (DfID) of the UK Government. WORLP's purpose is: sustainable livelihoods, particularly of the poorest, promoted in four districts in replicable ways by 2010.

The present study was taken up with the following specific objectives:

• Demonstrate the scientific watershed development approach using SWAT Hydrological Model framework on two pilot drainage basins of Suktel and Lant in the Bolangir District

• Demonstrate the procedure for creating hydrologically correct watershed boundaries for the two identified drainage systems of Suktel and Lant catchments of Bolangir District

• Create framework for Prioritization exercise for watersheds with the provided criteria

• Demonstrate procedure for Impact Assessment of development activities in micro-watersheds

• Procedure for establishing equity and evaluating sustainability of water resource.

• Bolangir District was identified as the pilot district. Two drainage basins of Suktel and Lant belonging to the Bolangir District were identified as pilot watersheds for the study.

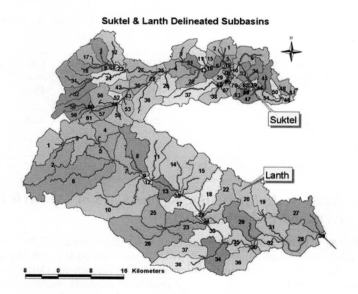

**Figure 13.** Suktel and Lanth subbasins delineated automatically.

The Suktel watershed is divided into 91 subbasins using a threshold value of 1,500 ha. Two of the tributaries of Suktel were further subdivided into a number of sub-watersheds in order to incorporate micro-watershed level modeling using plot level cadastral information using APEX model. Similarly, the Lanth watershed is delineated and subdivided into 39 subbasins by using a threshold value of 3,200 ha (IIT Delhi, 2006).

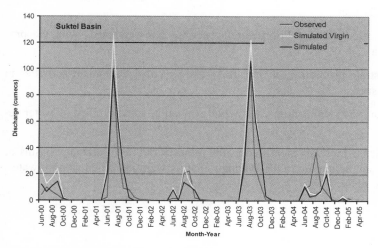

**Figure 14.** Monthly observed vs. simulated plot for Suktel basin.

176

The simulated monthly flow (cumecs) has been compared with the observed flow at M22 gage discharge station. Figure 14 shows the comparison of simulated vs. observed flows. It may be observed that the simulated flow (shown as simulated virgin in yellow) is higher than the observed flow consistently. The possible reason may be attributed to the fact that the model is simulating the basin as the virgin basin without any man-made interventions, whereas the observed flow corresponds to present baseline with appreciable interventions in the form of formed lands as well as watershed interventions. In order to implement logical baseline it has been assumed that every subbasin having an area greater than 500 ha has incorporated intervention of a collective capacity of 100 ham (hectare meter). The simulated flow (shown as simulated in blue) compares well with the observed flow. The correlation coefficient $R^2$ of 0.83 has been achieved.

## 9. Plot Level Hydrological Modeling for a Pilot Watershed of Suktel Basin

The impact of land forming on hydrological regime of a drainage basin can be depicted if we map the reformed land and use the same for hydrological modeling at the plot level. The SWAT model was not adequate to handle the layout at the cadastral level. However, a variation of the same model namely the APEX model is formulated to handle the farm level simulation. The same was used to demonstrate the impact of land forming vis-à-vis the natural areas on the hydrology.

APEX has been implemented for one subbasin of Suktel which consists of cadastral level information of Ghumer, Dabkani, Bagabhalli, Aenlatunga, Ghasian, and Tamian villages.

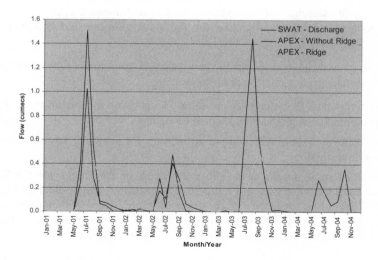

**Figure 15.** APEX simulation results.

Figure 15 shows the change in the flow regime due to reforming of the land with a 20 cm ridge around the plots. In the later situation all the water that was earlier flowing over the natural terrain is completely captured on to the plots surrounded by a ridge of 20 cm height. No water can escape the plot, unless the depth of the pool exceeds the ridge height. The impact of such reformation of land for agriculture purpose has been depicted in terms of the drastic reduction in runoff.

## 10. Small Hydropower Assessment Using GIS and Hydrological Modeling – Nagaland Case Study

Small and mini hydel potential can provide a solution for the energy problems in remote and hilly areas. Small hydro projects are useful since they allow installation of generation capacity in smaller increments to provide greater economic flexibility.

A Flow Duration Curve (FDC) provides an estimate of the percentage of time a flow discharge is exceeded over a historical period for a given drainage basin. In the case of small hydro projects most of the prospective sites are likely to be ungaged. For such potential sites, there are usually no flow data available for such analyses.

It was proposed to provide solutions using technologies of GIS and hydrological modeling to enable the users to assess the feasibility of proposed small-scale hydropower schemes. The study was sponsored by the Ministry of Non-conventional Energy Sources (MNES) presently known as MNRE (Ministry of New and Renewable Energy). Part of the Nagaland State was used as pilot drainage system to demonstrate the use of GIS based technologies and hydrological modeling for selection of hydropower sites. The following specific steps were used to achieve the set objective for the study (Gosain and Sandhya, 2007; INRM, 2004):

• Use of hydrological model for generation of continuous flow series at various locations of interest in the drainage system

• Derivation of flow duration curve for a location on the stream using the flow data generated through the hydrological modeling

Hydropower assessment is done at the sites for selecting key sites for more detailed investigation.

As an example, results of the above procedure on the Tapu system in Kohima District have been depicted in Figure 16. The extracted longitudinal profile using GIS has been used to identify all the drops of desired value within a desired horizontal distance set by the user. Four such sample locations have been identified where SWAT runs are made for flow generation and derivation of flow duration curves.

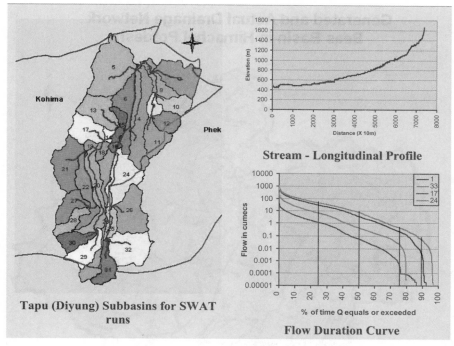

**Figure 16.** Tapu or Diyung stream, longitudinal profile and flow duration curve.

# 11. Small Hydropower Assessment Using GIS and Hydrological Modeling – Beas Basin in Himachal Pradesh Case Study

A similar exercise was undertaken but this time for a snow and glacier fed basin of Beas in the State of Himachal Pradesh (INRM, 2007). Figure 17 shows the drainage and the basin boundary of Beas. All the drainage profiles constructed from the DEM were analyzed for identification of natural drops. Watershed delineation was made at the identified points and SWAT was run to generate the flow series. Consequently flow duration curves were formulated.

Details of one such watershed namely Palachan has been given here. Since observed monthly discharge is available at the outfall from January 1988 to December 1991, validation of the model could be performed. Figure 18 shows the simulated flows for the available period at the outlet of watershed. It gives the coefficient of correlation as 0.89.

## Generated and Actual Drainage Network
## Beas Basin in Himachal Pradesh

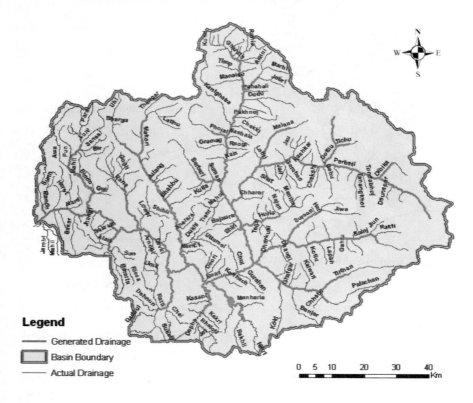

**Figure 17.** Drainage network of Beas basin in Himachal Pradesh.

The flow duration curve from the 7-year (1985-1991) simulated record of Palachan watershed is shown in Figure 19.

## Conclusion

These are only some of the applications of SWAT that have been reported here. The intent has been to report the range of applications as well as the scale of applications to which SWAT has been deployed in India. There have been many ongoing studies where SWAT is being used.

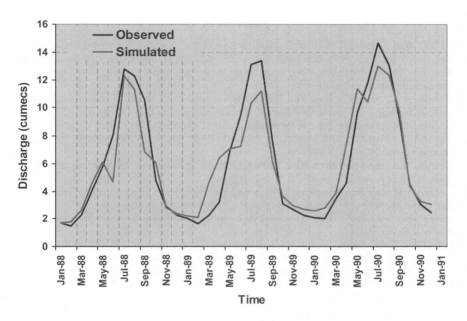

**Figure 18.** Observed vs. simulated discharge comparison (1988-1991).

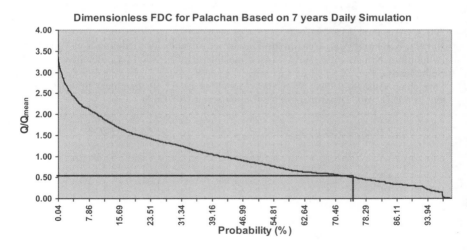

**Figure 19.** The flow duration curve from the 7-year simulated record of Palachan.

# References

**DFID, 2006.** Internal Report on 'Hydrological modelling with SWAT model in the Micro-watersheds of Madhya Pradesh and Himachal', by A. K. Gosain, Sandhya Rao, Debajit Basu Ray, Achraj Bhandari, Ian Calder, Jaime Amezaga, James Garratt, Low Base Flows and Livelihoods in India (R8171)

**Gosain, A.K., Sandhya Rao, and Debajit Basuray. 2006.** Climate change impact assessment on hydrology of Indian river basins, Current Science, Vol. 90 (3), pp 346-353.

**Gosain, A.K., Sandhya Rao, R. Srinivasan and N. Gopal Reddy. 2005.** Return-flow assessment for irrigation command in the Palleru river basin using SWAT model, Hydrological Processess. 19, pp 673-682.

**Gosain, A.K., and Sandhya Rao. 2004.** GIS-based Technologies for Watershed Management, Current Science, Vol. 87 (7).

**Gosain A.K. and Sandhya Rao. 2007.** Small Hydropower Assessment using GIS and Hydrological Modelling – Nagaland Case Study, in Renewable Energy and Energy Management (Eds.) S. C. Patra, B. C. Kusre and R. Kataki, International Book Distribution Co. Pp 33-46.

**IIT Delhi. 2006.** Internal report on 'Participatory Development of a Preliminary WORLP Water Management Strategy', Department of Civil Engineering, IIT Delhi.

**INRM. 2007.** Internal report on 'Flow Assessment of Streams of Beas Basin in Himachal Pradesh Using Hydrological Modelling and Hydropower Site Selection', MNRE/HP/M-1, INRM Consultants Pvt Ltd, New Delhi, India.

**INRM. 2004.** Internal report on GIS-Based Hydrological Modelling for Hydropower Assessment at Ungauged Sites in Nagaland, MNES, GoI, INRM Consultants Pvt Ltd, New Delhi, India

**Lodha, P.P. and A.K. Gosain. 2007.** Externalities in watershed management, Changes in Water Resources Systems: Methodologies to Maintain Water Security and Ensure Integrated Management (Proceedings of Symposium HS3006 at IUGG2007, Perugia, July 2007). IAHS Publ. 315, 2007.

**Narula, K.K. and A.K. Gosain. 2007.** Reaction Kinetics for Modeling Non-Point Source Pollution of Nitrate with SWAT Model, 4th International SWAT Conference, Delft, The Netherlands.

**Pasricha, Asutosh, 1999,** 'Watershed Modelling Using Geographical Information System', Ph.D. Thesis, Department of Civil Engineering, IIT Delhi.

# 2.5 Modeling Blue and Green Water Resources Availability in Iran

## Monireh Faramarzi[1], Karim C. Abbaspour[1], Rainer Schulin[2] and Hong Yang[1]

## Abstract

An exact knowledge of the internal renewable water resources of a country is a strategic information which is needed for long-term planning of a nation's water and food security, among many other needs. New modeling tools allow this quantification with high spatial and temporal resolution. In this study we used the program Soil and Water Assessment Tool (SWAT) in combination with the Sequential Uncertainty Fitting program (SUFI-2) to calibrate and validate a hydrologic model of Iran based on river discharges and wheat yield, taking into consideration dam operations and irrigation practices. Uncertainty analyses were also performed to assess the model performance. The results were quite satisfactory for most of the rivers across the country. We quantified all components of the water balance including blue water flow (water yield plus deep aquifer recharge), green water flow (actual and potential evapotranspiration), and green water storage (soil moisture) at subbasin level with monthly time steps. The spatially aggregated water resources and simulated yield compared well with the existing data. The study period was 1990-2002 for calibration and 1980-1989 for validation. The results show that irrigation practices have a significant impact on the water balances of the provinces with irrigated agriculture. Concerning the staple food crop in the country, 55% of irrigated wheat and 57% of rainfed wheat are produced every year in water scarce regions. The vulnerable situation of water resources availability has serious implications for the country's food security, and the looming impact of climate change could only worsen the situation. This study provides a strong basis for further studies concerning the water and food security and the water resources management strategies in the country and a unified approach for the analysis of blue and green water in other arid and semi-arid countries.

**Keywords:** SWAT, SUFI-2, internal water resources availability, irrigated wheat yield, uncertainty analysis, large-scale hydrologic modeling

---

© 2009 World Association of Soil and Water Conservation, *Soil and Water Assessment Tool (SWAT): Global Applications,* eds. Jeff Arnold, Raghavan Srinivasan, Susan Neitsch, Chris George, Karim Abbaspour, Philip Gassman, Fang Hua Hao, Ann van Griensven, Ashvin Gosain, Patrick Debels, Nam Won Kim, Hiroaki Somura, Victor Ella, Attachai Jintrawet, Manuel Reyes, and Samran Sombatpanit, pp. 183-209. The article has been reprinted from the original paper that appeared in Hydrological Processes Journal (2008), published by Wiley. WASWC is grateful for the permission granted.
[1]Eawag, Swiss Federal Institute of Aquatic Science and Technology, P.O. Box 611, 8600 Dübendorf, Switzerland. monireh.faramarzi@eawag.ch, abbaspour@eawag.ch
[2]ETH Zürich Institute of Terrestrial Ecosystem, Universitätstr. 16, 8092 Zürich, Switzerland. rainer.schulin@env.ethz.ch

# 1. Introduction

There are many studies concerning the increasing threat of water scarcity and vulnerability of water resources at regional and global scales (Postel et al., 1996; Cosgrove and Rijsberman, 2000; Vörösmarty et al., 2000; Oki and Kanae, 2006). As the agricultural sector is by far the largest water user, the main focus of most water scarcity studies is on the impact on agricultural and food security. Measures have been sought to produce more food with less water by increasing crop water productivity through effective development of genotypes and development of new technologies for integrated crop management (Kijne et al., 2003; Bouman, 2007).

Another way of dealing with water scarcity is through the use of "virtual water trade strategy" (Allan, 1997). At the global level, Yang et al. (2006) show that water saving results from virtual water trade because major flow of virtual water is from countries with large crop water productivity to countries with small crop water productivity. Within a country, virtual water trade can also result in water saving and water use efficiency at watershed and national levels. According to this concept, water scarce regions can use their water resources more efficiently by a combination of innovative local agricultural production (e.g. greenhouse and hydroponic production) and import from outside what they need to meet the local food demand. The import from outside can be thought of as 'virtual water' entering the region to compensate the local water shortages. At the national level, food self-sufficiency has been a desired objective of the Iranian government; nevertheless, large amounts of food are imported into the country in drought years. This is partly due to the lack of water for expanding agricultural production. Wheat import during the drought years of 1999 to 2001 accounted for 80% of the country's total domestic wheat supply, making Iran one the largest wheat importer of the world at the time (FAO, 2005).

Given the close relationship between water and food, a systematic assessment of water resources availability with high spatial and temporal resolution is essential in Iran for strategic decision-making on food security. Although initiatives have been taken to quantify water availability by the Ministry of Energy (MOE), the implementation has been slow and non-systematic so far. To our knowledge the national water planning report by the MOE (1998) is the only available source, which provides water resources availability data in surface water and harvestable groundwater resources on a regional scale for Iran. There is, however, a lack of information with adequate spatial and temporal resolution concerning the hydrological components affecting the availability of water resources in the country.

Water resource development through the water transfer projects, construction of dams, weirs and levees, and extraction of water for irrigation purposes can significantly alter the hydrology (Thoms and Sheldon, 2000). In arid and semi-arid countries such as Iran, due to the low rate, high variability and uneven distribution of precipitation, water resources in aquifers and rivers are subject to high levels of exploitation and diversion from their natural conditions (Abrishamchi and

Tajrishi, 2005). Accounting for these man-made changes in water courses presents a formidable challenge in hydrological modeling. Furthermore, irrigated agriculture, which uses more than 90% of total water withdrawal and more than 60% of total renewable water resources in the country (Keshavarz et al., 2005; Alizadeh and Keshavarz, 2005) has a major effect on the hydrological water balance. Therefore, incorporating water management practices (e.g. water storage by dams and irrigation in agriculture) is essential in obtaining more precise and realistic information on water resources availability in individual watersheds and in the country as a whole.

Against this background, the main objective of this study is first to calibrate and validate a hydrologic model of Iran at the subbasin level with uncertainty analysis. Second, to estimate water resources availability at the subbasin level on a monthly time step considering the impact of water resources management practices in the country. Third, to explicitly quantify hydrological components of water resources, e.g. surface runoff and deep aquifer recharge (blue water flow), soil water (green water storage) and actual evapotranspiration (green water flow). This work is intended to provide a basis for future scenario analysis of water resource management, virtual water trade and climate change in Iran. Model calibration and validation is based on river discharge data from 81 gaging stations and wheat yield data from irrigated regions. As crop yield is directly proportional to actual evapotranspiration (Jensen, 1968; FAO, 1986), model calibration using crop yield provides more confidence on the partitioning of water between soil storage, actual evapotranspiration and aquifer recharge than calibrations based on river discharge alone.

To satisfy the objectives of this study, the Soil and Water Assessment Tool (SWAT) (Arnold et al., 1998) was used to model the hydrology of Iran. SWAT is a continuous time and spatially distributed watershed model, in which components such as hydrology, crop growth related processes and agricultural management practices are considered. SWAT was preferred to other models in this project for various reasons. For example, CropWat and CropSyst (Confalonieri and Bocchi, 2005) are only capable of simulating crop growth related processes. WaterGAP 2 (Alcamo et al., 2003; Döll et al., 2003) consists of two independent components for hydrology and water use, but does not include crop growth and agricultural management practices. GIS based Erosion Productivity Impact Calculator (GEPIC) (Liu et al., 2007) addresses spatial variability of crop yield and evapotranspiration, but lacks an explicit component for large-scale hydrology. Soil and Water Integrated Model (SWIM) (Krysanova et al., 2005) was developed for use in mesoscale and large river basins (>100,000 km$^2$) mainly for climate change and land use change impact studies, and Simulation of Production and Utilization of Rangelands (SPUR) is an ecosystem simulation model developed mostly for rangeland hydrology and crops (Foy et al., 1999). For calibration and uncertainty analysis in this study, we used program SUFI-2 (Abbaspour et al., 2007a). SUFI-2 is a tool for sensitivity analysis, multi-site calibration, and uncertainty analysis. It is capable of analysing a large number of parameters and measured data from many gaging stations simultaneously. In a study Yang et al. (2008) found that SUFI-2 needed the smallest number of model runs to achieve a similarly good calibration and prediction uncertainty results in comparison with four other techniques. This efficiency is of great importance when dealing with computationally intensive, complex, and large-scale models. In addition, SUFI-2 is linked to SWAT (in the SWAT-CUP software, Abbaspour, 2007b) through an interface that includes also the programs Generalized Likelihood Uncertainty Estimation (GLUE) (Beven and Binley, 1992), Parameter Solution (ParaSol) (van Griensven and Meixner, 2006), and a Monte Carlo Markov Chain, MCMC, (Vrugt et al., 2003) algorithm.

## 2. Materials and Methods

### 2.1 The hydrologic simulator (SWAT)

SWAT is a computationally efficient simulator of hydrology and water quality at various scales. The program has been used in many international applications (Arnold and Allen, 1996; Narasimhan et al., 2005; Gosain et al., 2006; Abbaspour et al., 2007a; Yang et al., 2007; Schuol et al., 2008a,b). The model is developed to quantify the impact of land management practices on water, sediment and agricultural chemical yields in large complex watersheds with varying soils, land uses, and management conditions over long periods of time. The main components of SWAT are hydrology, climate, nutrient cycling, soil temperature, sediment movement, crop growth, agricultural management, and pesticide dynamics. In this study, we used Arc-SWAT (Olivera et al., 2006), where ArcGIS (ver. 9.1) environment is used for project development.

Spatial parameterization of the SWAT model is performed by dividing the watershed into subbasins based on topography. These are further subdivided into a series of hydrologic response units (HRU), based on unique soil and land use characteristics. The responses of each HRU in terms of water and nutrient transformations and losses are determined individually, aggregated at the subbasin level and routed to the associated reach and catchment outlet through the channel network. SWAT represents the local water balance through four storage volumes: snow, soil profile (0-2 m), shallow aquifer (2-20 m) and deep aquifer (>20 m). The soil water balance equation is the basis of hydrological modeling. The simulated processes include surface runoff, infiltration, evaporation, plant water uptake, lateral flow, and percolation to shallow and deep aquifers. Surface runoff is estimated by a modified Soil Conservation Service (SCS) curve number equation using daily precipitation data based on soil hydrologic group, land use/land cover characteristics and antecedent soil moisture.

In this study, potential evapotranspiration (PET) was simulated using Hargreaves method (Hargreaves et al., 1985). Actual evapotranspiration (AET) was predicted based on the methodology developed by Ritchie (1972). The daily value of the leaf area index (LAI) was used to partition the PET into potential soil evaporation and potential plant transpiration. LAI and root development were simulated using the 'crop growth' component of SWAT. This component represents the interrelation between vegetation and hydrologic balance. Plant growth was determined from leaf area development, light interception and conversion of intercepted light into biomass assuming a plant species-specific radiation use efficiency. Phenological plant development was based on daily accumulated heat units, potential biomass, and harvest index. Harvest index is the fraction of aboveground plant dry biomass that is removed as dry economic yield to calculate crop yield. Plant growth, in the model, can be inhibited by temperature, water, nitrogen and phosphorus stress factors. A more detailed description of the model is given by Neitsch et al. (2002).

## 2.2 Description of the study area

### i) Climate and hydrology

Iran, with an area of 1,648,000 km² is located between 25 and 40 degrees north latitude and 44 to 63 degrees east longitude. The altitude varies form -40 m to 5,670 m, which has a pronounced influence on the diversity of the climate. Although most parts of the country could be classified as arid and semiarid, Iran has a wide spectrum of climatic conditions. The average annual precipitation is 252 mm yr⁻¹.

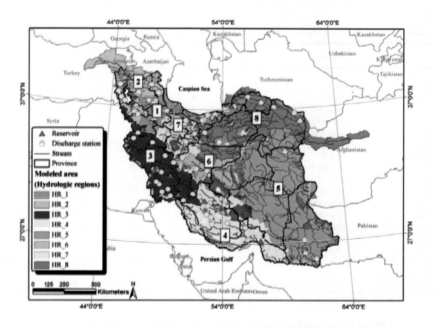

**Figure 1.** Study area and the main hydrologic regions. The dark green areas in the background include wetlands, lakes, marshes, etc., which needed to be cut from the DEM in order to have a correct river pattern. They are not included in the model.

The northern and high altitude areas found in the west receive about 1,600-2,000 mm yr$^{-1}$ (NCCO, 2003), while the central and eastern parts of the country receive less than 120 mm yr$^{-1}$. The per capita freshwater availability for the country was estimated at around 2,000 m$^3$ capita$^{-1}$ yr$^{-1}$ in the year 2000 and expected to go below 1,500 m$^3$ capita$^{-1}$ yr$^{-1}$ (the water scarcity threshold) by 2030 due to the population growth (Yang et al., 2003). Winter temperatures of -20°C and below in high altitude regions of much of the country and summer temperatures of more than 50°C in the southern regions have been recorded (NCCO, 2003).

**Table 1.** Watershed characteristics of the eight main hydrologic regions in Iran.

| Hydrologic region | Area[a] (km$^2$) | Mean precipitation[b] | Number of sub-basins | % Land use[c] BSVG | CRDY | CRGR | CRIR | CRWO | FODB | GRAS | SAVA | SHRB |
|---|---|---|---|---|---|---|---|---|---|---|---|---|
| HR 1 | 97,478 | 599 | 66 | - | - | 1.55 | 15.13 | 3.59 | 13.09 | 61.96 | 1.81 | 2.83 |
| HR 2 | 131,973 | 399 | 58 | - | 14.20 | - | - | 11.30 | - | 54.22 | 17.53 | 2.61 |
| HR 3 | 185,042 | 545 | 92 | 2.35 | 7.92 | - | - | 7.025 | - | 29.25 | - | 53.44 |
| HR 4 | 196,329 | 278 | 87 | 25.27 | - | - | - | 1.77 | - | 1.77 | - | 71.18 |
| HR 5 | 459,309 | 132 | 68 | 35.68 | 2.44 | 0.15 | 1.01 | 2.55 | 0.86 | 18.20 | 1.68 | 37.38 |
| HR 6 | 66,654 | 152 | 26 | 65.28 | - | 0.13 | 0.40 | - | - | 7.08 | - | 27.08 |
| HR 7 | 82,268 | 287 | 43 | 17.17 | - | - | - | - | - | 28.97 | - | 53.85 |
| HR 8 | 256,553 | 197 | 67 | 27.48 | 0.99 | - | - | 1.08 | - | 18.21 | - | 52.22 |

[a] Modeled area: area of sub-basins delineated in each HR were aggregated.
[b] Available from Ministry of Energy of Iran (1998) report.
[c] Extracted from USGS land use database using SWAT selected dominant land use and soil for each subbasin. BSVG: barren or sparsely vegetated, CRDY: dryland cropland pasture, CRGR: cropland-grassland mosaic, CRIR: irrigated cropland and pasture, CRWO: cropland-woodland mosaic, FODB: deciduous broadleaf forest, GRAS: grassland, SAVA: savanna, SHRB: shrub land.

**Table 2.** Characteristics of 19 large reservoirs included in the SWAT model.

| Name | River | Year of completion | Longitude (degree) | Latitude (degree) | Surface area (km$^2$) | Gross capacity (MCM)* |
|---|---|---|---|---|---|---|
| Aras | Aras | 1971 | 45.40 | 39.10 | 145 | 1,350 |
| Dez | Dez | 1962 | 48.46 | 32.61 | 62.5 | 2,600 |
| Doroudzan | Kor | 1973 | 52.49 | 30.16 | 55 | 993 |
| Gheshlagh | Gheshlagh | 1979 | 47.01 | 35.39 | 8.5 | 224 |
| Golpayegan | Ghom Rud | 1957 | 50.13 | 33.42 | 2.7 | 57 |
| Gorgan | Gorgan Rud | 1970 | 54.76 | 37.22 | 18.2 | 97 |
| Jiroft | Halil Rud | 1991 | 57.57 | 28.79 | 9.7 | 336 |
| Karaj | Karaj | 1961 | 51.09 | 35.95 | 3.9 | 205 |
| Karkheh | Karkheh | 2001 | 48.19 | 32.39 | 161 | 7,300 |
| Lar | Lar | 1982 | 52.00 | 35.89 | 29 | 960 |
| Latyan | Jaj Rud | 1967 | 51.68 | 35.79 | 2.9 | 95 |
| Maroun | Maroun | 1999 | 50.34 | 30.68 | 25.1 | 1,183 |
| Minab | Minab | 1983 | 57.06 | 27.15 | 18.2 | 344 |
| Panzdah-khordad | Ghom Rud | 1994 | 50.61 | 34.08 | 14.1 | 195 |
| Saveh | Vafregan | 1993 | 50.24 | 34.93 | 8.3 | 293 |
| Sefid Rud | Sefid Rud | 1962 | 49.38 | 36.75 | 46.4 | 1,765 |
| Shahid Abbaspour | Karun | 1977 | 49.61 | 32.06 | 51.7 | 3,139 |
| Shahid Rajayee | Tajan | 1998 | 53.30 | 36.35 | 4.1 | 191 |
| Zayandeh Rud | Zayandeh Rud | 1970 | 50.74 | 32.74 | 48 | 1,450 |

*MCM = million cubic meter.

According to the national water planning report by the MOE (1998), Iran can be divided into eight main hydrologic regions (HR) comprising a total of 37 river basins. We used the MOE hydrologic regions as the basis for comparison in our study. The eight main hydrologic regions are delineated in Figure 1.

Table 1 shows some pertinent characteristics of the eight hydrologic regions. Table 2 provides a list of dams on the major rivers that were included in the model.

In HR1, Sefid Rud and Haraz are the main rivers. Sefid Rud is 670 km long and rises in northwest Iran and flows generally east to meet the Caspian Sea. It is Iran's second longest river after Karun. A storage dam on the river was completed in 1962. Haraz is a river in northern Iran that flows northward from the foot of Mount Damavand to the Caspian Sea cutting through Alborz. A storage dam has been constructed on the Lar River which is an upstream tributary of the Haraz River. There are many other short rivers that originate from the Alborz Mountains and flow toward the Caspian Sea. This is a water-rich region in the country.

In HR2, Lake Urmiyeh is a permanent salt lake receiving several permanent and ephemeral rivers. Aras is an international river. It originates in Turkey and flows along the Turkish-Armenian border, the Iranian-Armenian border and the Iranian-Azerbaijan border before it finally meet with the Kura River, which flows into the Caspian Sea. This hydrologic region is important for agricultural activities, as the water resource availability and climatic conditions are suitable.

In HR3, Karkheh and Karun are the main rivers. They are the most navigable rivers in Iran, receiving many tributaries. HR3 is an arid and semi-arid region. Jarahi, Zohreh and Sirvan are the other main rivers in the region. Several storage dams have been constructed on the rivers and operated for many years. The region has large water resources but due to poor climatic conditions agricultural performance is moderate.

In HR4, all the rivers and streams provide relatively moderate water resources for agricultural activities. The Kor River flows into the Bakhtegan Lake at the end of its journey. The rivers Dalaki, Mond, Kol and southern coastal tributaries flow through this hydrologic region and end in the Persian Gulf.

HR5 has no major rivers. The region is classified as very arid. The only important rivers of the region are Halil Rud and Bampoor.

In HR6, the famous Zayandeh Rud is the only main river, which originates from the Zagros Mountains and ends in the Gavkhooni marsh after meandering for 420 km. There is a storage reservoir on the river with an average annual outflow of 47.5 $m^3 s^{-1}$.

In HR7, Karaj, Jaj Rud, Ghom Rud and Shor Rud are the main tributaries. The rivers originate from both the Alborz and Zagros Mountains and flow toward a Salt Lake at the central plateau of Iran.

In HR8, Atrak and Hari Rud are the most important of the six river basins. Atrak is a fast-moving river that begins in the mountains of northeastern Iran and flows westward to end at the southeastern corner of the Caspian Sea. Hari Rud is a riparian river recharged from tributaries of both Iran and Afghanistan.

Among all the trans-boundary rivers between Iran and its neighboring countries only the Hirmand River, located in HR5, was excluded from our modeling study, because its contributing area on the Iranian side only accounts for about 14% of the river basin (Chavoshian et al., 2005). This will not significantly affect the estimation of internal renewable water resources as the region is quite dry.

## ii) Cropping and irrigation

Roughly 37 million ha of Iran's total surface area is arable land. Of which, 18.5 million ha are devoted to horticulture and field crop production (Keshavarz et al., 2005). About 9 million ha of this land are irrigated using traditional and modern techniques, and 10 million ha are rainfed. Wheat is the core commodity of the Iranian food and agriculture system. It is grown on nearly 60 percent of the country's arable land. The average yield for irrigated wheat is approximately 3.0 tons ha$^{-1}$, compared to 0.95 ton ha$^{-1}$ for rainfed wheat (FAO, 2005).

In Iran, more than 90% of the total water withdrawal is used in the agricultural sector, mostly for irrigation. About 50% of the irrigation water is from surface sources and the other 50% from ground water (Ardakanian, 2005). Owing to the traditional method of irrigation and water conveying systems, the overall irrigation efficiency varies between 15% and 36% (Keshavarz et al., 2005). Therefore, a large fraction of diverted water is lost to evaporation and percolation. Irrigation practices in Iran have a large impact on the hydrological balances of the river basins.

In this study, irrigated wheat was incorporated in the modeling in order to obtain a sufficiently accurate representation of the hydrological balances, particularly for areas under irrigated agriculture. According to the information available from the Global Map of Irrigation Areas Version 4.0.1 (Siebert et al., 2007) and other sources, i.e. USDA (2003) and Statistical Center of Iran (SCI) (1990-2002), the major irrigated areas are distributed across 11 provinces (Table 3). Except for Kerman Province, where irrigated wheat is the second largest product in terms of area under irrigated farming, wheat production occupies the largest areas under irrigation in all other provinces. In this study, we use winter wheat as a representative crop for irrigated areas. To show the hydrological importance of irrigation, we ran the model with and without taking irrigated wheat into account.

## 2.3 Model inputs and model setup

Data required for this study were compiled from different sources. They include: Digital Elevation Model (DEM) that was extracted from the Global U.S. Geological Survey's (USGS, 1993) public domain geographic database HYDRO1k with a spatial resolution of 1 km (http://edc.usgs.gov/products/elevation/gtopo30/hydro/index.html). Land use map from the USGS Global Land Use Land Cover Characterization (GLCC) database with a spatial resolution of 1 km and distinguishing 24 land use/land cover classes (http://edcsns17.cr.usgs.gov/glcc/glcc.html).

**Table 3.** Proportion of irrigated areas under cultivation of wheat in different provinces.

| Province | (AIW / TIA)*100 |
|---|---|
| Bushehr | 61.27 |
| Esfahan | 43.16 |
| Fars | 49.10 |
| Ghazvin | 47.85 |
| Hormozgan | 25.40 |
| Kerman | 30.20 |
| Khorasan | 53.68 |
| Khozestan | 51.28 |
| Sistan Baluchestan | 50.82 |
| Tehran | 37.35 |
| Yazd | 37.47 |
| Zanjan | 65.96 |

Note: AIW = average (1990-2002) annual area under cultivation of irrigated wheat.
TIA = total irrigated area.

The soil map was obtained from the global soil map of the Food and Agriculture Organization of the United Nations (FAO, 1995), which provides data for 5,000 soil types comprising two layers (0-30 cm and 30-100 cm depth) at a spatial resolution of 10 km. Further data on land use and soil physical properties required for SWAT were obtained from Schuol et al. (2008a). The irrigation map was constructed from the Global Map of Irrigation Areas of the FAO (Siebert et al., 2007) which was developed by combining sub-national irrigation statistics with geospatial information on the position and extent of irrigation schemes (http://www.fao.org/ag/agl/aglw/aquastat/irrigationmap/index10.stm).

Information about the digital stream network, administrative boundaries depicting country and province boundaries, and reservoirs/dams was available from the National Cartographic Center of Iran, which provides information at a spatial resolution of 1 km.

Weather input data (daily precipitation, maximum and minimum temperature, daily solar radiation) were obtained from the Public Weather Service of the Iranian Meteorological Organization (WSIMO) for more than 150 synoptic stations. The distribution of the selected stations across the country was sufficiently representative, as the gaging station network was denser in mountainous areas. Time spans covered by the available data were from 1977 to 2004. They varied depending on the age of the weather stations. The WXGEN weather generator model (Sharpley and Williams, 1990), which is incorporated in SWAT, was used to fill in gaps in the measured records. The weather data for each subbasin is assigned automatically in SWAT using the closest weather station. River discharge data required for calibration-validation were obtained from MOE of Iran for about 90 hydrometric stations for the period of 1977 to 2002. Historical records on annual yield and area cultivated with irrigated wheat were obtained for the period of 1990 to 2002 from the Agricultural Statistics and the Information Center of Ministry of Jahade-Agriculture (MOJA) and SCI.

A drainage area of 600 km$^2$ was selected as the threshold for the delineation of watersheds. This threshold was chosen to balance between the resolution of the available information and a practical SWAT project size. This resulted in 506 subbasins which were characterized by dominant soil, land use, and slope. It should be pointed out that with the threshold of 600 km$^2$ the modeled area doesn't cover the entire land surface of the country, especially the coastal regions and some desert areas having a watershed area of less than 600 km$^2$. In these cases the results were linearly extrapolated from the closest modeled subbasins.

For a better simulation of the hydrology, the daily operation of 19 large reservoirs/dams was incorporated into the model. The operation data and parameters were obtained from the Water Resources Management Organization (WRMO) of Iran.

To simulate crop growth and crop yield, we used the auto-fertilization and auto-irrigation options of SWAT, using the available annual fertilizer use data from MOJA and assuming that there is no water stress in the production of irrigated wheat. The cumulative heat (growing degree day) required to reach maturity is almost 2,300 for wheat in Iran. The simulation period for calibration was from 1990-2002 considering 3 years as the warm up period, and for validation from 1980-1989 also using 3 years as warm up period. With the above specifications, a model run took about 15 minutes of execution time for each run in a 3 Ghz dual processor PC.

## 2.4 Calibration setup and analysis

Sensitivity analysis, calibration, validation, and uncertainty analysis were performed for the hydrology (using river discharge) as well as crop growth (using irrigated wheat yield). As these components of SWAT involve a large number of parameters, a sensitivity analysis was performed to identify the key parameters across different hydrologic regions. For the sensitivity analysis, 22 parameters integrally related to stream flow (Lenhart et al., 2002; Holvoet et al., 2005; White and Chaubey, 2005; Abbaspour et al., 2007a) and another 4 parameters related to crop growth (Ruget et al., 2002; Ziaei and Sepaskhah, 2003; Wang et al., 2005) were initially selected (Table 4). We refer to these as the 'global' parameters. In a second step, these global parameters were further differentiated by soil and land use in order to account for spatial variation in soil and land use (i.e. SCS curve number CN2 of agricultural areas was assigned differently from that of forested areas). This resulted in 268 scaled parameters, for which we performed sensitivity analysis using stepwise regression (Muleta and Nicklow, 2005).

As different calibration procedures produce different parameter sets

(Abbaspour et al., 1999; Abbaspour et al., 2007a; Schuol et al., 2008b; Yang et al., 2008), we used three different approaches here for comparison and to provide more confidence in the results. These include: (i) the 'global approach', where only the global parameters were used (26 parameters), (ii) the 'scaling approach', where parameters were differentiated by soil and land use (268 parameters), and (iii) the 'regional approach', where the scaling approach was used in each of the eight hydrologic regions, i.e. each region was calibrated separately.

The SUFI-2 (Abbaspour et al., 2007a) algorithm was used for parameter optimization according to the above schemes. In this algorithm all uncertainties (parameter, conceptual model, input, etc.) are mapped onto the parameter ranges, which are calibrated to bracket most of the measured data in the 95% prediction uncertainty (Abbaspour et al., 2007a). The overall uncertainty in the output is quantified by the 95% prediction uncertainty (95PPU) calculated at the 2.5% and 97.5% levels of the cumulative distribution of an output variable obtained through Latin hypercube sampling. Two indices are used to quantify the goodness of calibration/uncertainty performance: the *P-factor*, which is the percentage of data bracketed by the 95PPU band (maximum value 100%), and the *R-factor*, which is the average width of the band divided by the standard deviation of the corresponding measured variable. Ideally, we would like to bracket most of the measured data (plus their uncertainties) within the 95PPU band (*P-factor* ® 1) while having the narrowest band (*R-factor* ® 0).

In order to compare the measured and simulated monthly discharges we used a slightly modified version of the efficiency criterion defined by Krause et al. (2005):

$$\Phi = \begin{cases} |b|R^2 & for \quad |b| \leq 1 \\ |b|^{-1}R^2 & for \quad |b| > 1 \end{cases} \tag{1}$$

where $R^2$ is the coefficient of determination between the measured and simulated signals and $b$ is the slope of the regression line.

For multiple discharge stations, the objective function was simply an average of F for all stations within a region of interest:

$$g = \frac{1}{n}\sum_{i=1}^{n}\Phi_i \tag{2}$$

where $n$ is the number of stations. The function F varies between 0 and 1 and is not dominated by a few badly simulated stations. This is contrary to Nash-Sutcliffe, where a large negative objective function (i.e. a badly simulated station) could dominate the optimization process.

**Table 4.** Initially selected input parameters in the calibration process.

| Name[a] | Definition | t-value[b] | p-value[c] |
|---|---|---|---|
| v__SURLAG.bsn | Surface runoff lag time (days) | 3.091 | 0.00211 |
| v__SMTMP.bsn | Snow melt base temperature (°C) | 6.448 | $2.76 \times 10^{-10}$ |
| v__SFTMP.bsn | Snowfall temperature (°C) | 4.985 | 8.66E-07 |
| v__SMFMN.bsn | Minimum melt rate for snow during the year (mm/°C-day) | 2.95 | 0.00333 |
| v__TIMP.bsn | Snow pack temperature lag factor | 2.493 | 0.013 |
| r__CN2.mgt | SCS runoff curve number for moisture condition II | 19.801 | $2 \times 10^{-16}$ |
| v__ALPHA_BF.gw | Base flow alpha factor (days) | 2.179 | 0.02983 |
| v__REVAPMN.gw | Threshold depth of water in the shallow aquifer for 'revap' to occur (mm) | 2.146 | 0.03236 |
| v__GW_DELAY.gw | Groundwater delay time (days) | 3.633 | 0.00031 |
| v__GW_REVAP.gw | Groundwater revap. coefficient | 2.972 | 0.00311 |
| v__GWQMN.gw | Threshold depth of water in the shallow aquifer required for return flow to occur (mm) | 2.849 | 0.00457 |
| v__RCHRG_DP.gw | Deep aquifer percolation fraction | 5.184 | $3.20 \times 10^{-7}$ |
| v__ESCO.hru | Soil evaporation compensation factor | 5.568 | $4.28 \times 10^{-8}$ |
| r__SOL_AWC.sol | Soil available water storage capacity (mm $H_2O$/mm soil) | 8.841 | $2 \times 10^{-16}$ |
| r__SOL_K.sol | Soil conductivity (mm/hr) | 2.018 | 0.04414 |
| r__SOL_BD.sol | Soil bulk density (g/cm$^3$) | 7.908 | $1.79 \times 10^{-14}$ |
| v__SMFMX.bsn | Maximum melt rate for snow during the year (mm/°C-day) | 0.070 | 0.944 |
| v__EPCO.hru | Plant uptake compensation factor | 1.097 | 0.273 |
| r__OV_N.hru | Manning's n value for overland flow | 0.004 | 0.996 |
| r__SOL_ALB.sol | Moist soil albedo | 0.241 | 0.809 |
| v__CH_N2.rte | Manning's n value for main channel | 0.871 | 0.384 |
| v__CH_K2.rte | Effective hydraulic conductivity in the main channel (mm/hr) | 0.974 | 0.330 |
| v__HI | Harvest index | - | - |
| v__HEAT-UNITS | Crop required heat units | - | - |
| v__AUTO-WSTRS | Water stress factor | - | - |
| v__AUTO-NSTRS | Nitrogen stress factor | - | - |

[a] v__ : The parameter value is replaced by given value or absolute change; r__ : parameter value is multiplied by (1+ a given value) or relative change (See Abbaspour (2007b) for more detail).

[b] t-value indicates parameter sensitivity. The large the t-value, the more sensitive the parameter

[c] p-value indicates the significance of the t-value. The smaller the p-values, the less chance of a parameter being accidentally assigned as sensitive

The objective function in the global and scaling approaches was optimized based on 81 discharge stations across the modeled area. While in the regional approach, the function was optimized using the number of stations that fell in each of the eight hydrologic regions (Table 5).

## 3. Results and Discussions

### 3.1. Calibration-uncertainty analysis

The sensitivity analysis showed that most of the 22 'global parameters' of hydrology were sensitive to river discharge. Also, all crop parameters were sensitive to crop yield. These parameters are listed in Table 4 along with their $t$-value and $p$-value statistics representing their relative sensitivities. As expected, parameters such as CN2 (SCS runoff curve number), temperature parameters, and available soil water content (SOL_AWC) were most sensitive.

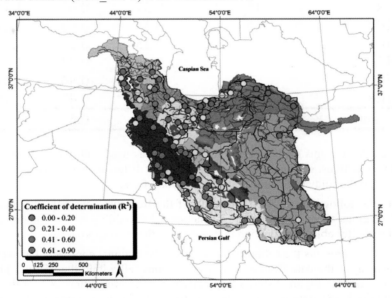

**Figure 2.** Comparison of observed and simulated discharges using coefficient of determination ($R^2$) for 81 stations across the country resulting from the regional approach calibration procedure.

Of the 268 parameters differentiated by soil and land use in the scaling and regional approach, 130 were also sensitive to hydrology and crop yield.

The three calibration procedures produced similar goodness of fit for the whole of Iran in terms of the objective function $g$, the *P-factor*, and the *R-factor*. The optimized parameter ranges, however, were different for the three procedures. Such non-uniqueness is typical for the calibration of hydrologic models. It states that if there is a model that fits the measurements, then there will be many such models with different parameter ranges. Yang et al. (2008) used four different calibration procedures, namely GLUE, MCMC, ParaSol, and SUFI-2 for a watershed in China. All four gave a very similar goodness of fit in terms of $R^2$, Nash-Sutcliffe, *P-factor* and *R-factor*, but converged to quite different parameter

**Table 5.** Calibration performances of regional approach procedure.

| Hydrologic region | Number of stations | Regional approach | | |
|---|---|---|---|---|
| | | Goal function | *P-factor* | *R-factor* |
| HR1 | 16 | 0.22 | 0.40 | 0.95 |
| HR2 | 10 | 0.20 | 0.52 | 0.82 |
| HR3 | 15 | 0.37 | 0.62 | 1.14 |
| HR4 | 15 | 0.32 | 0.65 | 1.89 |
| HR5 | 5 | 0.25 | 0.64 | 3.66 |
| HR6 | 7 | 0.43 | 0.43 | 1.80 |
| HR7 | 7 | 0.30 | 0.46 | 1.38 |
| HR8 | 6 | 0.28 | 0.47 | 2.26 |
| Country | 81 | 0.3 | 0.53 | 1.52 |

ranges. Also in this study, where only SUFI-2 was used with three different objective functions, all three procedures resulted in different final parameter values similar to the study of Schuol et al. (2008b) for Africa.

In the following, we used the result of the 'regional approach', because the eight regions accounted for more of the spatial variability in the country and a slightly better objective function than with the other two approaches.

Table 5 presents the calibration results for the regional approach. On average, 53 percent of the data from 81 discharge stations fell within the 95PPU. The *R-factor* was 1.52. Figure 2 shows the coefficient of determination ($R^2$) for the individual discharge stations across the country. Most of the stations in HR3, HR4, and HR6 were described with an $R^2$ of more than 0.5. There are still some poorly simulated stations with $R^2$ values of less than 0.15. The small *P-factor* and large *R-factor* values for these stations represent large uncertainties. Based on the information we obtained by consulting the local experts, possible reasons for the poor model calibration in some regions include insufficient accounting of agricultural and industrial water use in the model, inter-basin water transfer projects in humid and arid zones (Abrishamchi and Tajrishi, 2005), and the construction or operation of more than 200 reservoirs in the country during the period of study (Ehsani, 2005).

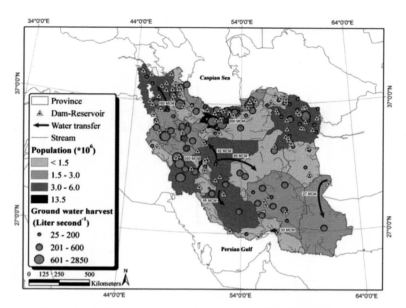

**Figure 3.** Water management map of the country showing some of the man's activities during the period of study. The map shows locations of dams, reservoirs, water transfers, and ground water harvest. Map's background shows Provincial-based population.

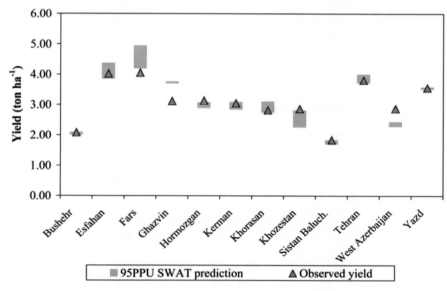

**Figure 4.** Comparison of observed and simulated (expressed as 95% prediction uncertainty band) annual wheat yield averaged over the years 1990-2002 for different provinces.

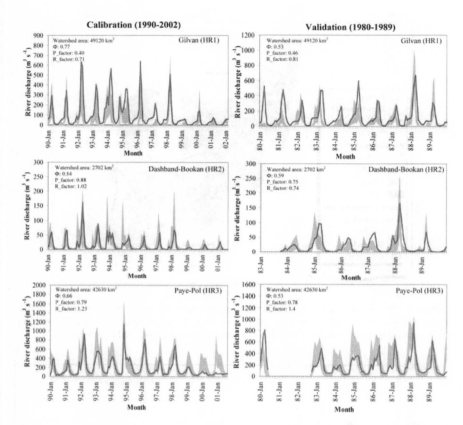

**Figure 5.** Comparison of the observed (red line) and simulated (expressed as 95% prediction uncertainty band) discharges for three hydrometric stations located in hydrologic regions HR1, HR2, and HR3. Calibration (left) and validation (right) results are shown.

We constructed a "water management map" for the country for the period of study as illustrated in Figure 3. This management map shows the spatial distribution of some of the man's activities influencing natural hydrology during the period of study. Regions with the highest activities have the worst calibration/validation results (compare with Fig. 2) as well as the largest uncertainties. The construction of dams, reservoirs, roads and tunnels can affect the local hydrology for many years. This is an important and often neglected source of uncertainty in large-scale hydrological modeling. As the extent of management in water resources development increases, hydrological modeling will become more and more difficult and will depend on the availability of detailed knowledge of the management operations.

Calibration of a large-scale distributed hydrologic model against river discharge alone may not provide sufficient confidence for all components of the water balance. Multi-criteria calibration is suggested by Abbaspour et al. (2007a) for

198

a better characterization of different components and as a way of dealing with the non-uniqueness problem (narrowing of the prediction uncertainty).

Because of the direct relationship between crop yield and evapotranspiration (FAO, 1986; Jensen, 1968), we included yield as an additional target variable in the calibration process in order to improve the simulation of ET, soil moisture, and deep aquifer recharge. Figure 4 shows the calibration results for the winter wheat yield across 12 major irrigated-wheat producing provinces. As illustrated, observed yields for all provinces are inside or very close to the predicted bands indicating good results. We are assuming that if yield is correct, then actual evapotranspiration and also soil moisture are simulated correctly. This in turn indicates that deep aquifer recharge is correct; hence, increasing our confidence on the calculated blue water, that is the sum of river discharge and deep aquifer recharge.

For validation (1980-1989), we used the parameters obtained by the regional approach to predict river discharges at the stations not affected by upstream reservoirs. Only these stations were chosen because data on daily outflow from reservoirs were not available for the validation period. In Figure 5, some examples of calibration and validation results are illustrated for individual stations in HR1-3. In general, the results of calibration and validation analysis based on river discharge and crop yield were quite satisfactory for the whole country. Next, we calculated water resources using the calibrated model and compared it with the available data as a further check of the performance of the model.

### 3.2 Quantification of water resources at provincial and regional levels

Monthly internal renewable blue water resources (IRWR, the summation of water yield and deep aquifer recharge) were calculated for all of 506 subbasins included in the model. Furthermore, the monthly IRWR of subbasins were aggregated to estimate the regional, provincial and national IRWR availability. Figure 6 compares the predicted regional IRWR with the values published by MOE (1998) and the prediction for the whole country with MOE and FAO estimates (FAO, 2003; Banaei et al., 2005). The MOE estimate is based on the long-term (1966-1994) averages of net precipitation, which is annual precipitation minus annual evapotranspiration. The FAO estimates are based on long-term (1961-1990) averages of annual surface and groundwater flow generated from precipitation. As shown in Figure 6, the FAO and MOE estimates are within or close to the 95PPU of our model predictions. Confidence in model results increases as most of the observed wheat yield (Fig. 4) and IRWR fall within the uncertainty band of model prediction.

Figure 7 shows the IRWR and actual ET or green water flow (Falkenmark and Rockstrom, 2006) for 30 provinces. For a better inter-provincial comparison we show also annual precipitation. In general, for some provinces uncertainty ranges of average annual IRWR are wide and this is especially true for the provinces with higher precipitation.

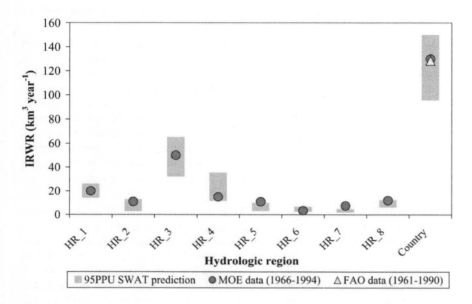

**Figure 6.** Comparison of simulated average (1990-2002) annual regional internal renewable blue water resources (IRWR) with the available data from the Ministry of Energy (MOE) and FAO for the entire country.

Similar results were also shown by Schuol et al. (2008a,b) in their study of water resources in Africa. A larger uncertainty band for some provinces might be due to higher conceptual model uncertainty as water management projects (not included in the model) could alter natural hydrology as discussed previously. A comparison of the results in Figure 7 and the "water management map" in Figure 3 shows the correspondence between high uncertainty provinces and the ones with substantial managements. It should be noted that the reported uncertainty includes both modeling uncertainties as well as natural heterogeneity. Despite the uncertainties, our results are quite realistic for most provinces as they were evaluated and confirmed by local experts (personal communications with local water resources experts, 2007).

We found that irrigation in particular has a large impact on hydrologic water balance. The main advantage of accounting for irrigated agricultural areas in the model is that actual ET and soil water are simulated adequately. For example, in the Zayandeh Rud river basin (Esfahan Province, HR6) the annual precipitation has an average of 126 mm. This river basin is agricultural and is intensively irrigated from various surface and groundwater sources. By ignoring irrigation, therefore, we could never produce an ET value of over 1,000 mm per year as reported by Akbari et al. (2007). This would have created an incorrect picture of water balance in this region.

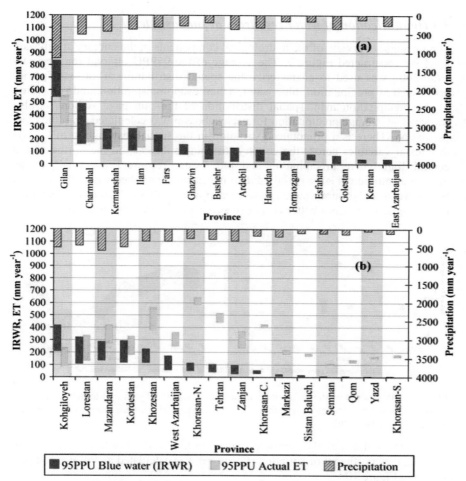

**Figure 7.** Modelled average (1990-2002) annual provincial internal renewable blue water resources (IRWR), actual evapotranspiration (ET) expressed as 95% prediction uncertainty, and precipitation.

To illustrate the impact of irrigation on water balances, we performed simulations with and without irrigation in the model. An example is shown in Figure 8 for Esfahan Province. Using the 95PPU band, the difference between ET with and without irrigation was calculated to have an average value of about 130 mm per year for the entire province. The difference becomes much larger if we take individual basins under irrigated agriculture within the province. For example, for the Zayandeh Rud river basin the calculations of ET with and without irrigation gave average values of about 850 mm and 135 mm per year, respectively. Aside from the bulk figures, the temporal distribution of the two scenarios shows pronounced differences as illustrated in Figure 8.

## 3.3 Quantification of water resources at subbasin level

For a general overview of the hydrological components in the country at subbasin level we constructed Figure 9. The average of the 95PPU interval for the years 1990-2002 was used to characterize the spatial distribution of various components such as precipitation, blue water, actual evapotranspiration, and soil water. In the precipitation map, spatial distribution of the rain gage stations is also shown. The average precipitation for each subbasin was calculated from the closest station. There is a pronounced variation in the spatial distribution of the hydrological variables across the country. In many subbasins in the northeast and central Iran where precipitation and blue water resources are small, actual evapotranspiration is large mainly due to irrigation from other water sources such as reservoirs and groundwater. The soil water map in Figure 9 shows areas where rainfed agriculture has a better chance of success due to larger soil moisture.

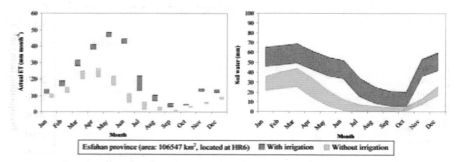

**Figure 8.** Illustration of the differences in predicted actual ET and soil moisture with and without considering irrigation in Esfahan Province. The variables are monthly averages for the period of 1990-2002.

To further illustrate the annual variations of blue water availability from 1990 to 2002, the coefficient of variation (CV in %) was calculated as follows and presented in Figure 10:

$$CV = \frac{\sigma}{\mu} \times 100$$

, (3)

where s is the standard deviation and µ is the mean of annual IRWR values for each subbasin. CV is an indicator of the reliability of the blue water resources from year to year. A large CV indicates a region experiencing extreme weather conditions such as drought; hence, having an unreliable blue water resource for development of rainfed agriculture. Figure 10 shows that central, eastern and southern parts of Iran fall into this category and have a high risk of food production in the absence of irrigation.

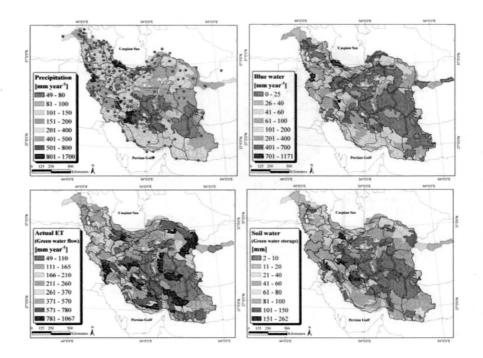

**Figure 9.** Average (1990-2002) simulated annual precipitation, internal renewable blue water resources (IRWR), actual evapotranspiration (ET), at subbasin level for the entire country.

To highlight the country's water scarcity situation, we plotted in Figure 11 the per capita internal renewable blue water availability in every subbasin. For this we used a 2.5-arcminute population map available from the Center for International Earth Science Information Network's in 2005 (CIESIN, http://sedac.ciesin.columbia.edu/gpw). As calculated here, for the entire country, the 95% prediction uncertainty of (blue) water resources availability (calculated from 1990-2002) stood at 1,310-2,060 m$^3$ per capita based on the population estimate in 2005. The spatial distribution of water resources availability in Figure 11, however, shows a large variation across the country. The five water stress levels given in the figure follow the widely used water stress indicators defined by Rijsberman (2006), Falkenmark et al. (1989) and Revenga et al. (2000). Taking 1,700 m$^3$ per capita per year as the water scarcity threshold, about 46 million people living on about 59% of the country's area are subject to water scarcity. According to the Global Geographic Distribution Map of Major Crops (Leff et al., 2004), which has a spatial resolution of 5 arcminutes and the findings from this study, about 53% of the area under cultivation of wheat in Iran is located in water scarce subbasins.

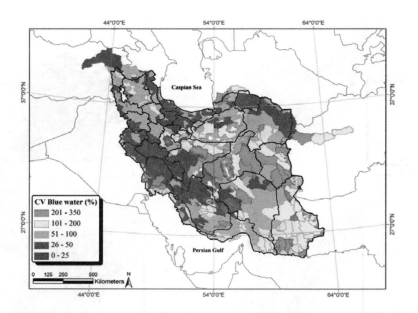

**Figure 10.** Coefficient of variation (CV) of the modeled annual (1990-2002) internal renewable blue water.

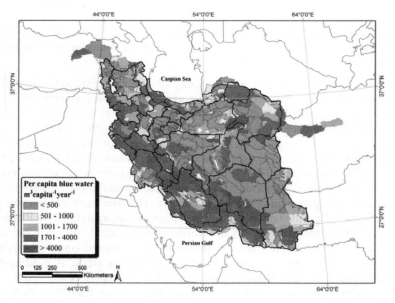

**Figure 11.** Per capita blue water availability at 506 modeled subbasins. Values of <500 indicate severe water stress, <1,000 are high water stress, 1,700 is water stress threshold, and >1,700 indicates adequate water availability.

Of the total wheat production in the country, 4.4 million tons of irrigated wheat and 1.9 million tons of rainfed wheat are produced every year in water scarce regions. In such a vulnerable situation of water resources availability, it can be expected that self-sufficiency in terms of wheat production will become even more difficult in the future, and the looming impact of climate change will further worsen the situation. All the more, it is of great importance to balance water budgets in water scarce regions and to improve the efficiency of water resources utilization.

## 4. Summary and Conclusion

Water resources availability, including internal renewable blue water, actual and potential ET as well as soil water, was estimated for Iran at the subbasin spatial and monthly temporal resolutions. The water components were then aggregated at sub-provincial, provincial, regional and country levels.

The study was performed using the process-based semi-distributed hydrologic model SWAT, which integrates hydrological, agricultural and crop growth processes. Extensive calibration, validation, as well as sensitivity and uncertainty analysis were performed to increase the reliability of the model outputs. The model was calibrated against crop yield as well as river discharge taking account of dam operation. Inclusion of irrigation was found to be essential for an accurate accounting of actual ET and soil water. SUFI-2 was used to calculate 95% prediction uncertainty band for the outputs to characterize model uncertainty.

Considering the conceptual model uncertainty (e.g. inter-basin water transfer, water use) as well as input data uncertainty and parameter uncertainty in such a large-scale hydrological model, presentation of the freshwater availability as 95PPU band is useful for the water resources management and planning in the individual regions and for the country as a whole.

This study provides a strong basis for further studies concerning water and food security in Iran. Producing more food with increasing water scarcity is a daunting challenge to the country. Water resources availability and wheat yield across provinces/regions in Iran as well as water scarcity distribution were successfully estimated, laying the basis for a systematic assessment of crop water productivity. Among other measures, with the current study, scenario analysis could be used to support the evaluation of the potential improvement in the regional and national water productivity and water use efficiency through regional crop structure adjustment and regional virtual water trade. The modeling approach in this study could be used for a high resolution analysis of water resources and a unified analysis of the blue and green water in other arid and semi-arid countries.

## Acknowledgments

This study was supported by the Swiss National Science Foundation (Project Nr: 205121-113890). The authors are especially grateful to the Iranian Water Resources Management Organization (WRMO), the Weather Service of the Iranian Meteorological Organization (WSIMO), the Ministry of Energy (MOE), the Agricultural Engineering Research Institute, the Ministry of Jahade-Agriculture, and the Isfahan University of Technology (IUT) for their collaboration, making available literature and data and valuable comments and discussions of this paper. We are also grateful to A. Liaghat from Tehran University, College of Agriculture and Natural Resources, and Saeed Morid from Tarbiat Modares University, Tehran, for their helpful comments and organization of meetings with local experts.

## References

**Abbaspour KC, Sonnleitner MA, Schulin R. 1999.** Uncertainty in estimation of soil hydraulic parameters by inverse modelling: Example lysimeter experiments. Soil Sci. Soc. Am. J. **63**: 501-509.

**Abbaspour KC, Yang J, Maximov I, Siber R, Bogner K, Mieleitner J, Zobrist J, Srinivasan R. 2007a.** Modelling hydrology and water quality in the pre-Alpine/Alpine Thur watershed using SWAT. *Journal of Hydrology* **333**: 413-430. DOI:10.1016/j.jhydrol.2006.09.014.

**Abbaspour KC. 2007b.** User Manual for SWAT-CUP, SWAT Calibration and Uncertainty Analysis Programs. Swiss Federal Institute of Aquatic Science and Technology, Eawag, Duebendorf, Switzerland. 93 pp.
http://www.eawag.ch/organisation/abteilungen/siam/software/swat/index_EN. Date last accessed, August 2008.

**Abrishamchi A, Tajrishi M. 2005.** Interbasin water transfer in Iran. In *Water conservation, reuse, and recycling: proceeding of an Iranian American workshop*, The National Academies Press: Washingon, D.C.; 252-271.

**Akbari M, Toomanian N, Droogers P, Bastiaanssen W, Gieske A. 2007.** Monitoring irrigation performance in Esfahan, Iran, using NOAA satellite imagery. *Agricultural Water Management* **88**: 99-109. DOI:10.1016/j.agwat.2006.10.019.

**Alcamo J, Döll P, Henrichs T, Kaspar F, Lehner B, Rosch T, Siebert S. 2003.** Development and testing of the WaterGAP 2 global model of water use and availability. *Hydrological Sciences Journal-Journal Des Sciences Hydrologiques* **48**: 317-337. DOI: 10.1623/hysj.48.3.317.45290.

**Alizadeh A, Keshavarz A. 2005.** Status of agricultural water use in Iran. In *Water conservation, reuse, and recycling: proceeding of an Iranian American workshop*, The National Academies Press: Washingon, D.C.; 94-105.

**Allan J.A. 1997.** 'Virtual Water': A Long Term Solution for Water Short Middle Eastern Economies?' *Occasional Paper. SOAS Water Issues Group*, King's College. UK.

**Ardakanian R. 2005.** Overview of water management in Iran. In *Water conservation, reuse, and recycling: proceeding of an Iranian American workshop*, The National Academies Press: Washingon, D.C.; 18-33.

**Arnold J.G., Allen P.M. 1996.** Estimating hydrologic budgets for three Illinois watersheds. *Journal of Hydrology* **176**: 57-77.

**Arnold J.G., Srinivasan R., Muttiah R.S., Williams J.R. 1998.** Large area hydrologic modeling and assessment - Part 1: Model development. *Journal of the American Water Re-*

sources *Association* **34**: 73-89.

**Banaei M.H., Moameni A., Bybordi M., Malakouti M.J.** 2005. *The soils of Iran: new achievements in perception, management and use.* Soil and Water Research Institute: Tehran; 481 pp.

**Beven K, Binley A.** 1992. The future of distributed models - model calibration and uncertainty prediction. *Hydrological Process* **6**: 279-298.

**Bouman B.A.M.** 2007. A conceptual framework for the improvement of crop water productivity at different spatial scales. *Agricultural Systems* **9**: 43–60. DOI:10.1016/j.agsy.2006.04.004.

**Chavoshian S.A., Takeuchi K., Funada S.** 2005. An overview to transboundary and shared water resources management in Iran, technical challenges and solutions. In *Role of Water Sciences in Transboundary River Basin Management,* Thailand; 189-195.

**Confalonieri R., Bocchi S.** 2005. Evaluation of CropSyst for simulating the yield of flooded rice in northern Italy. *European Journal of Agronomy* **23**: 315-326. DOI:10.1016/j.eja.2004.12.002.

**Cosgrove W.J., Rijsberman F.R.** 2000. *World Water Vision.* Earthscan Publications: London.

**Döll P., Kaspar F., Lehner B.** 2003. A global hydrological model for deriving water availability indicators: model tuning and validation. *Journal of Hydrology* **270**: 105-134. DOI:10.1016/S0022-1694(02)00283-4.

**Ehsani M.** 2005. A vision on water resources situation, irrigation and agricultural production in Iran. In *ICID 21st European Regional Conference on Integrated Land and Water Management: Towards Sustainable Rural Development,* Frankfurt, Germany, p. 7.

**Falkenmark M, Rockstrom J.** 2006. The new blue and green water paradigm: Breaking new ground for water resources planning and management. *Journal of Water Resources Planning and Management-ASCE* **132**: 129-132. DOI:10.1061/(ASCE)0733-9496(2006) 132:3(129).

**Falkenmark M., Lundquist J., Widstrand C.** 1989. Macro-scale water scarcity requires micro-scale approaches: aspects of vulnerability in semi-arid development. *Natural Resources Forum* **13**: 258-267.

**Food and Agriculture Organization.** 1995. *The digital soil map of the world and derived soil properties.* CD-ROM, Version 3.5, Rome.

**Food and Agriculture Organization.** 2003. *Review of the world water resources by country.* Water Report No. 23: Rome.

**Food and Agriculture Organization.** 1986. Yield response to water. *Irrigation and Drainage Paper* **33**. FAO, Rom, Italy.

**Food and Agriculture Organization.** 2005. FAO statistical database. Food and Agriculture Organization of the United Nations. Available on the World Wide Web: http://faostat.fao.org/.

**Foy J.K., Teague W.R., Hanson J.D.** 1999. Evaluation of the upgraded SPUR model (SPUR2.4). *Ecological Modelling* **118**: 149-165. DOI:10.1016/S0304-3800(99)00016-2.

**Gosain A.K., Rao S., Basuray D.** 2006. Climate change impact assessment on hydrology of Indian river basins. *Current Science* **90**: 346-353.

**Hargreaves G.L., Hargreaves G.H., Riley J.P.** 1985. Agricultural benefits for Senegal River Basin. *Journal of Irrigation and Drainage Engineering-ASCE* **111**: 113-124.

**Holvoet K., van Griensven A., Seuntjens P., Vanrolleghem P.A.** 2005. Sensitivity analysis for hydrology and pesticide supply towards the river in SWAT. *Physics and Chemistry of the Earth* **30**: 518-526. DOI:10.1016/j.pce.2005.07.006.

**Jensen, M.E.** 1968. Water consumption by agricultural plants. In *Water Deficits in Plant Growth (1).* Academic Press: New York; 1-22.

**Keshavarz A, Ashrafi SH, Hydari N, Pouran M, Farzaneh EA. 2005.** Water allocation and pricing in agriculture of Iran. In *Water conservation, reuse, and recycling: proceeding of an Iranian American workshop*, The National Academies Press: Washingon, D.C.; 153-172.

**Kijne JW, Barker R, Molden D. 2003.** Water productivity in agriculture: limits and opportunities for improvement. *Comprehensive Assessment of Water Management in Agriculture Series 1*. CAB7IWMI, Wallingford: Colombo.

**Krause P, Boyle DP, Bäse F. 2005.** Comparison of different efficiency criteria for hydrological model assessment. *Advanced Geosciences* **5**: 89-97.

**Krysanova V., Hattermann F., Wechsung F. 2005.** Development of the ecohydrological model SWIM for regional impact studies and vulnerability assessment. *Hydrological Processes* **19**: 763-783. DOI: 10.1002/hyp.5619.

**Leff B., Ramankutty N., Foley J.A. 2004.** Geographic distribution of major crops across the world. *Global Biogeochemical Cycles* **18**: GB1009. DOI: 10.1029/2003GB002108, 2004.

**Lenhart T., Eckhardt K., Fohrer N., Frede H.G. 2002.** Comparison of two different approaches of sensitivity analysis. *Physics and Chemistry of the Earth* **27**: 645-654. DOI:10.1016/S1474-7065(02)00049-9.

**Liu J., Williams J.R., Zehnder A.J.B., Yang H. 2007.** GEPIC - modelling wheat yield and crop water productivity with high resolution on a global scale. *Agricultural Systems* **94**: 478-493. DOI: 10.1016/j.agsy.2006.11.019.

**Ministry of Energy of Iran. 1998.** *An Overview of National Water Planning of Iran*. Tehran, Iran (available in Persian).

**Muleta M.K., Nicklow J.W. 2005.** Sensitivity and uncertainty analysis coupled with automatic calibration for a distributed watershed model. *Journal of Hydrology* **306**: 127-145. DOI:10.1016/j.jhydrol.2004.09.005.

**Narasimhan B., Srinivasan R., Arnold J.G., Di Luzio M. 2005.** Estimation of long-term soil moisture using a distributed parameter hydrologic model and verification using remotely sensed data. *Transactions of the ASAE* **48**: 1101-1113.

**NCCO. 2003.** Initial National Communication to United Nations Framework Convention on Climate Change. Published by Iranian National Climate Change Office at Department of Environment, Tehran, Iran.

**Neitsch S.L., Arnold J.G., Kiniry J.R., Williams J.R., King K.W. 2002.** *Soil and water assessment tool*. Theoretical documentation: Version 2000. TWRI TR-191. College Station, Texas: Texas Water Resources Institute.

**Oki T., Kanae S. 2006.** Global hydrological cycles and world water resources. *Science* **313**: 1068-1072. DOI: 10.1126/science.1128845.

**Olivera F., Valenzuela M., Srinivasan R., Choi J., Cho H.D., Koka S., Agrawal A. 2006.** ArcGIS-SWAT: A geodata model and GIS interface for SWAT. *Journal of the American Water Resources Association* **42**: 295-309.

**Postel S.L., Daily G.C., Ehrlich P.R. 1996.** Human appropriation of renewable freshwater. *Science* **271**: 785-788.

**Revenga C., Brunner J., Henninger N., Kassem K., Payne R. 2000.** *Pilot analysis of global ecosystems: Freshwater systems*. World Resources Institute: Washington DC, USA.

**Rijsberman F.R. 2006.** Water scarcity: Fact or fiction? *Agricultural Water Management* **80**: 5-22. DOI:10.1016/j.agwat.2005.07.001

**Ritchie J.T. 1972.** A model for predicting evaporation from a row crop with incomplete cover. *Water Resources Research* **8**: 1204-1213.

**Ruget F., Brisson N., Delecolle R., Faiver R. 2002.** Sensitivity analysis of a crop simulation model, STICS, in order to choose the main parameters to be estimated. *Agronomie* **22**: 133-158.

**Schuol J., Abbaspour K.C., Sarinivasan R., Yang H. 2008a.** Estimation of freshwater availability in the West African Sub-continent using the SWAT hydrologic model. *Journal of Hydroloy.* **352**: 30-42.

**Schuol J, Abbaspour K.C., Yang H., Srinivasan R., Zehnder A.J.B. 2008b.** Modelling blue and green water availability in Africa. *Water Resources Research* **44**: W07406, p. 18.

**Sharpley A.N., Williams J.R. 1990.** *EPIC-Erosion Productivity Impact Calculator: 1. model documentation.* U.S. Department of Agriculture, Agricultural Research Service, Tech. Bull. 1768.

**Siebert S., Döll P., Feick S., Hoogeveen J., Frenken K. 2007.** *Global Map of Irrigation Areas version 4.0.1.* Johann Wolfgang Goethe University, Frankfurt am Main, Germany / Food and Agriculture Organization of the United Nations, Rome, Italy.

**SCI (Statistical Center of Iran) 1990-2002.** Statistical year books of Iran, Tehran, Iran.

**Thoms M.C., Sheldon F. 2000.** Water resource development and hydrological change in a large dryland river: the Barwon-Darling River, Australia. *Journal of Hydrology* **228**: 10-21. DOI:10.1016/S0022-1694(99)00191-2.

**USDA. 2003.** *Production Estimates and Crop Assessment Division*, Foreign Agricultural Service. http://www.fas.usda.gov/pecad2/highlights/2003/12/iran_dec2003/index.htm

**USGS. 1993.** *Digital elevation model guide.* Washington, D.C.: U.S. Geological Survey. Available at: http://edc.usgs.gov/guides/dem.html. Accessed 15 March 2005.

**Van Griensven A., Meixner T. 2006.** Methods to quantify and identify the sources of uncertainty for river basin water quality models. *Water Science and Technology* **53**: 51-59.

**Vörösmarty C.J., Green P., Salisbury J., Lammers R.B. 2000.** Global water resources: vulnerability from climate change and population growth. *Science* **289**: 284-288. DOI: 10.1126/science.289.5477.284.

**Vrugt J.A., Gupta H.V., Bouten W., Sorooshian S. 2003.** A Shuffled Complex Evolution Metropolis algorithm for optimization and uncertainty assessment of hydrologic model parameters. *Water Resurses Research* **39**: 1201, p. 18.

**Wang X., Williams J.R., Izaurralde R.C., Atwood J.D. 2005.** Sensitivity and uncertainty analysis of crop yields and soil organic carbon simulated with EPIC. *Transactions of the ASAE* **48**:1041-1054.

**White K.L., Chaubey I. 2005.** Sensitivity analysis, calibration, and validations for a multisite and multivariable SWAT model. *Journal of the American Water Resources Association* **41**: 1077-1089. DOI:10.1111/j.1752-1688.2005.tb03786.x

**Yang H., Reichert P., Abbaspour K.C., Zehnder A.J.B. 2003.** A water resources threshold and its implications for food security. *Environmental Science and. Technology* **37**: 3048-3054.

**Yang, H., L. Wang, A.J.B. Zehnder, and K.C. Abbaspour. 2006.** Virtual Water Trade: an assessment of water use efficiency in the international food trade. *Journal of Hydrology and Earth System Sciences*, 10, 443-454.

**Yang J., Reichert P., Abbaspour K.C., Yang H. 2007.** Hydrological modelling of the Chaohe basin in China: Statistical model formulation and Bayesian inference. *Journal of Hydrology* **340**: 167-182. DOI:10.1016/j.jhydrol.2007.04.006.

**Yang J., Reichert P., Abbaspour K.C., Xia J., Yang H. 2008.** Comparing uncertainty analysis techniques for a SWAT application to Chaohe Basin in China. *Journal of Hydrology.* **358**: 1-23.

**Ziaei A., Sepaskhah A.R. 2003.** Model for simulation of winter wheat yield under dryland and irrigated conditions. *Agricultural Water Management* **58**: 1-17.

# 2.6 Application of the SWAT Model to the Hii River Basin, Shimane Prefecture, Japan

## H. Somura[1], D. Hoffman[2], J. Arnold[3], I. Takeda[1] and Y. Mori[1]

## Abstract

Using a daily time step, we evaluated SWAT's discharge simulation of the Hii River basin from 1986 to 2005. The Hii River basin is in the eastern part of Shimane Prefecture, Japan. It covers an area of about 900 $km^2$ and the length of the river from the source to Ootsu river discharge observation station, the outlet of whole basin, is about 150 km. About 80% of the basin is forest and 10% is paddy fields. The parameters were calibrated from 1993 to 1996 and validated from 1986 to 1992 and from 1997 to 2005. The parameters were automatically calibrated and they were CANMX, ALPHA_BF, SOL_AWC, SOL_Z, CH_K2, SMFMX, GWQMN, CN2, ESCO and SLOPE. Both calibration and validation results represented fluctuations of discharge relatively well, although some peaks were overestimated by SWAT. During the calibration period, $R^2$ varied from 0.65 to 0.77 and NSI was from 0.64 to 0.76. During the validation period from 1986 to 1992, $R^2$ varied from 0.58 to 0.74 and NSI was from 0.53 to 0.74. Lastly, from 1997 to 2005, $R^2$ varied from 0.51 to 0.71 and NSI was from 0.38 to 0.68.

**Keywords:** Runoff analysis, watershed management, subbasin, lake, GIS

## 1. Introduction

Impact assessment of land use change, population growth/decrease and watershed development to water quantity and quality is one of the most important topics in a basin. Integrated management of water environment from river basin to downstream, such as lake, is also very important for conservation and sustainable use of its resources. In recent years, water quality in lakes has been tried to be improved by putting an adequate sewage system in place and through the development of laws and environmental standards to control pollutant loads to lake and rivers. However, water quality in lakes has not improved. One of the reasons is pollutant loading from nonpoint sources such as agricultural lands.

© 2009 World Association of Soil and Water Conservation, *Soil and Water Assessment Tool (SWAT): Global Applications,* eds. Jeff Arnold, Raghavan Srinivasan, Susan Neitsch, Chris George, Karim Abbaspour, Philip Gassman, Fang Hua Hao, Ann van Griensven, Ashvin Gosain, Patrick Debels, Nam Won Kim, Hiroaki Somura, Victor Ella, Attachai Jintrawet, Manuel Reyes, and Samran Sombatpanit, pp. 211-221. This paper will be published in the Proceedings of the 4th International SWAT Conference, Delft, Netherlands, 2007. The paper is printed here with the permission of the 4th International SWAT Conference organizers. WASWC is grateful for the permission granted.
[1]Faculty of Life and Environmental Science, Shimane University, Japan som-hiroaki@life.shimane-u.ac.jp
[2]Blackland Research and Extension Center, U.S.A.
[3]Grassland Soil and Water Research Laboratory, U.S.A. jeff.arnold@ars.usda.gov

There are lakes in Shimane Prefecture, Japan, such as Lake Shinji and Lake Nakaumi, whose water quality has not improved. The Lake Shinji and Lake Nakaumi area has been designated as one of the Wetlands of International Importance by the Ramsar Convention in November 2005.

Many researchers have studied water quality in Lake Shinji and Lake Nakaumi from several perspectives (e.g. Seike et al., 2006; Sakuno et al., 2003). Also, there are some studies done on Hii River (Takeda et al., 1996; Ishitobi et al., 1988). However, few studies have been done about runoff analysis and quantitative analysis of pollutant loads by a model in the Hii River basin. When considering watershed management and improvement of water environment in lakes, both information of lakes and rivers are necessary. Thus, we tried to represent stream flow in the Hii River basin as a first step in water environment management.

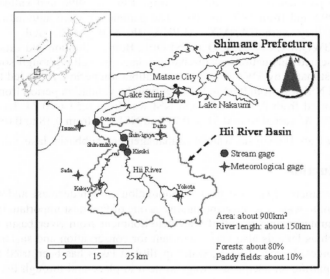

**Figure 1.** Location of Hii River Basin.

## 2. Study Area

The Hii River basin is located in the eastern part of Shimane Prefecture, Japan (Fig. 1). It covers an area of 914.4 km$^2$ and the length of the river from the source to the Ootsu river discharge observation station, which is the outlet of whole basin, is about 150 km. According to the Chugoku Regional Development Bureau in the Ministry of Land, Infrastructure and Transport Government of Japan (MLIT: http://www.cgr.mlit.go.jp/), yearly average discharge is about 40 m$^3$/s and the volume of total runoff is about 1,270 M m$^3$. About 80% of the land use in the basin is forest and 10% is paddy fields. As the Hii River dominates about 75% of watershed area flowing into the Lake Shinji, water quality and quantity of the river will considerably affect the lake.

212

# 3. Methodology

We tried to apply the SWAT model to this basin from 1986 to 2005 using daily time step. As a first step of application of the SWAT model to the basin, we paid attention to the discharge of the river. The Hii River basin was divided into four subbasins according to location of stream gages in the basin (Ootsu, Shinigaya, Shin-mitoya and Kisuki). The parameters were calibrated from 1993 to 1996 and validated from 1986 to 1992 and from 1997 to 2005. The ten parameters selected by ranking based on sensitivity analysis were optimized automatically for all subbasins using daily discharge data as shown in Table 1.

**Table 1.** Range and optimal values of SWAT2003 calibration parameters.

| Parameter name | Lower bound | Upper bound | Optimal value | Imet |
|---|---|---|---|---|
| CANMX: Maximum canopy storage (mmH$_2$O) | 0.0 | 10.0 | 0.009 | 1 |
| ALPHA_BF: Baseflow alpha factor (days) | 0.0 | 1.0 | 0.75 | 1 |
| SOL_AWC: Available water capacity of the soil layer (mmH$_2$O/mm soil) | -0.04 | 0.04 | 0.04 | 2 |
| SOL_Z: Depth from soil surface to bottom of layer (mm) | -50.0 | 600 | 588.2 | 2 |
| CH_K2: Effective hydraulic conductivity in main channel alluvium (mm/hr) | 0.0 | 150.0 | 150.0 | 1 |
| SMFMX: Melt factor for snow on June 21 (mmH$_2$O/°C-day) | 2.0 | 8.0 | 2.09 | 1 |
| GWQMN: Threshold depth of water in the shallow aquifer required for return flow to occur (mmH$_2$O) | 0.0 | 5000.0 | 0.35 | 1 |
| CN2: Initial SCS runoff curve number for moisture condition II | -8.0 | 8.0 | -6.6 | 2 |
| ESCO: Soil evaporation compensation factor | 0.001 | 1.0 | 0.89 | 1 |
| SLOPE: Average slope steepness (m/m) | 0.0 | 0.6 | 0.0002 | 1 |

Note: Imet means variation methods available in auto calibration (1: Replacement of initial parameter by value, 2: adding value to initial parameter)

## 3.1 Brief description of SWAT model

The Soil and Water Assessment Tool (SWAT) has been widely applied for modeling watershed hydrology and simulating the movement of nonpoint source pollution. The SWAT is a physically-based continuous time hydrologic model with an ArcView GIS interface developed by the Blackland Research and Extension Center and the USDA-ARS (Arnold et al., 1998) to predict the impact of land management practices on water, sediment and agricultural chemical yields in large complex basins with varying soil type, land use and management conditions over long periods of time. The main driving force behind the SWAT is the hydrological component. The hydrological processes are divided into two phases, the land phase, which controls the amount of water, sediment and nutrient loading in receiving waters, and the water routing phase which simulates movement through the channel network. The SWAT considers both natural sources (e.g. mineralization of organic matter and N-fixation) and anthropogenic contributions (fertilizers, manures and point sources) as nutrient inputs. The SWAT delineates watersheds into subbasins interconnected by a stream network and each subbasin is divided further into hydrologic response units (HRUs) based upon unique soil / land class characteristics, without any specified location in the subbasin. Flow, sediment and nutrient loading from each HRU in a subbasin are summed and the resulting loads are then routed through channels, ponds, and reservoirs to the watershed outlet (Arnold et al., 2001). The model includes a number of storage databases (i.e. soils, land cover/ plant growth, tillage and fertilizer) which can be customized for an individual basin. A single growth model in SWAT is used for simulating all crops based on the simplification of the EPIC crop model (Williams et al., 1984). Phenological development of the crop is based on daily heat unit accumulation. The model can simulate up to 10 soil layers if sufficiently detailed information is available. The SWAT is expected to provide useful information across a range of timescales, i.e. hourly, daily, monthly and yearly timesteps (Neitsch et al., 2002).

## 3.2 Input data description

The SWAT requires meteorological data such as daily precipitation, maximum and minimum air temperature, wind speed, relative humidity and solar radiation data. Spatial data sets including a digital elevation map (DEM), land cover and soil maps are required. Since some gaps were present in the climate data, the weather generator included in SWAT was used, based on statistical values (average monthly values of rain, maximum and minimum temperatures, standard deviation, skew coefficient, probability of wet day following a dry day in the month, probability of wet day following a wet day, average number of rainy days in the month) and computed on the basis of available daily values.

Meteorological data was obtained from the Japan Meteorological Agency (JMA: http://www.jma.go.jp/jma/index.html). Measuring gages of precipitation, air temperature and wind speed were located in and around the basin. We chose five gages for precipitation and three gages for air temperature and wind speed. However, there is no gage monitoring relative humidity in the basin. So, relative humidity data observed in Matsue city, located about 30 km away from the basin, was used instead. Solar radiation was calculated with the Angstrom formula (FAO, 1998) by using the data measured by Shimane University (http://www.ipc.shimane-u.ac.jp/weather/i/home.html) and actual sunshine duration in the basin obtained from the JMA because there was no monitoring gage of solar radiation in the basin. The average values of climatic data at each gage are shown in Table 2.

214

**Table 2.** Average annual precipitation and climatic variables from 1985 to 2005 at each gage.

| Gage name | EL. | Annual Precip. | Max. Air temp. | Min. Air temp. | Wind speed | Relative humidity | Solar radiation (calculated) |
|---|---|---|---|---|---|---|---|
| | (m) | (mm) | (deg. C) | (deg. C) | (m/s) | (%) | (MJ/m²) |
| Matsue | 16.9 | - | - | - | - | 75.6 (10.0) | - |
| Izumo | 20 | 1726 | 18.9 (8.3) | 10.3 (8.1) | 2.2 (1.2) | - | 11.1 (7.5) |
| Daito | 56 | 1778 | - | - | - | - | - |
| Sada | 100 | 2072 | - | - | - | - | - |
| Kakeya | 215 | 2046 | 18.0 (9.0) | 8.8 (8.3) | 1.3 (0.7) | - | - |
| Yokota | 369 | 1765 | 17.2 (9.3) | 7.5 (8.8) | 1.2 (0.7) | - | - |

Note: The values in the parenthesis indicate a standard deviation

Discharge data was prepared at four monitoring stations named Ootsu, Shin-igaya, Shin-mitoya and Kisuki in the basin. The data was furnished by the Izumo River Office in the MLIT.

DEM data was prepared with 50 m grid created from 1:25,000 topographic map of the Geographical Survey Institute.

Land use was categorized as paddy field, upland field, orchard, denuded land, forest, water and others. The land use data was obtained from the National-Land Information Office in the MLIT (http://nlftp.mlit.go.jp/). Each subbasin has almost similar land use. Forest area ranges from 59% to 87% and paddy fields area ranges from 9% to 18% spatially as shown in Table 3.

**Table 3.** Area and ratio of major land use in each subbasin.

| Gage name | Subbasin No. | Drainage area | Subbasin Area | Forests | Rice fields | Upland Fields and Orchard |
|---|---|---|---|---|---|---|
| | | (Km²) | (Km²) | (%) | (%) | (%) |
| Ootsu | Sub 1 | 914.4 | 183.9 | 74 | 16 | 3 |
| Shin-igaya | Sub 2 | 730.5 | 14.1 | 59 | 18 | 5 |
| Shin-mitoya | Sub 3 | 206.8 | 206.8 | 86 | 9 | 3 |
| Kisuki | Sub 4 | 509.6 | 509.6 | 87 | 10 | 2 |

Soil data was taken from Fundamental Land Classification Survey, a GIS soil map with a scale of 1:500,000 prepared by the MLIT (http://tochi.mlit.go.jp/ tockok/index.htm) (Fig. 2). Soil type was categorized into 10 groups of 14 soils such as Dystric Rhegosols, Fluvic Gleysols, Gleysols, Haplic Andosols, Helvic Acrisols, Humic Cambisols, Lithosols, Ochric Cambisols, Rhodic Acrisols and Vitric Andosols. Internal data of each soil such as the number of layers, soil depth and physicochemical properties was prepared based on soil profile in soil map and the data colleted up by Hirai (1995).

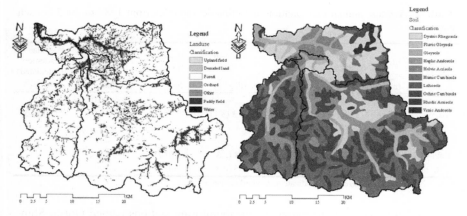

**Figure 2.** Land use and soil classification GIS data.

### 3.3 Model performance evaluation

The SWAT model was calibrated and validated using observed discharge data. The coefficient of determination ($R^2$) and Nash-Sutcliffe Index (NSI) were used to evaluate the model performance. The $R^2$ value is an indicator of strength of relationship between the observed and simulated values. The NSI value indicates how well the plot of the observed versus the simulated values fits the 1:1 line. The ranges of NSI value is between $\infty$ and one. If the $R^2$ and NSI values are less than or very close to zero, the model performance is considered unacceptable or poor. If the values are equal to one, then the model prediction is considered to be perfect.

$$NSI = 1.0 - \left( \frac{\sum_{i=1}^{n}(Q_{obs,i} - Q_{cal,i})^2}{\sum_{i=1}^{n}(Q_{obs,i} - \overline{Q}_{obs})^2} \right)$$

(Nash-Sutcliffe Index)

where $n$ represents the number of registered discharge data, $Q_{obs,i}$ is the observed discharge at time $i$, $Q_{cal,i}$ is the simulated discharge.

## 4. Results and Discussion

The model was applied to the Hii River basin, which has a low density of stream flow and climatic gages. The simulated and observed statistics for calibration and validation are shown in Table 4. The calibration procedures formulated consist of finding the most appropriate parameters for hydrologic routing model component. In this stage, the best fit was achieved with $R^2$ of 0.65 at subbasin 1, 0.75 at subbasin 2, 0.77 at subbasin 3, and 0.69 at subbasin 4. The best fit was done with

NSI of 0.64 at subbasin 1, 0.74 at subbasin 2, 0.76 at subbasin 3, and 0.67 at subbasin 4 for daily discharge. During the validation period (1986-1992), $R^2$ varied from 0.58 to 0.74 and NSI did from 0.53 to 0.74. From 1997 to 2005, $R^2$ varied from 0.51 to 0.71 and NSI did from 0.38 to 0.68. During the whole simulation period, subbasin 3, which is an independent subbasin, showed a relatively high reproducibility among the subbasins. Similarly, subbasins 2 and 4 also gave satisfactory simulation results except during the latter validation period (1997-2005) particularly for subbasin 4.

Simulated and observed discharge on a daily time step is shown in Figure 3. The gray line is observed flow and dotted black line is simulated flow. It is apparent that both results of calibration and validation at each subbasin captured the fluctuations of discharge relatively well, although some peaks were overestimated. This is particularly true on the 20th of October 2004, when the basin was struck by a big typhoon No. 23 and the observed precipitation was about 150 mm as observed at Yokota rain gage (a total of about 200 mm for 2 days), 120 mm at Kakeya rain gage (a total of 165 mm for 2 days), and 100 mm at Daito rain gage (a total of 150 mm for 3 days). Therefore, the simulated discharge during that day at all subbasins became big, particularly at subbasin 4. If the simulated results on that day were ignored, the NSI value would increase to 0.48 from 0.38.

**Table 4.** Simulated versus observed statistics for the Hii River calibration and validation.

| | Calibration period 1993-1996 | | Validation period | | | |
| | | | 1986-1992 | | 1997-2005 | |
| | $R^2$ | NSI | $R^2$ | NSI | $R^2$ | NSI |
|---|---|---|---|---|---|---|
| Sub 1 | 0.65 | 0.64 | 0.58 | 0.53 | 0.51 | 0.50 |
| Sub 2 | 0.75 | 0.74 | 0.67 | 0.60 | 0.64 | 0.62 |
| Sub 3 | 0.77 | 0.76 | 0.74 | 0.74 | 0.71 | 0.68 |
| Sub 4 | 0.69 | 0.67 | 0.70 | 0.69 | 0.59 | 0.38 |

Yearly averages for the water balance components are shown together with overall average for the simulated period in Table 5. The overall average of simulated river discharge (1,321 mm) was about 90% of observed average discharge (1,473mm). The average water balance is broken down as follows: precipitation 1,818 mm, percolation 921 mm, actual ET 428 mm, potential ET 985 mm, base flow 859 mm, lateral soil flow 400 mm, and surface flow 62 mm. It is considered that base flow accounts for about 65% and lateral flow does for about 30% of water yield in the simulation.

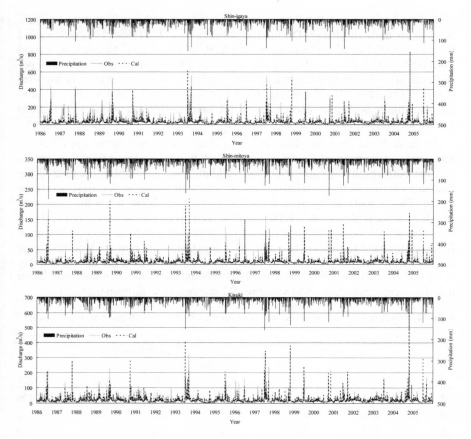

**Figure 3.** Simulated and observed discharge on a daily time step (calibration: 1993-1996, validation: 1986-1992 and 1997-2005).

By using the model parameter values used in the simulation, we tried to estimate the change in maximum and minimum discharge at each subbasin in case the annual total precipitation decreased or increased by 20% as shown in Table 6. The maximum and minimum flows were computed during the 20-year simulation period, keeping the other parameters constant. It was calculated that the maximum discharge at subbasin 1 became 1,200 $m^3$/s if the total precipitation amount increased by 20%. On the other hand, the maximum discharge became 558 $m^3$/s if the precipitation amount decreased by 20%. The minimum discharge at subbasin 1 became 3.76 $m^3$/s if the precipitation amount increased by 20% and 2.1 $m^3$/s if the amount decreased by 20%.

**Table 5.** Yearly averages of simulated water balance.

| Year | Precip. (mm) | Sur. flow (mm) | Lat. flow (mm) | Base flow (mm) | Perco. (mm) | Soil water (mm) | Actu. ET (mm) | Poten. ET (mm) | Water yield (mm) |
|------|------|------|------|------|------|------|------|------|------|
| 1986 | 1649 | 59 | 366 | 760 | 808 | 77 | 412 | 1112 | 1185 |
| 1987 | 1819 | 64 | 385 | 828 | 868 | 68 | 511 | 1152 | 1277 |
| 1988 | 1768 | 34 | 406 | 858 | 934 | 69 | 392 | 862 | 1298 |
| 1989 | 2193 | 76 | 498 | 1096 | 1169 | 71 | 436 | 889 | 1670 |
| 1990 | 1916 | 54 | 419 | 890 | 975 | 75 | 467 | 1053 | 1363 |
| 1991 | 1843 | 37 | 406 | 899 | 950 | 73 | 443 | 874 | 1342 |
| 1992 | 1475 | 8 | 323 | 730 | 778 | 71 | 381 | 954 | 1061 |
| 1993 | 2258 | 148 | 505 | 1079 | 1169 | 79 | 426 | 835 | 1732 |
| 1994 | 1340 | 23 | 263 | 649 | 665 | 78 | 388 | 1122 | 935 |
| 1995 | 1877 | 58 | 430 | 890 | 979 | 72 | 376 | 932 | 1378 |
| 1996 | 1607 | 45 | 340 | 738 | 789 | 68 | 474 | 944 | 1123 |
| 1997 | 2189 | 113 | 490 | 1043 | 1112 | 73 | 467 | 1005 | 1646 |
| 1998 | 1862 | 80 | 391 | 886 | 911 | 73 | 479 | 908 | 1357 |
| 1999 | 1707 | 52 | 367 | 757 | 862 | 73 | 425 | 919 | 1176 |
| 2000 | 1545 | 68 | 320 | 725 | 749 | 69 | 413 | 1053 | 1113 |
| 2001 | 1996 | 54 | 449 | 912 | 1018 | 71 | 473 | 1004 | 1415 |
| 2002 | 1621 | 10 | 365 | 792 | 855 | 74 | 381 | 996 | 1167 |
| 2003 | 2017 | 57 | 457 | 961 | 1044 | 73 | 465 | 899 | 1475 |
| 2004 | 1998 | 130 | 434 | 891 | 929 | 72 | 480 | 1129 | 1455 |
| 2005 | 1674 | 81 | 390 | 797 | 862 | 72 | 285 | 1066 | 1268 |
| **Ave.** | **1818** | **62** | **400** | **859** | **921** | **72** | **428** | **985** | **1321** |

**Table 6.** Change in maximum and minimum discharge due to decrease / increase of total precipitation amount (-20 %, 0% and +20 %).

| | Maximum flow ($m^3/s$) | | | Minimum flow ($m^3/s$) | | |
|------|------|------|------|------|------|------|
| | -20% | 0 | +20% | -20% | 0 | +20% |
| Sub 1 | 558 | 876 | 1200 | 2.1 | 2.87 | 3.76 |
| Sub 2 | 546 | 832 | 1120 | 1.5 | 2.07 | 2.70 |
| Sub 3 | 133 | 218 | 311 | 0.3 | 0.55 | 0.82 |
| Sub 4 | 440 | 656 | 872 | 0.9 | 1.32 | 1.72 |

**Table 7.** Yearly averages of simulated water balance components due to decrease/increase of total precipitation mount (-20 % and +20 %).

| Year | Precip. (mm) | Sur. flow (mm) | Lat. flow (mm) | Base flow (mm) | Perco. (mm) | Soil water (mm) | Actu. ET (mm) | Poten. ET (mm) | Water yield (mm) |
|------|------|------|------|------|------|------|------|------|------|
| -20 % | 1454 | 29 | 304 | 654 | 704 | 72 | 413 | 988 | 987 |
| +20 % | 2181 | 109 | 494 | 1059 | 1132 | 73 | 439 | 983 | 1662 |

In addition, the maximum discharge values resulting from precipitation of different return periods were estimated for each subbasin (Fig. 4). The precipitation at various probabilities was calculated using the software made by the Public Works Research Institute. Rainfall duration was set to 24 hours when calculating the rainfall intensity. Simulation period was 1 year and daily average precipitation for 21 years from 1985 to 2005 was prepared. Results showed that the highest monthly to yearly rainfall ratio occurred in July. Hence, the precipitation of a given probability was set on the day when the highest amount of rainfall was recorded in July. As a result, the maximum discharge was 1,490 m³/s at subbasin 1, 1,340 m³/s at subbasin 2,424 m³/s at subbasin 3, and 906 m³/s at subbasin 4 in case of 200-year return period. However, rainfall will continue for several days. Thus, maximum discharge will also continue to increase.

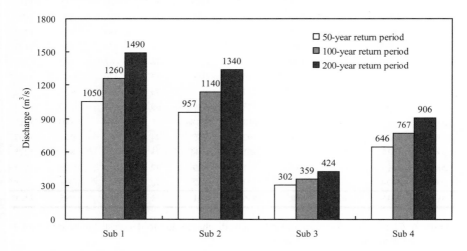

**Figure 4.** Maximum discharge at each subbasin due to precipitation of different return periods (rainfall duration was set to 24 hours).

## 5. Conclusion

The SWAT model performed well in simulating the general trend of river discharges at all subbasins over time for daily time intervals. Thus, this study showed that the SWAT model can be used for Japanese mountainous river basins. However, for more accurate modeling of hydrology and simulation of water quality, a large effort will be needed to improve the quality of available information concerning soils, land use, agricultural activity and climate of the basin.

## Acknowledgments

We wish to convey our special thanks to Ms. Nancy B Sammons, Ms. Georgie S Mitchell and Dr. Mauro Di Luzio of Grassland Soil and Water Research Laboratory, Temple, Texas who helped us to set up the model and input data. The discharge data was willingly furnished from the Izumo River Office in the Ministry of Land, Infrastructure and Transport Government of Japan. This research was supported by grant-in-aid of Shimane University priority research project.

# References

**Arnold, J.G., Srinivasan, R., Muttiah, R.S. and Williams, J.R. 1998.** Large area hydrologic modeling and assessment part I: model development. J. American Water Resources Association 34: 73-89.

**Arnold, J.G, Allen, P.M. and Morgan, D.S. 2001.** Hydrologic model for design and constructed wetlands. *Wetlands* 21 (2): 167-178.

**FAO. 1998.** Irrigation and Drainage Paper No.56 Crop evapotranspiration (guidelines for computing crop water requirements) by Richard G. Allen, Luis S. Pereira, Dirk Raes, Martin Smith, pp.290, ISBN 92-5-104219-5.

**Hirai, H. 1995.** Studies on the genesis of brown forest soils and their related soils in Japan, pp.146 (Doctoral Thesis).

**Ishitobi, Y., Kawatsu, M., Kamiya, H., Hayashi, K. and Esumi, H. 1988.** Estimation of water quality and nutrient loads in the Hii River by semi-daily sampling. *Jpn.J.Limnol.* 49 (1): 11-17.

**Nash, J.E. and Sutcliffe, J.V. 1970.** River flow forecasting through conceptual models. Part I - A discussion of principles -. *J. Hydrology* 10 (3), 282-290.

**Neitsch, S.L., Arnold, J.G., Kiniry, J.R., Srinivasan, R. and Williams, J.R. 2002.** Soil and Water Assessment Tool. User's Manual. Version 2000. GSWRL Report 02-02, BRC Report 2-06. Temple, Texas, USA.

**Sakuno, Y., Yamamoto M. and Yoshida T., 2003.** Estimation of Water Temperature and Turbidity in Lake Shinji and Lake Nakaumi Using ASTER Data, 2000-2002. *Laguna* 10: 65-72.

**Seike, Y., Kondo, K., Mitamura, O., Ueda, S., Senga, Y., Fukumori, R., Fujinaga, K., Takayasu, K, and Okumura, M. 2006.** Seasonal variation in nutrients and chlorophyll a in the stratified brackish lake Nakaumi, Japan. *Verh. Internat. Verein. Limnol.* 29: 1959-1965.

**Takeda, I., Fukushima A. and Mori Y. 1996.** An estimation of runoff loads of pollutants from River Hii to Lake Shinji. *Laguna* 3: 91-96.

**Williams, J.R., Jones, C.A. and Dyke, P.T. 1984.** A modeling approach to determining the relationship between erosion and soil productivity. *Trans. of the ASAE* 21: 129-144.

# 2.7 Development and Applications of SWAT-K (Korea)

## Nam Won Kim[1], Il Moon Chung[2], Chulgyum Kim[2], Jeongwoo Lee[2] and Jeong Eun Lee[3]

## Abstract

In Korea, accurate hydrological component analyses for proper water resources planning and management have become an urgent issue. To evaluate the variation and properties of the hydrological components and to produce well defined hydrologic model, SWAT-K (Korea) has been established with the financial support from the Sustainable Water Resources Research Center for 21st Century Frontier Research Project by MEST (Ministry of Education, Science and Technology). SWAT-K is the modified version of SWAT considering variation of water cycle structure (natural and artificial) and surface-groundwater interaction and so on. Major achievements are integrated surface-groundwater model SWAT-MODFLOW, Temporally Weighted Averaged CN technique, improved reservoir operation module, integrated SWAT-SWMM, modified EVT module SWAT-EVT and so forth. SWAT-K studies have been focused on two major topics. One thing is an accurate estimation of hydrologic components for proper planning and management of water resources in Korea and another is making the effective tool for water quality management in the watershed. SWAT-K is expected to be a useful tool for water resources planning and be a basic tool for TMDL management in Korea.

**Key Words**: SWAT- K (Korea), water resources planning, hydrological component analysis, TMDL management

## 1. Introduction

In Korea, accurate hydrological component analyses for proper water resources planning and management have become an urgent issue. As existing water budget model has some sources of errors, there have been many limitations in water resources planning and management due to incorrect input of water budget in Korean watershed.

---

© 2009 World Association of Soil and Water Conservation, *Soil and Water Assessment Tool (SWAT): Global Applications,* eds. Jeff Arnold, Raghavan Srinivasan, Susan Neitsch, Chris George, Karim Abbaspour, Philip Gassman, Fang Hua Hao, Ann van Griensven, Ashvin Gosain, Patrick Debels, Nam Won Kim, Hiroaki Somura, Victor Ella, Attachai Jintrawet, Manuel Reyes, and Samran Sombatpanit, pp. 223-252.

[1]Research Fellow, Korea Institute of Construction Technology (KICT), Goyang, South Korea nwkim@kict.re.kr
[2]Senior Researcher, Korea Institute of Construction Technology (KICT), Goyang, South Korea
[3]Researcher, Korea Institute of Construction Technology (KICT), Goyang, South Korea

To evaluate the variation and properties of the hydrological components and to produce well defined hydrologic model, SWAT-K (Korea) has been established with the financial support from the Sustainable Water Resources Research Center for 21$^{st}$ Century Frontier Research Project by MEST (Ministry of Education, Science and Technology). SWAT-K is the modified version of SWAT considering variation of water cycle structure (natural and artificial) and surface-groundwater interaction and so on. Major achievements are as below.

- SWAT-MODFLOW (Kim et al., 2008): integrated surface-groundwater model;

- Temporally Weighted Averaged CN technique (Kim and Lee, 2008): enhancement of runoff volume estimation by SWAT;

- SWAT-ROM (Kim et al., 2006b): improved reservoir operation module in SWAT;

- SWAT-SWMM (Kim and Won, 2004a,b): integrated modeling for urban watershed; and

- SWAT-EVT (Kim and Kim, 2004): modified EVT module for Korean watershed.

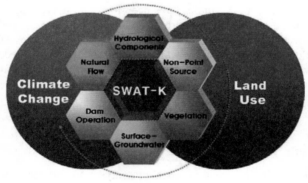

**Figure 1.** Overview of SWAT-Korea.

There have been a large number of applications involving use of SWAT-K in Korea. Brief descriptions of these studies have been presented below.

## 2. On the characteristics of flow duration curve according to the operation of multi-purpose dams in Han River basin, Korea

In Korea, about 70% of total rainfall is concentrated from June to September. Therefore, multi-purpose dams should store the water as well as reduce peak river flow during flood season, and they play an important role of original water supply, which stably provides the stored water to the downstream basin during dry seasons. Consequently, improving flow pattern to the downstream river is one of essential objectives for multi-purpose dam operations. However, there is no specific dam operation report on how large an effect of improving flow pattern is really indicated on the downstream river and with which amount of water storage the water supply is being attained. Accordingly, this study aimed to analyze and evaluate characteristics of flow pattern change depending on the operation of the Soyang and Chungju multi-purpose dams centered on Paldang dam which is located downstream of two larger dams. For this purpose, dam operation technique by using SWAT-K model is applied considering flow rate before and after dam construction. Also, it is aimed to quantitatively analyze and evaluate the virtual water storage effect of Soyang and Chungju dams.

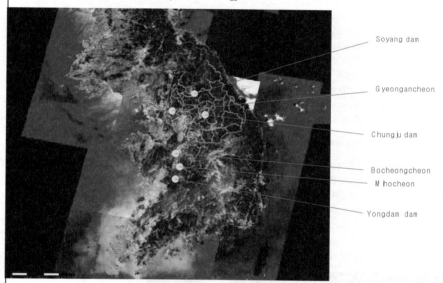

**Figure 2.** Study watersheds for SWAT application in Korea.

## 2.1 Concept and procedure for evaluating the characteristics of flow pattern changes depending on reservoir operation

The concept is that it is able to evaluate the storage shape and the storage operation in two multi-purpose dams as well as the evaluation of a flow pattern change, when being able to simulate runoff in the basin without Soyang and Chungju dams. Generally, the conceptual rainfall-runoff model, like the Tank model, the runoff simulation in the ungaged basin is very difficult and, moreover, the simulation on the basin of including reservoir is almost impossible. Fortunately, MEST (2004) had fully proven the application to the basin of including reservoir or the ungaged basin, through SWAT-K model, which is the modified version of SWAT (Arnold et al., 1993; Neitsch et al., 2001). Of course, a reservoir operation model is included in the SWAT itself, but this should be modified for application to Korean watershed. Consequently, SWAT-K's reservoir module is modified to apply the operation of each reservoir when a number of reservoirs are located within the basin. The following are the procedures that analyzed the flow pattern change in the Paldang dam by using this model:

(1) By using SWAT-K, applicability of model is examined by comparing the simulated runoff of upper basin of Paldang dam with the daily inflow of Paldang dam by forming the measured release of the upper stream basin of Soyang, Chungju and Hwacheon dams can be considered in a model.

(2) The daily inflow of the Paldang dam is simulated through the measured inflow of the Soyang and Chungju dams, through the measured release of Hwacheon dam, and through the runoff simulation in the remaining basin. At this time, it evaluates by subdividing an individual impact of the Soyang and Chungju dams.

(3) Performs the flow pattern analysis on a system of flow rate materials by scenario depending on the operation of the multi-purpose dam.

(4) Discusses the characteristics of two multi-purpose dams by using the result of flow pattern analysis.

## 2.2 Present status and runoff simulation of subject basin

As the Han River basin is located in the central part of the Korean Peninsula, and is the largest river with basin area of 26,919 km², river length of 481.7 km, average basin width of 54.4 km, and basin shape factor of 0.111, it possesses about 26.4 % of the entire area of 99,237 km² in South Korea. The basin area in the upper stream of Paldang dam is 23,800 km², within the basin is located 3 multi-purpose dams and 7 dams for hydroelectric power generation, for flood control, and for water supply (Fig. 3).

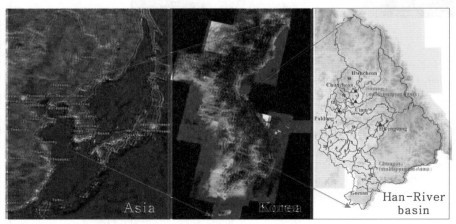

**Figure 3.** Present status of the subject basin.

226

For the purpose of SWAT-K modeling, daily based hydrometeorologic data from 16 weather stations are collected. Also, a digital thematic map is made up of Digital Elevation Model (DEM) from Korea Water Resources Corporation, land use map from Ministry of Environment, and soil map from Rural Development Administration.

Aiming to more exactly analyze a change in the flow duration curve at a spot of Paldang dam according to the operation of two multi-purpose dams, among the upper stream basins, the upper stream basin of Soyang, Chungju, Hwacheon, and Goesan dams were applied to a model by using the observed release and inflow data in each dam. Therefore, reservoir operations (target release) of Chuncheon, Uiam, and Cheongpyeong dams are performed in the North Han River system. The SWAT-K model is a physically based model, thus only its parameter is physically set, but optimization or other artificial manipulation is not easy.

Accordingly, parameter correction is virtually the same as the procedure of validation, and the correction comes to be attained within the physically proper range. Parameter calibration was performed using the observed and simulated daily inflows at the Paldang dam site during 1986~2000.

As shown in Figure 4, in consequence of performing the comparison of 1:1 in the observed value and the simulated value in daily units, the simulated value was indicated to be very good in coefficient of determination ($R^2$), which is about 0.91. To evaluate the water-budget balance of total runoff, it was compared the observed value and the simulated value in the accumulated inflow from the year of 1987 as shown in Figure 5(a). Given the attempt to consider objectives of a study aiming to analyze a change in runoff volume, the model, which is being currently applied, is excellent and efficient. Meanwhile, given the attempt to compare flow duration curve on the measured flow rate and the simulated flow rate in the Paldang dam, it can be seen to be almost consistent as shown in Figure 5(b).

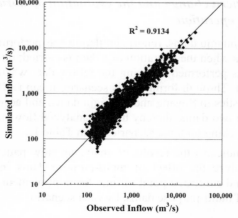

**Figure 4.** Comparison between the observed inflow and the simulated inflow at Paldang dam.

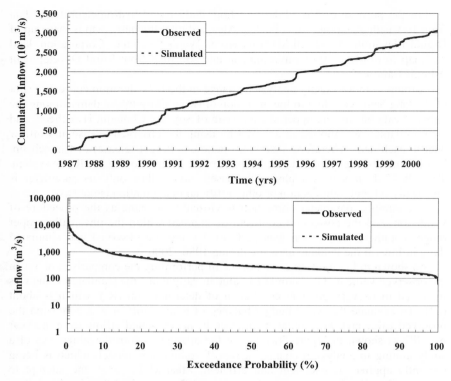

**Figure 5.** Comparison the measured-simulated inflow at Paldang dam: (a, upper) cumulative inflow; (b, lower) flow duration curve.

## 2.3 The flow pattern change and the evaluation of storage effect depending on reservoir operation

For Soyang and Chungju dams, runoff simulation was performed by using the observed release data when the operation of a dam is carried; on the other hand runoff simulation was performed by using the inflow data when the operation of a dam is not carried. Through forming this scenario, it can really inquire into even each of characteristics in Soyang and Chungju dams, and accordingly, can evaluate all the roles in two dams, thereby having analyzed flow pattern change at the Paldang dam by making up three scenarios as in Table 1.

As Figure 6 indicates the results of analyzing flow pattern change, it could quantitatively analyze the effect of multi-purpose dams in flood season and drought season, and confirm a point of time for improvement in flow pattern due to the operation of multi-purpose dams, by each scenario.

**Table 1.** The conditions of input materials by scenario and the situations of basin.

| Scenarios | Input | | Situations of basin |
|---|---|---|---|
| | Soyang dam | Chungju dam | |
| Current basin | Release | Release | When operation of Soyang and Chungju dams is proceeded |
| Scenario 1 | Inflow | Release | When there is no Soyang dam |
| Scenario 2 | Release | Inflow | When there is no Chungju dam |
| Scenario 3 | Inflow | Inflow | When there are no Soyang and Chungju dams |

In case of scenario 1 aiming to analyze the effect of Soyang dam on flow duration curve for a spot of the Paldang dam in the current basin situation, it can judge the effect of the Soyang dam, which reduced the peak flow as for high flow rate more than average 17.3 % (63 days) and improved flow pattern as for low flow rate less than it, during the simulation period. In other words, focusing on Paldang dam, the effect of operating the Soyang dam was indicated to store water in 9.1 billion tons over about 63 days every year and to regulate flow pattern during drought season. As the case of Scenario 2 that analyzed the effect of the Chungju dam, it could confirm the effect of improving flow pattern in a dam with a high flow rate and low flow rate as for average 7.7% (28 days). The period of storing water is shorter than the Soyang dam, but in case of storage capacity, it was shown that water in about 12.5 billion tons is stored in a high flow rate, and then flow pattern is improved again during the drought season, thereby having been indicated to be greater in the effect of improving flow pattern due to the Chungju dam, seeing the centering on the Paldang dam. Finally, given the case of scenario 3 that was aimed to simultaneously analyze the effect of the Soyang and Chungju dams, it brought about the effect of improving flow pattern in the remaining period, after storing water for the period of average 14.7% (54 days).

This is indicated to be the storage period due to the composite impacts of the Soyang and Chungju dams, and the storage capacity shows the storage effect about 21.6 billion tons, which are the sum total of two dams. The effective storage capacity in the Soyang and Chungju dams is 19 billion tons and 18 billion tons, respectively, thus the effective storage capacity in two dams is approximately 37 billion tons. However, it is known that the role in two dams can be averagely integrated into the storage effect of approximately 21.6 billion tons per year.

This is the first study of attempting to prove that this can be solved by using SWAT-K model, by paying attention to the fact that there has been no analysis on an effect of operating a dam due to the difficulty of interpreting flow pattern changes in the downstream river after constructing a dam.

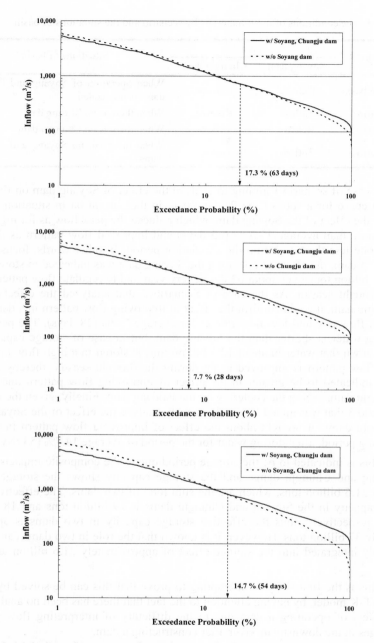

**Figure 6.** Analysis on flow pattern change by scenario: (a-upper) = Scenario 1; (b-middle) = Scenario 2, Lower - (c-lower) = Scenario 3.

## 3. Integrated modeling of surface water and groundwater by using combined SWAT-MODFLOW

Up until now, hydrologic component analysis in Korea has concentrated on surface water management, so problems related to groundwater were not dealt with in a rigorous manner. Additionally, the groundwater model was not adequately linked to surface water analysis, and thus the main focus was primarily on aquifer management. For instance, groundwater recharge could not be considered in terms of hydrological processes, which are directly related to precipitation, evapotranspiration and surface runoff. Groundwater recharge rate was an input to the groundwater model and thus has been determined from trial and error during calibration. The best solution for solving this problem is the construction of a long-term rainfall runoff model, which can effectively produce an integrated analysis for both the groundwater and surface water (Kim et al., 2006a). The main factors to consider for these kinds of models are: the land use, surface runoff, and other factors such as climate change. It is essential for the model to be able to examine the hydrologic effects and, at the same time, allowing hydraulic interaction between surface water and groundwater. To compute the quantity of groundwater runoff determined by runoff analysis from the watershed, SWAT (Arnold et al., 1993; Arnold et al., 1998) model and MODFLOW (McDonald and Harbaugh, 1988) model were fully combined (Kim et al., 2004a,b).

Although SWAT has its own module for groundwater components, the model itself is semi-distributed and thus distributed parameters such as hydraulic conductivity distribution could not be represented. Moreover, it causes difficulties in expressing the spatial distribution of groundwater levels. One of the most essential components of an efficient groundwater model is the accuracy of recharge rates amongst the input data. The conventional groundwater flow analysis performed by MODFLOW often overlooks the accuracy of the recharge rates that are required inputs to the model. Consequently, there is considerable uncertainty in the simulated runoff results. To overcome these disadvantages, we developed subroutines which exchanges flow data between the cells in MODFLOW and the HRUs (hydrologic response units) of SWAT. HRUs are defined by overlaying soil and land use and lumping similar soil/land use combinations. On the basis of these modifications, the groundwater model in SWAT was replaced with MODFLOW. Therefore, it was possible to establish a fully combined modeling program which is able to form a linkage in each time step. Sophocleous et al. (1997, 1999) already presented the development and implementation of a computer model SWATMOD which is capable of simulating the flow of surface water by SWAT, and groundwater and stream aquifer interactions by MODFLOW on a continuous basis for the Rattlesnake Creek basin in south-central Kansas.

In this study, the integrated SWAT-MODFLOW model (Kim et al., 2008) is described and tested in the Gyeongancheon watershed in Korea, where the area of the basin is 259.2 km$^2$. As shown in Figure 7, this drainage basin is divided into 9 subbasins, and the area of each subbasin ranges from 7 to 60 km$^2$. The channel length of each subbasin ranges from 5 to 20 km. AVS2000 (DiLuzio et al., 2001) was used to automate the development of model input parameters. Daily precipitation for Suwon gaging station that covers the entire watershed were obtained from the hydrologic database of MLTM (Ministry of Land, Transport and Maritime Affairs). Daily values of maximum and minimum temperatures, solar radiation, wind speed, and relative humidity were collected from the weather service data of KMA (Korea Meteorological Administration). Land use digital data (1:25,000) from the National Geographic Information Institute of MLTM were used. The detailed soil association map (1:25,000) from the NIAST (National Institute of Agricultural Science and Technology) was used for selection of soil attributes. Thirty-eight hydrologic soil groups within the Gyeongancheon watershed were used for analysis. Relational soil physical properties such as texture, bulk density, available water capacity, saturated conductivity, soil albedo etc. were obtained from the Agricultural Soil Information System (http://asis.rda.go.kr) of NIAST (2005).

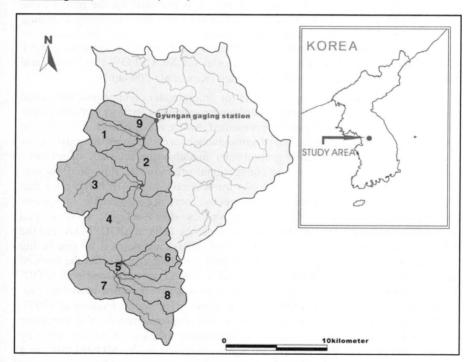

**Figure 7.** Division of subbasins of Gyeongancheon watershed.

HRUs in SWAT are formed based on the hydrologic soil group and land use. However, due to the semi-distributed features of SWAT, spatial locations of each HRU within subbasins is not determined. Hence, to reflect HRU locations to MODFLOW, spatially distributed HRUs using the DEM, with a cell size of 300

232

m, are used to match the discretized watershed with MODFLOW grids. An HRU-Grid conversion tool is made for this purpose. Within MODFLOW, the aquifers are represented as two layers, discretized into a grid of 126 rows and 123 columns. Groundwater information from National Groundwater Information Management and Service Center was used to determine the aquifer characteristics for MODFLOW inputs. Hydraulic conductivity in alluvial aquifer is $2.113 \times 10^{-3}$ cm/sec. Additionally, an assumption was made, according to a literature by Freeze and Cherry (1979), that the specific yield ranges from 0.1 to 0.3. Conductance of river bed was determined as one-tenth of the alluvial aquifer by trial-and-error procedure. The watershed boundaries were designated as no-flow cells. Recharge was distributed according to SWAT simulation outputs for each day. River-aquifer interaction was simulated using a RIVER package for MODFLOW. River stage of MODFLOW is imported from SWAT's daily simulation outputs.

Daily stream flow for year 1990 was calibrated against measured daily stream flow. Inputs to the model are physically based (i.e. based on readily observed or measured information). Several variables such as ESCO, AWC, CN2 were used for calibration. For the groundwater model, primary calibration parameters were the aquifer hydraulic conductivity and storativity. The hydraulic conductivity, the storativity and river bed conductance were then optimized by trial-and-error procedure. These variables were optimized by minimizing the low flow error during dry season. Calibration was performed on total stream flow. If simulated and measured flows are within 10%, the calibration is terminated. Observed and calibrated flows are shown in Figure 8(a). Total flow for the entire basin yielded an $R^2$ of 0.79. During 1991, daily stream flows were simulated by SWAT-MODFLOW model at the Gyungan gaging station in order to verify the performance of the calibrated SWAT-MODFLOW. The hydrograph was plotted using a log scale in order to emphasize the quality of low flow simulation. Figure 8(b) shows the SWAT-MODFLOW simulation during 1991. Total flow for the entire basin yielded an $R^2$ of 0.655 and Nash-Sutcliffe model efficiency of 0.647.

SWAT-MODFLOW is a grid based model, capable of calculating the spatially distributed groundwater table as shown in Figure 9. Figure 9 shows the distributions of groundwater head at 500, 800, 1000 days after running SWAT-MODFLOW. The gradual changes are shown in the figure.

The advanced pumping module, which is added to the SWAT-MODFLOW, is initially tested to Gyeongancheon watershed in Korea. For this purpose, the transfer command should be inserted to the data file We located a single discharge well at a certain cell (column=68, row=43) of MODFLOW in subbasin 4. The source is the shallow aquifer in subbasin 4, and the destination is the reach of subbasin 1.

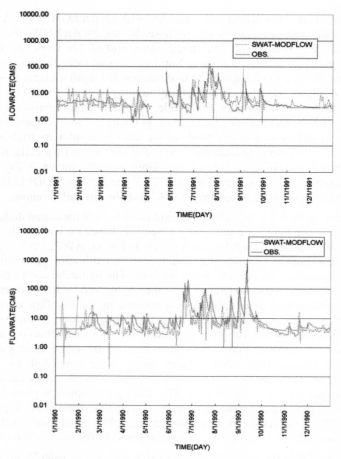

**Figure 8.** Simulation results by SWAT-MODFLOW (Kim et al., 2006): (a-upper) Calibration, (b-lower) Verification.

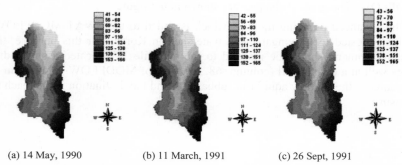

(a) 14 May, 1990          (b) 11 March, 1991          (c) 26 Sept, 1991

**Figure 9.** Spatial distribution of groundwater head simulated by SWAT-MODFLOW.

234

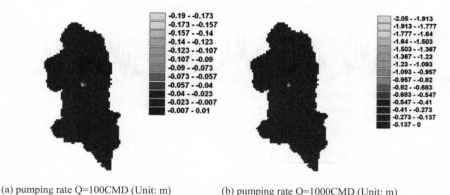

(a) pumping rate Q=100CMD (Unit: m)          (b) pumping rate Q=1000CMD (Unit: m)

**Figure 10.** Groundwater drawdown contour lines.

Two pumping scenarios, 100 m³/day and 1,000 m³/day, are applied. The groundwater variation and water budget variation according to pumping were examined. Figure 10 shows the groundwater drawdown contour lines with pumping rates of 100 m³/day and 1,000 m³/day.

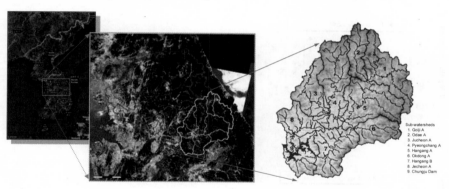

**Figure 11.** Han River basin and Chungju dam watershed.

235

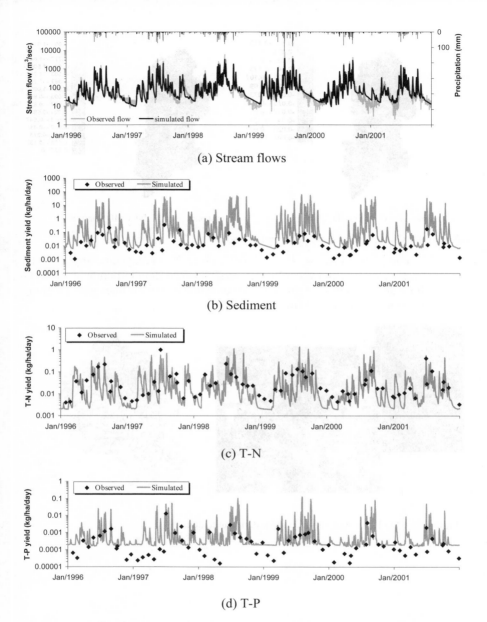

**Figure 12.** Calibration results of daily stream flows, sediment, T-N, and T-P loads at Chungju dam (Kim et al., 2007; Kim and Kim, 2008).

236

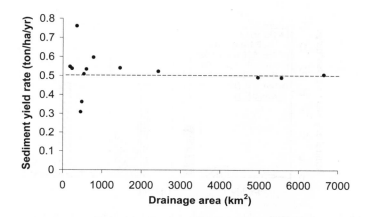

**Figure 13.** Sediment yield rates with drainage areas (Kim et al., 2007).

These results demonstrate that the advanced pumping module in the combined SWAT-MODFLOW model could effectively describe the water transfer in the watershed. Consequently, the combined SWAT-MODFLOW is introduced and applied to Gyeongancheon watershed in Korea. As model is fully combined, it is very useful to compute surface and groundwater components altogether. The application demonstrates a combined model which enables an interaction between saturated zones and channel reaches. This interaction plays an essential role in the runoff generation in the Gyeongancheon watershed. The comprehensive results show a wide applicability of the model that represents the temporal-spatial groundwater head distribution.

## 4. Watershed sediment and water quality modeling with SWAT-K

SWAT-K was applied to the Chungju dam upstream watershed through calibration and validation with physically based inputs and parameters, in order to quantify sediment, nitrogen, and phosphorus loads throughout the watershed, and investigate impacts of soil conservation practices.

The Chungju dam watershed is located in the main stream of the Han River basin, and covers 6,648 km² (6.7% of whole area of South Korea) with 375 km in length. For application of SWAT-K model, the watershed was divided into nine sub-watersheds based on TMDL unit-watershed of MOE (Ministry of Environment) (see Fig. 11), in which streamflow and water quality data have been measured at about 8-day intervals since August of 2004.

Figure 12 shows the calibration results for daily stream flows, sediment, total nitrogen (T-N), and total phosphorus (T-P) yields at Chungju dam site, the main outlet of the watershed, which accounts for reliable and accurate modeling in long-term periods.

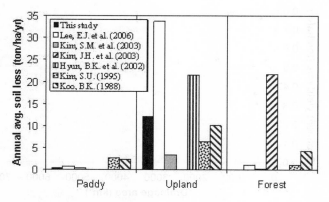

**Figure 14.** Annual average soil loss according to land use (Kim et al., 2007).

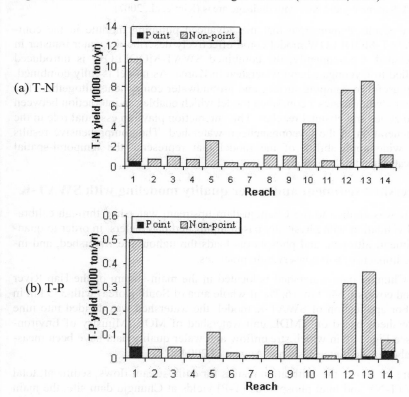

**Figure 15.** Pollutant yields of each reach with point and nonpoint sources (Kim and Kim, 2008).

238

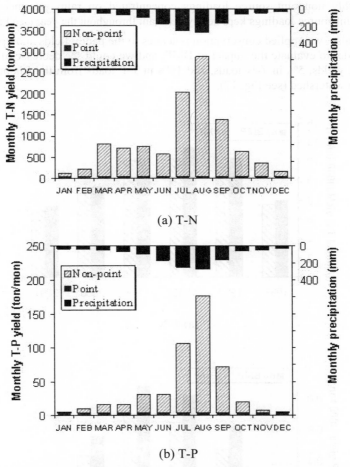

(a) T-N

(b) T-P

**Figure 16.** Monthly pollutant loads with point and nonpoint sources (Kim and Kim, 2008).

We could understand the spatial distribution of sediment yields in the watershed from the investigation on relationship between sediment yield rates and drainage areas in each watershed (see Fig. 13). And we could roughly estimate the amount of sediment yields and pollutant loads generated from each vegetation type (see Fig. 14).

In addition, we could grasp that in most forested upstream sub-watersheds of the Chungju dam upstream watershed, pollutant loadings from point sources are low, and total loadings by point and nonpoint sources are also insignificant. On the other hand, in #14 sub-watershed including Jecheon city, the loadings by point sources are relatively considerable (see Fig. 15). For the whole watershed, point sources account for 9% of T-N loads, and 16% of T-P loads.

Monthly nonpoint source loadings concentrated on rainy summer season, while point source loadings kept nearly constant throughout the year (see Fig. 16).

And also, we applied conservation practices to the paddy fields and upland areas in order to evaluate the impact of BMP, and we could see decrease of 18% in sediment yields, 5% in T-N loads, and 19% in T-P loads from the Chungju dam upstream watershed (see Fig. 17).

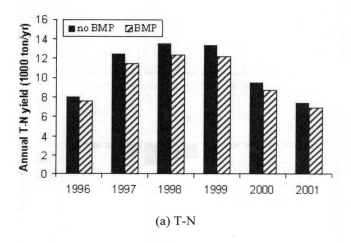

(a) T-N

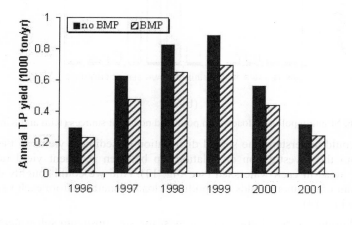

(b) T-P

**Figure 17.** Effect of conservation practices on annual T-N and T-P yields.

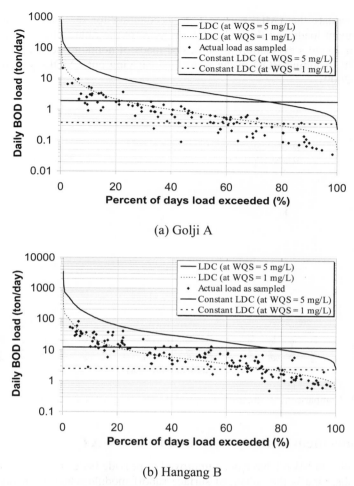

(a) Golji A

(b) Hangang B

**Figure 18.** TMDL test-evaluation by load duration curve.

SWAT-K was used to estimate flow duration curve (FDC) and standard flow for deriving LDC at each sub-outlet. In the Han River basin, TMDLs system currently is not in operation for most areas including the study watershed, and targeted WQS also has not been established yet, therefore we assumed WQS as 5 mg/L (corresponding to 'normal' in "Stream water quality level" by MOE), and 1 mg/L ('very good') for BOD, and performed test-evaluation of TMDLs with LDC and measured data for each sub-watershed. Figure 18 is an example result at Golji A in upstream and Hangang B in downstream, in which solid-lined and dotted-lined curves present LDCs obtained with WQS of 5 mg/L and 1 mg/L respectively, and parallel solid and dotted lines are allocated loads from the existing "averaged 10-year low flow". From the results we could more efficiently and reasonably evaluate the TMDLs using LDC accounting for seasonal varying non-point pollutant loads and flows through the year. In the future, it could be useful to perform TMDLs evaluation for allocated loads of nonpoint pollutants such as T-N or T-P including BOD in the watershed carrying out TMDLs system (Kim and Kim, 2009).

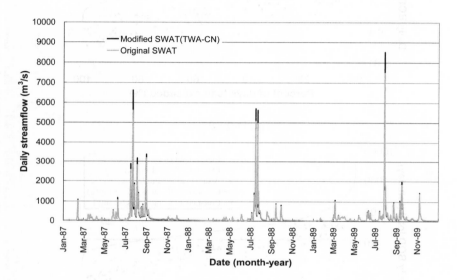

**Figure 19.** Comparison of streamflows simulated by original and modified versions of SWAT.

## 5. Enhancement of the runoff module in SWAT

Two modules in SWAT have been improved to provide better prediction of daily hydrographs. One is the enhanced surface runoff module which is incorporated with the temporally weighted average curve number (TWA-CN) method and the other is the additional channel routing module that is based on the nonlinear storage equation.

SWAT uses a procedure that links retention parameter with available water capacity of soil and uses the SCS runoff curve number method for estimating surface runoff depth. However, SWAT's weakness in predicting high and peak flows has been reported in recent articles. SWAT has a tendency to underestimate peak flows in high rainfall periods especially for lots of watersheds in South Korea.

Therefore, for providing better prediction of daily high and peak flows, the runoff module in SWAT has been enhanced by incorporating the TWA-CN method that is capable of reflecting the effect of the amount of rainfall for a given day as well as the antecedent soil moisture condition (Kim and Lee, 2008). In the modified version of SWAT with TWA-CN, the daily surface runoff volume is determined as a function of the weighted sum of $CN_t$ at the end of the previous day and $CN_{t+\Delta t}$ at the end of the current day.

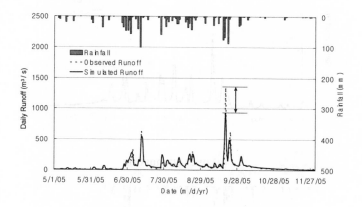

(a) Original version of SWAT

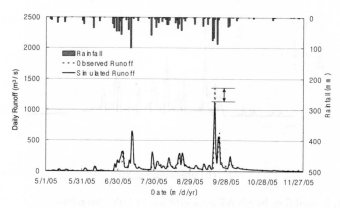

(b) Modified version of SWAT

**Figure 20.** Comparison of observed and simulated daily streamflow (Kim and Lee, 2008).

To assess the performance of the enhanced runoff module, the modified version of SWAT with TWA-CN method was applied to the Chungju dam watershed which is located in the middle of South Korea and covers a drainage area of 6,654 km². Figure 19 shows the hydrographs simulated by original and modified versions of SWAT. It is obvious that the peaks by modified SWAT are about 10-20% higher than those by original SWAT.

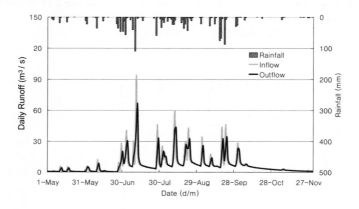

(a) over attenuation

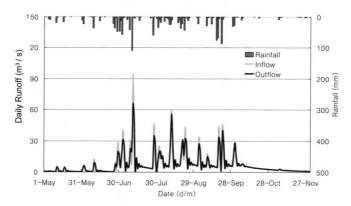

(b) unstable signal

**Figure 21.** Routed flow by SWAT for a subbasin of Mihocheon basin.

Simulation was also conducted for the Mihocheon basin (1,869 km²) located in the middle of South Korea to illustrate another performance of the modified version of SWAT with TWA-CN. Figures 20(a) and 20(b) show the results simulated by original and modified versions of SWAT, respectively. Figure 20(a) shows a satisfactory concurrence between measured and simulated hydrographs but it reveals a tendency to underestimate some of the peak flows. Even after a comprehensive calibration process, the original SWAT was not able to correctly reproduce the high flows for the Mihocheon basin. While using the modified

SWAT, as shown in Figure 20(b), an improved correspondence between the observed and predicted daily runoff was achieved. Visual inspection of the daily hydrographs shows the magnitude of peak flows simulated with reasonable accuracy.

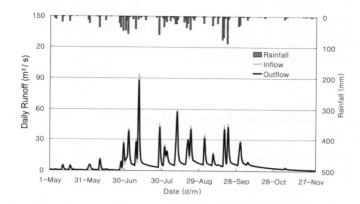

**Figure 22.** Routed flow by modified SWAT for a subbasin of Mihocheon basin.

Sometimes the channel routing module used in SWAT can be inappropriate for runoff simulation in small catchments that has a short travel time of much less than a day. As shown in Figures 21(a) and 21(b), simulated hydrographs showed an over attenuation of peak flow or a false signal during the recession periods when SWAT was applied to short tributaries within the Mihocheon River. This is due to the mathematical restriction of the Muskingum routing method in SWAT, which makes it difficult to calibrate routing parameters.

In order to enhance the channel routing module in SWAT for small catchments, an alternative routing technique in which Manning relationship is combined with a simple channel reach continuity equation has been added to the water routing module in SWAT. The advantage of the new routing technique is that parameters are readily available from channel morphological data and that it is applicable to small catchments. Figure 22 shows the routed flow by the modified version of SWAT. A little attenuation is found and the hydrograph is free from instability errors and produces realistic flow.

## 6. Assessment of forest vegetation effect on water balance in a watershed

To evaluate the effect of forest vegetation on the long-term water balance in a watershed, semi-distributed and physically based parameter model, SWAT was applied to the Bocheong watershed, and the variation of hydrological components such as evapotranspiration, surface flow, lateral flow, base flow, and total runoff was investigated with coniferous and deciduous forests, respectively. First,

245

SWAT model was modified to simulate the actual plant growth pattern of coniferous trees that have the uniform value of leaf area index all the seasons of the year. The modified model was applied to the watershed that is assumed to have only one land cover in the whole watershed, and the variation of the water balance components was investigated for each land cover. It was found that coniferous forest affected the increase in evapotranspiration and decrease in runoff more than deciduous forest. However, the age and the density of stand, the location, and soil characteristics and meteorological conditions including the tree species should be also considered to examine the effect more quantitatively and to reduce the uncertainties in simulated output from the hydrological model (Kim and Kim, 2004).

## 7. Runoff estimation from two mid-size watersheds using SWAT model

SWAT model was applied to estimate daily stream flow for Yongdam and Bocheong watersheds in Korea. The model was calibrated and validated for the two watersheds and a new routine was added to analyze runoff process in paddy fields. The model efficiencies for two watersheds were 0.77 and 0.65 for the calibration period, and 0.76 and 0.50 for the validation period, respectively. It showed that water balance method simulated the runoff from paddy fields more precisely than CN method in SWAT. As a result, the SWAT model is applicable to Korean watersheds, and more accurate estimation is possible using daily water balance method in paddy fields (Kim et al., 2004).

## 8. The development of coupled SWAT-SWMM model

### 8.1 Model development

From the continuous long-term rainfall-runoff standpoint, the urbanization within a watershed causes land use change due to the increase in impervious areas, the addition of manmade structures, and the changes in river environment. Therefore, rainfall-runoff characteristics change drastically after the urbanization. Due to these reasons, there exists the demand for rainfall-runoff simulation model that can quantitatively evaluate the components of hydrologic cycle including surface runoff, river flow, and groundwater by considering urban watershed characteristics as well as natural runoff characteristics. In this study, continuous long-term rainfall-runoff simulation model SWAT-SWMM is developed by coupling semi-distributed continuous long-term rainfall-runoff simulation model SWAT with RUNOFF block of SWMM, which is frequently used in the runoff analysis of urban areas in order to consider urban watershed as well as natural watershed. The coupling of SWAT and SWMM is described with emphasis on the coupling scheme, model limitations, and the schematics of coupled model (Kim and Won, 2004a).

## 8.2 Model characteristics and evaluation

The continuous long-term rainfall-runoff simulation model SWAT has an advantage of being able to account for various land use. However, SWAT lacks the capability of simulating the drainage characteristics of urban area. On the other hand, SWMM, which is the most popular model for runoff analysis of urban watershed, has the advantage of being capable of considering surface and drainage characteristics in urban area, but SWMM cannot easily account for land use other than urban area within a watershed. In this study, SWAT-SWMM model, which builds on the strengths of SWAT and SWMM, has been applied to the Osan River Watershed which is a tributary watershed to the Gyung-Ahn River. From the application, the results from coupled SWAT-SWMM model has been compared to the ones from SWAT for each hydrologic component such as evapotranspiration, surface runoff, groundwater flow, and watershed and channel discharge, and the runoff characteristics of two models for each hydrologic component has been discussed (Kim and Won, 2004b).

## 9. An evaluation of snowmelt effects using SWAT in Chungju dam Basin

The objective of this study is to evaluate the snowmelt effects on the hydrological components, especially on the runoff, by using the soil and water assessment tool (SWAT) which is a continuous semi-distributed long-term rainfall-runoff model. The model was applied to the basin located in the upstream of the Chungju dam. Some parameters in the snowmelt algorithm were estimated for the Chungju basin in order to reflect the snowmelt effects. The snowmelt effects were assessed by comparing the simulated runoff with the observed runoff data at the outlet of the basin. It was found out that the simulated runoff with consideration for the snowmelt component matches more satisfactorily to the observed one than without considering snowmelt effect. The simulation results revealed that the snowmelt effects were noticeable in March and April. Similar results were obtained at other two upstream gaging points. The effect of the elevation bands that distribute temperature and precipitation with elevation was analyzed. This study also showed that the snowmelt effect significantly affects the temporal distribution as well as quantity of the hydrological components. The simulated runoff was very sensitive to the change of temperature near the threshold temperature that the snowmelt can occur. However, the reason was not accounted for this paper. Therefore, further analyses related to this feature are needed (Kim et al., 2006).

## 10. Analysis of the characteristics of low-flow behavior based on spatial simulated flows

The drought flow analysis for small and medium sized river is very difficult because of the scarcity of drought flow observation data. This study concerns the generation of areal simulated flow from SWAT-the semi distributed hydrologic model, the estimation of drought flow and the analysis of its areal characteristics. The SWAT model is set up for the Chungju dam basin and is verified by comparing the observation-simulation daily flow of dam site with upper stream station. The specific flow rate of mean drought flow is increased with the area, which is identified from the slope of each subbasin and the areal characteristics of saturated hydraulic conductivity. It is also proved that the drought flow can be overestimated using observed flow data by comparing with previous results. This method can represent more reasonable drought flow than thereby areal-specific flow rate method. The physical characteristics of drought flow also can be evaluated by these results (Kim et al., 2007).

## 11. A new method of estimating groundwater recharge for sustainable water resources management in Korea

In Korea, there have been various methods of estimating groundwater recharge, which generally can be subdivided into three types: base flow separation method by means of groundwater recession curve, water budget analysis based on lumped conceptual model in watershed, and water table fluctuation method (WTF) by using the data from groundwater monitoring wells. However, groundwater recharge rate shows the spatial-temporal variability due to climatic condition, land use and hydrogeological heterogeneity, so these methods have various limits to deal with these characteristics. To overcome these limitations, we present a new method of estimating recharge based on water balance components from the SWAT-MODFLOW which is an integrated surface-groundwater model. Groundwater levels in the interest area close to the stream have dynamics similar to streamflow, whereas levels further upslope respond to precipitation with a delay. As these behaviors are related to the physical process of recharge, it is needed to account for the time delay in aquifer recharge once the water exits the soil profile to represent these features. In SWAT, a single linear reservoir storage module with an exponential decay weighting function is used to compute the recharge from soil to aquifer on a given day. However, this module has some limitations expressing recharge variation when the delay time is too long and transient recharge trend does not match to the groundwater table time series, the multi-reservoir storage routing module that represents more realistic time delay through vadose zone is newly suggested in this study. In this module, the parameter related to the delay time should be optimized by checking the correlation between simulated recharge and observed groundwater levels. The final step of this procedure is to compare simulated groundwater table with observed one as well as to compare simulated watershed runoff with observed one. This method is applied to Mihocheon watershed in Korea for the purpose of testing the procedure of proper estimation of spatio-temporal groundwater recharge distribution (Chung et al., 2007).

## 12. Estimation of runoff curve number for Chungju dam watershed using SWAT

The objective of this study is to present a methodology for estimating runoff curve number (CN) using SWAT model which is capable of reflecting watershed heterogeneity such as climate condition, land use, soil type. The proposed CN estimation method is based on the asymptotic CN method and particularly it uses surface flow data simulated by SWAT. This method has advantages to estimate spatial CN values according to subbasin division and to reflect watershed characteristics because the calibration process has been made by matching the measured and simulated streamflows. Furthermore, the method is not sensitive to rainfall-runoff data since CN estimation is on a daily basis. The SWAT based CN estimation method is applied to Chungju dam watershed. The regression equation of the estimated CN that exponentially decays with the increase of rainfall is presented (Kim et al., 2009).

## 13. Enhancement of coupling between soil water and groundwater in integrated SWAT-MODFLOW model

This study presents the effects of temporally varied groundwater table on hydrological components for the Musimcheon basin. To this end, the SWAT-MODFLOW model in which the groundwater module of SWAT is replaced with MODFLOW model has been used with a modification to enhance the coupling between the water content in soil profile and the groundwater in shallow aquifer. The variable soil layer construction technique (VSLT) is developed in the present work to represent the direct interaction of soil water and groundwater more realistically, and then the VSLT is incorporated into SWAT-MODFLOW model. In VSLT, when the simulated groundwater table rises within the soil zone, the soil layers below the water table is regarded as a portion of the shallow aquifer, so that those layers are excluded from the initially defined soil zone and are governed by the MODFLOW. From the simulation tests for the interested basin, the improved SWAT-MODFLOW model with VSLT is found to correctly capture the spatial distributions of overland flow, soil moisture, evapotranspiration according to the groundwater table variation (Kim et al., 2009).

## 14. The variation of probability flood according to the flow regulation by multi-purpose dams in Han River basin, Korea

The purpose of the present study is to evaluate the variation of probability flood according to the flow regulation by multi-purpose dams (Soyang and Chungju) in the Han River basin, Korea. SWAT-K was used in order to generate regulated and unregulated daily streamflows upstream of Paldang dam. Simulated flow regulated by the Soyang and Chungju dams was calibrated by comparison with the observed inflow data at Paldang reservoir. Generally the ratio of flood flows to daily streamflows is known to decrease with drainage area in a watershed.

Regulated and unregulated flood flows were obtained from the relationship between flood flows and daily streamflows. Extreme Type I distribution was applied for flood frequency analysis and L-moment method was used for parameter estimation. This is a novel approach capable of understanding the variation in flood frequency with dam operation for the relatively large watershed scale, and this will help improve the applicability of daily stream flow data for use in flood control as well as in water utilization (Kim and Lee, 2009).

## 15. Conclusion

As discussed above, SWAT-K studies have been carried out and some studies are going on. Especially our research is focused on two major topics. One thing is an accurate estimation of hydrologic components for proper planning and management of water resources in Korea and another is making the effective tool for water quality management in the watershed. Ministry of Land, Transport and Maritime Affairs performs the long-term water resources planning and management in Korea. For this purpose, verified and effective hydrologic model is essential. SWAT-K is expected to be a useful tool for this planning because it could analyze the hydrologic components according to the natural and artificial variation of watershed such as land use as well as the climate change. In addition, as Ministry of Environment operates Total Maximum Daily Load (TMDL) management system, it is essential to have an accurate and effective modeling technique for non-point source evaluation and estimation in watershed basis. SWAT-K is expected to be a basic tool for TMDL management. Therefore the future of SWAT-K is very promising.

## Acknowledgment

The authors wish to thank the Sustainable Water Resources Research Center (SWRRC) of the 21st Century Frontier Research Program for a grant with the code 2-2-3 that had enabled them to carry out this investigation.

## References

Arnold, J.G., P.M. Allen, and G. Bernhardt. 1993. "A comprehensive surface-groundwater flow model." *Journal of Hydrology,* Vol. 142. pp.47-69.

Arnold, J.G., R. Srinivasan, R.S. Muttiah, and J.R. Williams. 1998. "Large area hydrologic modeling and assessment part I: model development." Journal of American Water Resources Association, Vol. 34, No. 1, pp.73-89.

Chung, I.M., N.W. Kim, and J.W. Lee. 2007. "Estimation of Groundwater Recharge by Considering Runoff Process and Groundwater Level Variation in Watershed." *Journal of KOSSGE,* 12(5), pp.19-32 (in Korean).

DiLuzio, M., R. Srinivasan, and J. Arnold. 2001. *ArcView Interface for SWAT2000: User's Guide,* Blackland Research Center, Temple, Texas.

Freeze R. A. and J. A. Cherry. (1979). *Groundwater,* Prentice Hall.

Hyun, B.K., M.S. Kim, K.C. Eom, K.K. Kang, H. B. Yun, M. C. Seo, and K.S. Sung. 2002. "Evaluation on national environmental functionality of farming on soil loss using the

USLE and replacement cost method." *Journal of Korean Society of Soil Science and Fertilizer*, Vol. 35, No. 6, pp.361-371 (in Korean).

**Kim, C.G. and N.W. Kim. 2004.** "Assessment of forest vegetation effect on water balance in a watershed." *Journal of Korea Water Resources Association,* Vol 37, No. 9, pp.737-744 (in Korean).

**Kim, C.G. and N.W. Kim. 2008.** "Characteristics of pollutant loads according to types of sources for the Chungju Dam watershed." *Journal of Korean Society on Water Quality,* Vol. 24, No. 4, pp.465-472 (in Korean).

**Kim, C.G. and N.W. Kim. 2009.** "Assessment and TMDL development using load duration curve for the Chungju Dam watershed of the Han River in Korea." *The proceedings of the International SWAT Conference in Southeast Asia,* Chiang Mai, Thailand, Jan 5-8, 2009 (in press).

**Kim, C.G., H.J. Kim, C.H. Jang, and N.W. Kim. 2004.** "Runoff estimation from two mid-size watersheds using SWAT model." *Water Engineering Research*, Vol. 4, No. 4, pp.193-202 (in Korean).

**Kim, C.G., J.E. Lee, and N.W. Kim. 2007.** "Temporal and spatial characteristics of sediment yields from the Chungju Dam upstream watershed." *Journal of Korea Water Resources Association,* Vol. 40, No. 11, pp.887-898 (in Korean).

**Kim, J.H., K.T. Kim, and G.B. Yeon. 2003.** "Analysis of soil erosion hazard zone using GIS." *Journal of the Korean Association of Geographic Information Studies,* Vol. 6, No. 2, pp.22-32 (in Korean).

**Kim, N.W. and J. Lee. 2008.** "Temporally weighted average curve number method for daily runoff simulation." *Hydrological Processes*, Vol. 22, No.25, pp.4936-4948.

**Kim, N.W. and J.E. Lee. 2009.** "The Variation of Probability Flood according to the Flow Regulation by Multi-purpose Dams in Han-River Basin, Korea." *The proceedings of the International SWAT Conference in Southeast Asia,* Chiang Mai, Thailand, Jan 5-8, 2009 (in press).

**Kim, N.W., I.M. Chung, and Y.S. Won. 2004a.** "The development of fully coupled SWAT-MODFLOW model, (I) model development." *Journal of Korea Water Resources Association,* Vol. 37, No. 6, pp.503-512 (in Korean).

**Kim, N.W., I.M. Chung, and Y.S. Won. 2004b.** "The development of fully coupled SWAT-MODFLOW model, (II) evaluation of model." *Journal of Korea Water Resources Association,* Vol. 37, No. 6, pp.513-521 (in Korean).

**Kim, N.W., I.M. Chung, Y.S. Won, and J.G. Arnold. 2008.** "Development and Application of the Integrated SWAT-MODFLOW Model." *Journal of Hydrology*, Vol. 356, No. 1-2, pp.1-16.

**Kim, N.W., I.M. Chung, Y.S. Won, and J. Lee. 2006a.** "Development of combined watershed and groundwater models in Korea." *Proceedings of HIC 2006, Nice, France,* pp.1479-1486.

**Kim, N.W., J.E. Lee, B.J. Lee, and I.M. Chung. 2006b.** "Long-term runoff simulation with or without dams in Han River basin, Korea." *Proceedings of Hydroeco 2006*, pp.243-246.

**Kim, N.W., J. Lee, and J. Lee. 2009.** "Estimation of Runoff Curve Number for Chungju Dam Watershed Using SWAT." *Journal of Korea Water Resources Association,* Vol. 42, No. 1 (forthcoming issue, in Korean).

**Kim, N.W., J. Lee, I.M. Chung, and Y.S. Won. 2009.** "Enhancement of Coupling between Soil Water and Groundwater in Integrated SWAT-MODFLOW Model." *Journal of Korea Water Resources Association,* Vol. 42, No. 1 (forthcoming issue, in Korean).

**Kim, N.W. and Y.S. Won. 2004a.** "Development of coupled SWAT-SWMM model (I) Model Development." *Journal of Korea Water Resources Association*, Vol. 37, No. 7, pp.589-598 (in Korean).

**Kim, N.W. and Y.S. Won. 2004b.** "The Development of coupled SWAT-SWMM model (II) Model Characteristics and Evaluation." *Journal of Korea Water Resources Association*, Vol. 37, No. 7, pp.599-612 (in Korean).

**Kim, N.W., B.J. Lee, and J.E. Lee. 2006.** "An Evaluation of Snowmelt Effects Using SWAT in Chungju Dam Basin." *Journal of Korea Water Resources Association*, Vol. 39, No. 10, pp.833-844 (in Korean).

**Kim, N.W., B.J. Lee, and J.E. Lee. 2007.** "Analysis of the Characteristics of Low-flow Behavior Based on Spatial Simulated flows." *KSCE Journal of Civil Engineering*, Vol. 27, No. 4B, pp.431-440 (in Korean).

**Kim, S.M., S.W. Park, and M.S. Kang. 2003.** "Estimation of sediment yield to Asan Bay using the USLE and GIS." *Journal of Korea Water Resources Association,* Vol. 36, No. 6, pp.1059-1068 (in Korean).

**Kim, S.U. 1995.** "A study of the temporal change of soil loss of Kyungan river basin with GIS." Master's Thesis, Seoul National University (in Korean).

**Koo, B.K. 1988.** "A study on the analysis of land use and water quality relationships: case study of lake Eulam watershed." Master's Thesis, Seoul National University (in Korean).

**Lee, E.J., Y.K. Cho, S.W. Park, and H.K. Kim. 2006.** "Estimating soil losses from Saemangeum watershed based on cropping systems." *Journal of the Korean Society of Agricultural Engineers*, Vol. 48, No. 6, pp.101-112 (in Korean).

**McDonald, M.G. and A.W. Harbaugh. 1988.** *A Modular Three-Dimensional Finite-Difference Ground-water Flow Model,* U.S. Geological Survey Techniques of Water Resources Investigations Report Book 6, Chapter A1, 528 p.

**MEST. 2004.** *"Analysis and modeling for surface water hydrological components."* 21st Century Frontier R&D Program, Sustainable water resources research program, Korea Institute of Construction Technology (in Korean).

**Neitsch, S.L., J.G. Arnold, J.R. Kiniry, and J.R. Williams. 2001.** *"Soil and Water Assessment Tool Theoretical Documentation, Version 2000."*

**NIAST. 2005.** *Soil Database in Korea,* Report of 21century Frontier Research Program (in Korean).

**Sophocleous, M.S., S.P. Perkins, N.G. Stadnyk, and R.S. Kaushal. 1997.** *Lower Republican Stream-Aquifer Project, Final Report*, Kansas Geological Survey Open File Report 97-8, 1930 Constant Avenue, University of Kansas, Lawrence, KS 66047-3726.

**Sophocleous, M.S., J.K. Koelliker, R.S. Govindaraju, T. Birdie, S.R. Ramireddygari and S.P. Perkins. 1999.** "Integrated Numerical Modeling for Basin-Wide Water Management: The Case of the Rattlesnake Creek Basin in South-Central Kansas." *Journal of Hydrology,* Vol. 214, pp.179-196.

252

# 2.8 Predicting the Effects of Land Use on Runoff and Sediment Yield in Selected Sub-watersheds of the Manupali River Using the ArcSWAT Model*

## Nathaniel R. Alibuyog[1], Victor B. Ella[2], Manuel R. Reyes[3], Raghavan Srinivasan[4], Conrad Heatwole[5] and Theo Dillaha[6]

## Abstract

The quantitative prediction of environmental impacts of land use changes in watersheds could serve as basis for developing sound watershed management schemes, especially for Philippine watersheds with agroforestry systems. ArcSWAT, a river basin scale model developed to quantify the impact of land management practices on water, sediment, and agricultural chemical yields, was parameterized and calibrated in selected Manupali River sub-watersheds with an aggregate area of 200 ha to simulate the effects of land use on runoff volumes, sediment yield and streamflows.

Calibration results showed that ArcSWAT can adequately predict peaks and temporal variation of runoff volumes and sediment yields with Nash and Sutcliffe coefficient (NSE) ranging from 0.77 to 0.83 and 0.55 to 0.80, respectively. Simulation of land use change scenarios using the calibrated model showed that runoff volume and sediment yield increase by 3% to 14% and 200% to 273%, respectively, when 50% of the pasture area and grasslands are converted to agricultural lands. Consequently, this results to decrease in streamflows by 2.8% to 3.3%, with the higher value indicating a condition of the watershed without soil conservation intervention. More seriously, an increase of 15% to 32% in runoff volume occurs when the whole sub-watershed is converted to agricultural land. This accounts for 39% to 45% of the annual rainfall to be lost as surface runoff.

While simulation results are subject to further validation, this study has demonstrated that the Soil and Water Assessment Tool (SWAT) model can be a useful tool for modeling the impact of land use changes in Philippine watersheds.

**Keywords:** Land use change, runoff, sediment yield, SWAT modeling

---

© 2009 World Association of Soil and Water Conservation, *Soil and Water Assessment Tool (SWAT): Global Applications,* eds. Jeff Arnold, Raghavan Srinivasan, Susan Neitsch, Chris George, Karim Abbaspour, Philip Gassman, Fang Hua Hao, Ann van Griensven, Ashvin Gosain, Patrick Debels, Nam Won Kim, Hiroaki Somura, Victor Ella, Attachai Jintrawet, Manuel Reyes, and Samran Sombatpanit, pp. 253-266. The article has been reprinted from the paper published in the International Agricultural Engineering Journal (IAEJ). WASWC is grateful for the permission granted.

*This publication is part of the SANREM CRSP, which is supported by the United States Agency for International Development and the generous support of the American people through Cooperative Agreement No. EPP-A-00-00013-00.

[1]Assistant Professor and Director for Research and Development, Department of Agricultural Engineering, College of Agriculture and Forestry, Mariano Marcos State University, Batac City, 2906 Ilocos Norte, Philippines. natzalibuyog@yahoo.com *(Continued on next page)*

# 1. Introduction

Conversion of native forest to agricultural lands is prevalent in the Philippines. This is driven by the growing population and increasing demand for food as well as the short-term benefit derived from this newly opened often productive forest lands. The Manupali River watershed is a typical example of the many watersheds in the country today that had undergone land conversion and presently undergoing environmental degradation and causing off-site pollution and heavy sedimentation of rivers, reservoir and hydropower dams.

Manupali is an important watershed in the Philippines as it provides water to irrigate around 15,000 ha of ricelands (Daño and Midmore, 2002). It is rich in natural resources that had attracted many migrants from all over the country and pursue profitable economic activities in agriculture. Agriculture has become so extensive that it eventually led to the conversion of forest lands and grasslands into corn and other cropped land. Recently, expansions of sugar, banana, and corn cultivation at low altitudes and of vegetable and corn at higher altitudes have occurred substantially at the expense of perennial crops (Lapong, 2005). With the favorable climate and promise of high net return from growing cash crops in these areas, it is expected that upland farming will further increase and land conversion will eventually spread to higher altitude areas and more steeply sloping lands.

Obviously, intensive cultivation of annual crops coupled with the increase use of fertilizer, pesticides and other chemicals on vegetable crops cause serious soil erosion, aggravated by poor soil conservation practices. Soil erosion results to soil nutrient depletion or soil fertility reduction with the continuous detachment and transport of nutrient-rich particles from the top soil (Ella, 2005). The eroded sediment may also adsorb and transport agricultural contaminants such as pesticides, phosphate and heavy metals posing serious threat to aquatic life (Ella, 2005) and may create health problems for farm families and those living downstream. Moreover, soil erosion may result in several serious off-site effects including river and reservoir sedimentation affecting hydroelectric power generation and irrigation efficiencies (NWRB, 2004). Thus, unless conservation-oriented land management practices are employed, patterns of land use typically

[2]Professor, Land and Water Resources Division, Institute of Agricultural Engineering, College of Engineering and Agro-Industrial Technology, University of the Philippines Los Baños, College, Laguna 4031, Philippines vbella@up.edu.ph;

[3]Professor, Biological Engineering, Department of Natural Resources and Environmental Design, Sockwell Hall, North Carolina Agricultural and Technical State University, Greensboro, NC 27411-1080, U.S.A. mannyreyes@nc.rr.com, reyes@ncat.edu;

[4]Professor and Director Spatial Sciences Laboratory, Department of Ecosystem Science and Management, and Department of Biological and Agricultural Engineering, Texas A&M University, Texas, U.S.A. r-srinivasan@tamu.edu

[5]Associate Professor, and [6]Professor, Biological Systems Engineering Department, Virginia Tech, Blacksburg, VA 2406, U.S.A. dillaha@vt.edu

found in watershed such as the Manupali River watershed will generate substantial soil erosion and in the long run worsen the poverty of upland farmers as well as generate downstream costs (Paningbatan, 2005).

Developing a quantitative prediction model for assessing the environmental impacts of land use changes specifically on runoff and sediment yield in watersheds is therefore of paramount importance. It can serve as basis for developing policy interventions and for developing sound watershed management schemes, while ensuring the sustainability of the economic activities of the people.

Among the most widely used computer simulation modeling techniques for predicting runoff and sediment yield include the Soil and Water Assessment Tool (SWAT) model. However, this model has not yet been used in the Philippines particularly for predicting land use impacts. In fact, with the exception of the WEPP model application in small Philippine upland watersheds by Ella (2005), no other published report on the use of modern computer simulation modeling techniques for predicting hydrologic impacts of land use change in the Philippines exists.

Hence, this study was conducted to determine the effects of various land use patterns on runoff, and sediment yield in selected sub-watersheds of the Manupali River using the ArcSWAT model. Specifically, it aimed to parameterize, calibrate and use the ArcSWAT model in simulating the effects of various land use patterns on runoff and sediment yields.

ArcSWAT is a physically-based, river basin scale model developed to quantify the impact of land management practices on water, sediment, and agricultural chemical yields in large, complex watersheds with varying soils, land use, and management conditions over long period of time that runs on a daily time step. Major model components describe processes associated with water movement, sediment movement, soils, temperature, weather, plant growth, nutrients, pesticides and land management (Arnold et al., 1998). The watershed is subdivided into hydrologic response units (HRUs), which is a sub-watershed unit having unique soil and land use characteristics. The water balance of each HRU in the watershed is represented by several storage volumes. Surface runoff from daily rainfall is estimated using a modified SCS curve number method, and sediment yield is calculated with the Modified Universal Soil Loss Equation (MUSLE) developed by Williams and Berndt (1977).

## 2. Methodology

### 2.1 Description of study area

The Kiluya and Kalaignon are two sub-watersheds within the Manupali River watershed in Lantapan, Bukidnon, Philippines (Fig. 1). It encompasses a total area of about 200 ha and it is a typical area that practice intensive cultivation of corn and vegetables crops. The topography is rolling to hilly, and ranges in elevation from 900 m above mean sea level at the outlet of the two sub-watersheds to about

2,000 m at their upstream peak. Soils in these sub-watersheds are predominantly clayey due to the extent of fine-grained volcanic rocks, various sedimentary derivatives and pyroclastics (BSWM, 1985). Rainfall is evenly distributed throughout the year with an average annual rainfall of 2,347 mm with rainfall peaks from June to October. Mean temperature ranges from 17°C to 28°C. Relative humidity ranges from 86 to 98 percent. Existing land cover is comprised of 16.8% dense forest, 29.5% agricultural crops predominantly corn and vegetables, 53.0% grasslands, shrubs and small trees, and 0.7% footpath.

## 2.2 Preparation of the ArcSWAT model inputs

Spatial data required by the model include a digital elevation model (DEM), land use map and soil map. In this study, the DEM map was prepared by digitizing a 1:50,000 scale topographic map with contour intervals of 20 m in ArcGIS 9.2 software. This was converted into a raster map called the DEM map with pixel size of 10 m x 10 m using the topographic tool of ENVI 4.5. ArcSWAT used the DEM map to delineate the sub-watersheds and generate the slope map of the test watershed.

The land use map was generated from the Ikonos images taken in May 2007. The acquired Ikonos images came with two resolutions, namely 1 m x 1 m panchromatic and 4 m x 4 m multispectral images. Prior to land use classification, the multispectral image was fused to the panchromatic image to increase its resolution to 1 m x 1 m. The resulting image was then used to classify the various land uses present in the area. Four land uses were identified and classified as agricultural (29.5%), pasture/grasses (53.0%), forest (16.8%), and footpath (0.7%).

The soil map of the study area was extracted from the soil map of the Philippines prepared by the Bureau of Agricultural Research. Specific soil properties such as texture, organic matter content, soil erodibility, infiltration rate among others were compiled from various literatures (e.g. Lapong, 2005; Paningbatan, 2005; BSWM, 1985).

Time series of meteorological data such as rainfall, temperature, solar radiation, relative humidity, and wind speed were compiled into proper format required by ArcSWAT from previous weather data obtained from the automatic weather station of SANREM-CRSP installed at the study site. Time series of observed runoff volume and sediment yield were obtained from the work of Lapong (2005) and were used to calibrate the model.

## 2.3 Model development and calibration

ArcSWAT 2005 version 2.1.2a was used in this study. Using the generated DEM map and locations of four known gaging stations, the study area was delineated and subdivided into four sub-watersheds namely, lower and upper Kiluya and lower and upper Kalaignon within the ArcSWAT interface. Each sub-watershed was further subdivided into hydrologic response units (HRU) by overlaying the slope map, generated from the DEM, with the soils and land use maps.

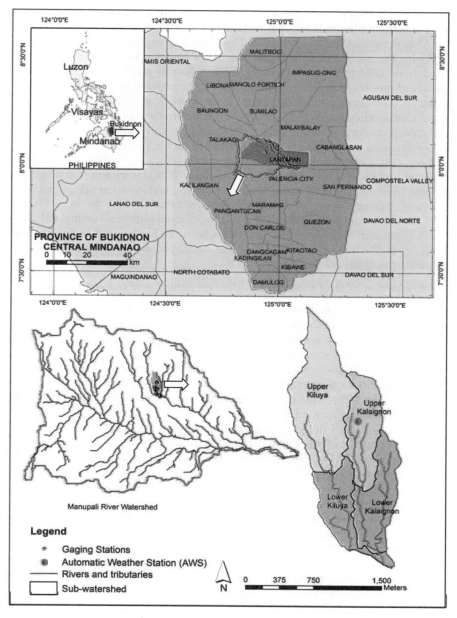

**Figure 1**. The Manupali River watershed and test sub-watersheds showing the locations of gaging stations and automatic weather station (AWS) and its location in the province of Bukidnon, Philippines.

The three major land uses were further subdivided into more specific land uses to better represent the spatial variation of vegetation in the watershed (Table 1). Also, the slope map was subdivided into four classes (Table 2).

Using the ArcSWAT default parameters, the watershed conditions were simulated from 1994 through 2004 using daily historical weather information. The simulated runoff and sediment yield in 2004 was compared to the runoff and sediment yield observed by Lapong (2005) in the same year in the same gaging stations. Considering that ArcSWAT is not a 'parametric model' with a formal optimization procedure to fit any data and it uses physically-based inputs, only few important parameters that are not well-defined physically such as runoff curve number, USLE cover and management factor (C factor), and infiltration rate were adjusted to provide a better fit. The curve number (CN2) were adjusted within 10 percent from the tabulated curve numbers to reflect conservation tillage practices and soil residue cover conditions of the watershed. Also, the linear factor (SPCON) and exponential factor (SPEXP) for channel sediment routing and filter width parameter were adjusted to provide a better fit to observed sediment yield in the area. The sequence of adjusting the model parameters were based on the procedures outlined by Santhi et al. (2001).

## 2.4 Evaluation of land use change effect on runoff and sediment yield

In order to develop sound management schemes of protecting the watershed and to have clear picture of the impact of land use changes specifically on runoff volume, streamflows, and sediment yield, the calibrated model was run to simulate eight land use change scenarios. Land use change scenarios are:

Scenario 1 - 50% of the present grasslands are converted to agricultural lands with soil conservation intervention;

Scenario 2 - 50% of the present grasslands are converted to agricultural lands without soil conservation intervention;

Scenario 3 - 100% of the present grasslands are converted to agricultural lands with soil conservation intervention;

Scenario 4 - 100% of the present grasslands are converted to agricultural lands without soil conservation intervention;

Scenario 5 - 100% of the present grassland and 50% of the present forest are converted to agricultural lands with soil conservation intervention;

Scenario 6 - 100% of the present grassland and 50% of the present forest are converted to agricultural lands without soil conservation intervention;

Scenario 7 - 100% of the present grassland and 100% of the present forest are converted to agricultural lands with soil conservation intervention; and

Scenario 8 - 100% of the present grassland and 100% of the present forest are converted to agricultural lands without soil conservation intervention.

For developing the scenarios, the key processes and related model parameters such as crops grown, P factor of USLE, infiltration rate, runoff curve number, and filter width were modified in the appropriate ArcSWAT input files. An USLE P factor of 0.6 and 1.0 were used in simulations to reflect the condition of the watershed with and without soil conservation intervention, respectively. Filter width of 10 m was m was provided in all simulation scenarios to partly reflect the vegetable agroforestry (VAF) technology being advocated by the Sustainable Agriculture and Natural Resources Management (SANREM) project. The microclimate effect of the VAF however was not simulated in this study. The simulated runoff volumes and sediment yields at the various scenarios were used as guide in developing recommendations for the sustainable management of the watershed.

## 2.5 Data analysis

The predicted and measured runoff volumes and sediment yield in 2004 were summarized and plotted weekly to compare their temporal distribution. The goodness of fit between the simulated and measured runoff volumes and sediment yields in the four sub-watersheds were evaluated by the coefficient of determination ($R^2$). Also, the efficiency of the model was evaluated using the Nash and Sutcliffe (1970) equation given as

$$E = 1 - \frac{\sum_{i=1}^{n}\left(X_{mi} - X_{pi}\right)^2}{\sum_{i=i}^{n}\left(X_{mi} - \overline{X}_m\right)^2}$$

where $E$ is the efficiency of the model, $X_{mi}$ and $X_{pi}$ are the measured and predicted values, respectively and $\overline{X}_m$ is the average measured values. A value of $E=1.0$ indicates a perfect prediction while negative values indicate that the predictions are less reliable than if one had used the sample mean instead. In addition, the root mean square error (RMSE) was used to evaluate how much of the prediction overestimates or underestimates the measured values. In each scenario, the mean runoff volume, streamflow and sediment yield over a 5-year simulation excluding a six-year precondition simulation period were obtained and used to assess the impact of the land use change.

**Table 1.** Land use classification of the study area.

| LANDUSE | AREA (ha) | % of TOTAL |
|---|---|---|
| Agricultural | | |
| Corn | 35.3 | 17.7 |
| Cabbage | 11.8 | 5.9 |
| Potato | 11.8 | 5.9 |
| Pasture/Grassland | | |
| Ranged grasslands | 74.2 | 37.1 |
| Pasture with brushes | 31.8 | 15.9 |
| Forest | | |
| Mixed forest | 23.5 | 11.8 |
| Deciduous trees | 10.1 | 5.0 |
| Foot path | 1.4 | 0.7 |
| TOTAL | 199.8 | 100.0 |

**Table 2.** Slope classification of the study area.

| Slope (%) | Area (ha) | % of Total |
|-----------|-----------|------------|
| 0-8 | 45.4 | 22.71 |
| 8-18 | 0.1 | 0.03 |
| 18-30 | 57.6 | 28.82 |
| Above 30 | 96.7 | 48.44 |
| TOTAL | 199.8 | 100.0 |

**Table 3.** Comparison between the simulated and observed runoff volumes in the four sub-watersheds.

| WATERSHED | WEEKLY MEAN RUNOFF VOLUME ($m^3$) | | RMSE | $R^2$ | NSE |
|-----------|----------|-----------|------|-------|-----|
| | Observed | Simulated | | | |
| Lower Kiluya | 3809 | 4098 | 3014 | 0.88 | 0.82 |
| Upper Kiluya | 2610 | 2820 | 1977 | 0.88 | 0.83 |
| Lower Kalaignon | 2992 | 2848 | 2368 | 0.90 | 0.80 |
| Upper Kalaignon | 1470 | 1449 | 1323 | 0.87 | 0.77 |

**Table 4.** Comparison between the simulated and observed sediment yield in the four sub-watersheds

| WATERSHED | WEEKLY MEAN SEDIMENT YIELD (tons) | | RMSE | $R^2$ | NSE |
|-----------|----------|-----------|------|-------|-----|
| | Observed | Simulated | | | |
| Lower Kiluya | 1.95 | 2.09 | 1.84 | 0.82 | 0.80 |
| Upper Kiluya | 0.84 | 3.39 | 4.17 | 0.70 | -5.16 |
| Lower Kalaignon | 3.96 | 2.53 | 5.83 | 0.80 | 0.55 |
| Upper Kalaignon | 1.03 | 1.12 | 1.45 | 0.58 | 0.58 |

## 3. Results and Discussion

### 3.1 Prediction of runoff volume

The daily simulated runoff volumes in each of the four sub-watersheds were lumped into weekly totals and compared with the measured runoff volumes in the area. Results show that the simulated and measured runoff volumes at the four sub-watershed outlets matched well (Fig. 2). **Further agreement between measured and simulated runoff volumes at the four sub-watershed outlets are shown by the coefficient of determination, $R^2$, ranging from 0.87 to 0.90 (Table 3). The adequacy of the Arc-SWAT model to simulate the runoff volumes is also indicated by high NSE values ranging from 0.77 to 0.83.** The adequacy of the model is further indicated by its clear response to extreme rainfall events resulting in high runoff volumes (Fig. 2). These results indicate that hydrologic processes in ArcSWAT are modeled realistically and can be extended to simulate other hydrologic process including peak flows and streamflows at various land use change scenarios.

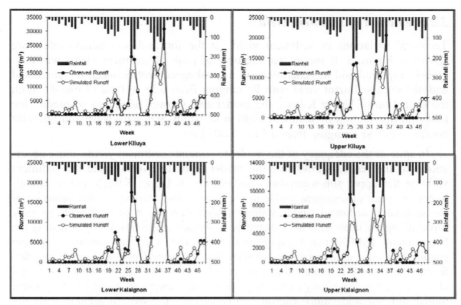

**Figure 2.** Observed and calibrated simulated runoff volumes at the four sub-watersheds superimposed with the weekly rainfall amount in the study area.

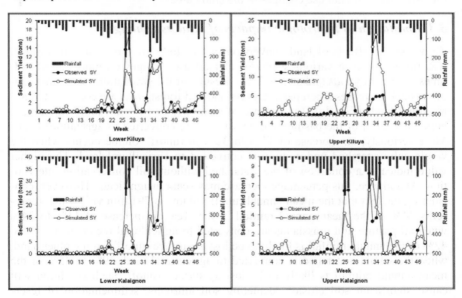

**Figure 3.** Observed and simulated sediment yields at the four sub-watersheds superimposed with the weekly rainfall amount in the study area during calibration period.

## 3.2 Prediction of sediment yield

Temporal variations of sediment yields at the four sub-watershed outlets are shown in Figure 3. It shows that the time of peak of sediment yields was adequately captured and in general shows a good agreement between the simulated and observed sediment yield with $R^2$ ranging from 0.58 to 0.82 (Table 4). With the exception of Upper Kiluya, the model also showed adequacy to predict the temporal distribution of sediment yield in the study area with Nash and Sutcliffe coefficient (NSE) ranging from 0.55 to 0.80 (Table 4).

In spite of the adequacy of the model to simulate sediment yields, close observation of the results shows that the model tends to overestimate the sediment yield in the upper sub-watersheds particularly in Upper Kiluya and underestimates the peak of sediment yields in the lower sub-watersheds. This behavior of the simulated sediment yields indicates high deposition of sediments as they travel along the channel. This was partly addressed in ArcSWAT by adjusting the linear factor (SPEXP) and exponential factor (SPCON) for channel sediment routing to their maximum values of 0.01 and 2, respectively. The remaining difference between the simulated and observed values may also be attributed to the channel erosion, especially during high flows, and other factors which the present model did not adequately capture. Nevertheless, the overall adequacy of the model to simulate sediment yields in the watershed indicates its usefulness to predict the effects of land use changes in the study area.

## 3.3 Simulation of hydrologic impacts of land use change

To assess the effects of land conversion in the study area, the calibrated model was run to simulate various scenarios of land use changes on more runoff volumes, sediment yields and streamflows. Results of the simulations show that runoff volume increases when pasture/grassland and forest areas are converted to agricultural lands (Fig. 4a). An increase of about 3% to 14% in runoff volume occurs when 50% of the pasture and grasslands are converted to agriculture lands. More seriously, an increase of 15% to 32% in runoff volume occurs when the whole sub-watershed under study is converted to agricultural land. The higher value indicates a condition of the watershed without soil conservation intervention. At a glance, this percentage increase may seem insignificant. However, considering the fact that the mean annual runoff volume is 791 mm yr$^{-1}$, which represents 34% of the mean annual rainfall in the area, an increase of 11% to 24% when all pasture and grasslands are converted to agricultural means that 37% to 42% of the annual rainfall is likely to be lost as surface runoff. On the other hand, when the whole watershed is converted to agricultural land, 39% to 45% of the mean annual rainfall is likely to be lost as surface runoff. Such condition will cause significant soil erosion, depleting soil nutrients, sedimentation of reservoirs, and flooding of low lying areas at the downstream. The eroded sediment may also adsorb and transport agricultural contaminants such as pesticides, phosphate and heavy metals posing serious threat to aquatic life (Ella, 2005) and may create health problems for farm families and those living downstream. Furthermore, there will be a significant decrease in groundwater baseflow due to reduced infiltration. This impacts the wildlife and fish in the streams and also the water supply of the watershed especially during dry periods.

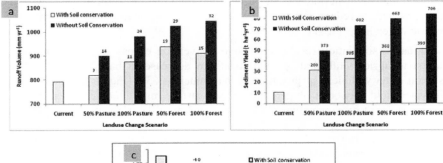

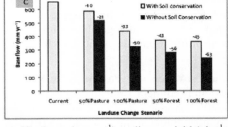

**Figure 4.** Simulated runoff volume (mm yr$^{-1}$), sediment yield (t ha$^{-1}$ yr$^{-1}$), baseflow (mm yr$^{-1}$) in the study area as affected by percentage pasture and forest areas converted to agricultural land. The numbers on top of the bars indicate the percentage change from its current value.

It should be noted that more dramatic increase in runoff volumes can be expected in the test watershed than our simulation results. This is because we assumed in all simulations that converted areas are planted with agricultural crops all year round. Such assumption is considerably valid since only about 1.5 to 1.75 percent of the total existing agricultural areas is classified as fallow (Lapong, 2005). On the other hand, despite this assumption, a dramatic increase in sediment yields is predicted as pasture, grassland and forest areas are converted to agricultural lands, even with the intervention of soil conservation practices such as contouring (Fig. 4b). Converting 50% of the pasture and grasslands to agricultural crops is likely to increase the current sediment yields of 10.4 t ha$^{-1}$yr$^{-1}$ to about 31 t ha$^{-1}$yr$^{-1}$ and up to 49 t ha$^{-1}$yr$^{-1}$ when no soil conservation intervention is employed. Likewise, converting the whole watershed to agricultural lands is likely to increase the sediment yield to 51 t ha$^{-1}$yr$^{-1}$ and up to 84 t ha$^{-1}$yr$^{-1}$. Again, this dramatic increase in sediment yields could be even worse when portions of the converted areas to agricultural lands are left fallow and bare. Our simulation results show that mean annual sediment yield in fallow areas is about 296 t ha$^{-1}$, compared to areas planted to corn, cabbage, and potato having sediment yields of 40 t ha$^{-1}$, 34 t ha$^{-1}$, and 59 t ha$^{-1}$, respectively. The current sediment yield of the watershed of 10.43 t ha$^{-1}$ yr$^{-1}$ is in fact near the upper limit of tolerable soil loss of 11.2 t ha$^{-1}$ yr$^{-1}$ (Hudson, 1995). Thus, rather than expanding the current agricultural areas to increase crop production, efforts should be exerted to improve present crop cultural management practices of farmers and train them to employ soil conservation practices to reduce soil erosion rate, thereby rehabilitating and sustaining the whole watershed.

Finally, simulation results show that conversion of pasture, grasslands and forest to agricultural land use will result to decrease in baseflow (defined as stream water yield less surface runoff) to as much as 63% (Fig. 4c). This decrease in water yield may be attributed to increased surface runoff and decreased infiltration as a result of conversion of forest to agricultural land use. Forest vegetation dissipates raindrop energy, retards surface runoff velocity, increases evapotranspiration rates and increases the soil organic matter content, all of which lead to greater infiltration and lower surface runoff. According to Paningbatan (2005), forest areas in the study area have an infiltration rate of about 100 mm hr$^{-1}$ while agricultural land planted with corn and vegetables with and without soil conservation intervention has an infiltration rate of 60 mm hr$^{-1}$ and 17 mm hr$^{-1}$, respectively.

Considering that the test watershed is a part of the Manupali river basin, an increase in surface runoff and sediment yield and decrease in baseflow will have serious environmental and economic effects not only to the communities living in the study area but also those living at the downstream. Efforts should therefore be exerted to address forest conversion to agricultural crops. Policies addressing this problem should be done both at the local and national level. Likewise, an intensive information and education campaign on the consequences of forest conversion and ways of rehabilitating the watershed should be done. Finally, this study recommends that alternative livelihood opportunities for upland farmers should be considered in policy implementation.

## 4. Summary and Conclusions

The ArcSWAT model was parameterized and calibrated in selected Manupali River sub-watersheds in the Philippines with an aggregate area of 200 ha to simulate the effects of land use on runoff volumes, sediment yield and streamflows. Results showed that ArcSWAT adequately predicted the runoff volumes of the test watershed with NSE ranging from 0.77 to 0.83. Both the peaks and temporal variation of runoff volumes at the four sub-watersheds of the test watershed were adequately captured by the model. Likewise, with the exception of Upper Kiluya, the model adequately predicted the sediment yields of the test watershed with NSE ranging from 0.55 to 0.80.

In order to develop sound management schemes for protecting the watershed and to have clear picture of the impact of land use changes specifically on runoff volume, streamflows and sediment yield, the calibrated model was also run to simulate eight land use change scenarios. Results showed that converting pasture, grasslands and forest to agricultural crops will likely result in increased runoff volumes, increased sediment yields, and decreased streamflows. Converting 50% of the pasture and grassland to agricultural crops increases predicted runoff volumes and sediment yields by 3% to 14% and 200% to 273%, respectively with the higher value indicating a condition of the watershed when no soil conservation intervention is applied. Consequently, this will result to decrease in streamflows by about 45% to 63%. More seriously, an increase of 15% to 32% in runoff volume is likely to occur when the whole sub-watershed under study is converted to agricultural land. This accounts for 39% to 45% of the annual rainfall to be lost as surface runoff. Such condition will cause significant soil erosion depleting soil nutrients, sedimentation of reservoirs, and flooding of low lying areas at the downstream.

These simulated effects of pasture and forest conversion to agricultural crops clearly indicate an alarming situation of watersheds elsewhere having the same land use pattern as our test watershed. Efforts should therefore be exerted to address forest conversion to agricultural crops. In our test watershed, we recommend that policies addressing this problem should be formulated both at the local and national level. Parallel to this, an intensive information and education campaign on the consequences of forest conversion and ways of rehabilitating the watershed should likewise be done. Finally, alternative livelihood opportunities for the upland farmers should be considered in policy implementation.

While simulation results are subject to further validation, this study showed that the Soil and Water Assessment Tool (SWAT) model can be a useful tool for modeling the impact of land use changes in Philippine watersheds.

## Acknowledgments

This project was made possible through support provided by the United States Agency for International Development (USAID) and the generous support of the American people for the Sustainable Agriculture and Natural Resources Management Collaborative Research Support Program (SANREM CRSP) under terms of Cooperative Agreement Award No. EPP-A-00-04-00013-00 to the Office of International Research and Development (OIRED) at Virginia Polytechnic Institute and State University (Virginia Tech); and terms of sub-agreement 19070A-425632 between Virginia Tech and North Carolina Agricultural and Technical State University (NCA&T). The authors also thank Dr. David J. Midmore and Engr. Edward R. Lapong for providing the data used in the calibration of the model.

## References

Arnold, J.G., R. Srinivasan, R.S. Muttiah, and J.R. Williams. 1998. Large-area hydrologic modeling and assessment: Part I. Model development. *J. American Water Res. Assoc.* 34(1):73-89.

Bureau of Soils and Water Management, Department of Agriculture (BSWM). 1985.

Land resources evaluation report for Bukidnon province: the physical land resources volume 1. BSWM-DA, Manila, Philippines.

**Daño, A.M., and D.J. Midmore. 2002.** Analyses of soil and water conservation technologies in vegetable based upland production system of Manupali Watershed. 12$^{th}$ ISCO Conference, Beijing.

**Ella, V.B. 2005.** Simulating soil erosion and sediment yield in small upland watersheds using the WEPP model. In: I. Coxhead and G.E. Shively, eds., Land use change in tropical watersheds: Evidence, causes and remedies. CABI publishing. Wallingford, Oxfordshire, UK. pp 109-125.

**Hudson, N. 1995.** Soil conservation. BT Batsford Limited, London. 391 pp.

**Lapong, E.R. 2005.** Effect of land use patterns on runoff, sediment yield, and pesticide loading in selected microcatchments in Manupali Watershed, Lantapan, Bukidnon, Philippines. Unpublished Master's thesis, University of the Philippines at Los Baños, College, Laguna, Philippines. 178 pp.

**National Water Resources Board (NWRB). 2004.** Water for food: Aiming for self-sufficiency and rural development. In: Ella, V.B. 2005. Simulating soil erosion and sediment yield in small upland watersheds using the WEPP model. In: I. Coxhead and G.E. Shively, eds., Land use change in tropical watersheds: Evidence, causes and remedies. CABI publishing. Wallingford, Oxfordshire, UK. pp 109-125.

**Nash, J. E., and J.E. Sutcliffe. 1970.** River flow forecasting through conceptual models: Part I. A discussion of principles. *J. Hydrol.* 10:282-200.

**Paningbatan, Jr. E.P. 2005.** Identifying soil erosion hotspots in the Manupali River watershed. In: I. Coxhead and G.E. Shively, eds., Land use change in tropical watersheds: Evidence, causes and remedies. CABI publishing. Wallingford, Oxfordshire, UK. pp 126-132.

**Santhi, C., R. Srinivasan, J.G. Arnold, and J.R. Williams. 2006.** A modeling approach to evaluate the impacts of water quality management plans implemented in Texas. Environmental Modeling and Software. 21:1141-1157.

**Williams, J.R., and H.D. Berndt. 1977.** Sediment yield prediction based on watershed hydrology. *Trans. ASAE.* 20(6): 1100-1104.

# 2.9 Hydrological Modeling with SWAT under Conditions of Limited Data Availability: Evaluation of Results from a Chilean Case Study

## Alejandra Stehr[1], Patrick Debels, Francisco Romero and Hernan Alcayaga

## Abstract

Water resources from the Biobío basin are of high strategic importance for economic development in Chile, both at the regional level as well as for the country as a whole. Advances in the capacity to describe and predict - in a spatially explicit manner - the impact of climate and anthropogenic forcing on the hydrology of the Biobío River basin are therefore urgently required. The work presented in this manuscript pretends to set the basis for future modeling applications within Biobío by analyzing the applicability of a readily available modeling tool, the SWAT model, to a subbasin of it. Modeling results show that the model performs well in most parts of the study basin. The SWAT model application for the Vergara basin confirms that SWAT is a useful tool and can already be used to make preliminary assessments of the potential impacts of land use and climate changes on basin hydrology.

**Keywords:** hydrological modeling, SWAT, calibration, Chile, Biobío

## 1. Introduction

The integrated management and adequate allocation of water resources between different water uses under changing conditions of land use and climate are major challenges which many societies already face, or will have to face during the next decades (Simonovic, 2002). In this context, the analysis of the impact of land use and climate changes on river hydrology and surface water availability can be addressed by means of spatially distributed rainfall-runoff model applications (Harrison and Whittington, 2002; Eckhardt and Ulbrich, 2003; Haverkamp et al., 2005). Well-known models that are commonly applied at the basin scale are the Hydrologic Simulation Package Fortran (HSPF; Holtan and Lopez, 1971), the Système Hydrologique Européen (SHE; Abbott et al., 1986a,b), the Soil and Water Assessment Tool (SWAT; Arnold et al., 1998) and the Hydrologic Engineering Centre Hydrologic Modeling System (HEC-HMS; HEC, 2000), amongst others.

© 2009 World Association of Soil and Water Conservation, *Soil and Water Assessment Tool (SWAT): Global Applications,* eds. Jeff Arnold, Raghavan Srinivasan, Susan Neitsch, Chris George, Karim Abbaspour, Philip Gassman, Fang Hua Hao, Ann van Griensven, Ashvin Gosain, Patrick Debels, Nam Won Kim, Hiroaki Somura, Victor Ella, Attachai Jintrawet, Manuel Reyes, and Samran Sombatpanit, pp. 267-284. This paper has been published in the Hydrologic Sciences Journal (2008). WASWC is grateful for the permission granted by the copyright holders International Association of Hydrological Sciences (IAHS).

[1]All authors are from the Centre for Environmental Sciences EULA-CHILE, University of Concepción, P.O. Box 160-C, Concepción, Chile. Contact pdebels@gmail.com, pdebels@udec.cl

These models that produce hydrographs as well as water yields and provide possibilities for continuous simulation can be operated at different time steps, and have varying numbers of input parameters (Mishra and Singh, 2004). However, for practical applications in meso- or macro-scale basins, in Chile as well as in many other places of the world, available meteorological data will restrict choice to those models that offer possibilities for using daily (or coarser) data for performing water balance calculations. Most applications of the previously described models found today in the literature correspond to case studies from the developed world, where data availability may be very different from those typically encountered elsewhere.

In Central Chile, the Biobío basin (24.371 km$^2$) is of high strategic importance for economical development, both at the regional and the national level. The continuously growing pressures on the basin's water resources, together with the need to preserve its unique aquatic biodiversity, make it very difficult to achieve a consensus-based and sustainable equilibrium between availability and demand, unless a better understanding of basin hydrology and of its sensitivity to climate variability and changes in climate and land use can be provided. Advances in the capacity to describe and predict - in a spatially explicit manner - the impact of climate and anthropogenic forcing on the hydrology of the Biobío River basin are therefore urgently required. In this context, the work presented herein attempts to set the basis for future modeling applications within the Biobío basin, by analyzing the applicability of the SWAT model (Arnold et al., 1998; Neitsch et al., 2002a,b) to the Vergara basin (4.265 km$^2$), a subbasin of the Biobío River system that is especially important for the forestry industry (plantations). Selection of SWAT for this project was based on the following: it is an existing, readily available and well-documented modular modeling tool. Its graphical user interface (GUI), AVSWAT (Di Luzio et al., 2002), comes embedded in the popular and widely used GIS environment ArcView 3.2 (ESRI, 1999). Both the availability of good manuals as well as the ArcView-based GUI are aspects that make the model also attractive to potential end-users, such as government agencies and decision-makers. With SWAT, basic applications can be built for hydrological modeling and later extended, e.g. for analyzing water quality issues as well. An additional interesting aspect of SWAT is the ongoing development that is taking place, with contributions coming from different groups, from different parts of the world. SWAT also offers different options for calculating runoff and evapotranspiration, each option having different requirements with regard to input data. This is important, as in Chile, just as in many other places in the world, meteorological data are typically available at the daily time step only. By using the SCS Curve Number approach for runoff calculations and the Hargreaves method for evapotranspiration (both offered by SWAT - see The SWAT Model Section), this limitation can be easily addressed. Departing from the former analysis, one of our goals was to test the practical applicability of SWAT on a case study basin for which data availability can be described as "typical of many Chilean basins". It is thought that interpretation of the results obtained from this case study holds the potential for users from other parts of the world to evaluate the appropriateness of this tool - under similar conditions of basin characteristics and data availability - for their specific water resources applications.

## 2. Selection of the Study Area

The Biobío River basin is the third largest Chilean basin. It is located in central Chile, between 36°45'-38°49'S and 71°00'-73°20'W. The basin stretches from the continental divide in the east (Andes, Chilean-Argentinean border) to the Pacific Ocean in the west. It covers approximately 3% of the Chilean continental territory, and is influenced by the temperate climates of the south as well as by the Mediterranean climate of central Chile. Due to its location in a climatic transition zone, the study area is rich in biodiversity, which is characterized by a high degree of species endemism. At the same time, the area constitutes the country's most important centre for forestry activities (both pulp mills and exotic species forestry plantations) and contains a major portion of the Chilean agricultural soils. The basin also plays a predominant role in the national energetic supply (hydroelectricity), and its main river, the Biobío, is the principal provider of drinking water for one of Chile's major cities: Concepción (population: 700,000).

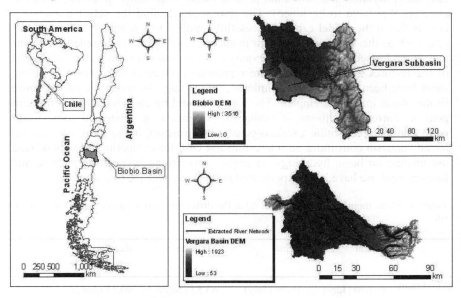

**Figure 1.** Location of the Bíobio and Vergara basins.

The flow regime of the Biobío River is pluvio-nival, with a very marked difference in discharge between dry and wet season: maximum and minimum monthly mean values near the mouth are 1,823 and 279 m$^3$/s during the months of July (winter, wet season) and February (summer, dry season), respectively. In the central valley part of the basin (where most agricultural activities take place), irrigation practices are very important during the Austral summer.

The main tributaries to the Biobío are the Duqueco, Bureo, Vergara and Laja rivers. Together these rivers drain 50% of the basin's total surface area. The rainfall-runoff modeling application described in this paper focuses on one of these subbasins: the Vergara River basin. This subbasin has an area of 4,265 km², covering approximately 17% of the total surface area of the Biobío basin. It is located in the southern part of the Biobío basin (Fig. 1), between 37°29'-38°14'S and 71°36'-73°20'W. Maximum and minimum mean monthly discharges occur during July and February-March respectively (Table 1). Its selection as a test area for the application of the SWAT model is based on: (a) the availability of a typical set of basic input data which should allow for the model to be calibrated and validated; (b) the absence of either hydropower infrastructure or major irrigation works; and (c) the reduced amount of snowfall in the basin, and the consequent small contribution of snowmelt to total river discharge. These last two aspects are considered important: the snowmelt contributions, as well as the presence of major flow deviations and/or abstractions, would require special attention during the modeling, due to their impact on the timing and magnitude of observed discharge values. This would require additional processes to be modeled, and thus further complicate the calibration and validation process (more uncertainty involved; more parameters that have to be tuned). The philosophy behind the selected approach here is that if the model can be successfully applied to a relatively 'simple' testcase such as the Vergara basin, then in successive steps more complex subbasins may be addressed, e.g. those where one or a (progressive) combination of several of the features mentioned above are represented. Once all successive modeling steps have been successfully completed, then finally the modeling of the entire Biobío basin may be attempted. The former should be considered as a long-term goal, as current conditions of availability of data (e.g. related to snow water equivalent) still constitute a serious constraint. However, in the short term, the selected subbasin constitutes an interesting test case for evaluating impacts of land use change on basin hydrology, as major conversions between agriculture and forestry land use have been experienced in this area over the past decades.

**Table 1.** Mean monthly discharges (m³/s) at the different control points in the Vergara basin.

|         | Tijeral         | Rehue          | Mininco         | Renaico        |
|---------|-----------------|----------------|-----------------|----------------|
| Maximum | 153.70 (July)   | 16.79 (July)   | 43.57 (July)    | 90.17 (June)   |
| Minimum | 7.52 (February) | 0.28 (February)| 2.16 (February) | 6.71 (March)   |
| Mean    | 56.32           | 5.85           | 16.21           | 42.66          |

# 3. The SWAT Model

Development of the Soil and Water Assessment Tool (SWAT, Arnold et al., 1998; Neitsch et al., 2002a,b) was started in the 1990s at the United States Department of Agriculture (USDA). SWAT is a process-based and spatially semi-distributed hydrological and water quality model designed to calculate and route water, sediments and contaminants from individual drainage units (subbasins) throughout a river basin towards its outlet. It is a versatile tool that has been used in many parts of the world to predict the impact of management practices on water, sediment and agricultural chemical yields in large complex basins with varying soils, land use and management conditions, over long periods of time (Eckhardt et al., 2005).

A complete description of the SWAT model can be found in Neitsch et al., (2002a,b). Below, we limit ourselves to a short overview of the most relevant aspects related to the hydrology component, as this has been the main focus of attention in the presented work.

Within the SWAT conceptual framework, the representation of the hydrology of a basin is divided into two major parts: (a) the land phase of the hydrological cycle, and (b) the routing of runoff through the river network. For modeling the land phase, the river basin is divided in subbasins, each one of which is composed of one or several hydrological response units (HRUs), which are areas of relatively homogeneous land use/land cover and soil types. The characteristics of the HRUs define the hydrological response of a subbasin. For a given time step, the contributions to the discharge at each subbasin outlet point is controlled by the HRU water balance calculations (land phase). The river network then connects the different subbasin outlets, and the routing phase determines movement of water through this network towards internal control points, and finally towards the basin outlet (Neitsch et al., 2002a).

For the land phase water balance, within SWAT evapotranspiration can be calculated using one of either three methods: Penman-Monteith, Hargreaves or Priestley-Taylor. The Penman-Monteith method offers a better process description, but has high input data requirements which for practical applications will be hard to fulfil in many parts of the world. Although less physically based, the Hargreaves or Priestley-Taylor methods have the advantage of less stringent input data needs; under minimal conditions of data availability, the Hargreaves method can even be used with temperature time series as the only required measured input (Heuvelmans et al., 2005). For surface runoff calculations, SWAT gives the user two alternatives: (a) the use of the Soil Conservation Service curve number (SCS CN) procedure, and (b) the Green and Ampt infiltration method. For the latter method, input data at a finer-than-daily time resolution are required, whereas the CN method is lumped over time (Johnson, 1998); the SCS CN approach can typically be applied using daily rainfall values. Runoff contributions from snowmelt can be incorporated by means of a temperature index, a method commonly used in water resources management applications (Walter et al., 2005).

Due to this flexibility, SWAT has been used in many parts of the world (USA, Europe, India, New Zealand, etc.; Abu El-Nasr et al., 2005; Cao et al., 2006; Gosain et al., 2005; Govender and Everson, 2005; Tripathi et al., 2006). However, at present, almost no case study applications of SWAT in Latin America have been documented in the international scientific literature.

## 4. Data Sources

### 4.1 GIS data layers

The 90m-resolution topography data from the Shuttle Radar Topography Mission (SRTM DEM, final version) were used as a basis for the modeling process (Fig. 1). The GIS layer representing land use/cover in the basin (Fig. 2) was based on an interpretation of aerial photographs (scale 1:70 000/1:115 000 from 1996-1998; CONAMA-CONAF-BIRF, 1999), combined with information from the "Chilean Inventory of Native Vegetation Resources". The methodology used is based on the land occupation map developed by the Centre of Phytosociological and Ecological Studies L. Emberger, Montpellier, France (Etienne and Prado 1982; CONAMA-CONAF-BIRF, 1999). The GIS layer representing the different soils in the basin (Fig. 3) was obtained from the "Agrological Study of the VIII and IX Region" (CIREN, 1999a,b).

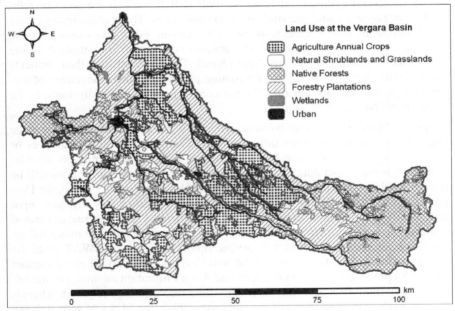

**Figure 2.** Land use/cover.

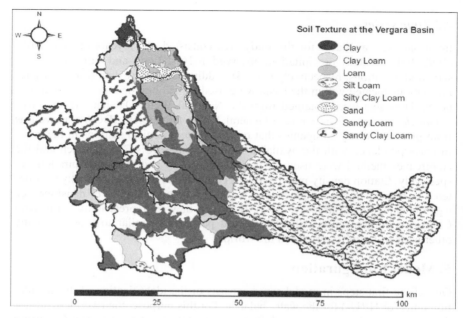

**Figure 3.** Soil types for the Vergara.

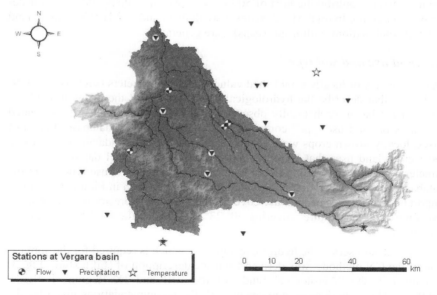

**Figure 4.** Meteorological and gaging stations used for modeling (the figure also shows the river network extracted by means of the SWAT GIS interface).

## 4.2 Time series

Input data sets available for the study area consisted of 11 years of time series (1992-2002) of daily precipitation, observed at 16 stations, and temperature, observed at 3 stations, respectively (Fig. 4). Additionally, flow data from four gaging stations located within the basin were used for calibration and validation purposes. Data sets were obtained from the National Water Databank (*Banco Nacional de Aguas*) of the Chilean General Water Directorate (DGA), as well as from private forestry companies that operate meteorological stations in the zone. In correspondence with the available input data, the SCS CN approach and the Hargreaves method were used for calculating runoff and evapotranspiration, respectively. Station density may be low as compared to densities typically encountered in many parts of the developed world (for some examples of densities, see e.g. Samaniego and Bárdossy, 2005). However, they are representative of general Chilean conditions (especially the central part), and similar to those of many other parts of Latin America and the world.

## 5. Model Configuration

One of the first steps in model setup consists of the identification of the calculation units (or HRUs) for the water balance. For this purpose, the river network for the Vergara basin was extracted from the digital elevation data (DEM), using standard analytical techniques contained in the AVSWAT GIS interface (a minimum upstream contributing area of 50 km$^2$ was used as a threshold value for defining river cells). In total 51 subbasins were defined and 272 HRUs (unique land use/soil combinations within subbasins) were generated.

### 5.1 Land use and soil type

Due to the lack of locally established values for the parameters (such as SCS CN, LAI, etc.) that describe the hydrological characteristics of the different land use types in the basin, each locally observed crop or land use type was associated with a "crop/land use type" contained in the SWAT model database. For most cases, locally grown crops were also contained in the SWAT database. For those local crops/land uses that were not represented in this model database, the parameter values corresponding to the most closely related land use types from the database were used as a first approximation. As can be seen in Figure 2, the most important major types of land use/cover in the basin are: forestry plantations, native forest and agriculture, covering 40, 23 and 22% of the total basin area, respectively.

For each soil series, the hydrological group - which is required for the application of the CN method - was derived from the description of soil texture (Fig. 3) contained in the "Agrological Study of the VIII and IX Region" (CIREN, 1999a,b). This was done in agreement with the recommendations given by the USDA (1986). Conductivity values were obtained from Liu et al. (2002, cited in Campos, 2005), horizon depth from CIREN (1999a,b), and the available water

274

capacity was estimated using Soil Water Characteristics calculator (Saxton and Willey, 2005; Saxton and Rawls, 2006).

## 5.2 Snow

In the upper part of the basin, where snowfall may occur during winter, ten elevation bands were considered. Parameterization of the snowmelt module (e.g. mean air temperature at which precipitation is equally likely to be rain or snow, threshold temperature for snow melt, maximum and minimum melt factors) was done based on data from the Chilean literature (Peña et al., 1985; Escobar, 1992). The precipitation and temperature lapse rates were obtained using the available meteorological data sets.

# 6. Calibration and Validation

The SWAT model includes a large number of parameters that describe the different hydrological conditions and characteristics across the basin. During a calibration process, model parameters are subject to adjustments, in order to obtain model results that correspond better to discharge rates observed in the field. The range of parameter values used in the calibration process must be physically plausible (Eckhardt et al., 2005), so that the model can be applied afterwards for assessing the impact of change scenarios and/or management options.

Time series of discharge data from four limnigraph stations ('control points') were used for calibration and validation purposes. One of the stations corresponds to a subbasin (Rehue) that is nested in a bigger subbasin (Tijeral), which is also gaged. Together, the four stations cover 80.5% of the total drainage area of the Vergara basin (Fig. 5). For the calibration period, the model was run using rainfall and temperature data from 1998-2002 as input. The first 2 years of the modeling period were reserved for 'model warm-up'.

Prior to the calibration exercise, a sensitivity analysis was executed for each control point, in order to determine the eight parameters to which the model results are most sensitive. At each point, these eight parameters are then used in the calibration process. A ranking of the 'most sensitive' parameters, determined by means of a LH-OAT analysis (Latin Hypercube Sampling - One at A Time; incorporated in the latest model version, SWAT2005) (van Griensven et al., 2006) is given in Table 2.

An automated calibration procedure implemented in SWAT2003 called PARASOL (Parameter Solution Method; van Griensven and Bauwens, 2003) was applied separately to each one of the four subbasins. This procedure used the Shuffle complex evolution algorithm as optimization method, which is a global search algorithm for the minimization of a single function for up to 16 parameters (Duan et al., 1992). It combines the direct search method of the simplex procedure with the concept of a controlled random search, a systematic evolution of points in the direction of global improvement, competitive evolution and the concept of complex shuffling (van Griensven and Bauwens, 2003).

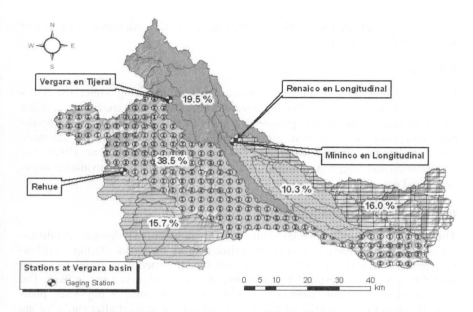

**Figure 5.** Location of the four gaging stations used for calibration and validation stations and percentage of the total basin area cover by each one of them (Rehue and Tijeral are nested).

**Table 2** Ranking of the eight most sensitive parameters per subbasin (1= most sensitive) and their variation range for autocalibration.

| Parameter | Description | Pl | P2 | P3 | P4 | Range |
|---|---|---|---|---|---|---|
| GWQMN | Threshold water depth in the shallow aquifer for flow | 2 | 3 | 4 | 2 | 0–5000 mm |
| GW_REVAP | Groundwater revap coefficient* | | 4 | | 8 | 0.02–0.20 |
| ESCO | Soil evaporation compensation factor | 7 | 6 | 6 | 7 | 0–1 |
| SLOPE | Average slope steepness | 8 | | | 5 | −5% to 5 % |
| CN2 | Initial SCS CN II value | 1 | 2 | 1 | 1 | −15% to 15% |
| SOL_AWC | Available water capacity | 3 | 5 | 2 | 4 | −10% to 10 % |
| GW_DELAY | Groundwater delay | | 8 | | | 0–50 days |
| rchrg_dp | Deep aquifer percolation fraction | 4 | 1 | 3 | 3 | 0.5–1 |
| canmx | Maximum canopy storage | 6 | | 5 | | 0–10 mm |
| sol_k | Saturated hydraulic conductivity | 5 | | 8 | 6 | −10% to 10 % |
| sol_z | Soil depth | | 7 | 7 | | −25% to 25% |

To obtain the optimum solution the sum of the squares of the residuals (SSQ) was used; this is similar to the mean square error method (MSE), as it aims to match a simulated series to a measured time series. The parameters and variation range considered in the autocalibration are given in Table 2. The upper and lower bound of: GWQMN, GW_REVAP, ESCO, GW_delay, canmx and Sol_z were selected considering the default values cited by Van Liew et al. (2005) and the range of SLOPE, rchrg_dp, sol_K, CN2 and SOL_AWC were selected on the basis of the results of previous SWAT calibration studies (e.g. Eckhardt et al., 2005; Van Liew et al., 2005; Srinivasan, personal communication, 2005).

**Table 3** Statistical indicators used to evaluate model performance.

| Name | Formula | Name | Formula |
|---|---|---|---|
| Relative root Mean square error | $RRMSE = \sqrt{\dfrac{\sum\limits_{i=1}^{n}(S_i - O_i)^2}{n}} \dfrac{1}{\overline{O}}$ | Goodness of fit | $R^2 = \left[ \dfrac{\sum\limits_{i=1}^{n}(O_i - \overline{O})(P_i - \overline{P})}{\sqrt{\sum\limits_{i=1}^{n}(O_i - \overline{O})^2}\sqrt{\sum\limits_{i=1}^{n}(P_i - \overline{P})^2}} \right]^2$ |
| Mean absolute error | $ABSERR = \dfrac{\sum\limits_{i=1}^{n}\left|O_i - S_i\right|}{n}$ | PBIAS | $PBIAS = \dfrac{\sum\limits_{i=1}^{n}(O_i - S_i)}{\sum\limits_{i=1}^{n}O_i} \cdot 100$ |
| Nash-Sutcliffe modelling efficiency | $EF = \dfrac{\sum\limits_{i=1}^{n}(O_i - \overline{O})^2 - \sum\limits_{i=1}^{n}(S_i - O_i)^2}{\sum\limits_{i=1}^{n}(O_i - \overline{O})^2}$ | | $O_i$: observed streamflow (m³/s) $S_i$: simulated streamflow (m³/s) $\overline{O}$ : Mean observed streamflow during evaluation period (m³/s) |

**Table 4** Statistical indicators of model performance (monthly output) calculated at the different control points within the Vergara basin: model calibration / model validation.

| Index | Tijeral | Rehue | Mininco | Renaico |
|---|---|---|---|---|
| RRMSE | 0.30 / 0.31 | 0.51 / 0.63* | 0.50 / 0.33 | 0.82 / 0.42 |
| ABSERR | 11.64 / 8.24 | 1.99 / 2.15* | 6.31 / 2.98 | 24.16 / 9.12 |
| EF | 0.93 / 0.93 | 0.82 / 0.75* | 0.72 / 0.92 | 0.54 / 0.82 |
| $R^2$ | 0.96 / 0.93 | 0.88 / 0.80* | 0.76 / 0.94 | 0.71 / 0.83 |
| PBIAS | 11.78 / 2.77 | 21.35 / 32.75* | 8.32 / 9.13 | 32.04 / 7.88 |

Additionally, the surface lag time (SURLAG) for flow routing was also included in the calibration process, in this case the variation range (0.5-10) was chosen considering recommendations done by Van Liew et al. (2005). In the case of the nested subbasins Rehue and Tijeral, calibration was done first for the 'internal' basin.

Even though the SWAT performs the simulation at a daily level, model calibration was evaluated at monthly level. The statistical indicators used for evaluating model performance are: relative root mean squared error (RRMSE); mean absolute error (ABSERR); the Nash-Sutcliffe modeling efficiency index (EF); the goodness-of-fit ($R^2$) and the % of deviation from observed stream flow (PBIAS). Table 3 gives the equations used for calculating these indicators, whereas Table 4 gives the value obtained for each one of these indicators during the calibration period. The closer the values of RRMSE and ABSERR to zero, and those of $R^2$ and EF to unity, the better the model performance is evaluated (Abu El-Nasr et al., 2005). For PBIAS, the optimal value is 0; a negative value indicates an overestimation of observed discharge values, whereas a positive value indicates underestimation. Van Liew et al. (2005) specify the following criteria for interpreting model performance:

(a)  An absolute value for PBIAS of less than 20% is considered 'good', values between ±20% and ±40% are considered 'satisfactory', and those greater than ±40% are considered 'not satisfactory'; and

(b) An EF index value greater than 0.75 is considered 'good', values between 0.75 and 0.36 are considered 'satisfactory' and values below 0.36 are considered 'not satisfactory'.

From the results shown in Table 4, it can be seen that best model performance is obtained for the subbasin that closes at Tijeral (i.e. the biggest of the studied subbasins). The poorest results are obtained for Renaico, which has a relatively bigger proportion of its surface area within the Andes, and for which the representativeness of available weather stations may be bad. Overall performance for Rehue (a subbasin of Tijeral) is poorer than for Tijeral as a whole, but water yield for Rehue is proportionally much lower than for the remaining part of the Tijeral basin, so pre-calibration of the Rehue model has a relatively low impact on calibration and model performance at Tijeral. In general the performance over the 3-year calibration period ranges from 'very good' to 'satisfactory' according to the criteria mentioned above.

## 6.1 Validation

For model validation, a time series of discharge data from the 1992-1999 period was used. Again, the first 2 years from this period were discarded for the evaluation of model performance, as they were considered to correspond to 'model warm-up'. The evaluation was thus based on output generated for the years 1994-1999. Table 4 gives the values of the different statistical indicators. It can be seen that for the Renaico subbasin (and to a lesser extend for Mininco), model performance during validation is substantially better than during the calibration period. A possible explanation can be found in the extreme discharge rates observed during the calibration period (Fig. 6); such extreme discharges are typically (still) not well represented by the model.

## 7. Discussion of Results

The accuracy of model results was evaluated at the four control points for which time series of observed discharge data were available. Evaluation was done by means of different statistical indicators and by a visual interpretation of observed versus modeled (calibration and validation) discharge time series (Fig. 6). Best model performance (Table 4) was obtained for the Tijeral subbasin, where the Nash-Sutcliffe index (EF) calculated from monthly runoff values was 0.93 for both the calibration and validation period. The EF index for other subbasins ranged from 'good' to 'satisfactory' for the calibration period; based on this same index the model performance was 'good' for all subbasins during validation. For the indicator PBIAS, Tijeral and Mininco present a good performance, whereas Rehue and Renaico can be considered satisfactory. However, over the long term as well as for the peak flows the model typically underestimates the runoff. One possible explanation for this may be found in an inadequate description of the

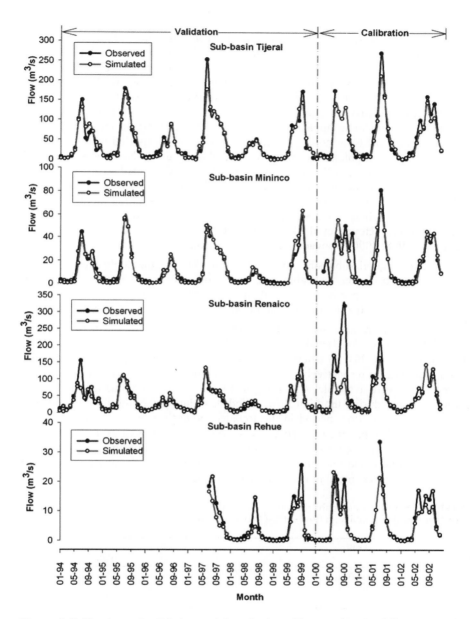

**Figure 6.** Calibration and validation model results (monthly output) at the different control points.

rainfall input field, caused by the limited number of available meteorological stations, as well as by their poor representation in areas of higher altitudes (orographic effects). It is relevant to remember in this context that climate information represents the main forcing data for a hydrological model (Hattermann et al., 2005). Even when the importance of spatial variability of rainfall in simulating runoff was recognized already more than three decades ago (Osborn and Keppel, 1966; Rodda, 1967; Dawdy and Bergman, 1969), the assumption of uniform rainfall over relatively large surface areas remains a common practice in many hydrological modeling applications (Chaubey et al., 1999). In this context, discrete improvements in model performance may still be expected from the testing of alternative interpolation techniques, rather than by using the 'nearest neighbor' assignment (~Thiessen Polygons), which is the standard method in AVSWAT. For this reason, future research on the Vergara basin will include an evaluation of the effects of better descriptions of the spatially variable rainfall input fields, using methods such as: inverse distance weighting, kriging, co-kriging, radial basis functions, etc. (Hevesi et al., 1992; Daly et al., 1994; Martínez-Cob, 1995; Hutchinson, 1998, 2000; Goovaerts, 2000; Hattermann et al., 2005).

For the Tijeral subbasin, which represents 54% of the study area, the total volumetric error over the calibration and validation period was approximately 12% and +3%, respectively. The volumetric error for the other subbasins ranged from +8 to +32% (calibration set) and from +8 to +33% (validation set).

Model performance was further analyzed separately for the period of low flows (November-April) and high flows (May-October). Table 5 shows the Nash-Sutcliffe EF and PBIAS calculated from pooled monthly output data for the dry and rainy season respectively, for the three stations for which the long validation time series were available. According to EF, in all the subbasins the model performed better during the high flow period than during the low flow period. Results for the low flow period in the Renaico subbasin were not satisfactory according to this parameter. PBIAS was good for both periods in Tijeral and Renaico, but was not satisfactory for the low flow period in Mininco. In this context, it can be noted that of the three stations included in the analysis, Mininco also has the lowest mean monthly discharge values for the low flow period.

**Table 5.** Statistical index for the validation period, separately evaluated for the low flow (November-April) and high flow (May-October) periods.

| Basin | EF | | PBIAS | |
|-------|------|------|-------|------|
| | Low | High | Low | High |
| Tijeral | 0.69 | 0.89 | −3.14 | 3.62 |
| Mininco | 0.63 | 0.89 | 47.72 | 1.96 |
| Renaico | 0.24 | 0.71 | 5.21 | 8.47 |

The sensitivity analysis showed a high sensitivity of model results to the SCS CN2 parameter (Table 2). National or regional databases relating CN to local land use/cover and/or soil types are currently not available for Chile. Development of such a database based on (a) local empirical data combined with (b) the results from modeling applications may improve both model performance as well as its usefulness for practical management purposes. It may be worthwhile to further analyze the spatial and temporal variability of CN2 as well as the pre-specified ranges used in the calibration process. Substantial additional research at the national level will be required in this area. In the currently used version of the AVSWAT model, the standard option included for describing the spatial variability of rainfall fields (assignment of nearest station rainfall value to each subbasin) is rather simplistic. Improvements in this area by means of the testing of different interpolation techniques (e.g. Hattermann et al., 2005) may further contribute to better model performance, especially where orographic effects are important. Potential improvements, however, will depend at least partially on the local availability of weather station data (especially critical at higher altitudes) and on the length and quality of the available time series.

## 8. Conclusions

Under local conditions of data availability, the performed SWAT model application for the Vergara basin confirms that SWAT is a useful tool that can already be used to make preliminary assessments of the potential impact of land use and climate changes on the hydrology of this basin. These assessments will consequently be based on the best currently available knowledge for the study area. However, further improvements in model performance should be sought. Meanwhile, when using outcome from the model, the limitations inherent in the modeling approach used should be taken into account.

The present work should be considered as a first step in the development of a bigger model application involving the entire Biobío basin. However, current conditions of data availability do not yet allow such an application. Current results can already be used to establish priorities for obtaining additional field data sets, which should allow such an application in the long term.

Future research on the Vergara model itself should address the aspects of spatial variability of rainfall fields, inter- and intra-annual variability of CNs and the development of a regional/national database relating CN to local land use/cover types.

### Acknowledgments

The present research was conducted in the framework of the TWINBAS project, which was co-financed by the European Community through its Sixth Framework Programme for Research and Technological Development (Priority Area "Global Change and Ecosystems", Contract No. 505287). The authors wish to express their sincere gratitude to the Chilean General Water Directorate DGA, and in particular to the staff of the Biobío Division, the Chilean Meteorological Directorate (DMC), the Chilean National Environmental Commission CONAMA (Bío Bío Division), the 'Mininco' and 'Bosques Arauco' Forestry Companies, as well as to all other data providers not explicitly mentioned above. We also wish to thank the two anonymous reviewers for their valuable contributions to the further improvement of the manuscript.

# References

**Abu El-Nasr, A., Arnold, J.G., Feyen, J. and Berlamont, J. 2005.** Modelling the hydrology of a catchment using a distributed and a semi-distributed model. *Hydrol. Processes* **19**, 573–587.

**Arnold, J.G., Srinivasan, R., Muttiah, R.S. and Williams, J.R. 1998.** Large area hydrologic modeling and assessment – Part I: model development. *JAWRA* **34**(1), 73–89.

**Campos, A. 2005.** Modelo hidrológico integrado a un sistema de información geográfica para una cuenca agroforestal de la VIIIa Región. Thesis, Universidad de Concepción, Concepción, Chile.

**Cao, W. Bowden, W.B., Davie, T. and Fenemor, A. 2006.** Multi-variable and multi-site calibration and validation of SWAT in a large mountainous catchment with high spatial variability. *Hydrol. Processes* **20**, 1057–1073.

**Chaubey, I., Haan, C.T., Salisbury, J.M. and Grunwald, S. 1999.** Quantifying model output uncertainty due to the spatial variability of rainfall. *JAWRA* **35**(5), 1113–1123.

**CIREN (Centro de Información de Recursos Naturales) 1999a.** Estudio Agrológico, VIII Región, Tomos I y II. Centro de Información de Recursos Naturales, Chile.

**CIREN (Centro de Información de Recursos Naturales) 1999b.** Estudio Agrológico, IX Región. Centro de Información de Recursos Naturales, Chile.

**CONAMA-CONAF-BIRF (Corporación Nacional Forestal – Comisión Nacional del Medio Ambiente – Banco Interamericano de Reconstrucción y Fomento) 1999.** Catastro y evaluación de los recursos vegetacionales nativos de Chile. Informe Regional, Octava Región. CONAF-CONAMA, Santiago, Chile.

**Daly, C., Neilson, R.P. and Phillips, D.L. 1994.** A statistical-topographic model for mapping climatological precipitation over mountainous terrain. *J. Appl. Met.* **33**,140–158.

**Dawdy, D. R. & Bergman, J. M. 1969.** Effect of rainfall variability on streamflow simulation. *Water Resour. Res.* **5**, 958–966.

**Di Luzio, M., Srinivasan, R., Arnold, J.C. and Neitsch, S.L. 2002.** *ArcView Interface for SWAT2000. User's Guide.* Texas Water Resources Institute, College Station, Texas, USA.

**Duan, Q., Gupta, H.V. and Sorooshian, S. 1992.** Effective and efficient global minimalization for conceptual rainfall–runoff models. *Water Resour. Res.* **28**, 1015–1031.

**Eckhardt, K., Fohrer, N. and Frede, H.G. 2005.** Automatic model calibration. *Hydrol. Processes* **19**, 651–658.

**Eckhardt, K. and Ulbrich, U. 2003.** Potential impacts of climate change on groundwater recharge and streamflow in a central European low mountain range. *J. Hydrol.* **281**, 244–252.

**ESRI (Environmental Systems Research Institute Inc.) 1999.** Arc View GIS 3.2.

**Escobar, F. (1992)** Aplicacion del modelo "SRM3-11" (Snowmelt runoff model) en cuencas de los Andes centrales. Segundas Jornadas de Hidráulica Francisco Javier Domínguez, Santiago, Chile.

**Etienne, M. and Prado, C. 1982.** Descripción de la vegetación mediante cartografia de ocupacion de tierras. Ciencias Agrícolas no. 10, Universidad de Chile, Facultad de Cs. Agrarias y Forestales. UNESCO-MAB.

**Goovaerts, P. 2000.** Geostatistical approaches for incorporating elevation into the spatial interpolation of rainfall. *J. Hydrol.* **228**,113–129.

**Gosain, A. K., Rao, S., Srinivasan, R. and Reddy, N. G. 2005.** Return-flow assessment for irrigation command in the Palleru river basin using SWAT model. *Hydrol. Processes* **19**, 673–682.

**Govender, M. and Everson, C.S. 2005.** Modelling streamflow from two small South African experimental catchments using the SWAT model. *Hydrol. Processes* **19**, 683–692.

**Harrison, G.P. and Whittington, H. W. 2002.** Vulnerability of hydropower projects to climate change. *IEE P-Gener Transm D* **149**(3), 249–255.

**Hattermann, F., Krysanova, V., Wechsung, F. and Wattenbach, M. 2005.** Runoff simulations on the macroscale with the ecohydrological model SWIM in the Elbe catchment—validation and uncertainty analysis. *Hydrol. Processes* **19**, 693–714.

**Haverkamp, S., Fohrer, N. and Frede, H.G. 2005.** Assessment of the effect of land use patterns on hydrologic landscape functions: a comprehensive GIS-based tool to minimize model uncertainty resulting from spatial aggregation. *Hydrol. Processes* **19**, 715–727.

**HEC (Hydrologic Engineering Center) 2000.** *Hydrologic Modeling System HEC-HMS. User's Manual, Version 2.* Hydrologic Engineering Center; US Army Corps of Engineers, Davis, California, USA.

**Heuvelmans, G., Garcia-Qujano, J.F., Muys, B., Feyen, J. and Coppin, P. 2005.** Modelling the water balance with SWAT as part of the land use impact evaluation in a life cycle study of CO2 emission reduction scenarios. *Hydrol. Processes* **19**, 729–748.

**Hevesi, J.A., Istok, J.D. and Flint, A.L. 1992.** Precipitation estimation in mountainous terrain using multivariate statistics. Part I: Structural analysis. *J. Appl. Met.* **31**,661–676.

**Hutchinson, M.F. 1998.** Interpolation of rainfall data with thin plate smoothing splines: II. Analysis of topographic dependence. *GIDA* **2**(2), 168–185.

**Hutchinson, M.F. 2000.** *ANUSPLIN Version 4.1. User Guide.* Centre for Resource and Environmental Studies, Australian National University, Canberra, Australia.

**Johnson, R.R. 1998.** An investigation of curve number applicability to watersheds in excess of 25000 hectares (250 km$^2$). *J. Environ. Hydrol.* **6** (Paper 7), 10.

**Liu, Y., Gebremeskel, S., De Smedt, F. and Pfister, L. 2002.** Flood prediction with Wetspa model on catchment scale. In: *Flood Defense 2002*, Science Press New York Ltd, New York, USA.

**Martínez-Cob, A. 1995.** Multivariate geostatistical analysis of evapotranspiration and precipitation in mountainous terrain. *J. Hydrol.* **174**,19–35.

**Mishra, S.K. and Singh, V.P. 2004.** Long-term hydrological simulation based on the Soil Conservation Service curve number. *Hydrol. Processes* **18**, 1291–1313.

**Neitsch, S.L., Arnold, J.C., Kiniry, J.R., Williams, J.R. and King, K.W. 2002a.** *Soil and Water Assessment Tool Theoretical Documentation. Version 2000.* Texas Water Resources Institute, College Station, Texas, USA.

**Neitsch, S.L., Arnold, J.C., Kiniry, J.R., Williams, J.R. and King, K.W. 2002b.** *Soil and Water Assessment Tool User's Manual. Version 2000.* Texas Water Resources Institute, College Station, Texas, USA.

**Osborn, H.B. and Keppel, R.V. 1966.** Dense rain gauge network as a supplement to regional networks in semiarid regions. In: Proc. Symp. on the Design of Hydrological Networks, Quebec, 15-22 June 1965, vol. 2, 675–687. IASH Publ. 68. IAHS Press, Wallingford, UK.

**Peña, H., Vidal, F. and Escobar, F. 1985.** Estimación de tasas de derretimiento de nieve. VII Congreso Nacional, Sociedad Chilena de Ingenieria Hidraulica, Concepcion, Chile.

**Rodda, J. C. 1967.** The systematic errors in rainfall measurement. *J. Instn Water Engrs* **21**, 173–177.

**Samaniego, L. and Bárdossy, A. 2005.** Robust parametric models of runoff characteristics at the mesoscale. *J. Hydrol.* **303**, 136–151.

**Saxton, K.E. and Rawls, W.J. 2006.** Soil water characteristic estimates by texture and organic matter for hydrologic solutions. *Soil Sci. Soc. Am. J.* **70**, 1569–1578.

**Saxton, K.E. and Willey, P.H. 2005.** The SPAW Model for agricultural field and pond hydrologic simulation. Ch. 17 in: *Mathematical Modeling of Watershed Hydrology* (ed. by

283

V.P. Singh & D. Frevert), **pages?** CRC Press LLC, Boca Raton, Florida, USA.

**Simonovic, S.P. 2002.** World water dynamics: global modeling of water resources. *J. Environ. Manage.* **66**, 249–267.

**Tripathi, M.P., Raghuwanshi, N.S. and Rao, G.P. 2006.** Effect of watershed subdivision on simulation of water balance components. *Hydrol. Processes* **20**, 1137–1156.

USDA (1986). *Urban Hydrology for Small Watersheds*, TR 55. US Dept Agriculture.

**van Griensven, A. and Bauwens, W. 2003.** Multiobjective autocalibration for semidistributed water quality models. *Water Resour. Res.* **39**(12), 1348.

**van Griensven, A., Meixner, T., Grunwald, S., Bishop, T. and Srinivasan, R. 2006.** A global sensitivity analysis tool for the parameters of multi-variable catchment models. *J. Hydrol.* **324**, 10–23.

**Van Liew, M.W., Arnold, J.G. and Bosch, D.D. 2005.** Problems and potential of autocalibrating a hydrologic model. *Trans. Am. Soc. Agric.* **48**(3), 1025–1040.

**Walter, M.T., Brooks, E.S., McCool, D.K., King, L.G., Molnau, M. and Boll, J. 2005.** Process-based snowmelt modeling: does it require more input data than temperature-index modeling? *J. Hydrol.* **300**, 65–75.

# 2.10 Continental Scale Simulation of the Hydrologic Balance

## J.G. Arnold[1], R. Srinivasan[2], R.S. Muttiah[2] and P.M. Allen[3]

## Abstract

This paper describes the application of a continuous daily water balance model called SWAT (Soil and Water Assessment Tool) for the conterminous U.S. The local water balance is represented by four control volumes; (1) snow, (2) soil profile, (3) shallow aquifer, and (4) deep aquifer. The components of the water balance are simulated using 'storage' models and readily available input parameters. All the required databases (soils, land use, and topography) were assembled for the conterminous U.S. at 1:250,000 scale. A GIS interface was utilized to automate the assembly of the model input files from map layers and relational databases. The hydrologic balance for each soil association polygon (78,863 nationwide) was simulated without calibration for 20 years using dominant soil and land use properties. The model was validated by comparing simulated average annual runoff with long-term average annual runoff from USGS stream gage records. Results indicate over 45 percent of the modeled U.S. are within 50 mm of measured, and 18 percent are within 10 mm without calibration. The model tended to underpredict runoff in mountain areas due to lack of climate stations at high elevations. Given the limitations of the study (i.e. spatial resolution of the databases and model simplicity), the results show that the large-scale hydrologic balance can be realistically simulated using a continuous water balance model.

**Keywords:** surface water hydrology, modeling/statistics, evapotranspiration, plant growth, geographic information systems

---

© 2009 World Association of Soil and Water Conservation, *Soil and Water Assessment Tool (SWAT): Global Applications,* eds. Jeff Arnold, Raghavan Srinivasan, Susan Neitsch, Chris George, Karim Abbaspour, Philip Gassman, Fang Hua Hao, Ann van Griensven, Ashvin Gosain, Patrick Debels, Nam Won Kim, Hiroaki Somura, Victor Ella, Attachai Jintrawet, Manuel Reyes, and Samran Sombatpanit, pp. 285-304. This paper has been published by the *J. of the American Water Resources Association* (JAWRA) Vol. 35 (1999), Issue 5, pp. 1037-1051. WASWC is grateful for the permission granted by the copyright holders JAWRA.

[1]Agricultural Engineer, USDA-Agricultural Research Service, 808 East Blackland Road, Temple, Texas 76502, U.S.A. arnold@brc.tamus.edu
[2]Associate Research Scientists, Texas Agricultural Experiment Station, 808 East Blackland Road, Temple, Texas 76502, U.S.A. r-srinivasan@tamu.edu
[3]Professor of Engineering Geology and Hydrology, Department of Geology, Baylor University, P.O. Box 97354, Waco, Texas 76798, U.S.A.

# 1. Introduction

The renewable water resources for the conterminous United States are derived from an average annual precipitation of 760 mm. Seventy percent of this rainfall is consumed through evaporation and transpiration. The remaining 30 percent of precipitation constitutes an average annual runoff of about 230 mm (WRC, 1978). Management and utilization of these resources depends upon the spatial distribution of rainfall, location of reservoirs, evapotranspiration (ET) potential, soil and groundwater storage, and water quality. All of these factors vary from basin to basin. Continental-scale maps representing some of the above components have been prepared such as annual runoff (Langbein, 1980) and precipitation-evaporation (Winter, 1990). While important in illustrating regional trends, these studies do little toward assessing the potential interaction of the components of the water balance. Basin-scale assessments have been made to determine the adequacy of water supply regions (WRC, 1968, 1978; Hirsch et al., 1990) and make projections based on estimates of population and land use, but again are not designed to account for interactions between the components of the system. Projections are made by predicting average values into the future without regard to potential thresholds or feedback loops within the system.

Water balance models attempt to predict the partitioning of water among the various pathways inherent to the hydrologic cycle (Dooge, 1992). Early models developed in the 1940s are essentially bookkeeping procedures that estimate the balance between inflow (precipitation and snowmelt) and outflow (ET, stream flow, and groundwater) (Alley, 1984). While generalized global water balance maps have been prepared, they often lack the necessary scale to be useful in even the simplest modeling efforts (UNESCO, 1978). More advanced water balance models have been used to assess the effects of land management, seasonal irrigation demands, prediction of stream flow and lake levels, recharge to the groundwater system, groundwater storage, and as a means of assessing the impact of vegetation on water yield (runoff, soil flow, and groundwater flow) and sediment yield (Chiew and McMahon, 1990; Winter, 1981; Essery, 1992; Thomas et al., 1983; Bultot et al., 1990; Arnold et al., 1993). Robbins Church et al. (1995) developed a simple water balance equation using measured precipitation and runoff to compute ET and runoff precipitation ratios for the northeast United States. More recently, general circulation models (GCMs) have linked atmospheric models to land-surface water balance models and emphasized the importance of the land based hydrologic cycle to global energy fluxes (Wood et al., 1992), and conversely, the effects of atmospheric contaminants ($CO_2$), on land surface runoff (Miller and Russell, 1992). Recent research on the land based component of the water balance using simplified inputs of potential evapotranspiration and soil water holding capacity (0.5 degree resolution) have shown the importance of soil storage control in the regional water balance (Milly, 1994). Liang et al. (1994) used a simple 2-layer soil storage model with a vegetation component to model surface water and energy fluxes for GCMs.

The SWAT model (Arnold et al., 1998) provides the modeling capabilities of the HUMUS (Hydrologic Unit Model of the United States) project (Srinivasan et al., 1993). The major components of the HUMUS project are: (1) SWAT to simulate surface and subsurface water quality and quantity; (2) a Geographic Information System (GIS) to collect, manage, analyze, and display the spatial and temporal inputs and outputs (Srinivasan and Arnold, 1994); and (3) relational databases required to manage the non-spatial data (Fig. 1). HUMUS simulates the hydrologic budget, sediment and nutrient movement for approximately 2,100 8-digit hydrologic unit areas as delineated by the USGS. Findings of the project are being used in the Resource Conservation Act (RCA) Assessment conducted by the Natural Resources Conservation Service. Planning scenarios include agricultural and municipal water use, tillage and cropping system trends, and fertilizer/manure management.

The purpose of this study is to present findings of the HUMUS continental-scale modeling effort of all the major river basins of the conterminous United States as they relate to regional runoff and water supply. This modeling effort has been validated against average annual runoff using all existing gaging stations of the USGS. The modeled results allow assessment of spatial variations in runoff of the conterminous United States. If runoff can be simulated with reasonable accuracy, the model can then be validated for sediment and nutrient yields for further NRCS national agricultural policy scenarios. Results should also allow for more accurate assessments of the effects of land use changes and water management initiatives as well as provide a tool for parameterization of GCMs.

## 2. Theoretical Framework

### 2.1 Overview

The overriding objective of this study is to develop the most realistic physical representation of the water balance possible while utilizing data that is readily available for large regions of the U.S. This requires that model input parameters are physically based and that calibration is not attempted. Most model input parameters are physically defined such as topography (slopes and flow lengths), soil properties (texture, bulk density, saturated conductivity, etc.) and plant characteristics (biomass to energy conversions, maximum height and rooting depth, etc.). Some of the relationships used in the model, such as the curve number, are based on physical properties such as soil type and land use and do not require calibration (i.e. measured stream flow and ET are not required). However, there is often considerable uncertainty in model inputs due to spatial variability and measurement errors. In most watershed studies, inputs are allowed to vary within a realistic uncertainty range for calibration and validation then is performed on another period of data. In this study, the model was only validated using average annual runoff.

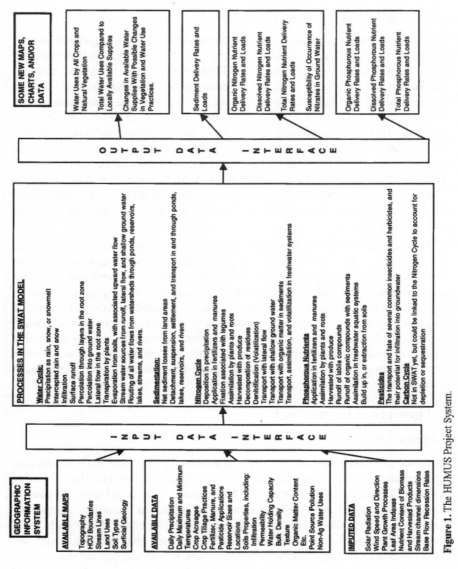

**Figure 1.** The HUMUS Project System.

The other main objective of this study is to develop the ability to simulate the impact of climate and land use changes on the water balance. Climate change scenarios include projected annual and seasonal changes in precipitation, temperature, and $CO_2$. Land use scenarios include vegetative changes (i.e. forest to agricultural land) and cropping system changes. This requires the ability to simulate tillage systems and nutrient/pesticide application scenarios.

## 2.2 Spatial and temporal variability

A common approach in simulating the water balance of large areas is to subdivide the area into homogeneous modeling subareas. Although there are numerous discretization schemes that are possible, we chose to use soil associations as the basis for modeling subareas. The dominant (by area) soil series, and the corresponding physical properties, for each soil association polygon were used. While, there is considerable variability in soil hydraulic properties even at relatively small scales (Warrick and Nelson, 1980), some lumping of soil properties must be made since available regional-scale data bases do not include sufficient spatial detail.

Vertical variability within the polygon is modeled by dividing the water balance into three control volumes: the soil profile, shallow aquifer, and deep aquifer. The soil profile can be subdivided further to account for soil horizons that may have a significant impact on percolation, surface runoff, and root growth. The shallow aquifer is directly below the soil profile and is assumed to (1) actively circulate groundwater and respond rapidly to changes in discharge and recharge, (2) have relatively short travel times, and (3) supply a large percentage of baseflow to the stream (Moody, 1990). Seepage from the shallow aquifer recharges the deep aquifer. The deep aquifer does not contribute to stream flow in the model.

To represent temporal variability, the model continuously updates the water balance on a finite time step (one day). Thus, the model can run continuously for many years and describe annual and seasonal variability. A long-term regional database of weather data at subdaily time steps is not currently available at similar spatial resolution as daily weather data. Also, a monthly time step cannot account for the variation in individual surface runoff events within the month. Daily weather data is readily available and daily stochastic weather generators (for a point) have been parameterized and such an approach has been in use for many years (Richardson, 1981).

## 2.3 Description of algorithms

Water storage is divided into four distinct components as shown in Figure 2: (1) snow profile (above the ground surface), (2) soil profile (0-2 m), (3) shallow aquifer (2-50 m), and (4) deep aquifer (> 50 m). Equations and detailed descriptions are found in Arnold et al. (1998).

**Snow cover.** The control volume for snow cover is bounded above by the snow-atmosphere interface and below by the snow-soil interface. The mass balance of water in the snow control volume consists of snow fall, snow melt and sublimation.

**Soil profile.** The upper boundary of the soil profile is the soil-atmosphere (or soil-snow if snow is present) interface. The lower boundary corresponds to the average rooting depth of the vegetation. This normally coincides with the depth that the soils have been characterized in soil surveys and is less than 2 meters. Since a modeling subarea is considered homogeneous, the horizontal extent of the soil control volume is irrelevant (soil heterogeneity and topographic effects are neglected). However, it should be noted that horizontal water flux between subareas is not considered. Processes simulated include: surface runoff, lateral soil flow, percolation, evapotranspiration, soil temperature, plant growth, and management (irrigation, fertilization and residue management).

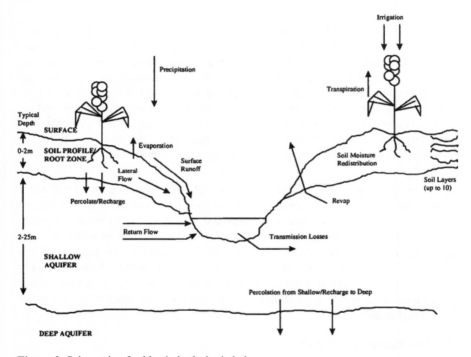

**Figure 2.** Schematic of subbasin hydrologic balance.

**Shallow aquifer.** Ground water flow systems can be classified into three types of depth and proximity to surface drainage features: (1) shallow, (2) intermediate, and (3) regional flow systems (Toth, 1963). The shallow flow systems: (1) actively circulate groundwater and respond rapidly to changes in discharge and recharge, (2) have relatively short travel times, and (3) supply a large percentage of base flow to the stream (Cannon, 1989). The shallow groundwater flow component in SWAT is intended for general use where extensive field work to obtain inputs (pump tests, etc.) is not feasible and thus the model must use readily available inputs. For more detailed, site-specific studies, Sophocleous et al. (1999)

have linked SWAT to MODFLOW, a two-dimensional groundwater flow model.

The shallow aquifer control volume is bounded above by the soil-shallow aquifer interface and below by the interface with the deep aquifer. Typical depth of the shallow aquifer is 2-25 m and processes simulated include return flow, plant water uptake, percolate to the deep aquifer, and water withdrawals. A complete description of the groundwater flow component is found in Arnold et al. (1993).

**Deep Aquifer.** It is assumed that there is no interaction between the deep aquifer and the stream. Also, no underflow is allowed to occur from one modeling subarea to another. Processes simulated in the deep aquifer are percolate from the shallow aquifer and water withdrawals.

## 3. Previous Model Validation

Ideally, we would like to validate all simulated components of the hydrologic balance (surface runoff, groundwater flow, ET, recharge, etc.) with measured estimates for the entire U.S. Unfortunately, measured estimates of the individual components of the hydrologic balance are not generally available. However, the SWAT model has been compared against measured components of the hydrologic balance at several locations throughout the U.S. Table 1 shows the location, reference, basin area, and validated components for each location. These locations represent a wide range of soils, land use, climate, and topography. The most comprehensive testing was performed for three basins in Illinois (Arnold and Allen, 1996). Schicht and Walton (1961) used precipitation, stream flow, and groundwater level data to ascertain groundwater recharge, runoff, and ET for all three basins. This data was then compared against SWAT simulated results with reasonable agreement.

A component of the model that has had limited testing is ET. Monthly simulated ET was compared against measured ET from lysimeters growing corn and bluegrass. The impact of irrigation on annual ET and corn yields at Bushland, Texas, was simulated by the model illustrating corn yield response to increasing volumes of irrigation water (Arnold and Williams, 1985). Arnold and Stockle (1991) demonstrated the models ability to simulate dryland wheat yields under extreme differences in climate and soil conditions. While the runoff validation in this study only compares average annual values, it is important to note that the model has been validated against monthly time series and is capable of simulating seasonal variability. Numerous studies (Table 1) confirm that this modeling approach is capable of simulating realistic monthly time series of runoff, and several other components of the hydrologic balance across the U.S.

**Table 1.** Model validation studies.

| | Location | Reference | Drainage Area (km²) | Water Yield/ Streamflow | Soil Water | Surface Runoff | Base Flow | Soil ET | GW ET | GW Recharge | Plant Biomass |
|---|---|---|---|---|---|---|---|---|---|---|---|
| 1. | Middle Bosque River, Texas | Arnold et al. (1993) | 471 | X | | X | X | | | X | |
| 2. | Coshocton, Ohio | Arnold and Williams (1985) | lysimeter | | | | | X | | | |
| 3. | Bushland, Texas | Arnold and Williams (1985) | field plot | | | | | X | | | X |
| 4. | Riesel, Texas | Savabi et al. (1989) | 1.3 | X | X | | | X | | | |
| | Sonora, Texas | Savabi et al. (1989) | 4.1 | X | X | | | | | | |
| 5. | Seco Creek, Texas | Srinivasan and Arnold (1994) | 114 | X | | | | | | | |
| 6. | Neches River Basin, Texas | King et al. (1999) | 25,032 | X | | | | | | | |
| 7. | Colorado River Basin, Texas | King et al. (1999) | 40,407 | X | | | | | | | |
| 8. | Lower Colorado, Texas | Rosenthal et al. | 8,927 | X | | | | | | | |
| 9. | White Rock Lake, Texas | Arnold and Williams (1987) | 257 | X | | | | | | | |
| 10. | North Carolina | Jacobson et al. (1995) | 4.6 | X | | X | | | | | |
| 11. | Goose Creek, Illinois | Arnold and Allen (1996) | 246 | X | X | X | X | X | X | X | |
| 12. | Hadley Creek, Illinois | Arnold and Allen (1996) | 122 | X | X | X | X | X | X | X | |
| 13. | Panther Creek, Illinois | Arnold and Allen (1996) | 188 | X | X | X | X | X | X | X | |
| 14. | Goodwin Creek Watershed, Mississippi | Binger et al. (1996) | 21.3 | X | | | | | | | |
| 15. | Watersheds in: Oklahoma, Ohio, Georgia, Idaho, Mississippi, Vermont, Arizona | Arnold and Williams (1987) | 9.0-538 | X | | | | | | | |
| 16. | Bushland, Texas Logan, Utah Temple, Texas | Arnold and Stockle (1991) | field plot | | | | | | | | X |

# 4. Application

The model presented in the section entitled 'Theoretical Framework' was tested for its ability to reproduce components of the annual water balance. The test region is the entire conterminous United States. The first part of this section describes how the input variables were estimated. All the required databases (soils, land use and DEM) were assembled at 1:250,000 scale. A GIS interface

(Srinivasan and Arnold, 1994) was utilized to automate the assembly of the model input files from map layers and relational databases. The hydrologic balance for each soil association polygon (78,863 nationwide) was simulated for 20 years using dominant soil and land use properties. Channel and impoundment routing were not simulated and thus inputs were not developed.

## 4.1 Estimation of inputs

**Digital Elevation Model (DEM) attributes** – Overland slope and slope length for each subbasin was estimated using the 3-arc second DEM. Overland slope was estimated using the neighborhood technique (Srinivasan and Engel, 1991) for each cell and calculating an average slope for the entire subbasin.

**Land use attributes** – The USGS-LUDA (land use/land cover) data (USGS, 1990) were used to develop plant inputs to the model. The dominant land use was used for each subbasin and a plant parameter database was used to characterize each crop. The broad classification used in the LUDA was urban, agriculture/ pasture, range, forest, wetland, and water as categories. A heat unit scheduling algorithm was used to find probable planting dates of a land use based on location (latitude and longitude) of a subbasin, monthly mean temperature, and land use type. Due to lack of information about specific crops from the LUDA database, this study used corn as the agricultural crop across the U.S., which was thought to be appropriate since corn is the major crop grown in many parts of the U.S. and since it will have a similar impact on the water balance as other summer crops.

**Soils attributes** – The STATSGO-soil association map (USDA, 1992) was used for selection of soil attributes for each subbasin. Each polygon contains multiple soil series, and the areal percentage of each is given (without regard to spatial location). The dominant soil series (largest area) was selected by the GIS interface. Once the soil series was selected, the interface extracted the properties for the model from a relational database. Soil physical properties include texture, bulk density, saturated conductivity, available water capacity, and organic carbon. The curve number (CN) was assigned to each subbasin, based on land use and the hydrologic soil group of the dominant soil series.

**Irrigation attributes** – This study used the STATSGO database to identify locations using irrigation due to lack of spatial irrigation databases showing irrigated agricultural areas. STATSGO reports irrigated crop yield for any crop in this table, and if the land use (from the USGS-LUDA) was agriculture, the entire subbasin was assigned as irrigated agriculture. Figure 3 shows the location of irrigated agriculture identified through above process. Using this irrigation layer the input interface created input parameters for automated irrigation application for each subbasin. The model automatically irrigates a subbasin and replenished soil moisture to field capacity when the crop stress reaches a user defined level.

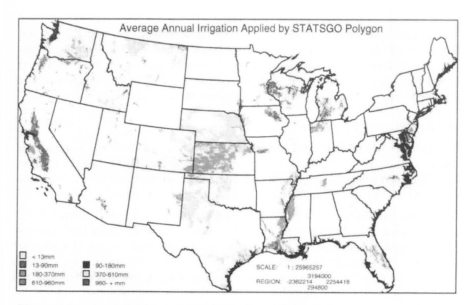

**Figure 3.** Location and amount of annual irrigation water applied.

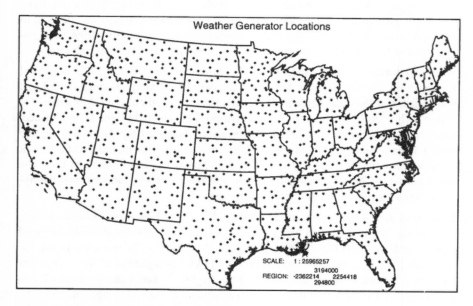

**Figure 4.** Location of weather generator parameter sites.

**Weather attributes** – The model utilized monthly weather generator parameters from approximately 1,130 weather stations to simulate daily precipitation, maximum and minimum temperatures, solar radiation, wind speed, and relative humidity. The GIS interface selected the nearest weather station for each subbasin. (Fig. 4). The interface also extracted and stored the monthly weather parameters in a model input file for each subbasin.

## 4.2 Comparisons with observed runoff for entire U.S.

The model was run for 20 years to obtain average annual values of runoff to compare against observed runoff. Observed runoff was determined by Gebert et al. (1987) from measured stream flow from 5,951 gaging stations that were unaffected by reservoirs, diversions or return flow. This analysis covered the entire U.S. for the period 1951-1980. Modeled runoff is defined as the sum of surface, lateral flow from the soil profile, and groundwater flow from the shallow aquifer which corresponds to observed runoff determined by Gebert et al. (1987). The model assumes that groundwater flow returns within the subbasin and that there is no net groundwater inflow or outflow. No calibration was performed and model inputs were taken without modification from the existing databases. Stream flow and potential ET were not used in developing model inputs. The modeled and observed annual runoff estimates are shown in Figures 5a and 5b. The large-scale features of the observed runoff are apparent in the simulated runoff. High values of runoff are observed from the Northeast States through the Appalachian mountain, down to the northern coast of the Gulf of Mexico. Runoff decreases from east to west between the Mississippi River and the Rocky Mountains. The high runoff of the Pacific Northwest rainforest is also simulated by the model.

The difference between observed and simulated runoff is shown in Figure 6. Negative values identify areas where the model overpredicts while positive numbers signify model underprediction. The model has a general tendency to underpredict runoff in mountain areas. This is evident in Figure 6 in the Appalachian Mountains and the western U.S. This is attributed to the lack of weather data in higher elevations. Typically, weather stations in the western U.S. are located in the valleys that generally have lower precipitation. There was no attempt in this study to correct precipitation and temperature for elevation. The model tends to overpredict runoff in areas that are irrigated (see Fig. 3). This may be due to previous assumption used in the model where irrigation was applied to the entire subbasin when the database reports that cropland within that subbasin may be irrigated. This is the limitation of the irrigation database as well as using only the dominant soil and land use for each subbasin. It should be noted that the spatial resolution of the simulated runoff (Fig. 5b) is considerably finer than the observed runoff (Fig. 5a). Some discrepancies in the two maps may be due to lack of resolution in the observed runoff, fewer stations, and more smoothing of the data set.

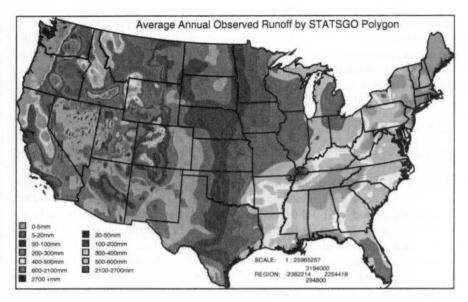

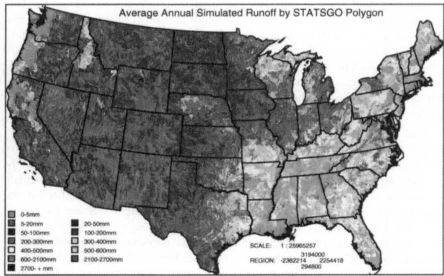

**Figure 5.** (a) Observed average annual runoff for U.S. from USGS stream flow records (top); and (b) Simulated average annual runoff for U.S. (bottom).

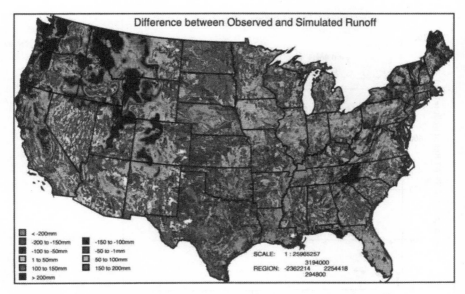

**Figure 6.** Difference between observed and simulated averaged annual runoff.

Summation of runoff errors show that over 45 percent of runoff difference between modeled and observed falls within 50 mm and 18 percent fall within 10 mm. This compares well considering input uncertainty and the fact that no calibration was performed. It also compares favorably with others studies (Milly, 1994). The simple water balance model of Liang et al. (1994) produced major errors in peak runoff. However, the purpose of evaluation was to provide evidence that the model is producing a reasonable soil water balance to GCMs. For that purpose the runoff simulations of Liang et al. (1994) were judged adequate.

Regression analysis was performed by state (Fig. 7) and by soil association polygon (Fig. 8). Average runoff by state compares well with a regression slope of 0.95 and $R^2$ of 0.18. The $R^2$ determined by comparing measured and simulated runoff for each of the 78,863 soil association polygons was lower at 0.66. The model displayed a general tendency to underpredict subareas with high runoff. This is again attributed to both the use of only the dominant soil in each polygon and a lack of more precise irrigation database.

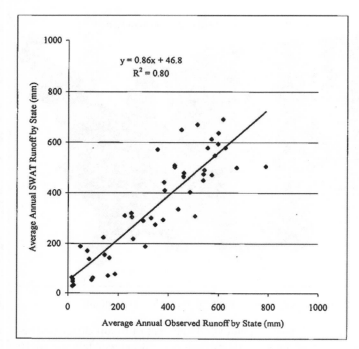

**Figure 7.** Regressiion of observed and simulated runoff by state.

Figure 9 shows simulated potential and actual ET. Although validation was not performed, expected large-scale features were evident and potential ET compares favorably to the method of Thornwaite (Legates and Willmott, 1990).

## 4.3 Limitations and implications for future studies

**Databases.** There are several limitations of the databases used in this study. Soil properties for each series are reported as a range and the midpoint was selected for model input. Within each soil association polygon only areal percentages of soil series are given without regard to spatial position within the polygon. Selecting the dominate soil to represent the entire polygon can cause runoff errors of 30 percent or more (Arnold, 1992). Using the dominant land use for each subbasin can similarly impact model output as the runoff is a function of soil and land use combinations.

Another database limitation involves the location of the weather stations. Elevation and orographic effects are not considered since the vast majority of the weather stations in the coterminous U.S. are located near airports or in valleys next to cities and not distributed in the higher elevations. This can significantly affect the hydrologic balance and is the probable reason for the discrepancies between measured and predicted runoff in the western mountain areas.

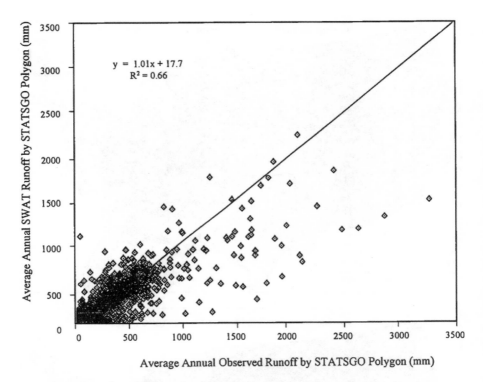

$$y = 1.01x + 17.7$$
$$R^2 = 0.66$$

Average Annual SWAT Runoff by STATSGO Polygon (mm)

Average Annual Observed Runoff by STATSGO Polygon (mm)

**Figure 8.** Regression of observed and simulated runoff by soil association polygons.

**Model algorithms.** Selection of a rainfall runoff model is a compromise between model complexity and available input data. While more complex models may better represent the physical processes, the assumption that they lead to more reliable results has been questioned (Loague and Freeze, 1985). They have shown that the simpler, less data intensive models provided as good or better prediction than the physically based models. An empirical model is a representation of data and has no real theoretical basis. A physically based model is one that has a theoretical basis and whose parameters and variables are measurable in the field (Beven, 1983). In reality, many empirical relationships are used for parameter esti -mation by the 'physically based' models (Wilcox et al., 1990). The SCS runoff equation is basically an empirical model that came into common use in the 1950s and is the product of more than 20 years of studies of rainfall-runoff relationships from small rural watersheds. The model was developed to provide a consistent basis for estimating the amounts of runoff under varying land use and soil types (Rallison and Miller, 1981). No other rainfall-runoff model has been used as successfully or as often on ungaged rangeland adequate procedure to use in regional estimates of runoff.

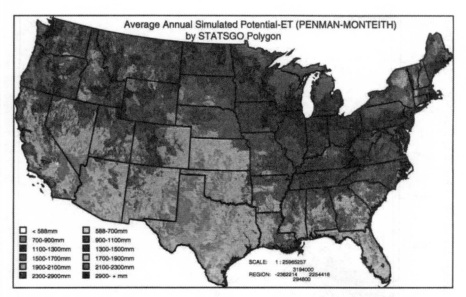

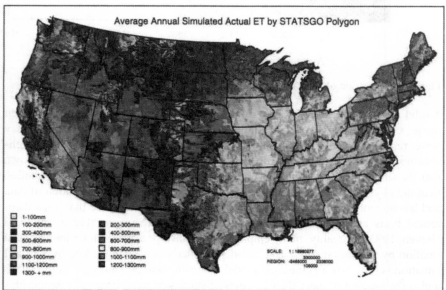

**Figure 9.** (a) Average annual simulated potential ET for U.S. (top); and (b) Average annual simulated actual ET for U.S. (bottom).

Other model components (snow melt, soil water routing, and shallow aquifer storage) are also rather simplistic and may not be representative of the actual flow system. However, inputs are readily available for large regions and the algorithms have provided reasonable results without calibration. It also has been assumed that there is no deep flow from one subbasin to another. While this assumption is incorrect, it is not believed to cause major error in the overall model output due to the small percentage of the overall water budget involved in recharging the deep aquifer system.

## 5. Summary

This paper describes the application and validation of a model of continuous daily water balance. The local water balance was represented by four control volumes; (1) snow, (2) soil profile, (3) shallow aquifer, and to a lesser extent (4) deep aquifer and the components of the water balance were simulated using 'storage' models and readily available input parameters. The model operates on a daily time step and is able to predict seasonal variations, which are important for water resources planning. The control volumes have been found to be critical in timing of flows, surface runoff occurs in hour to days, soil lateral flow in days to weeks, shallow aquifer in months to years, and deep aquifer flow (not simulated) in years to decades.

It is also important to simulate management/land use and climate scenarios since the model is being used by NRCS in national agricultural policy planning and by EPA in TMDL (Total Maximum Daily Load) analysis. Algorithms are included to simulate plant growth including the impact of various land use and cropping systems on the hydrologic balance. The impact of climate is also considered including precipitation, temperature which directly effects plant growth (indirectly ET), snow fall and melt, and soil temperature. Carbon dioxide concentration directly impacts ET and plant biomass growth.

The model was validated by comparing simulated average annual runoff (20 year model simulation) with long-term average annual runoff from USGS stream gage records. Comparisons show that over 45 percent of the conterminous U.S. within 50 mm of measured, and 18 percent within 10 mm. This was accomplished without calibration. Given the errors associated with model inputs (spatial variability, measurement errors, etc.), these results appear realistic. In this study, at the continental scale, only average annual runoff was validated. Examples of previous model validation at numerous sites across the U.S. were used to show that the model was capable of simulating other components of the hydrologic balance (surface runoff, groundwater flow, and ET) and of producing monthly and daily time series of runoff.

### Literature Cited

**Alley, W.M. 1984.** On the Treatment of Evapotranspiration, Soil Moisture Accounting, and Aquifer Recharge in Monthly Water Balance Models. Water Resources Research 20

(8):1137-1149.

**Arnold, J.G. 1992.** Spatial Scale Variability in Model Development and Parameterization. Ph.D. Dissertation, Purdue University, West Lafayette, Indiana.

**Arnold, J.G., R. Srinivasan, R.S. Muttiah, and J.R. Williams. 1998.** Large Area Hydrologic Modeling and Assessment. Part I: Model Development. J. Amer. Water Resources Assoc. 34(1):73-89.

**Arnold, J.G. and P.M. Allen. 1996.** Estimating Hydrologic Budgets for Three fllinois Watersheds. Journal of Hydrology, 176(1996): 55-77.

**Arnold, J.G., P.M. Allen, and G. Bernhardt. 1993.** A Comprehensive Surface-Groundwater Flow Model. Journal of Hydrology 142:47-69.

**Arnold, J.G. and C.O. Stockle. 1991.** Simulation of Supplemental Irrigation from On-Farm Ponds. ASCE Journal of Irrigation and Drainage Division 117(3):408-424.

**Arnold, J.G. and J.R. Williams. 1985.** Evapotranspiration in a Basin Scale Hydrologic Model. In: Advances in Evapotranspiration. Proc. ASAE Symp., pp. 405-413.

**Arnold, J.G. and J.R. Williams. 1987.** Validation of SWRRB — Simulator for Water Resources in Rural Basins. ASCE Journal of Water Resour. Plann. and Manage. 113: (2):243-256.

**Bales, J. and R.P. Betson. 1981.** The Curve Number as a Hydrologic Index. In: Rainfall Runoff Relationship, V. P. Singh (Editor). Water Resources Publication, Littleton, Colorado, pp. 371-386.

**Beven, K. 1983.** Surface Water Hydrology-Runoff Generation and Basin Structure. Rev. Geophys. 21 (3):721-730.

**Binger, R.L., C.V. Alonso, J.G. Arnold, and J. Garbrecht. 1996.** Validation of the GRASS-TOPAZ-SWAT Sediment Yield Scheme Using Measurements from the Goodwin Creek Watershed. Federal Interagency Sedimentation Conference, Las Vegas, Nevada.

**Bultot, F., G.L. Dupriez, and D. Gellens. 1990.** Simulation of Land Use Changes and Impacts on Water Balance — A Case Study in Belgium. Journal of Hydrology 114 (1990):327-348.

**Cannon, M.R. 1989.** Shallow and Deep Ground Water Flow Sys-tems. In: Summer of the U.S. Geological Survey and U.S. Bureau of Land Management National Coal-Hydrology Program, 1974-1984, L. J. Britton et al. (Editors). USGS Professional Paper 1964, pp 136-141.

**Chiew, F.H.S. and T.A. McMahon. 1990.** Estimating Groundwater Recharge Using a Surface Watershed Modeling Approach. Journal of Hydrology 114:285-304.

**Dooge, J.C.I. 1992.** Hydrologic Models and Climate Change. Jour-nal of Geophysical Research 97(D3):2677-2686.

**Essery, C.I. 1992.** Influence of Season and Balance Period on Construction of Catchment Water Balance. Journal of Hydrology 130:171-187.

**Gebert, W.A., D.J. Graczyk, and W.R. Krug. 1987.** Average Annual Runoff in the United States 195 1-1980. U.S. Geological Survey Hydrologic Investigations, Atlas HA-7 10. Graf, W. L., 1988. Fluvial Processes in Dryland Rivers. Springer Verlag, New York, New York, 346 pp.

**Hirsch, R.M., J.F. Waller, J.C. Day, and R. Kallio. 1990.** The Influence of Man on Hydrologic Systems. In: Surface Water Hydrology, M. G. Wolman and H. C. Riggs (Editors). Geological Society of America, Vol. 0-1. pp. 329-359.

**Jacobson, B.M., J. Feng, G.D. Jennings, and K.C. Stone. 1995.** Watershed Scale Non-Point Source Model Evaluation for the North Carolina Coastal Plain. Proc. Intl. Symp. on

Water Quality Modeling, ASAE Publ No. 05-95, Orlando, Florida, pp. 186-191.

**King, K.W., J.G. Arnold, R. Srinivasan, and J.R. Williams. 1999.** Sensitivity of River Basin Hydrology to $CO_2$ and Temperature. ASCE J. of Water Resources Planning and Management (in review).

**Langbein, W.B. 1980.** Distribution of the Difference Between Precipitation and Open Water Evaporation in North America, Plate (2). In: Surface Water Hydrology, M. G. Wolman (Editor). Geological Society of America, Vol. 0-1.

**Legates, D.R. and C.J. Willmott. 1990.** Mean Seasonal and Spatial Variability in Global Surface Air Temperature. Theor. Appl. Climatology 42:11-21.

**Liang, X., D.P. Lettenmaier, E.F. Wood, and S.J. Burges. 1994.** A Simple Hydrologically Based Model of Land Surface Water and Energy Fluxes for General Circulation Models. J. of Geophysical Research 99(D7): 14,415-14,428.

**League, K.M. and R.A. Freeze. 1985.** A Comparison of Rainfall Runoff Modeling Techniques on Small Upland Catchments. Water Res. Research 21(2):229-248.

**Miller, J.R. and B. Russell. 1992.** The Impact of Global Warming on River Runoff. Journal of Geophysical Research 97(D3):2757-2764

**Milly, P.C.D. 1994.** Climatic Soil Water Storage, and the Average Annual Water Balance. Water Resources Research 30(7):2143. 2156.

**Moody, P.W. 1990.** Groundwater Contamination in the United States. Journal of Soil and Water Conservation 45(2):170-179.

**Rallison, R.E. and N. Miller. 1981.** Past, Present, and Future SCS Runoff Procedure. In: Rainfall Runoff Relationship, V. P. Singh (Editor). Water Resources Publication, Littleton, Colorado, pp. 353-364.

**Richardson, C.W. 1981.** Stochastic Simulation of Daily Precipitation, Temperature, and Solar Radiation. Water Resources Res. 17(1): 182-190.

**Rosenthal, W.D., R. Srinivasan, and J.G. Arnold. 1995.** Alternate River Management Using a Linked GIS-Hydrology Model. Trans. ASAE 38(3):783-790.

**Robbins Church, M., G.D. Bishop, and D.L. Cassell. 1995.** Maps of Regional Evapotranspiration and Runoff/Precipitation Ratios in the Northeast United States. J. of Hydrology 168(1995):283-298.

**Savabi, M. G., J.G. Arnold, and C.W. Richardson. 1989.** Modeling the Effect of Brush Control on Rangeland Water Yield. Water Resources Bull. 25(4):855-865.

**Schicht, R.J. and W.C. Walton. 1961.** Hydrologic Budgets for Three Small Watersheds in flhinois. Illinois State Water Survey, Report of Investigations 40, 40 pp.

**Sophocleous, M.A., J.K. Koelliker, R.S. Govindaraju, T. Birdie, S.R Ramireddygani, and S.P. Perkins. 1999.** Integrated Numer-ical Modeling for Basin-Wide Water Management: The Case of the Rattlesnake Creek Basin in South-Central Kansas. J. of Hydrology 214(1999):179-196.

**Srinivasan, R. and B.A. Engel. 1991.** A Knowledge Based Approach to Extract Input Data from GIS. ASAE Paper No. 91-7045. ASAE Summer Meeting, Albuquerque, New Mexico.

**Srinivasan, R., J. Arnold, R.S. Muttiah, C. Walker, and P.T. Dyke. 1993.** Hydrologic Unit Model of the United States (HUMUS). In: Proc. Adv. in Hydro-Science and Eng. Univ. of Mississippi, Oxford, Mississippi.

**Srinivasan, R. and J.G. Arnold. 1994.** Integration of a Basin-Scale Water Quality Model with GIS. Water Resources Bulletin (30)3: 453-462.

**Thomas, H.A., C.M. Mann, M.J. Brown and M.B. Piering. 1983.** Methodology for Water Resources Assessment Report to the U.S. Geological Survey. Rept. NTIS 84-12163, National Tech. Info. Service, Springfield, Virginia.

**Toth. J. 1963.** A Theoretical Analysis of Groundwater Flow in Small Drainage Basins. Jour. Geophys. Res. 68(16):4795-4812.

**UNESCO. 1978.** World Water Balance and Water Resources of the Earth, Including Atlas of World Water Balance. UNESCO Press, Paris, France, 663 pp.

**USDA. 1992.** STATSGO — State Soils Geographic Data Base. Soil Conservation Service, Publication Number 1492, Washington, D.C.

**USGS. 1990.** Land Use and Land Cover Digital Data from 1:250,000 and 1:100,000 Scale Maps. Data User Guide 4, Reston, Virginia, 33 pp.

**Warnick, A.W. and D.R. Nielsen. 1980.** Spatial Variability of Soil Physical Properties in the Field. In: Applications of Soil Physics, D. Hillel (Editor). Academic, San Diego, California, 385 pp.

**Water Resources Council. 1968.** The Nation's Water Resources. Water Resources Council, U.S. Gov. Printing Office, Washington, D.C., misc. pages.

**Water Resources Council. 1978.** The Nation's Water Resources. Water Resources Council, U.S. Coy. Printing Office, Washington, D.C., misc. pages.

**Wilcox, B.P., W.J. Rawls, D.L. Brakensiek, and J.R. Wight. 1990.** Predicting Runoff from Rangeland Catchments: A Comparison of Two Models. Water Res. Research 26 (10):2401-2410.

**Winter, T.C. 1981.** Uncertainties in Estimating the Water Balance of Lakes. Water Resources Bulletin 17( 1):82-115.

**Winter, T.C. 1990.** Distribution of the Difference Between Precipitation and Open Water Evaporation in North America, Plate (2). In: Surface Water Hydrolog M. G. Wolman (Editor). Geological Society of America, Vol. 0-1.

**Wood, E.F., D.O. Lettenmaier, and V.G. Zartanian. 1992.** A Land Surface Hydrology Parameterization with Subgrid Variability for General Circulation Models. Journal of Geophysical Research 97:2717-2728.

# Part 3
# Using SWAT Software

# 3.1 MapWindow Interface for SWAT (MWSWAT)

## Prepared by Luis F. Leon

## June 2007

(Slightly modified for this book and its accompanying DVD)

### MWSWAT (MapWindow SWAT)

### Step by Step Setup for the San Juan (Mexico) and Linthipe Watersheds (Malawi)

### Contents

# Figures:

# 1. Environment and Tools Required

1. Microsoft Windows (any version, as far as we are aware)
2. Microsoft Access, as the interface uses an Access database
3. A tool like WordPad or NotePad that enables you to read ASCII text files.
4. A tool like WinZip that can uncompress .zip files

# 2. Installation

- Install MapWindow by running **MapWindow46SR.exe** (which is version 4.6) found in the DVD under *Software\MapWindow_GIS*, or a later version if available from www.mapwindow.org. Use the default folder *C:\Program Files\MapWindow* as the installation folder.

- Install MWSWAT by running **MWSWAT.exe**, found in *Software\MWSWAT*. It will create a folder *C:\Program Files\MapWindow\Plugins\MWSWAT* containing

- **createHRU.dll** and **MWSWAT.dll** - these constitute the MWSwat plugin

- **mwswat.mdb** - a database that will be copied for new projects

- **crop.dat**, **fert.dat**, **pest.dat**, **till.dat**, **urban.dat** - SWAT data files, in a sub-folder *Databases*

- **swat2005.exe** - this is the SWAT executable

- **SWAT2005**.mdb - SWAT reference data, in the subfolder *Databases*

- A collection of weather generator (.wgn) files in the subfolder *Databases\USWeather*

- From the folder *Global_Weather_Data* in *Software\MWSWAT\DATA*, get **stnlist.txt** and **2000.zip** to **2005.zip**. Place stnlist.txt and the zip files in one folder (e.g. *Weather*) and unzip them. You will get subfolders *2000* to *2005*. The weather data includes precipitation and temperature data.

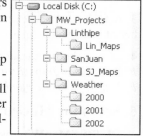

- From the folder *SWATEditor*, found in *Software*, unzip the installation archive SwatEditor_Install_2.1.2bRelease.zip and run **Setup.exe** to install the SWAT input file editor. Use the default folder *C:\Program Files\SWAT\SWAT 2005 Editor* as the installation folder.

- Create a folder to store the digital source data (e.g. *SJ_Maps* sub-folder under each project directory) and refer to the geo-processing document. This is where the DEM, landuse, and soil grids generated according to that document should be placed.

# 3. Structure and Location of Source Data

The "Step by Step Geo-Processing and Set-up of the Required Watershed Data for MWSWAT (MapWindows SWAT)" document (*Geo-Process.pdf*) describes the pre-processing of digital map data (DEM, Landuse and Soil). The document may be found in *Software\MWSWAT\MWSWAT_Manual*. Following that document you can create the required DEM, landuse and soil maps for the two watersheds by clipping and reprojecting the appropriate files from global data. Alternatively, for the San Juan example, you may prefer to skip this step and instead unzip the *Geo_processed.zip* archives in the *SJ_Maps* folder found in *Software\MWSWAT\DATA*. (The Linthipe example set can be downloaded from http://www.waterbase.org/.)

After either geo-processing or unzipping the archives you should have at least the following maps available. For the San Juan watershed in *SJ_Maps*: *sj_dem_clip_utm.asc*, *sj_land_clip_utm.tif*, *sj_soil_clip_utm.tif*, and *sj_washd_utm.shp*. For the Linthipe watershed in *Lin_Maps*: *lin_dem_clip_utm.asc*, *lin_land_clip_utm.tif*, *lin_soil_clip_utm.tif* and *lin_out.shp*.

# 4. Structure and Location of Output Data

We will be establishing a project called *Proj*, say, in a folder *F*. This will automatically create:

1. A folder *F\Proj* containing the project file *proj.mwprj*. If we later want to re-open the project this will be the file we look for. This folder also contains the project database *proj.mdb*.

2. A folder *F\Proj\Scenarios\Default\TxtInOut* that will contain all the SWAT input and output files.

3. A folder *F\Proj\Source* that will contain copies of our input maps and a number of intermediate maps generated during watershed delineation.

4. If we choose to save a SWAT run as *Run1*, for example, then a folder *F\Proj\\Scenarios\Run1\TxtInOut* will be created (a copy of *F\Proj\Scenarios\Default\TxtInOut*).

# 5. Setup for Mexico: San Juan River Watershed

1. Start **MapWindow** and check that you have plugins "**Watershed Delineation**" and "**MWSWAT**" available. Both these should be checked in the **Plug-ins** menu.
2. Start **MWSWAT**.
3. The main MWSWAT interface will be displayed. Click the box *New Project*.

310

4. A browser will be displayed requesting a name for the new project. Type **SJ_MWSwat** in the text box labeled *File name* (under the *SanJuan* folder) See Figure 1.

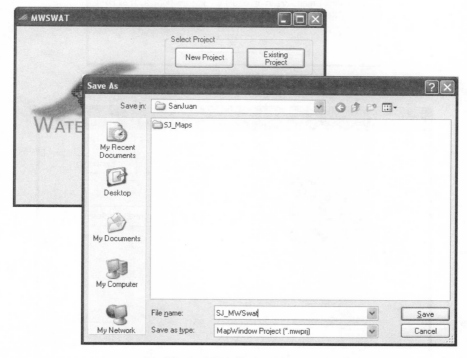

**Figure 1: Naming a project**

At this point you get a reminder (Figure 2) that (1) all your maps should be in an equal area projection (probably, but not necessarily, UTM)[1]; you also need to make sure that the map's units of measure are meters, and (2) that the Watershed Delineation plugin needs to be selected. If some of your maps need re-projecting you can use the MapWindow *GIS Tools* plug-in to do it.

Some of your files may not come with associated projection information, and MapWindow will ask if they have the right projection. If you are sure they have the same projection as your other files you just confirm that they should be loaded and given the same projection as the rest of the project.

If you are ready to proceed with MWSWAT, click *OK*.

---

[1]While UTM is not truly an equal area projection, it is close enough in most cases for SWAT.

**Figure 2: Reminders**

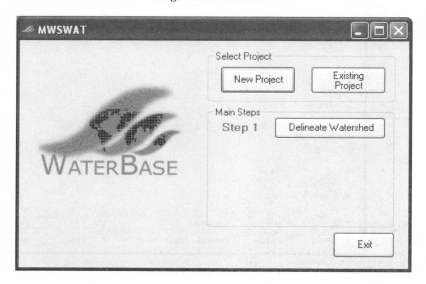

**Figure 3: About to do step 1**

The interface now presents a step-by-step configuration to be followed in order to prepare the SWAT simulation, starting with Step 1 (Figure 3).

5. If you need to set up some database tables for your project, this is a good time to do it, as the database has just been created in the *SJ_MWSwat* folder. See section 8 on *Using Your Own Data*.

## 5.1 Step 1. Process DEM (Watershed Delineation)

6. To start the automatic watershed delineation click the *Delineate Watershed* button. When the prompt box is opened *Select Base DEM*.

7. Browse to the *SJ_Maps* folder in *Software\MWSWAT\DATA* and open the file *sj_dem_clip_utm.asc*  (Figure 4)

8. Click the *Process DEM* button to load the DEM file and activate the *Automatic Watershed Delineation* plug-in. This may take a few minutes.

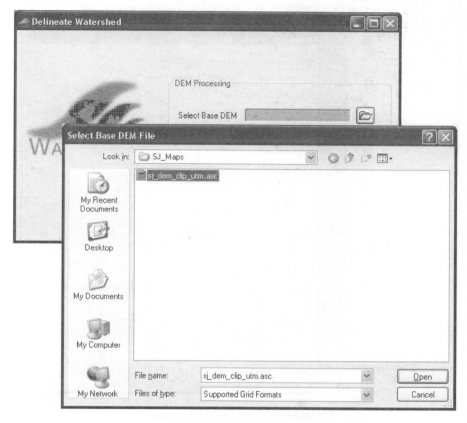

**Figure 4: Selecting the DEM**

9. The name of the elevation map grid will be displayed in the *DEM* text box on the *Automatic Watershed Delineation* (AWD) dialog box. Make sure the *Elevation Units* are *Meters* (and that this is appropriate for your DEM!) and that the *Burn-in Existing Stream Polyline* option is not checked. For this watershed we have a shape file we will use as a focusing mask; select the *Use a Focusing Mask* option, click the *Use Grid or Shapefile for Mask* option if not already marked, click the file selection icon, and find and open the file *sj_washd_utm.shp* in the *SJ_Maps* folder, and click the first *Run* button (Figure 5). The first part of the watershed delineation tool will be run. This can take a few minutes.

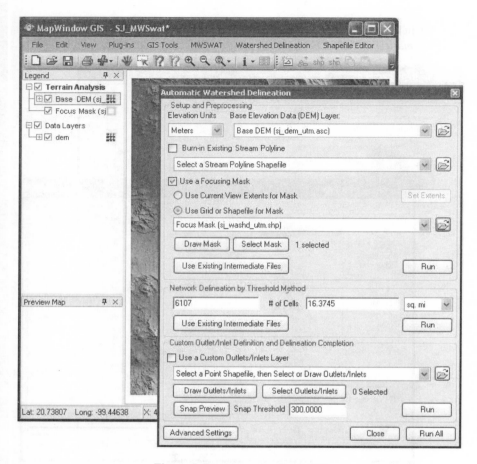

**Figure 5: Preprocessing the DEM**

10. The threshold size for subbasins is set next. It can be set by area, in various units such as sq km or hectares, or by number (#) of cells. Change the threshold method to use sq km, change the number of sq km to 50, and press *Enter*: the number of cells will be adjusted to the corresponding value (7200). Now click the second *Run* button to delineate the stream network. This can take a few minutes, and when complete the MapWindow display will be as illustrated in Figure 6. (You may have to move the Focus Mask entry above the Base DEM entry in the Legend panel to get exactly this view.)

314

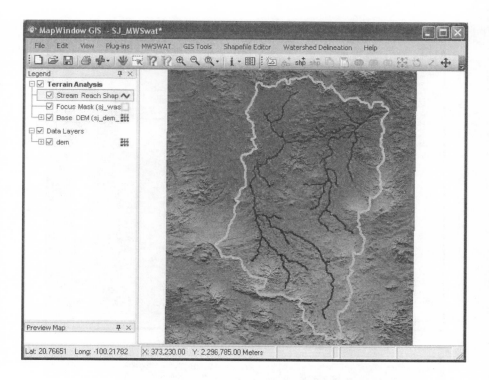

**Figure 6: Stream networks displayed**

11. To complete the watershed delineation we need to select an outlet point, which will be in the form of a shapefile. In the AWD form make sure that *Use a Custom Outlets/Inlets Layer* is checked, and use MapWindow to zoom into the area of the map where you want to locate the outlet. Click *Draw Outlets/Inlets*. Confirm in the new window that pops up that you want to create a new outlets/inlets shapefile, and in the next dialogue give it the name sj_out. Use the mouse to mark the outlet point on the MapWindow display (where the stream network meets the mask boundary), and click *Done* (Figure 7).

12. *n version 4.4 of AWD there was a bug which causes the network delineation parameters to be reset when the Outlets/Inlets shapefile is selected. If this happens, reset the number of cells to 7200 and press Enter.*

13. Then in the AWD form click the third *Run*. The outlets and subbasin delineation will be performed, which can take a few minutes, and the MapWindow display will show the river network draining to the outlet point and the subbasin boundaries. The AWD part is now completed and you can *Close* the AWD form (Figure 8).

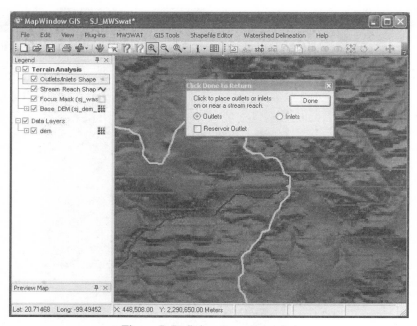

**Figure 7: Defining the outlet point**

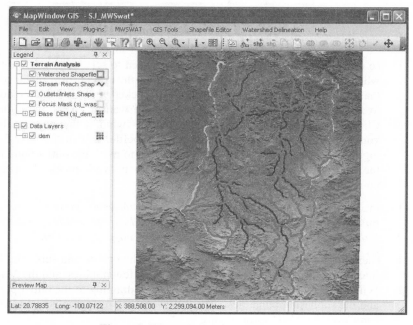

**Figure 8: Watershed delineation complete**

14. The MWSWAT interface will mark the *Process DEM* as done and enable the second step (Figure 9).

It is strongly recommended to save the project (via the menu of MapWindow) at this stage.

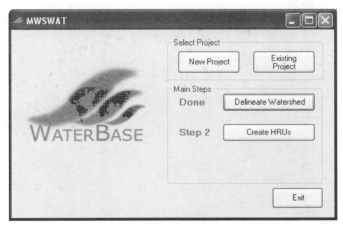

**Figure 9: About to do step 2**

## 5.2 Step 2. Create HRUs

15. Having calculated the basins, we want to calculate the details of the Hydrological Response Units (HRUs) that are used by SWAT. We can divide basins into smaller pieces each of which has a particular soil/ landuse(crop)/slope range combination.

16. To do this we click *Create HRUs*, select *sj_land_clip_utm.tif* as the *Landuse Map*, select *sj_soil_clip_utm.tif* as the *Soil Map*, select *global_landuses* as the *Landuse Table*, and select *global_soils* as the *Soil Table*. . The last two will take a few seconds as the relevant database tables are read.

17. We will form HRUs based on slope as well as landuse and soil. We add an intermediate point for slopes (e.g. 10) to divide HRUs into those with average slopes for 0-10% and those with average slopes in the range 10% to the top limit. Type 10 in the box and click *Insert*. The *Slope bands* box shows the intermediate limit is inserted.

18. To read in the data from the DEM, landuse, soil and slope maps and prepare to calculate HRUs, click *Read* (Figure 10). This may take a few minutes.

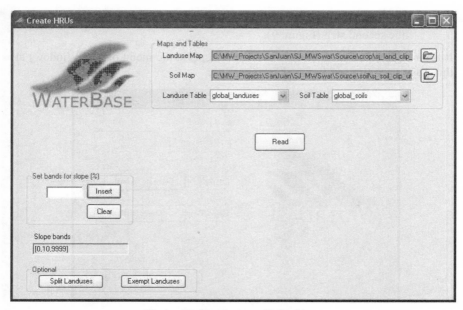

**Figure 10: Ready to read the maps**

19. After reading the grids you will notice a number of changes to the MapWindow display (Figure 11):

- The subbasins have been numbered.
- A Slope bands map has been created and added. This allows you to see where the areas of the two slope bands selected for this project are located. If no intermediate slope limits are chosen this map is not created.
- The legends for the landuse map sj_land_utm and the soil map sj_soil_utm include the landuse and soil categories from the SWAT database.
- A shapefile FullHRUs has been created and added. This allows you to see where in each subbasin the potential Hydrological Response Units (HRUs) are physically located. If, for example, we zoom in on subbasin 15, in the Legend panel select (left button) FullHRUs, open its attribute table (right button), set the mouse to Select (MapWindow toolbar ) and click on the box just above the number 15 in the map, then we get a view like Figure 12. We see that this potential HRU is composed of two parts, has the landuse FOEN, the soil I-K-E-c-4749, and the slope band 0-10. Its area of 396.5ha is only 4.1% of the subbasin. Close the Attribute Table Editor.

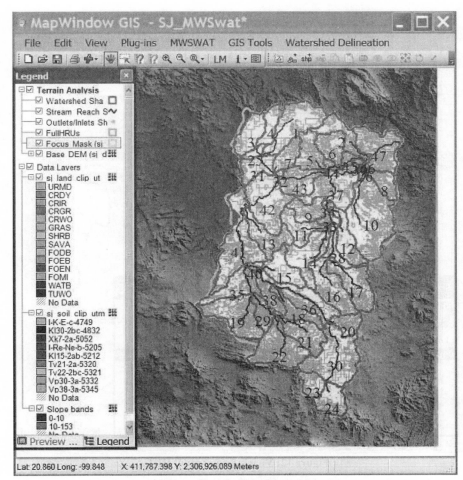

**Figure 11: After reading grids**

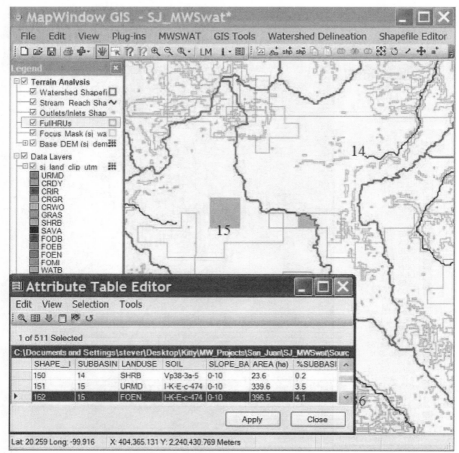

**Figure 12: Viewing a potential HRU**

20. Before we continue with HRU definition, if we look at the main MWSWAT window we see that a new item *Reports* is available and we can choose to view just two reports at this point, which are the *Elevation* and *Basin* reports. The elevation report gives information about how much land is at each elevation from the lowest to the highest, both for the watershed as a whole and for each subbasin (Figure 13). The basin report lists the landuse, soil and slope-band areas for each subbasin (Figure 14).

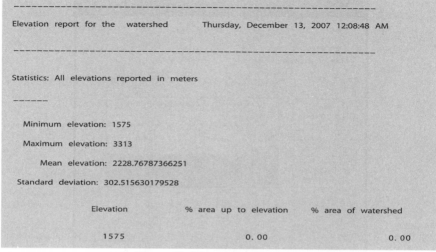

Statistics: All elevations reported in meters

Minimum elevation: 1575

Maximum elevation: 3313

Mean elevation: 2228.76787366251

Standard deviation: 302.515630179528

| Elevation | % area up to elevation | % area of watershed |
|---|---|---|
| 1575 | 0. 00 | 0. 00 |

**Figure 13: Elevation report (start)**

| | | Area [ha] | %Watershed | %Subbasin |
|---|---|---|---|---|
| Subbasin 47 | | 15081.24 | 3.65 | |
| Landuse | | | | |
| | SHRB | 6943.05 | 1.68 | 46.04 |
| | GRAS | 8138.19 | 1.97 | 53.96 |
| Soil | | | | |
| | Vp30-3a-5332 | 3127.78 | 0.76 | 20.74 |
| | K130-2bc-4832 | 11297.21 | 2.73 | 74.91 |
| | Xk7-2a-5052 | 656.25 | 0.16 | 4.35 |
| Slope | | | | |
| | 0-10 | 6952.08 | 1.68 | 46.10 |
| | 10-153 | 8129.16 | 1.97 | 53.90 |

**Figure 14: Basin report (fragment)**

21. At this point we have the options to split landuses, and to exempt landuses, both of which will affect how HRUs are defined.

- Splitting landuses allows us to define more precise landuses than our landuse map provides. If, say, we know that in this basin 60% of the CRIR (Irrigated cropland and pasture) is used for corn, we could split CRIR into 60% CORN and 40% CRIR (Figure 15).

- Exempting landuses allows us to ensure that a landuse is retained in the HRU calculation even if it falls below the thresholds we will define later. For example, we might decide to exempt the urban landuse URMD (Figure 16).

321

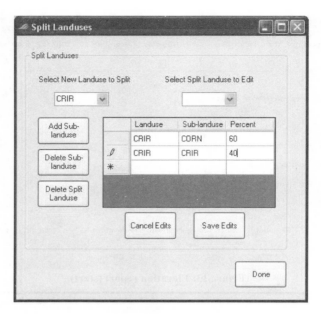

Figure 15: Splitting a landuse

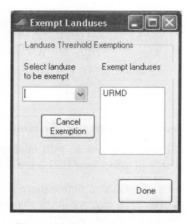

Figure 16: Exempting a landuse

In this example we will not split or exempt any landuses. Now we need to exclude HRUs that are insignificant by considering percentage thresholds or area thresholds. This is the "multiple" HRU option. The "single" option just uses each basin as one HRU, giving it the dominant soil, landuse and slope range for that basin.

22. Once all the data has been read in and stored, the *Single/Multiple HRU* choice is enabled. Select *Multiple HRUs*, and then select *By Percentage*. Now select thresholds for landuse, soil and slope. The idea of this option is that we will ignore any potential HRUs for which the landuse, soil or slope is less than the selected threshold, which is its percentage in the subbasin. The areas of HRUs that are ignored are redistributed proportionately amongst those that are retained. The value of 33 as the maximum we can choose for landuse indicates that there is a subbasin where the max value for a landuse is 33%: if we chose a higher value than 33% we would be trying to ignore all the landuse categories in that subbasin. Hence 33% is the min across the subbasins of the max landuse percentage in each subbasin. Select 20% for landuse, by using the slider or by typing in the box, and click *Go*. The interface then computes the min-max percentage for a soil as 51%. Select 10 for Soil, click *Go*, 5 for slope, and click *Create HRUs* (Figure 17). It should report 195 HRUs formed in 47 subbasins. Click *OK*.

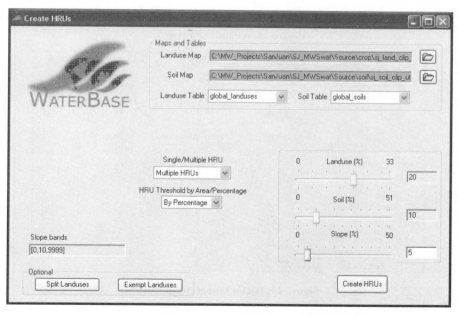

**Figure 17: Creating multiple HRUs by percentage**

23. *Create HRUs* is now reported as done and the third step is enabled (Figure 18). If you look at the *Reports* now available you will find that there is an *HRUs* report that only includes the landuses, soils and slope bands left after HRU selection, and also gives details of the HRUs that have been formed (Figure 19). If you wish to change the HRU thresh-

olds then you can click the *Create HRUs* button again, change the thresholds and/or the landuses to be split or exempted, and rerun the *Create HRUs* step.

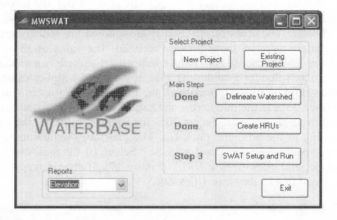

**Figure 18: About to do step 3**

| | Area [ha] | %Watershed | %Subbasin |
|---|---|---|---|
| Subbasin 47 | 15081.24 | 3.65 | |
| Landuse | | | |
| SHRB | 6943.05 | 1.68 | 46.04 |
| GRAS | 8138.19 | 1.97 | 53.96 |
| Soil | | | |
| Vp30-3a-5332 | 3210.49 | 0.78 | 21.29 |
| K130-2bc-4832 | 11870.75 | 2.87 | 78.71 |
| Slope | | | |
| 0-10 | 7011.57 | 1.70 | 46.49 |
| 10-153 | 8069.67 | 1.95 | 53.51 |
| HRUs: | | | |
| 188   SHRB/Vp30-3a-5332/10-153 | 800.00 | 0.19 | 5.30 |
| 189   SHRB/Vp30-3a-5332/0-10 | 1384.72 | 0.33 | 9.18 |
| 190  SHRB/K130-2bc-4832/10-153 | 2366.66 | 0.57 | 15.69 |
| 191   SHRB/K130-2bc-4832/0-10 | 2391.66 | 0.58 | 15.86 |
| 192  GRAS/Vp30-3a-5332/10-153 | 381.45 | 0.09 | 2.53 |
| 193   GRAS/Vp30-3a-5332/0-10 | 644.32 | 0.16 | 4.27 |
| 194  GRAS/K130-2bc-4832/10-153 | 4521.55 | 1.09 | 29.98 |
| 195   GRAS/K130-2bc-4832/0-10 | 2590.87 | 0.63 | 17.18 |

**Figure 19: HRUs report (fragment)**

24. It is strongly recommended to save the project (via the menu of MapWindow) at this stage.

## 5.3 Step 3. SWAT Setup and Run

25. At this point almost everything is ready to write the SWAT input files and run SWAT. Click *SWAT Setup and Run* (Figure 20).

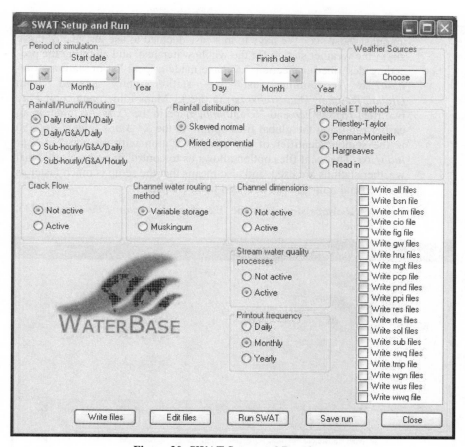

**Figure 20: SWAT Setup and Run form**

26. The first thing to do on this form is to set the period for the SWAT run. Select 1 January 2000 as the *Start date* and 31 December 2001 as the *Finish date*.

27. Next we have to choose the source of weather data. Click the *Choose* button for *Weather Sources*. MWSWAT is set up to use actual weather data for maximum and minimum temperature and precipitation, and a weather generator file that will simulate other weather factors (solar radiation, wind speed, and relative humidity). So you need to provide a weather generator file for your basin, and data for precipitation and temperature. Normally for the first run you would choose the option *Global files*, and choose *Global_Weather_Data\stnlist.txt* as the *Weather Stations File*. Then MWSWAT looks for the nearest 6 weather stations in that file, generates the temperature and precipitation data for them, and

then associates each subbasin with the nearest weather station from amongst those six. We have in this case decided to use just one of those six as the weather station for the whole watershed, and adopting the procedure described in Section 7.8, have made a local list of stations, *sanjuan1.txt* (containing just one station entry copied from *Global_Weather_Data\stnlist.txt*) in the *SJ_*Maps folder, and copied the two files *765850.pcp* and *765850.tmp*, made in the *TxtInOut* folder in an earlier run using the global files option, to the *SJ_Maps* folder. 765850 is the station identifier of the weather station with an entry in *sanjuan1.txt*. The local files option allows us to control more precisely what weather stations are used, and also means that the setup is much faster as the .pcp and .tmp files do not need to be created.

28. Choose *SJ_Maps\sj.wgn* as the *Weather Generator File* (Figure 21). Click *Done*.

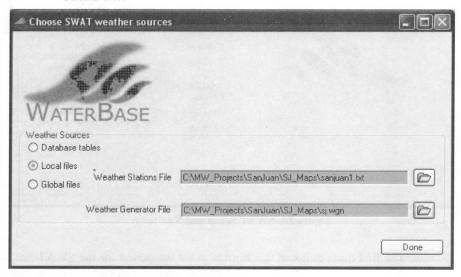

**Figure 21: Choosing weather sources**

29. Click *Write all files* in the list box (Figure 22) and click the *Write files* button. This can take a few minutes, especially if your simulation covers several years, but is fast in this case as the weather data is prepared already.

30. The interface reports that the SWAT input files are written. They can be found in the *TxtInOut* folder. Click *OK*.

31. Click *Run SWAT* to launch the SWAT executable in a DOS prompt window (Figure 23).

326

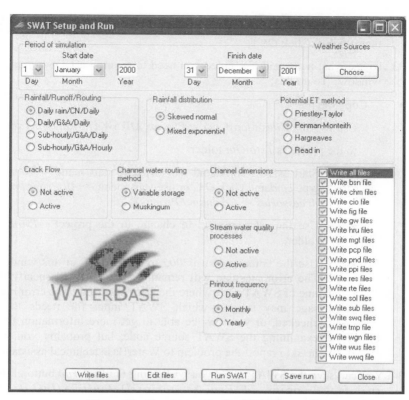

Figure 22: About to write the SWAT input files

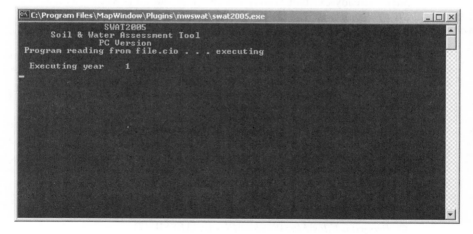

Figure 23: Running SWAT

32. When done a message box will say that SWAT was run successfully, or that it failed. Click *OK*.

33. To see what happened if it failed you need to rerun in a DOS command window. To do this:

- Copy the file

  *C:\Program Files\MapWindow\Plugins\MWSWAT\swat2005.exe*

  to the project's *TxtInOut* folder.

  - Start a DOS command window (use start menu -> *Run...* , type *cmd* and click *OK*, or use start menu -> *All Programs* -> *Accessories* -> *Command Prompt*).

  - Use the *cd* command to change to the project's *TxtInOut* folder.

  - Use the command *swat2005* to run SWAT in this window. The error message will remain visible and will specify the line of SWAT code where the error occurred. The error message may suggest which SWAT input file needs to be checked, or you may be able to get more information from examining the SWAT source code, but probably you will need to report the problem to WaterBase technical assistance.

34. You can save the SWAT run if you wish using the *Save run* button. This in fact copies *F\Proj\Scenarios\Default\TxtInOut* to *F\Proj\Scenarios\Save1\TxtInOut* if you choose to save as *Save1*. If *Save1* already exists it is overwritten. This button is live as soon as the *SWAT Setup and Run* form is opened, so you can if you wish use the form to save an earlier run before you start writing the files for this one. (But note that if you changed the watershed delineation or the HRU parameters the report files will be wrong, so in this case you should do the save manually before starting the interface.)

35. You can use the *Edit files* button to run the SWAT Editor to edit any of the input files and database files if you wish. See Figure 24. Note that the parameters for the editor should be set as follows:

- SWAT Project Geodatabase: *F\Proj\Proj.mdb*
- SWAT Parameter Geodatabase:
  *C:\Program Files\MapWindow\Plugins\MWSWAT\Databases\SWAT2005.mdb*

  - SWAT Executable folder:
  *C:\Program Files\MapWindow\Plugins\MWSWAT\*
  (Note the final "\", which must not be omitted.)

For information on using the SWAT Editor, see chapters 9 through 15 of the *ArcSWAT_Documentation.pdf* in *Software\SWATEditor* on the DVD.

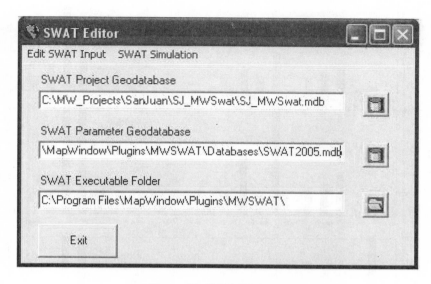

**Figure 24: SWAT Editor**

From the reach output file, the monthly values for the outlet were extracted and the following plots (Figure 25) created (note: precipitation values for San Juan are for the two nearest rain gauges).

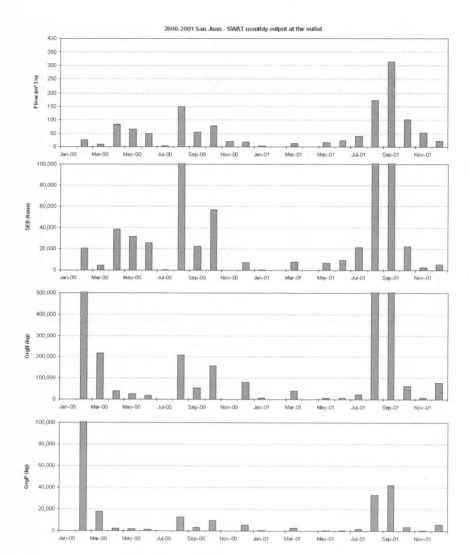

**Figure 25: San Juan output plots**

# 6. Setup for Malawi: Linthipe Watershed

Note: Be sure to read Sections 1-3 of this document before beginning the Linthipe Watershed setup. Example data for Linthipe is not available on the DVD, but may be downloaded from Waterbase at http://www.waterbase.org/download_mwswat.html.

330

1. Start **MapWindow** and check that you have plugins "**Watershed Delineation**" and "**MWSWAT**" available. Both these should be checked.

2. Start **MWSWAT**.

3. The main interface will be displayed. Click the box beside *New Project*.

4. A browser will be displayed requesting a name for the new project. Type **Lin_MWSwat** in the text box labeled *File Name* (under the *Linthipe* folder).

At this point you get a reminder that (1) all your maps should be in an equal area projection (probably, but not necessarily, UTM)[1]; you also need to make sure that the maps units of measure are meters, and (2) that the Watershed Delineation plugin needs to be selected. If some of your maps need re-projecting you can use the MapWindow *GIS Tools* plug-in to do it.

Some of your files may not come with associated projection information, and MapWindow will ask if they have the right projection. If you are sure they have the same projection as your other files you just confirm that they should be loaded and given the same projection as the rest of the project.

If you are ready to proceed with MWSWAT, click *OK*.

The interface now presents a step-by-step configuration to be followed in order to prepare the SWAT simulation, starting with Step 1 (Figure 26).

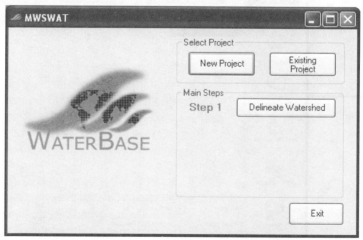

**Figure 26: About to do step 1**

[1]UTM, while not truly an equal area projection is close enough in most cases for SWAT.

5. If you need to set up some database tables for your project, this is a good time to do it, as the database has just been created in the *Lin_MWSwat* folder. See section 8 on *Using Your Own Data*.

## 6.1 Step 1. Process DEM (Watershed Delineation)

6. To start the automatic watershed delineation click the *Delineate Watershed* button. When the prompt box is opened *Select Base DEM*.

7. Browse to the *Lin_Maps* folder and open the file *lin_dem_clip_utm.asc* (Figure 27).

8. Click the *Process DEM* button to activate the *Automatic Watershed Delineation* plug-in. This will also load the DEM grid, which may take a few minutes.

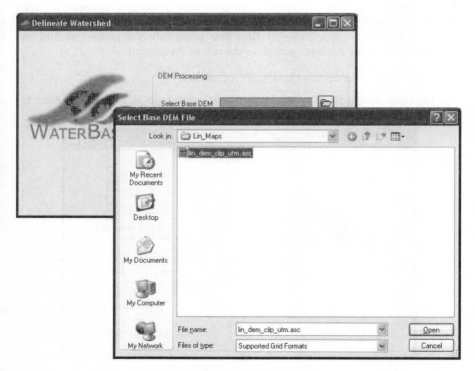

**Figure 27: Selecting the DEM**

9. The name of the elevation map grid will be displayed in the *DEM* text box on the *Automatic Watershed Delineation* (AWD) dialog box. Make sure the *Elevation Units* are *Meters* (and that this is appropriate for your DEM!) and that the *Burn-in Existing Stream Polyline* and *Use Focusing*

*Mask* options are not checked. The threshold size for subbasins is set next. It can be set by area, in various units such as sq km or hectares, or by number (#) of cells. Change the threshold method to use sq km, change the number of sq km to 150, and press Enter: the number of cells will be adjusted to the corresponding value (18646).

10. To complete the watershed delineation we need to select an outlet point, which will be in the form of a shapefile. In the AWD form make sure that *Use a Custom Outlets/Inlets Layer* is checked, and browse for the file *lin_out.shp*.

11. *In version 4.4 of AWD there was a bug which causes the network de-lineation parameters to be reset when the Outlets/Inlets shapefile is se-lected. If this happens, reset the number of cells to* 18646 *and press En-ter* (Figure 28).

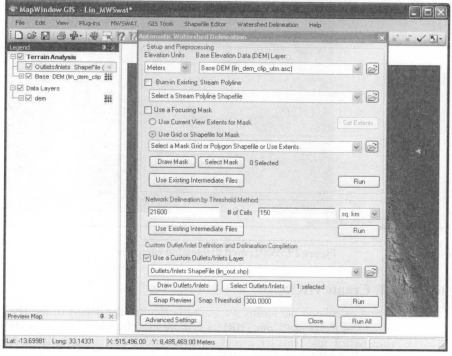

**Figure 28: Running Automatic Watershed Delineation**

12. Click *Run All*. All the watershed delineation steps will be performed, which can take a few minutes, and the MapWindow display will show the river network draining to the outlet point and the subbasin

boundaries. The AWD part is now completed and the AWD form will be closed automatically. (Figure 29).

13. The MWSWAT interface will mark the *Process DEM* as done and enable the second step. It's strongly recommended to save your project at this point.

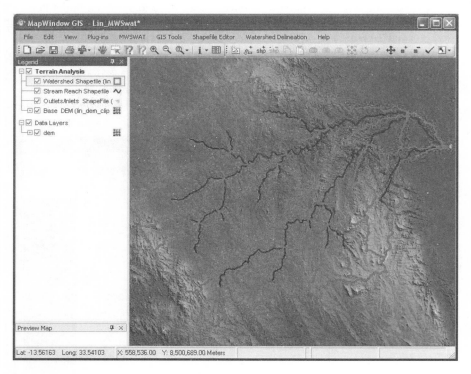

**Figure 29: Watershed delineation complete**

# 6.2 Step 2. Create HRUs

14. Having calculated the basins we want to calculate the details of the Hydrological Response Units (HRUs) that are used by SWAT. We can divide basins into smaller pieces each of which has a particular soil/landuse(crop)/slope range combination.

15. To do this we click *Create HRUs*, select *lin_land_clip_utm.tif* as the *Landuse Map*, select *lin_soil_clip_utm.tif* as the *Soil Map*, select *global_landuses* as the *Landuse Table*, and select *global_soils* as the *Soil Table*. The last two will take a few seconds as the relevant database tables are read.

16. We will form HRUs based on slope as well as landuse and soil. We add an intermediate point for slopes (e.g. 10) to divide HRUs into those with average slopes for 0-10% and those with average slopes in the range 10% to the top limit. Type 10 in the box and click *Insert*. The *Slope bands* box shows the intermediate limit is inserted.

17. To read in the data from the DEM, landuse, soil and slope maps and prepare to calculate HRUs, click *Read* (Figure 30). This may take a few minutes.

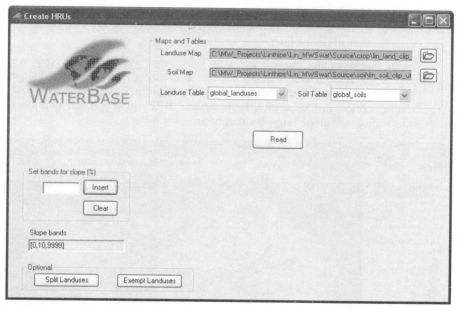

**Figure 30: Ready to read the maps**

18. After reading the grids you will notice a number of changes to the Map-Window display (Figure 31):

   a. The subbasins have been numbered.

   b. S*lope bands* map has been created and added. This allows you to see where the areas of the two slope bands selected for this project are located. If no intermediate slope limits are chosen this map is not created.

   c. The legends for the landuse map *lin_land_clip_utm* and the soil map *lin_soil_clip_utm* include the landuse and soil categories from the SWAT database.

d. A shapefile *FullHRUs* has been created and added. This allows you to see where in each subbasin the potential Hydrological Response Units (HRUs) are physically located.

19. At this point we have the options to split landuses, and to exempt landuses, both of which will affect how HRUs are defined.

   a. Splitting landuses allows us to define more precise landuses than our landuse map provides.

   b. Exempting landuses allows us to ensure that a landuse is retained in the HRU calculation even if it falls below the thresholds we will define later.

20. In this example we will not split or exempt any landuses. Now we need to exclude HRUs that are insignificant by considering percentage thresholds or area thresholds. This is the "multiple" HRU option. The "single" option just uses each basin as one HRU, giving it the dominant soil, landuse and slope range for that basin.

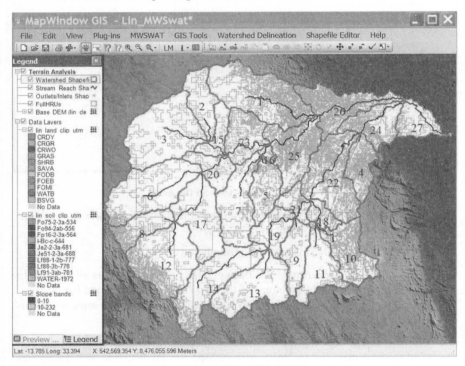

**Figure 31: After reading grids**

21. Once all the data has been read in and stored, the *Single/Multiple HRU* choice is enabled. Select *Multiple HRUs*, and then select *By Percentage*. Now select thresholds for landuse, soil and slope. The idea of this option is that we will ignore any potential HRUs for which the landuse, soil or slope is less than the selected threshold, which is its percentage in the subbasin. The areas of HRUs that are ignored are redistributed proportionately amongst those that are retained. The value of 34 as the maximum we can choose for landuse indicates that there is a subbasin where the max value for a landuse is 34%: if we chose a higher value than 34% we would be trying to ignore all the landuse categories in that subbasin. Hence 34% is the minimum across the subbasins of the maximum landuse percentage in each subbasin. Select 20% for landuse, by using the slider or by typing in the box, and click *Go*. The interface then computes the min-max percentage for a soil as 37%. Select 10 for Soil, click *Go*, 5 for slope, and click *Create HRUs* (Figure 32). It should report 120 HRUs formed in 27 subbasins. Click *OK*.

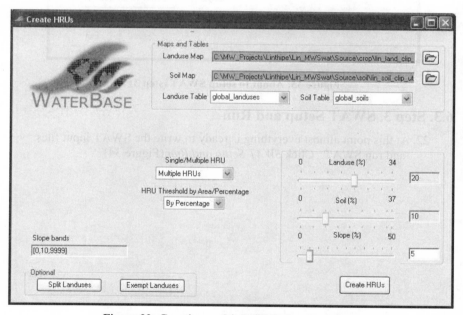

**Figure 32: Creating multiple HRUs by percentage**

*Create HRUs* is now reported as done and the third step is enabled (Figure 33). If you look at the *Reports* now available you will find that there is an *Elevation* report that gives information on the elevation profile of the basin and each subbasin, a *Basins* report that lists the landuse, soil and slope-band areas for each subbasin and also an *HRUs* report that only includes the landuses, soils and slope bands left after HRU selection, and also gives details of the HRUs that have been formed. If you wish to change the HRU thresholds then you can click the *Create HRUs* button again, change the thresholds and/or the landuses to be split or exempted, and rerun the *Create HRUs* step.

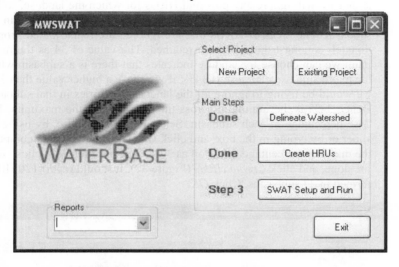

**Figure 33: About to setup SWAT (step 3)**

## 6.3. Step 3. SWAT Setup and Run

22. At this point almost everything is ready to write the SWAT input files and run SWAT. Click *SWAT Setup and Run* (Figure 34).

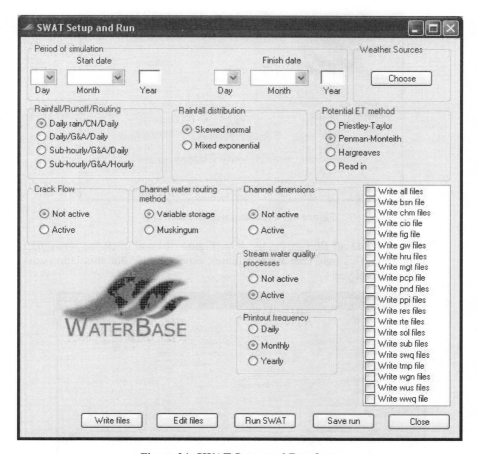

**Figure 34: SWAT Setup and Run form**

23. The first thing to do on this form is to set the period for the SWAT run. Select 1 January 2000 as the *Start date* and 31 December 2001 as the *Finish date*.

24. Next we have to choose the source of weather data. Click the *Choose* button for *Weather Sources*. MWSWAT is set up to use actual weather data for maximum and minimum temperature and precipitation, and a weather generator file that will simulate other weather factors (solar radiation, wind speed, and relative humidity). So you need to provide a weather generator file for your basin, and data for precipitation and temperature. Choose the option *Global files*, choose *Global_Weather_Data\stnlist.txt* as the *Weather Stations File* and *Lin_Maps\lin.wgn* as the *Weather Generator File* (Figure 35). Click *Done*.

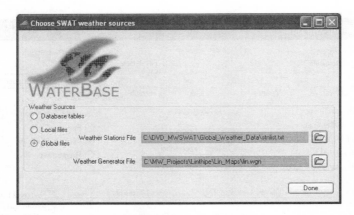

**Figure 35: Choosing weather sources**

25. Click *Write all files* in the list box (Figure 36) and click the *Write files* button. This may take a few minutes, especially if your simulation covers several years.

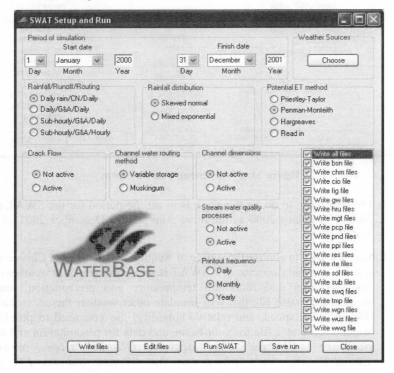

**Figure 36: About to write the SWAT input files**

26. The interface reports that the SWAT input files are written. They can be found in the *TxtInOut* folder. Click *OK*.

27. Click *Run SWAT* to launch the SWAT executable in a DOS prompt window (Figure 37).

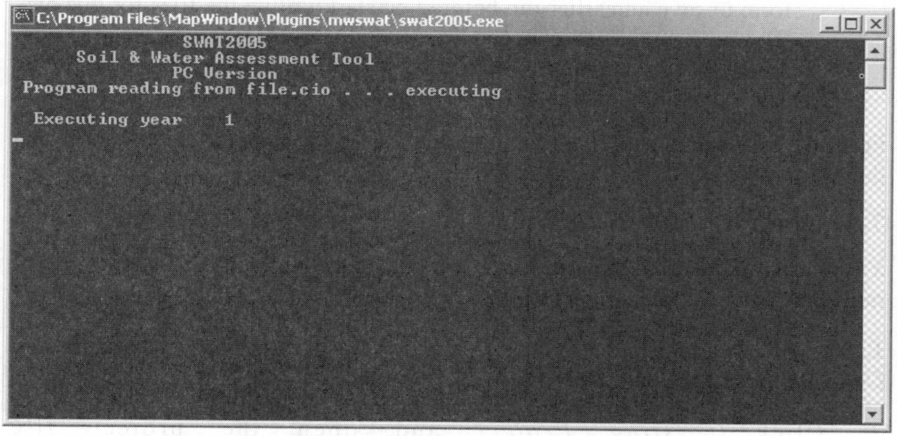

**Figure 37: Running SWAT**

28. When done a message box will say that SWAT was run successfully, or that it failed. Click *OK*.

29. To see what happened if it failed you need to rerun in a DOS command window:

   a. Copy the file

   *C:\Program Files\MapWindow\Plugins\MWSWAT\swat2005.exe*

   to the project's *TxtInOut* folder.

   b. Start a DOS command (use start menu -> *Run...*, type *cmd* and click *OK*, or use start menu -> *All Programs -> Accessories -> Command Prompt*).

   c. Use the *CD* command to change to the project's *TxtInOut* folder.

   d. Use the command *swat2005* to run SWAT in this window. The error message will remain visible and will specify the line of SWAT code where the error occurred. The error message may suggest which SWAT input file needs to be checked, or you may be able to get more information from examining the SWAT source code, but probably you will need to report the problem to WaterBase technical assistance.

30. You can save the SWAT run if you wish using the *Save run* button. This in fact copies $F \backslash Proj \backslash Scenarios \backslash Default \backslash TxtInOut$ to $F \backslash Proj \backslash Scenarios \backslash Save1 \backslash TxtInOut$ if you choose to save as *Save1*. If *Save1* already exists it is overwritten. This button is live as soon as the *SWAT Setup and Run* form is opened, so you can if you wish use the form to save an earlier run before you start writing the files for this one. (But note that if you changed the watershed delineation or the HRU parameters the report files will be wrong, so in this case you should do the save manually before starting the interface.)

From the reach output file, the monthly values for the outlet were extracted and the following plots created (Figure 38).

# 7. Rerunning MWSWAT

You may want to rerun the interface because you want to change some of the parameters. This section explains how to do so.

1. Start MapWindow and make sure that the plugins *MWSWAT* and *Watershed Delineation* are selected. Start *MWSWAT*.

2. Click *Existing Project* and open the project file $F \backslash SJ\_MWSwat \backslash SJ\_MWSwat.mwprj$ (remember that we started the new project *SJ_MWSwat* in folder *F*).

3. The *Process DEM* step is marked as already done. You can rerun it if you want to use a new DEM, change the subbasin threshold, or move the outlet point, or add additional inner inlets, reservoirs, or outlets.

4. In the *Create HRUs* step you will find that the landuse and soil maps are already set to the files you used before (or, rather, the copies that were made of them and stored in the project folder tree) and the database tables are set to *global_landuses* and *global_soils*. These can be changed if you want to use different maps.

5. Assuming you keep the same landuse and soil maps, you are offered the options to *Read from previous run* or *Read from maps*. The former is much faster, and can be used unless you want to change the slope limits. Changing the slope limits requires a re-read of the maps because cells are allocated to potential HRUs by their subbasin number, landuse type, soil type, and slope range.

6. After reading or rereading you are offered the same choice as before between removing insignificant HRUs by percentages or area thresholds, and the values you used last time are preselected. You can switch between area and percentage, you can change the values, and you can change landuse splits and exemptions, or you can just immediately click *Create HRUs*, keeping the old values.

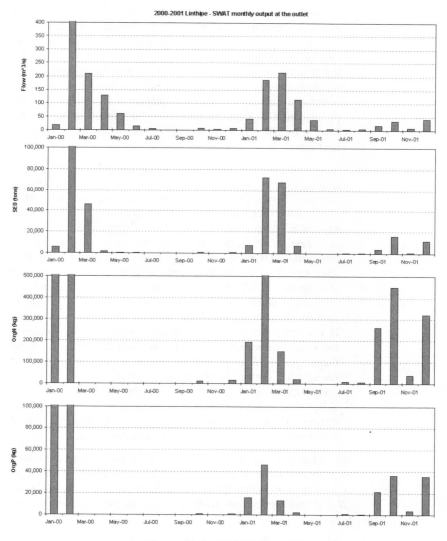

**Figure 38: Linthipe output plots**

7. You can now start the final form *SWAT Setup and Run*. Here you can change the Start and Finish dates, the weather sources, and any other of the options shown.

8. There are three ways to select the weather sources:

      •   You can use the global weather data that is supplied on the DVD. This provides a worldwide list of weather stations *stlnlist.txt*. In the folder *Global_Weather_Data* containing *stnlist.txt* there are subfolders *2000, 2001* etc containing data for each year. In the *Choose SWAT weather sources* form choose the option *Global files* and find the *stnlist.txt* file for the *Weather Stations File*. MWSWAT will later select the six weather stations closest to your basin, and then from them select the one nearest to each subbasin. It will also create precipitation and temperature files for each weather station for use by SWAT. This is what we did when we ran for the first time.

- You can reuse the files generated by using the previous option as follows. In the *TxtInOut* folder you will find files of the form *nnnnnn.pcp* and *nnnnnn.tmp. nnnnnn* is a weather station identifier from *stnlist.txt*. Create a new file, *sj_list.txt*, say, in SJ_Maps, and cut and paste the relevant lines from *stnlist.txt into it*. It does not matter if you insert some header lines first: MWSWAT will only start reading at the first line starting with 6 digits. You don't need to all six weather stations for which *.pcp* and *.tmp* files exist, and you can use different weather stations if you wish (but make sure there is data for them in *yyyy/JAN.txt*, where *yyyy* is your start year). If you have put into your weather stations list only stations for which there are *.pcp* and *.tmp* files in *TxtInOut*, copy these files to *SJ_Maps* and in your next run you can use the *Local files* option in the *Choose SWAT weather sources* form, selecting *sj_list.txt* as your *Weather Stations File*. When this option is chosen only those stations in the weather stations file are used, and the *.pcp* and *.tmp* files are looked for in the same folder as the weather stations file.

If you have in your weather stations list some stations for which you do not have *.pcp* and *.tmp* files in *TxtInOut* then copy *sj_list.txt* to the same folder as *stnlist.txt* and next time use the *Global files* option but with *sj_list.txt* as the weather stations file.

- The third alternative is to use tables in the database *SJ_MWSwat.mdb*, which you will find in the *F\SJ_MWSwat* folder. The first run will generate a table *weather_sources* , six tables *pcpnnnnnn*, and six tables *tmpnnnnnn*. These tables can be reused by selecting *Database tables* as the weather source, and *weather_sources* as the table.

Note that if you use different start or end dates in later runs you must ensure with the local or database options that your precipitation and temperature files or tables include the whole simulation period, and with the global option that the *Global_Weather_Data* folder has sub-folders for all the years required.

You can also use the *SWAT Editor* to edit any of the SWAT input files. The SWAT Editor is described in its own documentation and in further detail in chapters 9-15 of the *ArcSWAT_Documentation.pdf*, both of which can be found in *Software\SWATEditor* on the DVD.

# 8. Using Your Own Data

The data supplied with MWSWAT is obtained from the web, and you may have your own data which you want to use. This section explains how to do so.

## 8.1 DEM

The digital elevation map (DEM) is selected at the start of the interface. It can be any resolution, but (a) it must be projected to an "equal area" projection, or to a projection such as UTM which comes close enough to equal area in most cases – use MapWindow's *GIS Tools* plugin to do any reprojection – and (b) the elevations must be in meters.

## 8.2 Landuse and Soil Maps

You can substitute your own landuse and/or soil maps. This is a little more complicated since you have to provide the information on how the categories of landuse or soil that your maps use are to be interpreted by SWAT. For each differently categorized landuse or soil map that you use you have to prepare a table like *global_landuses* or *global_soils* and put it into either *C:\Program Files\MapWindow\Plugins\MWSWAT\mwswat.mdb* or the project database *Proj.mdb* in the *Proj* folder. In the first case it will be copied into every new project database, but you must be careful to keep it and replace it if you ever reinstall MWSWAT. In the second case it will only be used on the particular project. The project database is created (by copying *mwswat.mdb*) by the *New Project* action, so after this, before *Step 1*, is the best time to add any extra tables you need for a particular project.

1. In the case of a landuse map, the table should have the string *landuse* in its name. Then it will be offered as an option for a landuse table. It must have the same structure as the table *global_landuses* in *mwswat.mdb*. So it must contain at least the columns LANDUSE_ID (type Long Integer) and SWAT_CODE (type Text). The LANDUSE_ID corresponds to the values in the landuse grid. It is possible that more than one of your LANDUSE_IDs maps to the same SWAT_CODE, where your data makes more distinctions than are

supported by SWAT. The SWAT_CODE strings are 4 letters long and all the ones used in your map must be found in a table *crop* (or a table *urban* if the SWAT_CODE starts with a 'U') found in

 a. The project database, or
 b. The SWAT reference database

These databases are examined in this order.

2. In the case of a soil map, the table should have the string *soil* in its name. Then it will be offered as an option for a soil table. You should copy the structure of the table *global_soils* in *mwswat.mdb*. So it must contain at least the columns SOIL_ID (type Long Integer) and SNAM (type Text). The SOIL_ID corresponds to the values in the soil grid. You may map more than one of your soil categories to the same SWAT soil, where your data makes more distinctions than are supported by SWAT, but this is much less likely than it is for landuses. All the the SNAM strings you use must be found in a table *usersoil* found in

 a. The project database, or
 b. The SWAT reference database

MWSWAT uses by default *global_soils* whose characteristics are defined in the table *usersoil* defined in *mwswat.mdb* and hence in your project database. If you need to define your own soils then you need to rename *usersoil* in the project database to something else (when the default will be the *usersoil* table in the SWAT reference database) and, if the SWAT reference table is not appropriate, replace it with another table of the same name and design. Or you can just add your own soils to *usersoil*, provided they have new names.

## 8.3 Weather Sources

You can also use the database option in *Choose weather sources* to use your own precipitation and temperature data if you have it. You need to prepare and put into your project database:

1. A table containing weather station data like *weather_sources,* with columns (at least) STATIONID, LATITUDE, LONGITUDE and ELEVATION. The first of these is type Text, the other three are type Double. The table should have a name that includes the string *weather* (but should not be called *weather_sources* or it is likely to be overwritten at some point by MWSWAT.)

2. For each STATIONID *id* in the first table there should be a table called *pcpid* and a table called *tmpid*. Each of these must have an column OID of type *Integer* that is marked as an index (with no duplicates) containing 1, 2, 3 etc., a column DATE of type *Text*, and the dates in this column must be consecutive days in one of four formats:

    a. Julian date *yyyyddd*

    b. *yyyy/mm/dd*

    c. *dd/mm/yyyy*

    d. *mm/dd/yyyy*

    MWSWAT decides which format is being used, using the first two dates in the table in the case of non-Julian dates.

    These tables can start and end with any date, not necessarily the first or last date of a year.

3. The tables called *pcpid* must have a column PCP of type Double giving the precipitation in mm on that day. The value -99 indicates missing data.

4. The tables called *tmpid* must have columns MAX and MIN of type Double defining the maximum and minimum temperatures on that day in degrees Celsius. -99 indicates missing data.

Text files with comma (or some other character)-separated values, or of fixed format, can be easily imported to make the *pcpid* and *tmpid* tables.

# 3.2 Step by Step Geo-Processing and Setup of the Required Watershed Data for MWSWAT (MapWindow SWAT)

## Luis F. Leon

## December 2007

(Slightly modified for this book and its accompanying DVD)

## Contents

# 1. Source Data

## 1.1 DEM Source Data

### 1.1.1 SRTM Processed 90m Digital Elevation Data Version 3:

Format: ArcView Ascii Grid Files in 5° x 5° tiles (Lat/Long, decimal degrees)
Source: http://srtm.csi.cgiar.org/
Metadata included in header:

| | |
|---|---|
| ncols | 6000 |
| nrows | 6000 |
| xllcorner | -120 |
| yllcorner | 25 |
| cellsize | 0.000833333333333 |
| NODATA_value | -9999 |

*Contents of the Readme file:*

**PROCESSED SRTM DATA**

The data distributed here are in ARC GRID format, in **decimal degrees** and **datum WGS84**. They are derived from the **USGS/NASA SRTM** data. CIAT have processed this data to provide seamless continuous topography surfaces. Areas with regions of no data in the original **SRTM data have been filled** in using interpolation methods. A full technical report on this method is in preparation.

**DISTRIBUTION**

Users are prohibited from any commercial, non-free resale, or **redistribution without explicit written permission from CIAT**. Users should acknowledge CIAT as the source used in the creation of any reports, publications, new data sets, derived products, or services resulting from the use of this data set. CIAT also request reprints of any publications and notification of any redistributing efforts.

**NO WARRANTY OR LIABILITY**

CIAT provides these data without any warranty of any kind whatsoever, either express or implied, including warranties of merchantability and fitness for a particular purpose. CIAT shall not be liable for incidental, consequential, or special damages arising out of the use of any data downloaded.

## ACKNOWLEDGMENT AND CITATION

We kindly ask any users to cite this data in any published material produced using this data, and if possible link web pages to the CIAT SRTM website (http://gisweb.ciat.cgiar.org/sig/90m_data_tropics.htm).

*Citations should be made as follows:*

Hole-filled seamless SRTM data V1, 2004, International Centre for Tropical Agriculture (CIAT), available from http://gisweb.ciat.cgiar.org/sig/90m_data_tropics.htm

**Downloaded Data**

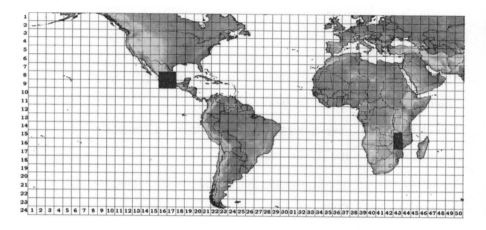

| Tiles for Mexico: | Tiles for Malawi: |
|---|---|
| srtm_16_08 | srtm_43_15 |
| srtm_16_09 | srtm_43_16 |
| srtm_17_08 | |
| srtm_17_09 | |

*From the header info on each of these tiles, a simple shape file was created to quickly identify the required tiles when the user zooms in the area of interest (see World_Data_Grids folder and ZIP file).*

The zipped DEM files for the San Juan example, such as **srtm_16_08.zip,** as well as for Cambodia, Indonesia, Laos, Malaysia, Philippines, Thailand, and Vietnam are packaged in the DVD under *Software\MWSWAT\DATA\DEMs*. DEMs for other areas can be downloaded from **http://srtm.csi.cgiar.org/**. We use the

351

ArcInfo ASCII format. The suggested location to prepare the clipped versions to use in MWSWAT is a temporary folder (e.g. *C:\temporary\dems*). Once the DEM is merged and/or clipped for the area of interest it is strongly suggested to move the resulting output grid (*filename*.asc) to the MW_project location.

## 1.1.2 Basic Supporting Geographic Data:

HYDRO1k Elevation Derivative Database: http://edc.usgs.gov/products/elevation/gtopo30/hydro/index.html

Format: ArcView Shapefile Format (Lambert Azimuthal Equal Area projection)

Documentation: http://edc.usgs.gov/products/elevation/gtopo30/hydro/readme.html

### *Drainage Basins:*

Africa - http://edcftp.cr.usgs.gov/pub/data/gtopo30hydro/af_bas.tar.gz

Origin (Longitude = 20° E ; Latitude = 5° N)

Asia - http://edcftp.cr.usgs.gov/pub/data/gtopo30hydro/as_bas.tar.gz

Origin (Longitude = 100° E ; Latitude = 45° N)

Australasia - http://edcftp.cr.usgs.gov/pub/data/gtopo30hydro/au_bas.tar.gz

Origin (Longitude = 135° E ; Latitude = 15° S)

Europe - http://edcftp.cr.usgs.gov/pub/data/gtopo30hydro/eu_bas.tar.gz

Origin (Longitude = 20° E ; Latitude = 55° N)

North America - http://edcftp.cr.usgs.gov/pub/data/gtopo30hydro/na_bas.tar.gz

Origin (Longitude = 100° W ; Latitude = 45° N)

South America - http://edcftp.cr.usgs.gov/pub/data/gtopo30hydro/sa_bas.tar.gz

Origin (Longitude = 60° W ; Latitude = 15° S)

The above files are already projected in latitude-longitude and available in the distribution DVD under the ***Global_Basins_latlong*** folder *in Software\MWSWAT\Data.* The vertices were also smoothed with 500m threshold.

Format: ArcView Shapefile Format (lat/long)

*Projected Basins:*

Africa –         af_bas_ll_r500m.zip

Asia –           as_bas_ll_r500m.zip

Australasia –    au_bas_ll_r500m.zip

Europe –    eu_bas_ll_r500m.zip

North America – na_bas_ll_r500m.zip

South America – sa_bas_ll_r500m.zip

It is suggested to unzip the contents of the files to a folder in the user's hard drive (e.g. *C:\unu_waterbase\Global_Basins_latlong*). The above figure, with the basins in different color for each continent, was created with MapWindow.

## 1.2 Landuse Source DATA:

The landuse data was provided by Dr Karim Abbaspour of Eawag (http://www.eawag.ch/index_EN):

Landuse data was constructed from the USGS Global Land Cover Characterization (GLCC) database (http://edcsns17.cr.usgs.gov/glcc/glcc.html). This map has a spatial resolution of 1 kilometre and 24 classes of landuse representation. The parameterization of the landuse classes (e.g. leaf area index, maximum stomatal conductance, maximum root depth, optimal and minimum temperature for plant growth) is based on the available SWAT landuse classes and literature research.

*Pre-processing note:*

Due to the huge size of the uncompressed files, after importing the file with Arc-View the grids were divided into tiles for each continent. The resulting files were still rather slow to load and manipulate in MapWindow, and were therefore re-sampled at half the original resolution. Both the original and resampled (*newres*) tiles are available on the DVD. We think that there will typically be little difference in the results from SWAT between the two resolutions. When you are starting to use MapWindow and MWSWAT we suggest you use the resampled tiles. It is possible to get much better speed with the original tiles if you hide their display before clipping, but this is likely to be confusing to new users. We give an explanation of this in the sections on generating landuse maps.

*Files exported as GeoTiff raster (distributed in the DVD – folder Software\MWSWAT\DATA\Global_Landuse_Data):*

- North America – na_landuse.zip, na_landuse_newres.zip (na_land_1, na_land_2, na_land_3)

- South America – sa_landuse.zip, sa_landuse_newres.zip (sa_land_1, sa_land_2)

- Europe & Asia – ea_landuse.zip, ea_landuse_newres.zip (ea_land_1, ea_land_2, ea_land_3, ea_land_4)

- Africa – af_landuse.zip, af_landuse_newres.zip (af_land_1, af_land_2)

- Australia & Pacific – ap_landuse.zip, ap_landuse_newres.zip (ap_land_1)

# 1.3 Soil Source DATA:

The soil data was provided by Dr Karim Abbaspour of Eawag (http://www.eawag.ch/index_EN):

Soil map was produced by the Food and Agriculture Organization of the United Nations (FAO, 1995). Almost 5000 soil types at a spatial resolution of 10 kilometres are differentiated and some soil properties for two layers (0-30 cm and 30-100 cm depth) are provided. Further soil properties (e.g. particle-size distribution, bulk density, organic carbon content, available water capacity, and saturated hydraulic conductivity) were obtained from Reynolds et al. (1999) or by using pedotransfer functions implemented in the model Rosetta (http://www.ars.usda.gov/Services/docs.htm?docid=8953).

Reynolds, C.A., Jackson, T.J., Rawls W.J., 1999. Estimating available water content by linking the FAO soil map of the world with global soil profile database and pedo-transfer functions. Proceedings of the AGU 1999 spring conference. Boston, MA.

*Files exported as GeoTiff raster (distributed in the DVD – folder: Software\MWSWAT\DATA\Global_Soil_Data):*

- North America – na_soil.zip (na_soil_1, na_soil_2, na_soil_3)

354

- South America – sa_soil.zip (sa_soil_1, sa_soil_2)
- Europe & Asia – ea_soil.zip (ea_soil_1, ea_soil_2, ea_soil_3, ea_soil_4)
- Africa – af_soil.zip (af_soil_1, af_soil_2)
- Australia & Pacific – ap_soil.zip (ap_soil _1)

## 1.4 Note on Projection Warnings

Sometimes when adding a layer to MapWindow you may see a warning like the following:

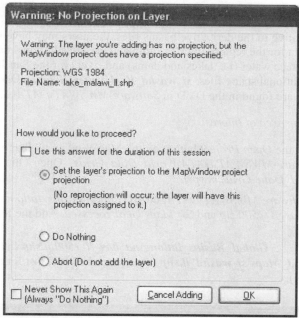

This is because one of the maps already added has projection information, which has set the current project projection, and the new map does not. To be safe you can select *Cancel Adding*, and use *File\Settings* to look at the *Project Projection*. For a lat/long projection this should say (for the maps we are using) Geographic Coordinate Systems, World, and WGS 1984. For a UTM projection it should say (again for the maps we are using) Projected Coordinate Systems, Utm - Wgs 1984, and WGS 1984 UTM Zone plus either 14N (for San Juan) or 36S (for Linthipe). Provided the new layer is intended to be lat/long or UTM respectively you can select the default action of setting the new layer's projection to the MapWindow project projection. This, as the associated text indicates, does not change the layer data, it merely stores an extra .prj file for the layer being added.

If you are adding a new layer that has a different projection from the current project projection, for example as the result of reprojection, then you get a similar warning titled *Projection Mismatch*. In this case the best thing to do usually is *Cancel Adding*, then clear all layers (which removes the current project projection) before adding the differently projected layer.

## 2. Setup for Mexico: San Juan River Watershed

### 2.1 Elevation maps (DEMs)

### 2.1.1 Pre-Process of DEM Data

*Objective: Merge and clip the SRTM files for the area of interest.*

As an alternative to the derivative basins files, the users may have available their own map data for the region. In this example, there are additional datasets for watersheds, surface water (i.e. lakes and dams) and rivers for the San Juan River watershed. (additional shape files: *sj_washd_ll, sj_water_ll* & *sj_rivers_ll*; all in lat/long). These are found in the DVD in *Software\MWSWAT\DATA\ SJ_Maps*.

*Clip DEM for Area of Interest:*

• Click the *Open Project* button on the MapWindow toolbar and navigate to *Software\MWSWAT\DATA\World_Data_Grids* Open the project file, *World_Data_Grids.mwprj*.

• In *Software\MWSWAT\DATA*, unzip *Global_Basins_latlong/ na_bas_ll_r500.zip* and *SJ_Maps\GeoProcessed*. Add the following layers

 ➕ ▾ : *Global_Basins_latlong\na_bas_ll_r500m.shp* (lat/long basins) and *SJ_Maps\sj_washd_ll.shp* (user watershed file, just for reference purposes).

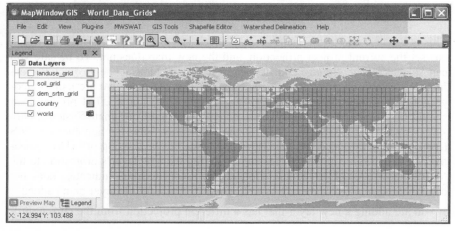

- Zoom in to the required level and create a shape file with a rectangle around the area of interest. To make such a rectangle:

1. Use ![icon] to open a new shapefile.

2. Using the button by the Filename textbox, navigate to the *SJ_Maps* folder and set the new shapefile's name to *sj_clip_box_ll.shp* and its type to *Polygon*

3. Click *OK* on the warning about the extents of the new shapefile.

4. Use ![icon] to add a regular shape, select Rectangle, ignore the width and height settings, click somewhere near the center of the watershed to place the initial rectangle. If the Add Regular Shape dialog box is no longer visible, find it on the task bar to bring it back to the front. Click *Done* to stop adding shapes.

5. Make sure the new rectangle is selected, then click on ![icon] to move the vertices of the initial rectangle one by one so that it easily includes the watershed. The next two pictures show (a) the situation after moving the first vertex and (b) the situation after moving all four vertices and setting *Show Fill* for the shapefile to false. To do this, use the right mouse button on the legend entry for *sj_clip_box_ll*, select *Properties*, and change *Show Fill*.

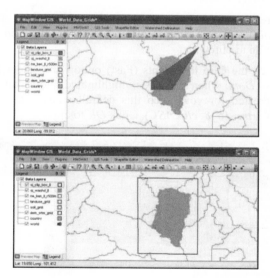

- With the *dem_srtm_grid* active, identify ![icon] the four DEM files that needed to be clipped and merged (S_16_08, S_16_09, S_17_08 & S_17_09).

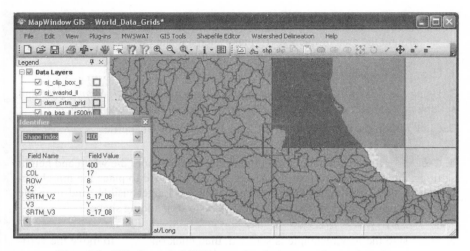

- Close MapWindow: do NOT save the changes to the project.

- Unzip **srtm_16_08.zip** and move **srtm_16_8.ASC.** to the folder, **temporary\dems.** Now add it as a view (being patient – it takes a few minutes). Also add the shapefile **SJ_Maps\sj_clip_box_ll.shp** found in *Software\MWSWAT\DATA\.*

- Make sure that *GIS Tools* is selected as a Plug-in, and select *GIS Tools\Raster\Clip Grid With Polygon*. Select the dem grid to clip and the box shapefile to clip with.

- Don't check the Clip to Extents (Fast) option and select the shape (clip box), press *Done* when the box is highlighted. Note that the output file name is created for you (keep this default name and location: ***temporary\dems\srtm_16_8_clip.ASC***). Click *OK* to clip.

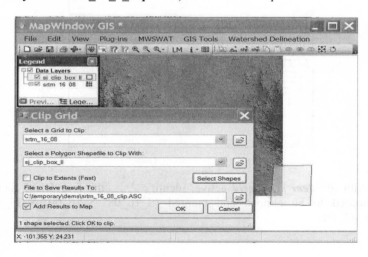

- When the clipping is done, remove the large dem layer (*srtm_16_8.ASC*) and repeat the process for the other three tiles (*srtm_16_9.ASC, srtm_17_8.ASC, & srtm_17_9.ASC*). Don't forget to remove them from the view after clipping, leaving only the clipped files.

- Merge the four clipped grids with *GIS Tools\Raster\Merge Grids*. It is possible to merge all four in one step, but this often leaves strips of No-Data cells at the joins. It is safer to merge two at a time. We start by merging **srtm_16_8_clip.ASC** and **srtm_17_8_clip.ASC**. Select these two clipped grids (press Ctrl while selecting) and click Open.

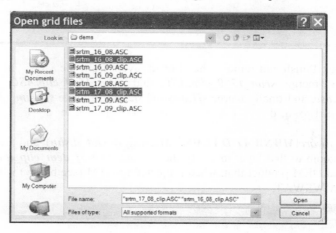

- When done, the Select Grids window will display the information for each of the files.

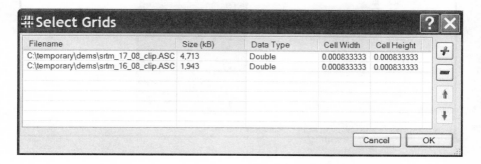

- Click OK to start merging. Name the result sj1.

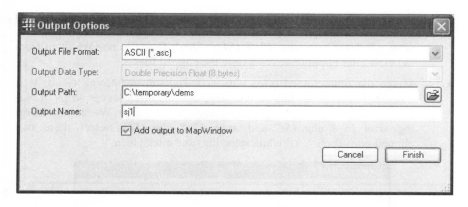

- Click Finish and remove the clipped layers from the view. In the same way merge **srtm_17_9_clip.ASC** and **srtm_16_9_clip.ASC** to make **sj2.asc**, and finally merge **sj1.asc** and **sj2.asc** to make **sj_dem_clip_ll.asc**. R e l o a d     t h e     w a t e r s h e d     l a y e r (*Software\MWSWAT\DATA\SJ_Maps\sj_washd_ll.shp*) and use  to zoom to that layer to verify the extents. This **sj_dem_clip_ll.asc** is the final DEM product that, when projected to UTM (see below) will be used in MWSWAT.

## 2.1.2 Re-project DEM to UTM

*Objective: Re-project the clipped DEM files to UTM and re-clip for the area of interest.*

Due to the fact that MWSWAT needs meter units and an equal area projection to perform slope and area calculations, the clipped DEM need to be re-projected to UTM coordinates. (While UTM is not truly an equal area projection, it is close enough for SWAT in most cases.) In this example, there is an additional dataset for the San Juan River watershed already projected in UTM. (additional shape file: *sj_washd_utm*: Zone 14N).

Re-project DEM and re-clip for Area of Interest:

- Select *GIS Tools\Raster\Reproject Grids*.

- Select the clipped DEM in lat/long (*temporary\dems\sj_dem_clip_ll.asc*), and when loaded click OK to re-project.

- Choose projection details: Projected Coordinate System, Datum WGS 1984 and Zone 14N and the current projection values if MapWindow couldn't determine them (Geographic Coordinate, World Projections, Datum: WGS 1984).

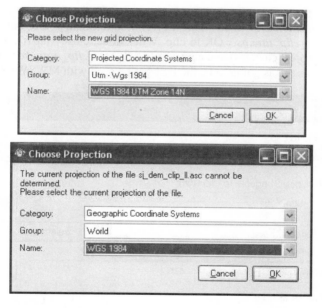

- A new file will be created (*SJ_Maps\sj_dem_clip_ll_Reprojected.asc*). Do not add this layer when asked, as its projection is different from the current one. Clear all layers and then add the layer **SJ_Maps\sj_dem_clip_ll_Reprojected.asc**. Also add the watershed in UTM (*SJ_Maps\sj_washd_utm.shp*).

- Create a new clipping box in this UTM view (this will remove all the missing values generated with the rotation of the grid when re-projected).

- Clip the re-projected dem with the UTM clip box. Select *GIS Tools\Raster\Clip Grid With Polygon* and rename the output file as *sj_dem_clip_utm.asc*. OK to clip. When done, close MapWindow (do not save project changes) and copy the file *sj_dem_clip_utm.asc* to the project folder as this is going to be the DEM to be used with MWSWAT.

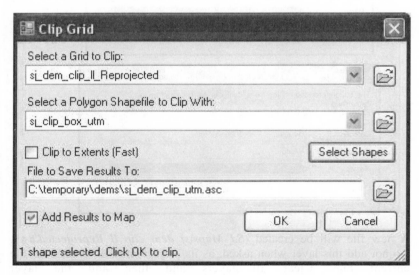

## 2.2 Landuse Data

## 2.2.1 Pre-Process of Landuse Data

*Objective: Clip the Landuse file for the area of interest.*

362

Clip Landuse for Area of Interest:

- Open the project *World_Data_Grids.mwprj* again. This shows that the tile we need for our area of interest is *na_land_3*.

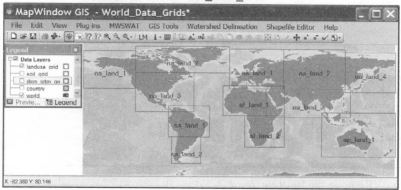

- Extract *na_land_3.tif* together with the corresponding .bmp, .bpw and .mwleg files from *na_landuse_newres.zip* (found in the DVD in the *Software\MWSWAT\DATA\Global_Landuse_Data*). Store them in, say, *temporary\land*.

- Close MapWindow. Do NOT save the project data.

- Add Layer ![plus icon] and select: *temporary\land\ na_land_3.tif*.

- *Hint: you can choose instead of **na_landuse_newres.zip** to use the tile from **na_landuse.zip**, the original landuse files. These tiles are large and take some time to display, and are also slow to react to any changes in the display. So as soon as such a tile is loaded, remove the tick from its leg-end, i.e. change* ![na_land_3 checked] *to* ![na_land_3 unchecked] *This removes the display of the map. You can still proceed with the following steps of loading a clip box and clipping, but you can't see so clear- ly what is happening.*

- Add the layer for the clip box (*SJ_Maps\sj_clip_box_ll.shp*).

- Select *GIS Tools\Raster\Clip Grid With Polygon*. Select the landuse layer and the box to clip with from the ones just loaded into the view.

- Check the Clip to Extents (Fast) option and select the shape (clip box), press Done when the box is highlighted. Note that the output file name is created for you. Rename this to: *temporary\land\sj_land_ll_clip.tif*. Click OK to clip.

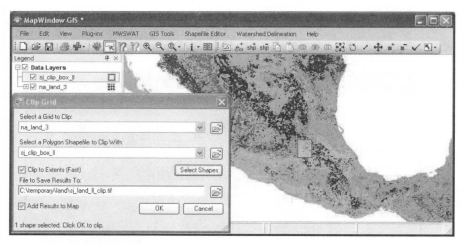

- Remove the layer **na_land_3**.

- Use 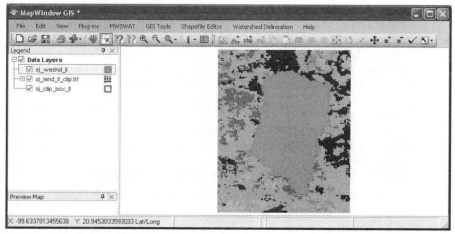 to zoom to the layer of **sj_clip_box_ll**, and use Add Layer

  to reload the watershed layer (**SJ_Maps\sj_washd_ll.shp**) to verify the extents. This **sj_land_ll_clip.tif** is the final landuse product that, when projected to UTM (see below) will be used in MWSWAT.

## 2.2 Re-project Landuse to UTM

*Objective: Re-project the clipped landuse file to UTM and re-clip for the area of interest.*

Due to the fact that MWSWAT needs meter units and an equal area (or close to equal area) projection to perform area calculations, the clipped landuse file needs to be re-projected to UTM coordinates. In this example, there is an additional dataset for the San Juan River watershed already projected to UTM. (additional shape file: *sj_washd_utm*: Zone 14N).

Re-project Land and re-clip for Area of Interest:

- Clear all the layers and select *GIS Tools\Raster\Reproject Grids*.

- Open the clipped landuse file in lat/long (*temporary\land\ sj_land_ll_clip.tif*). When loaded click OK to re-project.

- Choose projection details: Projected Coordinate System, Datum WGS 1984 and Zone 14N and the current projection values if MapWindow couldn't determine them (Geographic Coordinate, World Projections, Datum: WGS 1984).

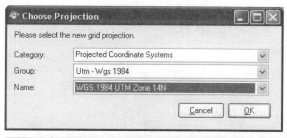

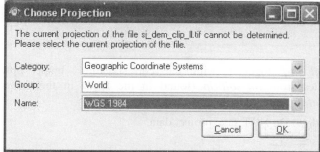

- A new file will be created (*temporary\land\sj_land_clip_ll_Reprojected.tif*). Do not add the layer when asked, as it has a different projection, but clear all layers and then add it. Also add the watershed in UTM (*SJ_Maps\sj_washd_utm.shp*).

- Load the clipping box in UTM view (*SJ_Maps\sj_clip_box_utm.shp*) to re-clip and remove all the missing values generated with the rotation of the grid when re-projected.

- Clip the re-projected landuse with the UTM clip box. Select *GIS Tools\Raster\Clip Grid With Polygon* and rename the output file as *sj_land_clip_utm.tif*. OK to clip. When done, close MapWindow (do not save project changes) and copy the file *sj_land_clip_utm.tif* to the project folder as this is going to be the landuse file to be used with MWSWAT.

## 2.3 Soil Data

### 2.3.1 Pre-Process of Soil Data

*Objective: Clip the Soil file for the area of interest.*

Clip Soil for Area of Interest:

- Open the project *World_Data_Grids.mwprj* again. This shows that the soil tile we need is *na_soil_3*.

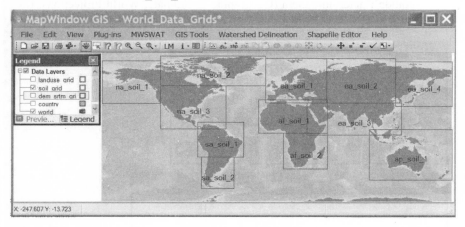

- Extract *na_soil_3.tif* together with the corresponding .bmp, .bpw and .mwleg files from *na_soil.zip* (found in the DVD in the folder *Global_Soil_Data*). Store them in, say, *temporary\soil*.

- Close MapWindow. Do NOT save project data.

- Add Layer ➕ ▾ and select: *temporary\soil\ na_soil_3.tif*. Also add the layer for the clip box (*SJ_Maps\sj_clip_box_ll.shp*).

- Select *GIS Tools\Raster\Clip Grid With Polygon*. Select the soil layer and the box to clip with from the ones just loaded into the view.

- Check the Clip to Extents (Fast) option and select the shape (clip box), press Done when the box is highlighted. Note that the output file name is created for you. Rename this default name to ***tempo-rary\soil\sj_soil_ll_clip.tif***. Click OK to clip.

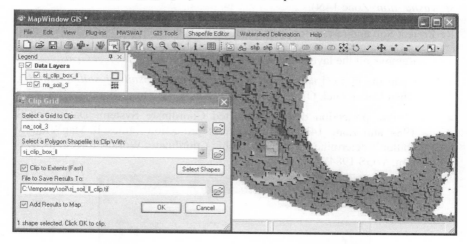

- Remove the layer ***na_soil_3***. With Add Layer 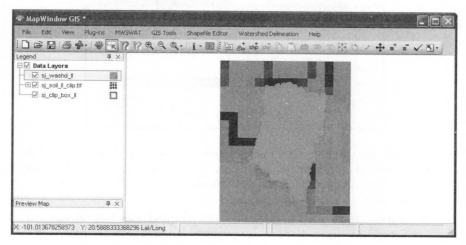 reload the watershed layer (***SJ_Maps\sj_washd_ll.shp***) to verify the extents. This ***sj_soil_ll_clip.tif*** is the final soil product that, when projected to UTM (see below) will be used in MWSWAT.

## 2.3.2 Re-project Soil to UTM

*Objective: Re-project the clipped soil file to UTM and re-clip for the area of interest.*

Due to the fact that MWSWAT needs meter units and a projection that is close to equal area to perform area calculations, the clipped soil file need to be re-projected to UTM coordinates. In this example, there is an additional dataset for the San Juan River watershed already projected in UTM. (additional shapefile: *sj_washd_utm*: Zone 14N).

Re-Project Soil and re-clip for Area of Interest:

- Remove all the layers and select *GIS Tools\Raster\Reproject Grids*.

- Open the clipped soil file in lat/long (*temporary\soil\ sj_soil_ll_clip.tif*), when loaded click OK to re-project.

- Choose projection details: Projected Coordinate System, Datum WGS 1984 and Zone 14N and the current projection values if MapWindow couldn't determine them (Geographic Coordinate, World Projections, Datum: WGS 1984).

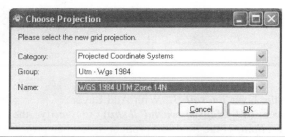

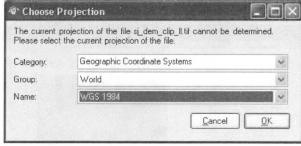

- A new file will be created (*temporary\soil\sj_soil_clip_ll_Reprojected.tif*). Do not add the layer when asked, as it has a different projection, but clear all layers and then add it. Also add the watershed in UTM (*SJ_Maps\sj_washd_utm.shp*).

- Load the clipping box in UTM view (**SJ_Maps\sj_clip_box_utm.shp**) to re-clip and remove all the missing values generated with the rotation of the grid when re-projected.

- Clip the re-projected soil with the UTM clip box. Select *GIS Tools\Raster\Clip Grid With Polygon* and rename the output file as *sj_soil_clip_utm.tif*. OK to clip. When done, close MapWindow (do not save project changes) and copy the file *sj_soil_clip_utm.tif* to the project folder as this is going to be the soil file to be used with MWSWAT.

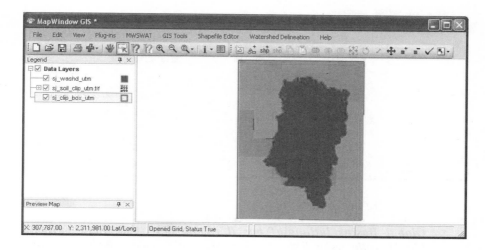

## 3. Setup for Malawi: Linthipe Watershed

## 3.1 Elevation Data (DEMs)

### 3.1.1 Pre-Process of DEM Data
*Objective: Clip the SRTM file for the area of interest.*

As an alternative to the derivative basins files, the users may have available their own map data for the region. Data sets for the Linthipe example are not included on the DVD but can be downloaded from http://www.waterbase.org. In this example, there are additional datasets for: Malawi rivers, Lake Malawi and for the Linthipe watershed. (additional shapefiles: *malawi_rivers_ll, lake_malawi_ll* & *lin_wshd_ll*; all in lat/long).

Clip DEM for Area of Interest:

- Click the *Open Project* button on the MapWindow toolbar and navigate to *Software\MWSWAT\DATA\World_Data_Grids* Open the project file, *World_Data_Grids.mwprj.*

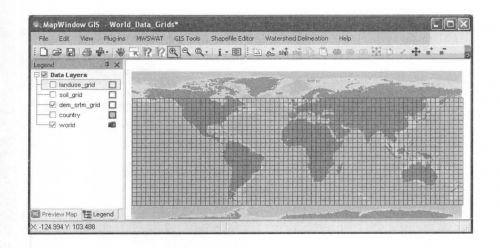

- A d d    t h e    f o l l o w i n g    l a y e r s    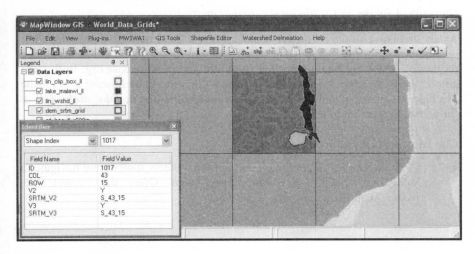 :
  *Global_Basins_latlong\af_bas_ll_r500m.shp* (lat/long basins),
  *Lin_Maps\lin_wshd_ll.shp and Lin_Maps\lake_malawi_ll.shp* (user wa-
  tershed file and Lake Malawi, just for reference purpose).

- Zoom in to the required level and create a shape file with a rectangle
  around the area of interest (namely the shape file
  *Lin_Maps\lin_clip_box_ll.shp*).

- For this watershed only one dem tile is required (*srtm_43_15*), easily identified ![i], so the only process left to do is clipping for the area of interest.

- Close MapWindow: Do NOT save the changes to the project.

- Unzip *srtm_43_15.zip* to extract *srtm_43_15.ASC*, storing it in **temporary\dems** and add it is a layer (being patient – it takes a few minutes). Also add the shapefile *Lin_Maps\lin_clip_box_ll.shp*.

- Make sure that *GIS Tools* is selected as a Plug-in, and select *GIS Tools\Raster\Clip Grid With Polygon*. Select the dem grid to clip and the shapefile to clip with..

- Check the Clip to Extents (Fast) option and select the shape (clip box), press Done when the box is highlighted. Note that the output file name is created for you (rename this file: *temporary\dems\lin_dem_clip_ll.asc*). Click OK to clip.

- This *lin_dem_clip_ll.asc* is the final DEM product that, when projected to UTM (see the projection section) will be used in MWSWAT. When the clipping is done, remove the large DEM layer (*srtm_43_15.ASC*).

- Reload the watershed (*Lin_Maps\lin_wshd_ll.shp*) to verify the extents.

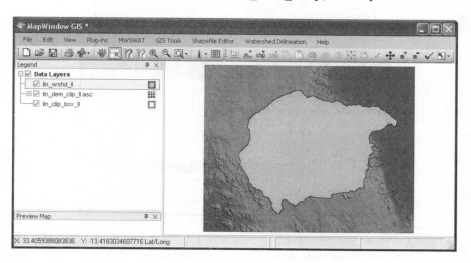

## 3.1.2 Re-project DEM to UTM

*Objective: Re-project the clipped DEM files to UTM and re-clip for the area of interest.*

Due to the fact that MWSWAT needs meter units and an equal area projection to perform slope and area calculations, the clipped DEM needs to be re-projected to UTM coordinates (which is close enough to an equal area projection for our purposes). In this example, there is an additional dataset for the Linthipe watershed already projected in UTM. (additional shapefile: *lin_wshd_utm*: Zone 36S).

Re-Project DEM and re-clip for Area of Interest:

- Select *GIS Tools\Raster\Reproject Grids*.

- Open the clipped DEM in lat/long (*temporary\dems\lin_dem_clip_ll.ASC*), when loaded click OK to re-project.

- Choose projection details: Projected Coordinate System, Datum WGS 1984 and Zone 36S and the current projection values if MapWindow couldn't determine them (Geographic Coordinate, World Projections, Datum: WGS 1984).

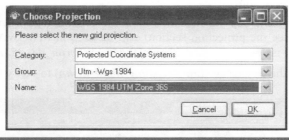

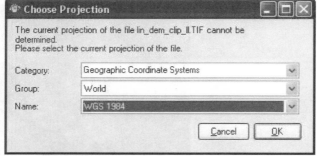

- A new file will be created (*temporary\dems\lin_dem_clip_ll_Reprojected.asc*). Do not add this layer when asked, as it has a different projection. Clear all layers, then add the reprojected DEM and and the watershed in UTM (*Lin_Maps\lin_wshd_utm.shp*).

- Create a new clipping box in this UTM view (this will remove all the missing values generated with the rotation of the grid when re-projected).

372

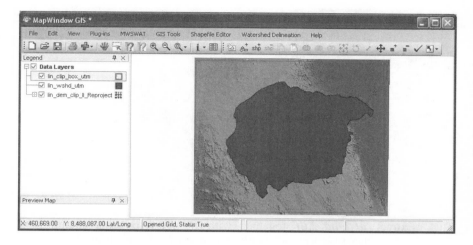

- Clip the re-projected DEM with the UTM clip box. Select *GIS Tools\Raster\Clip Grid With Polygon* and rename the output file as *lin_dem_clip_utm.asc*. OK to clip. When done, close MapWindow (do not save project changes) and copy this final file to the project folder as this is going to be the DEM to be used with MWSWAT.

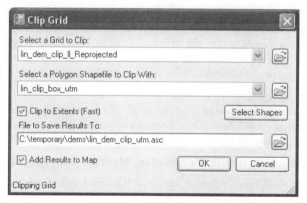

## 3.2 Landuse Data

## 3.2.1 Pre-Process of Landuse Data

*Objective: Merge and clip the Landuse files for the area of interest.*

Clip Landuse for Area of Interest:

- Close MapWindow, and open the project *World_Data_Grids.mwprj* again. This shows that the tile we need for our area of interest is *af_land_2*.

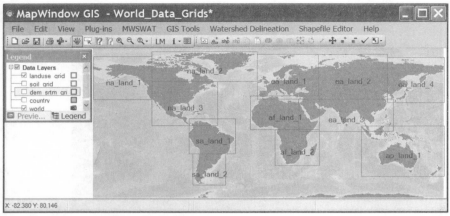

- Extract *af_land_2.tif* together with the corresponding .bmp, .bpw, and .mwleg files from *af_landuse_newres.zip* (found in the DVD in the folder *Global_Landuse_Data*). Store them in, say, *temporary\land*.

- Close MapWindow. Do NOT save the project data.

- Add Layer and select: *temporary\land\ af_land_2.tif* (note: be patient! MapWindow takes a few minutes to load the file).

- *Hint: you can choose instead of* **na_landuse_newres.zip** *to use the tile from* **na_landuse.zip,** *the original landuse files. These tiles are large are large and take some time to display, and are also slow to react to any changes in the display.  So as soon as such a tile is loaded, remove the tick from its legend, i.e. change* af_land_2 *to* af_land_2 *This removes the display of the map. You can still proceed with the following steps of loading a clip box and clipping, but you can't see so clearly what is happening.*

- Add the layer for the clip box (*Lin_Maps\lin_clip_box_ll.shp*).

- Select *GIS Tools\Raster\Clip Grid With Polygon*. Select the landuse layer and the box to clip with from the ones just loaded into the view.

- Check the Clip to Extents (Fast) option and select the shape (clip box), press Done when the box is highlighted.  Note that the output file name is created for you. Rename this default name: *temporary\land\lin_land_ll_clip.tif*. Click OK to clip.

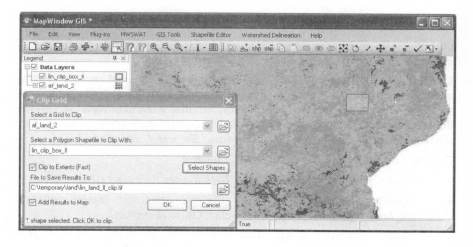

- Remove the layer *af_land_2*.

- Use 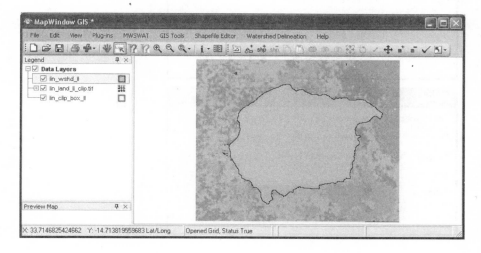 to zoom to the layer of *lin_clip_box_ll* and with Add Layer

  reload the watershed layer (*Lin_Maps\lin_wshd_ll.shp*) to verify the extents. This *lin_land_ll_clip.tif* is the final landuse product that, when projected to UTM (see below) will be used in MWSWAT.

## 3.2.2 Re-project Landuse to UTM

*Objective: Re-project the clipped landuse file to UTM and re-clip for the area of interest.*

Due to the fact that MWSWAT needs meter units and an equal area (or close to equal area) projection to perform area calculations, the clipped landuse file need to be re-projected to UTM coordinates. In this example, there is, in file downloaded from WaterBase, an additional dataset for the Linthipe watershed already projected to UTM. (additional shape file: *lin_wshd_utm*: Zone 36S).

Re-Project Landuse and re-clip for Area of Interest:

- Clear all the layers and select *GIS Tools\Raster\Reproject Grids*.

- Open the clipped landuse file in lat/long (*temporary\land\ lin_land_ll_clip.tif*), when loaded click OK to re-project.

- Choose projection details: Projected Coordinate System, Datum WGS 1984 and Zone 36S and the current projection values if MapWindow couldn't determine them (Geographic Coordinate, World Projections, Datum: WGS 1984).

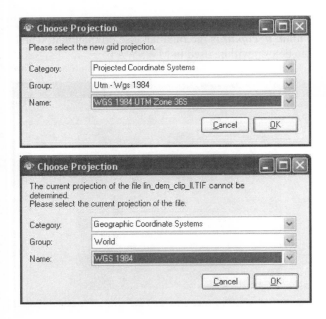

- A new file will be created (*temporary\land\Lin_land_clip_ll_Reprojected.tif*). Do not add the layer when asked, as it has a different projection, but clear all layers and then add it. Also add the watershed in UTM (*Lin_Maps\lin_wshd_utm.shp*).

- Load the clipping box in UTM view (*Lin_Maps\sj_clip_box_utm.shp*) to re-clip and remove all the missing values generated with the rotation of the grid when re-projected.

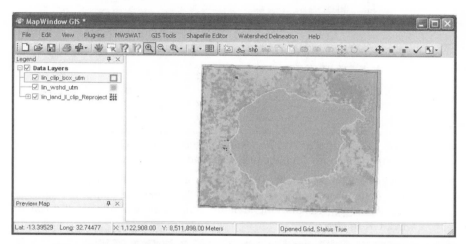

- Clip the re-projected landuse with the UTM clip box. Select *GIS Tools\Raster\Clip Grid With Polygon* and rename the output file as *lin_land_clip_utm.tif*. OK to clip. When done, close MapWindow (do not save project changes) and copy the file *lin_land_clip_utm.tif* to the project folder as this is going to be the landuse file to be used with MWSWAT.

## 3.3 Soil Data

### 3.3.1 Pre-Process of Soil Data

*Objective: Clip the soil file for the area of interest.*

Clip Soil for Area of Interest:

- Open the project *World_Data_Grids.mwprj* again. This shows that the soil tile we need is *af_soil_2*.

- Extract *af_soil_2.tif* together with the corresponding .bmp, .bpw and .mwleg files from **af_soil.zip** (found in the DVD in the folder *Software\MWSWAT\DATA\Global_Soil_Data*). Store them in, say, *temporary\soil*.

- Close MapWindow. Do NOT save project data.

- Add Layer and select: *temporary\soil\ af_soil_2.tif*. Also add the layer for the clip box (*Lin_Maps\lin_clip_box_ll.shp*).

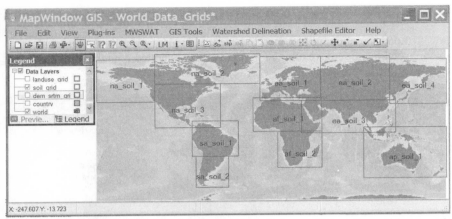

- Select *GIS Tools\Raster\Clip Grid With Polygon*. Select the soil layer and the box to clip with from the ones just loaded into the view.

- Check the Clip to Extents (Fast) option and select the shape (clip box), press Done when the box is highlighted. Note that the output file name is created for you. Rename this default name: *temporary\soil\lin_soil_ll_clip.tif*. Click OK to clip.

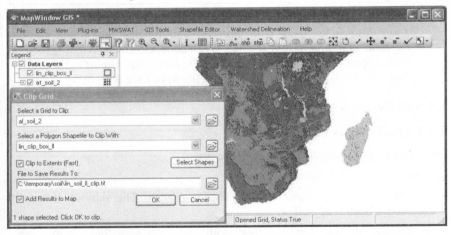

- Remove the layer *af_soil_2*.

- Zoom out and with Add Layer [icon] reload the watershed layer (*Lin_Maps\lin_wshd_ll.shp*) to verify the extents. This *lin_land_ll_clip.tif* is the final landuse product that, when projected to UTM (see below) will be used in MWSWAT.

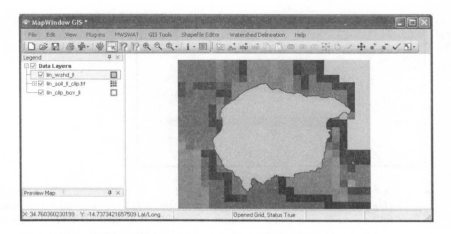

## 3.3.2 Re-project Soil to UTM

*Objective: Re-project the clipped soil file to UTM and re-clip for the area of interest.*

Due to the fact that MWSWAT needs meter units and an equal area (or nearly equal area) projection to perform area calculations, the clipped soil file need to be re-projected to UTM coordinates. In this example, there is an additional dataset for the Linthipe watershed already projected in UTM. (additional shapefile: ***lin_wshd_utm***: Zone 36S).

Re-Project Soil and re-clip for Area of Interest:

- Remove all the layers and select *GIS Tools\Raster\Reproject Grids*.

- Open the clipped soil file in lat/long (***temporary\soil\ lin_soil_ll_clip.tif***), when loaded click OK to re-project.

- Choose projection details: Projected Coordinate System, Datum WGS 1984 and Zone 36S and the current projection values if MapWindow couldn't determine them (Geographic Coordinate, World Projections, Datum: WGS 1984).

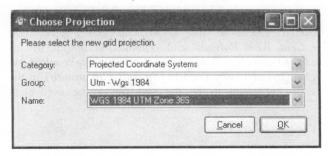

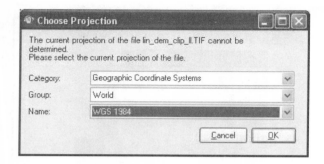

- A new file will be created (***temporary\soil\lin_soil_clip_ll_Reprojected.tif***). Do not add the layer when asked, as it has a different projection, but clear all layers and then add it. Also add the watershed in UTM (***Lin_Maps\lin_wshd_utm.shp***).

- Load the clipping box in UTM view (***Lin_Maps\sj_clip_box_utm.shp***) to re-clip and remove all the missing values generated with the rotation of the grid when re-projected.

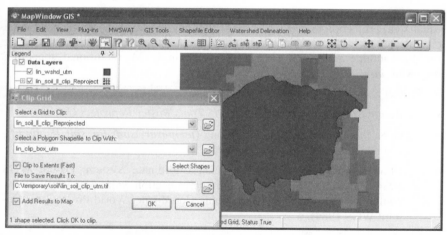

- Clip the re-projected soil with the UTM clip box. Select *GIS Tools\Raster\Clip Grid With Polygon* and rename the output file as ***lin_soil_clip_utm.tif***. OK to clip. When done, exit from MapWindow (do not save project changes) and copy the file (***lin_soil_clip_utm.tif***) in the project folder as this is going to be the soil file to be used with MWSWAT.

# 3.3 SWAT Output Plotting and Graphing Tools (SWATPlot and SWATGraph)

## Chris George

## Version 1.1 June 2008

## 1. Introduction

SWATPlot and SWATGraph are companion tools to the MWSWAT tool that generates inputs for and runs the SWAT watershed modelling tool. SWATPlot is a tool designed to make it easy to select SWAT output values from the files output.rch, output.sub, output.hru, output.rsv and output.wtr. (The last two only include output values if you have reservoirs and ponds respectively in your SWAT model.) The normal way to plot such values is to import the SWAT output file into Excel, use an Excel filter to select the reach, subbasin, hru, reservoir or hru, respectively, and then use Excel graphing facilities to draw graphs or histograms. This is a relatively tedious process, especially if you want to use outputs from different runs to compare them. SWATPlot makes this process much simpler. It also allows you to include a file of observed results if you have them.

SWATPlot generates a comma-separated (.csv) file of the results of which you want to draw a graph or histogram. It automatically invokes the second tool SWATGraph to display the graph or histogram. However, if you wish to do some further processing, or use Excel's graphing or calculational capabilities, you can import this intermediate .csv file into Excel, or any other tool you may have.

The design philosophy of both tools is maximum simplicity, to keep the interface clean and easy to use. They are not intended to replace all the features of tools like Excel, but to make the normal display of comparative results simple and fast.

Like MWSWAT, SWATPlot and SWATGraph are free, open source tools produced by the WaterBase project http://www.waterbase.org.

## 2. Installation

The tools come in a self installing executable. They use two files, mschrt20.ocx and msflxgrd.ocx, that are if necessary installed in your C:\WINDOWS\system32 folder and registered. This means that if you don't already have these files you will need administrator privileges to do the installation.

The installer suggests the folder C:\Program Files\MapWindow\Plugins\MWSWAT as the installation folder, but you may choose somewhere else if you wish. A shortcut to SWATPlot will appear on your desktop.

## 3. Running SWATPlot

When you start SWATPlot you see the view in Figure 1.

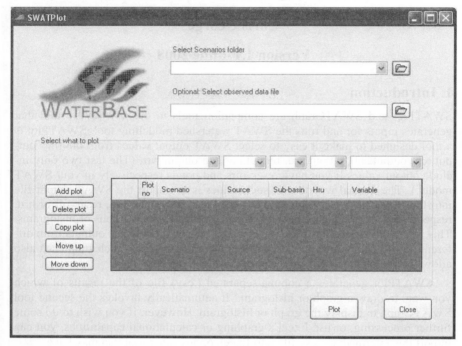

**Figure 1: Initial screen**

The first thing to do is to select the Scenarios folder, which is contained in the SWAT project folder. You can find it using the folder search button. The tool keeps a list of up to 10 Scenarios folders, so you can later select one you worked with previously. You select one from the drop-down list as in Figure 2.

Select Scenarios folder

C:\MW_Projects\ArcSWATExample1\example1\Scenarios
C:\MW_Projects\India\Jalgaon\Scenarios
C:\MW_Projects\India\Suk\Scenarios
C:\MW_Projects\Linthipe\Lin_MWSwat\Scenarios
C:\MW_Projects\SanJuan\SJ_MWSwat\Scenarios
C:\MW_Projects\India\Karso\Scenarios

**Figure 2: Selecting a previously used scenario**

Selecting the Scenarios folder of a SWAT project allows you to input data from any scenarios you have produced with SWAT in that project. The latest one is always called Default, but you may have saved earlier runs as part of the same project, and you can combine data from any of them. We will see later how compatible these runs need to be (in terms of how you have divided the watershed into subbasins and HRUs, and the periods and reporting intervals of the runs).

There is also an option to include a file of observed outputs. We will deal with this later in Section 5.

When you have selected the scenarios folder you are ready to choose your data for the first plot. Click *Add plot* and an empty line appears in the table. Now click the arrow in the leftmost of the pull-down boxes above the table, the one above the heading *Scenario*, and you will see something like Figure 3. Here, as well as the *Default* scenario we have saved two earlier ones, called *adjusted* and *unadjusted*. We are going to compare the flows out of the watershed for these two runs.

We select *unadjusted* for the first plot. We now proceed from left to right choosing the next value from each pull-down box in turn. The second one, *Source*, offers a choice of *reach*, *subbasin*, and *hru*. In addition, if there are ponds (water impoundments) in your model you will see the possible source *water*, and if there are reservoirs you will see the possible source *reservoir*. These sources refer to the SWAT output files output.rch, output.sub, output.hru, output.wtr, and output.rsv respectively. We choose *reach*.

Now in the Subbasin pull-down box we have a choice of all the subbasins in the watershed. We would have the same choice here if we had chosen *subbasin* or *hru* as the source. If we had chosen *water* or *reservoir* we would only see the numbers of the subbasins containing ponds or reservoirs respectively. We want to compare the final flows from the watershed, so we choose subbasin 1, which (for SWAT runs prepared with MWSWAT) is always the most downstream subbasin[1].

---

[1]This was true until MapWindow version 4.5, when the subbasin with the highest number became the outlet subbasin.

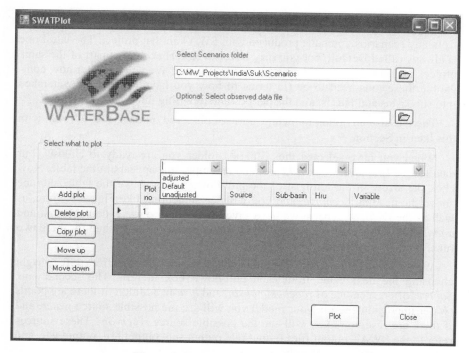

**Figure 3: Ready to choose the scenario**

Sources *reach*, *subbasin*, and *reservoir* are based on subbasins, so the *Hru* box is not needed – it is marked by "-". If we had chosen *hru* or *water* we would choose from the Hru pull-down box one of the hrus within the chosen subbasin.

Finally we choose which variable we want to plot. The Variable pull-down box gives us a choice of all the variables in the output file selected by our choice of Source. We select *FLOW OUT cms* and we see something like Figure 4.

Our first plot definition is complete. Now we want to add the second. We could use *Add plot* and continue as before. But since the second will be mostly like the first, instead we click *Copy Plot*. This makes a copy of the selected plot (shown by ▶), and we then just use the Scenario pull-down box to change the scenario for this one to *adjusted*. We get Figure 5.

We can now add more plots, change the selections we have made, or delete ones we decide we don't need. We can also change the order using the *Move up* and *Move down* buttons: the horizontal ordering of histograms in the graph display will be plots numbered 1 2 etc left to right.

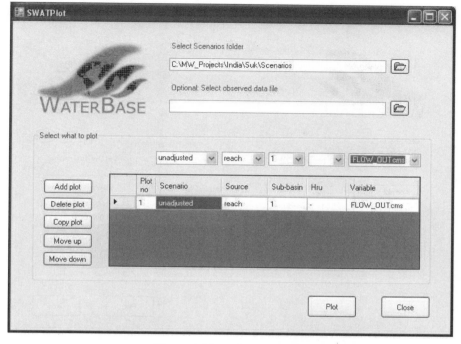

**Figure 4: First plot completed**

When we have completed the plot selections we click *Plot*. This invites us first to choose a .csv file to save the data. We can if we wish later import this into, for example, Excel if we wish to do further manipulations or use Excel's graphing tools.

Once the data is written to the .csv file SWATGraph is automatically started to display the data graphically: see Figure 6. The data has been displayed as histograms, labelled by months as that was the time interval of our SWAT output. We can change the display to lines using the *Chart Type* pull-down box and clicking *Update Graph*.

Other options include importing another (similarly created) .csv file, using *New File to Plot*, and saving the graph to the clipboard, using *Copy chart to clipboard*, so we can then for example paste it into the Paint tool to make an image file.

The data from the .csv file is also displayed. The column headings, also shown in the graph legend, take the form *Scenario-Source-Number-Variable*, where *Number* is the subbasin number if the source is reach, subbasin or reservoir, and the hru number if the source is hru or water.

You can fill in the *Chart Title* and *Y Axis Title*s if you wish, and change the *X Axis Title*.

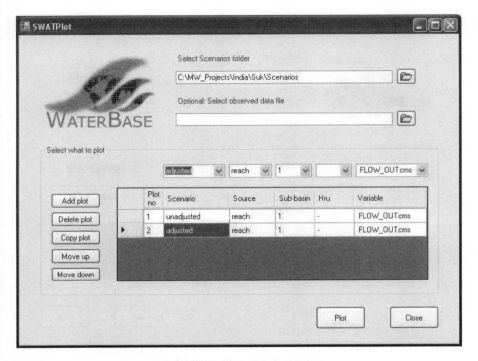

**Figure 5: Second plot completed**

At the bottom of the screen some statistics are displayed. These are correlation and Nash coefficients for each pair of plots. Some of these may be meaningless, of course, if for example you choose to plot four things that are really two pairs, but it is quicker as well as simpler to calculate them all than it is to ask the users what they want.

## 4. How compatible do different scenarios need to be?

Obviously, they need to use the same time period, and the same time interval (monthly, daily or yearly). In fact, the number of records in the data is determined by the first plot, so if necessary this can be shorter. Start dates are assumed to be the same; they are not checked.

You also need to be reasonably confident that the things you want to compare are indeed comparable, so if you are comparing hrus, for example, they should be the same hru in each scenario. But if you are comparing reach 1 in each scenario, which (for MWSWAT) gives figures for the whole watershed[2], it doesn't matter how the subbasins and hrus in each were selected.

---

[2]For MapWindow version 4.5 and above it is the subbasin with the maximum number that gives the watershed outlet

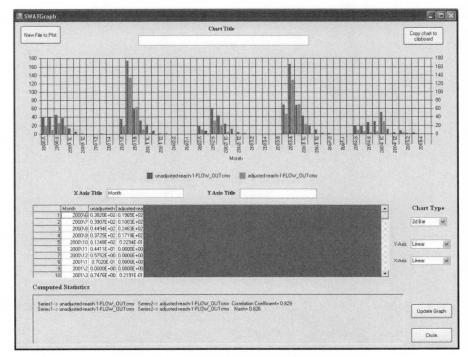

**Figure 6: SWATGraph**

## 5. Including observed data

To include observed data you need to prepare a .csv file, i.e. a text file where each line consists of the same number of items (one or more), separated by commas.

The first line should be comma-separated text strings, which will be used as the labels in the graph. If the first string is DATE, or Date, or indeed these four letters in any case, it and the data in the first column are ignored. The dates are assumed to be the same as in the SWAT output plots; they are not checked.

The data on lines two to the end should be numeric.

If you include such an observed data file in SWATPlot then *observed* will appear as an additional Scenario in its pull-down box. (You will be asked to rename one of your SWAT scenarios and start again if it is also called *observed*.) Source, Subbasin and Hru boxes will then be unavailable, but you need to choose a Variable. The choices in the Variable pull-down box will be the labels in the first line of the .csv file.

## 6. Reporting problems

If you have problems or suggestions send them to <u>waterbase.contact@waterbase.org</u>.

# 3.4 SWAT Calibration and Uncertainty Procedures (SWAT-CUP)

## Karim C. Abbaspour

SWAT Calibration and Uncertainty Procedures (SWAT-CUP) is a standalone computer program for calibration of SWAT models. SWAT-CUP is a public domain program, and as such may be used and copied freely. The program links GLUE, ParaSol, SUFI2, and MCMC procedures to SWAT. It enables sensitivity analysis, calibration, validation, and uncertainty analysis of a SWAT model. The interface of the program is user-friendly and allows graphical illustration of calibration results including prediction uncertainty ranges. The overall program structure is as shown in the Figure below.

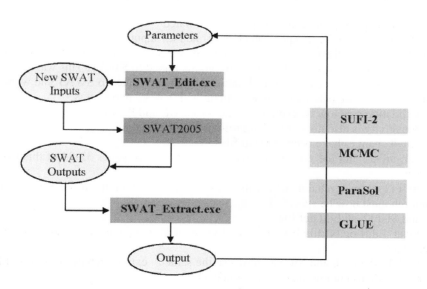

The program and its manual may be downloaded from:
http://www.eawag.ch/organisation/abteilungen/siam/software/swat/index_EN

Questions and comments should be forwarded to Dr Karim C. Abbaspour at:
abbaspour@eawag.ch

Users are encouraged to visit the above site regularly for new updates.

*Last minute update from Dr. Karim Abbaspour, January 6, 2009:*

**A new version of SWAT-CUP can be downloaded from:**
http://www.eawag.ch/organisation/abteilungen/siam/software/swat/index_EN

New Implementations
The differences between the present version and the previous version is that swEdit_2005.exe has been replaced with the same SWAT_Edit.exe program, which works in the same manner for all four algorithms. SWAT_Edit has improved capabilities including:

1- Parameters of all soil layers can now be calibrated (see pages 32-34)
2- Next to landuse, texture, subbasin, and hydrologic unit, slope can also be accounted for
3- Management parameters can all be calibrated including each rotation and operation
4- All crop parameters can be explicitly calibrated
5- Rainfall in the file pcp.pcp can be calibrated for input uncertainty
6- At the end of the file *.gw, 20 auxiliary parameters can be specified as R1, R2, ..., R20, which can be used by other programs linked to SWAT. This was done at the request of some users that had linked their own routines to SWAT and wanted to calibrate those parameters as well along with SWAT parameters.
- Validation can now be explicitly done for GLUE and ParaSol.
- Sensitivity is also done for all algorithms.
- Small changes have been made to files:
- par_inf.sf2 and the way parameters are specified (see pages 32-34 of this manual),
- SUFI2_extract_rch.def, where the number of total columns in the SWAT output.rch must now be specified
- and SUFI2_swEdit.def file
- Swat_EditLog.txt file lists the actual value of all the parameters that have been changes.
- GLUE, ParaSol, and MCMC now use the same *_extract_rch.def file as SUFI2 and can all accept missing observation data.
- Other small changes to GLUE, ParaSol, and MCMC files can be found in the examples provided by the SWAT-CUP program.

Dr. Karim C. Abbaspour
Swiss Federal Institute for Aquatic Science and Technology, Eawag
Ueberlandstr. 133, P.O. Box 611, 8600 Duebendorf, Switzerland
phone: +41 44 823 5359; Fax: +41 44 823 5375
email: abbaspour@eawag.ch; http://www.eawag.ch/index_EN

# 3.5 Contents of SWAT DVD Version 1 (January 2009)

**I. SWAT Theoretical Documentation**
    A. SWAT Theoretical Documentation. Version 2005.pdf
    B. SWAT Input-Output File Documentation. Version 2005.pdf

**II. Software**
    A. MapWindow GIS
        1. MapWindow46SR.exe
        2. MapWindow User Guides
            a. Quick_Guide_to_MapWindow_GIS.pdf
            b. Introduction_to_MapWindow_GIS_Ver_4_3.pdf

    B. MWSWAT
        1. MWSWAT.exe Version 1.4.0.0
        2. MWSWAT Manual
            a. Geo-Process.pdf
            b. MWSWAT Setup.pdf
        3. DATA
           a) DEMs
            a. Global_Basins_latlong
            b. Global_Landuse_Data
            c. Global_Soil_Data
            d. Global_Weather_Data
            e. SJ_Maps
            f. World_Data_Grids

    C. SWAT Editor
        1. SwatEditor_Install_2.1.2bRelease.zip
           a) README.txt
           b) Setup.Exe
           c) Setup.Ini
           d) SwatEditorInstall.msi
        2. SWATEditor_Documentation.pdf
           a) ArcSWAT_Documentation.pdf (See Chapt. 9-15)

    D. SWAT Plot_and_SWAT Graph
        1. SWATPlot.exe
        2. SWATPlot and SWATGraph.pdf

*(Continued on next page)*

E. SWAT-CUP
    1. SWAT-CUP User Manual
       a) SWAT_CUP_Description.pdf
       b) Usermanual_Swat_Cup.pdf
    2. SWAT-CUP Setup
       a) ExternalData
          a. Example_projects
          b. SourceData
          c. References

F. ACROBAT Reader

# Index for Models, Abbreviations and Acronyms

# Geographical INDEX

# Subject INDEX

233, 248, 276
HYDRO1k – A digital stream network 101
Hydrograph 44, 66, 233, 242, 243, 244, 245, 268,
Hydroinformatics 125, 139, 140
Hydrological model 97, 98, 99, 100, 102, 163, 173, 177, 178, 185, 186, 198, 205, 267, 268, 280,
Hydrologic assessments 35, 48
Hydrologic balance 70
Hydrologic balance, large-scale 285
Hydrologic cycle 8
Hydrologic inputs 65
Hydrologic interface 71
Hydrologic response unit (HRU) 5, 12, 72
Hydrologic simulator 186
Hydrology 4, 6, 7, 11, 16, 25, 27, 28, 57, 59, 66, 67, 72, 125, 128, 167, 177, 184, 185, 186, 187, 192, 195, 198, 200, 213, 220, 267, 268, 270, 271, 281, 285,
Hydrology Handbook of SCS 15

ICT – Information and Communication Tool 125
IITM – Indian Institute of Tropical Meteorology, Pune 160
Impact 3, 4, 5, 6, 11, 25, 26, 27, 28, 33, 34, 35, 47, 56, 57, 58, 59, 63, 64, 65, 66, 67, 68, 69, 70, 72, 73, 115, 126, 127, 133, 145, 146, 147, 152, 153, 160, 161, 163, 171, 172, 174, 175, 177, 178, 183, 184, 185, 186, 190, 200, 201, 205, 211, 213, 226, 229, 237, 240, 253, 255, 258, 259, 262, 263, 264, 265, 267, 268, 270, 271, 275, 278, 281, 286, 288, 289, 291, 293, 298, 301,
Impoundments 47, 293
Indictors 69
Infiltration 6, 13, 14, 28, 29, 31, 47, 71, 128, 129, 186, 256, 258, 263, 264, 271
In-stream process 19
Integrated Surface and Sub-surface model (ISSm) 68
Integration 4, 125, 126, 130, 131, 133, 140,
Interfaces of SWAT 67
Interflow 14, 31, 44, 72, 135,
Interflow functions 31
Intermittent stream 15, 34, 106,
IOSWAT – InputOutputSWAT software package 32
Irrigation 5, 13, 19, 29, 30, 47, 68, 70, 72,

116, 118, 120, 165, 166, 171, 173, 183, 184, 185, 190, 191, 192, 200, 202, 204, 205, 270, 286, 290, 291, 293, 294, 295, 297
Irrigation project 107, 165, 166
IRWR – internal renewable water resource 199
iSWAT – A generic interface of SWAT program 32
i_SWAT – An interactive SWAT software 32
ISSm – An Integrated Surface and Subsurface model 68
ITE$^2$M – Integrated Tool for Ecological and Economical Modeling 134, 135, 136, 137

Jahade-Agriculture, Ministry of (Iran) 192
Joint research project 127
JMA – Japan Meteorological Agency 214

Karst characteristics 60
Key inputs 63
Kinematic wave model 129
KINEROS2 – A model 32
Kinetic functions 74

L95PPU 101
LAI – Leaf area index 186
Land cover 6, 15, 100, 214
Land management practice 3, 161, 186, 213, 253, 254, 255
Landscape services 134
Land use 28, 64, 253
Land use effects 65
Land use impacts 56
Land use in India 166
Lane's method 15
Lateral flow 14, 16
LCA - Life cycle assessment 65
Leaf area index 13, 31
LH-OAT – Latin Hypercube – One Factor at a Time 60, 131, 275
Life cycle assessment (LCA) 65
Limitations 5, 73, 116, 120, 130, 223, 246, 248, 281, 285, 298
Long-term benefits 147
Low-flow behavior 247
Management 19 and many more pages
Management inputs 29
Manning relationship 245
Manning's Formula 14

Safe drinking water 98
SANREM CRSP – Sustainable Agriculture and Natural Resources Management Collaborative 256
SCE – Shuffled Complex Evolution 61, 62, 63
SCE-UA 132
SCS – Soil Conservation Service (now NRCS – Natural Resources Conservation Service) 5, 14, 15, 27, 100, 128, 147, 186, 192, 195, 242, 255, 268, 271, 274, 276, 280, 299
Sediment, found in page 3 and most pages after that
Sediment concentration 21
Sediment loads 51, 52, 53, 54, 67, 75, 129,
Sediment movement 3, 4, 27, 75, 186, 255,
Sediment studies 51
Sediment, suspended 21, 54
Sediment transport 4, 5, 18, 21, 27, 31, 54, 75, 129, 148
Sediment yield 4, 5, 16, 17, 27, 30, 36, 52, 53, 54, 56, 59, 64, 69, 145, 147, 153, 154, 158, 172, 173, 236, 237, 239, 240, 253, 255, 256, 258, 259, 261, 262, 263, 264, 265
Sediment yield, annual 54, 263
Sensibility, calibration and uncertainty analyses 59
Sensitivity analyses 25
Shuffled complex evolution (SCE) 61
Sichuan 149
Simulate, simulation, simulator: These words first appear in page 3 and in many pages after that.
Simulation, continental scale 285
Simulation of BMPs 72
Simulation, long-term 4
Skylark bird habitat 70
SLOPE – relating to slope steepness 151, 211, 276
Slope classes 100
SLSUBBSN – relating to average slope length 151
SMDR – Soil Moisture Distribution and Routing 67
Snow cover 29
Snowmelt 29, 247
Snowmelt-related applications 45, 46
Soil conservation measures 30, 237, 253, 254, 258, 263, 264, 265

Soil erosion 59, 70, 145, 146, 149, 152, 153, 161, 254, 255, 262, 264, 265,
Soil organic carbon 18
Soil management 135
Soil moisture 45, 61, 67, 112, 120, 183, 186, 199, 202, 242, 249, 293,
Soil moisture variability 45
Soil moisture variables 61
Soil temperature 11, 13, 28, 128, 186, 290, 301
Soil type 28, 63, 72, 74, 101, 104, 107, 135, 149, 155, 191, 213, 215, 249, 271, 273, 274, 280, 287, 299,
Soil water 6, 8, 45, 97, 98, 108, 115, 119, 147, 185, 186, 195, 200, 202, 205, 249, 275, 286, 297, 300
Soil water availability 16
Soil water routing 300
Southern Hemisphere 5
SPARROW – a model 67
SPUR – Simulation of Production and Utilization of Rangelands 185
SOL_AWC – relating to soil water content 195
SOL_ORGN – initial soil organic N concentration 151
SOL_ORGP – initial soil organic P concentration 151
SOL_Z1 – relating to the depth of the top layer of Aledo soil 151
SPCON – relating to the linear factor 258, 262
SPEXP – relating to the exponential factor 258
SSURGO – Soil Survey Geographic 32, 65, 130
STATSGO – USDA-NRCS State Soil Geographic 32, 65, 130, 293
Stomatal conductance 31, 58
Storage effect 14, 225, 228, 229
Streambed 15, 20
Stream channel 11, 75
Streamflow 5, 14, 36, 44, 48, 58
Streamflow predictions 61, 63
Streamflow variation 153
Subbasin 6, 14, 15, 113, 213, 233
Subbasin command loop 9
Sub-country level 117
Subdaily rainfall pattern 10
Subsidy schemes 146

# ADDENDUM

# WASWC: Its History and Operations

## By Bill Moldenhauer and David Sanders (2003)

## Updated by Samran Sombatpanit (2007, 2008)

WASWC was established in 1983 with the help and support of the Soil and Water Conservation Society (SWCS) of the U.S.A. The original purpose was to support international activities of both SWCS and the International Soil Conservation Organization (ISCO). The world was divided into nine regions with at least one Vice President from each region. Since there was little contact among ISCO participants from one biennial conference to the next, our first priority was to publish a quarterly newsletter with meeting announcements, international conservation news, book reviews, member news, etc. From the beginning, we tried to give recognition to, and a forum for, workers in the international field who had published mainly in the "gray literature" (company, Government (GO) and non-governmental (NGO) agency and organization reports that had had very small circulation).

This continues to be one of our most vital functions. By 1986 there was great interest in the Food and Agriculture Organization (FAO) of the United Nations and many GOs and NGOs in just how effective their international programs were in solving problems in developing countries. WASWC and SWCS organized a workshop in Puerto Rico with the help of several donor organizations and invited speakers to address the success (or failure) of donor sponsored soil and water conservation and land husbandry programs in developing countries worldwide.

This was a very successful conference and resulted in two publications published by SWCS, *Conservation Farming on Steep Lands* and *Land Husbandry: A Framework for Soil and Water Conservation.* Since our Puerto Rico workshop we have held a workshop in Taiwan in 1989, one in Solo, Central Java, Indonesia, in 1991, and one in Tanzania and Kenya in 1993. These have all been published and were circulated by SWCS.

Our Vice President for Europe, Dr. Martin Haigh, has initiated a series of meetings on Environmental Regeneration in Headwaters in various parts of the globe. Our Vice President for the Pacific Region, Dr. Samir El-Swaify, has initiated a series on "Multiple Objective Decision Making for Land, Water and Environmental Management." Four of our members—Samran Sombatpanit, Michael Zoebisch, David W. Sanders, and Maurice Cook have edited a book titled, *Soil Conservation Extension: From Concepts to Adoption.* David Sanders, Paul

Huszar, Samran Sombatpanit and Thomas Enters have edited a book titled, *Incentives in Soil Conservation: From Theory to Practice.* Lately, Samran Sombatpanit has edited a voluminous book, *Response to Land Degradation,* with five other editors in 2001 and *Ground and Water Bioengineering for Erosion Control and Slope Stabilization,* with four other editors in 2004. Besides the above publications, past WASWC President Hans Hurni initiated a long-term program, "World Overview of Conservation Approaches and Technologies (WOCAT)," based in Berne, Switzerland in 1992 and had a landmark WOCAT Global Overview book *"where the land is greener"* published in 2006. WASWC has supported Jim Cheatle's "Organic Matter Management Network" based in Nairobi, Kenya. WASWC is also closely allied with Reseau Erosion, a project of Vice President Eric Roose, based in Montpellier, France, and operating mainly in Africa. WASWC is closely allied to ISCO and cooperates fully with planning and conducting its biennial conferences. WASWC is requested and very willing to co-sponsor conferences, symposia and workshops it feels will further its philosophy and objectives.

**The WASWC Philosophy:** WASWC philosophy is that the conservation and enhancement of the quality of soil and water are a common concern of all humanity. We strive to promote policies, approaches and technologies that will improve the care of soil and water resources and eliminate unsustainable land use practices.

**WASWC Vision:** A world in which all soil and water resources are used in a productive, sustainable and ecologically sound manner.

**WASWC Mission:** To promote worldwide the application of wise soil and water management practices that will improve and safeguard the quality of land and water resources so that they continue to meet the needs of agriculture, society and nature.

**WASWC Slogan:** Conserving soil and water worldwide – join WASWC

**The Objectives of WASWC:** The basic objective of WASWC is to promote the wise use of our soil and water resources. In doing so WASWC aims to:
• Facilitate interaction, cooperation and links among its members.
• Provide a forum for the discussion and dissemination of good soil and water conservation practices.
• Convene and hold conferences and meetings and conduct field studies connected with the development of better soil and water conservation.

• Assist in developing the objectives and themes for ISCO conferences and collaborate in their running.

• Produce, publish and distribute policies, guidelines, books, papers and other information that promote better soil and water conservation.

• Encourage and develop awareness, discussion and consideration of good conservation practices among associated organizations.

• Liaise, consult and work in conjunction with environmental organizations on the development and promulgation of global environmental and conservation policies, strategies and standards.

**Recent Developments:** The WASWC has had to face some serious problems in recent years and, as a result, some important changes have taken place. The cost of running WASWC has increased over the years and, at the same time, membership numbers dropped to below 400. The drop in numbers was partly because a membership fee of even US$10 per year is a considerable amount of money for many members from developing countries. Added to this, is the problem of paying in dollars and transferring relatively small sums of money internationally. To overcome these problems, a number of important steps have been taken. *First,* a concerted effort has been made to recruit new members. As part of this campaign, an effort has been made to improve the services provided to members. This has included improving the quality and length of the quarterly newsletter and distributing it by e-mail. *Second,* a flexible system of membership fees has been introduced which means that members can join for as little as US$5 and US$10 per year for respectively developing and developed countries. *Third,* a program of decentralization has also been launched with the appointment of several more Vice Presidents and the establishment of National Representatives, now covering approximately 100 countries. This program is not only bringing our association closer to members but has also provided other advantages including a system whereby it is now possible for local organizations to collect membership fees in local currencies and to pay the secretariat in bulk. *Fourth,* the WASWC council has become more actively involved in encouraging regional and local meetings, conferences and other useful activities. *Fifth,* the WASWC council offers 1-year Guest membership to persons who have participated at any technical meeting worldwide, if they wish so. As a result of these measures, membership has risen to several thousands in 2007.

Another major change has been the move of the WASWC secretariat from the SWCS in the U.S.A. to Beijing in China, on April 1, 2003. It is now hosted by the Ministry of Water Resources. The WASWC appreciates the generous help that it received from the SWCS over the 20 years that the SWCS ran its secretariat and intends to maintain a close association with it in the future. However, the Council believes that this move will have a number of advantages. Our Chinese hosts have offered very generous terms for the running of the secretariat; we will have the opportunity to work in a country where running costs are relatively low and where there is considerable technical expertise available and of interest to many of our members. The most recent development is the establishment of our main website at the Guangdong Institute of Eco-Environmental and Soil Sciences in Guangzhou, in the southern part of China, to offer services to our members along with the other one in Tokyo, Japan, supported by ERECON.

## WASWC Council
(For the period up to December 2010)

1. President: Miodrag Zlatic, Serbia miodrag.zla@sbb.rs, mizlatic@yahoo.com
2. Deputy President: Machito Mihara, Japan m-mihara@nodai.ac.jp
3. Treasurer: John Laflen, U.S.A. laflen@wctatel.net
4. Executive Secretary: Henry Lu Shunguang, China sglu@mwr.gov.cn
5. Imm. Past President: Samran Sombatpanit, Thailand (& Coordinator General) sombatpanit@yahoo.com, samran_sombatpanit@yahoo.com
6. Li Dingqiang, P.R. China dqli@soil.gd.cn, lloydli@hotmail.com
7. Suraj Bhan, India bhan_suraj2001@yahoo.com
8. Surinder Singh Kukal, India sskukal@rediffmail.com
9. Rachendra Shrestha, Thailand rajendra@ait.ac.th
10. Stanimir Kostadinov, Serbia kost@eunet.yu, kost@yubc.net
11. Tom Goddard, Canada tom.goddard@gov.ab.ca
12. Li Rui, P.R. China lirui@ms.iswc.ac.cn
13. V.N. Sharda, India vnsharda1@rediffmail.com
14. Rachid Mrabet, Morocco rachidmrabet@gmail.com
15. Richard Fowler, South Africa rmfowler@iafrica.com
16. Roberto Peiretti, Argentina sdrob@idi.com.ar
17. Kristie Watling, Australia kristie.watling@nrw.qld.gov.au
18. Mike Fullen, United Kingdon m.fullen@wlv.ac.uk
19. Eric Roose, France roose@mpl.ird.fr, eric.roose@mpl.ird.fr
20. Doug Wimble, Australia dougwimble@spraygrass.com.au
21. José Rubio, Spain jose.l.rubio@uv.es, kertesza@helka.iif.hu,
22. One Councilor that represents ISCO
23. Winfried Blum, Austria herma.exner@boku.ac.at
24. Ian Hannam, Australia ian.hannam@ozemail.com.au
25. Rolf Derpsch, Paraguay rderpsch@telesurf.com.py

**With Vice Presidents in ~100 countries, 6 Special Representatives and 30 members of the Translators' Club**

## Past Presidents
1983-1985: William C. Moldenhauer, U.S.A.
1986-1988: Norman W. Hudson, UK
1989-1991: Rattan Lal, U.S.A.
1992-1997: Hans Hurni, Switzerland

1997-2001: David W. Sanders, UK
2002-2004: Samran Sombatpanit, Thailand
January-March 2005: Martin Haigh, UK
April 2005-June 2006: Samran Sombatpanit, Thailand (Acting)
July 2006-December 2007: Miodrag Zlatic, Serbia

**WASWC Secretariat and Websites:** See p. vi, this volume.

# WASWC Publications
– Published in association with other institutions or publishers –

*1988*
• *Conservation Farming on Steep Lands.* Edited by W.C. Moldenhauer and N.W. Hudson, ISBN 0935734198
*1989*
• *Land Husbandry – A Framework for Soil and Water Conservation.* by T.F. Shaxson, N.W. Hudson, D.W. Sanders, E. Roose and W.C. Moldenhauer, ISBN 0935734201
*1990*
• *Soil Erosion on Agricultural Land.* Edited by J. Boardman, I.D.L. Foster and J.A. Dearing, ISBN 0471906027 (From a meeting co-sponsored by WASWC)
*1991*
• *Development of Conservation Farming on Hillslopes.* Edited by W.C. Molden-hauer, N.W. Hudson, T.C. Sheng and San-Wei Lee, ISBN 0935734244
• *Soil Management for Sustainability.* Edited by R. Lal and F.J. Pierce, ISBN 0935734236
*1992*
• *Conservation Policies for Sustainable Hillslope Farming.* Edited by S. Arsyad, I. Amien, Ted Sheng and W.C. Moldenhauer, ISBN 0935734287
• *Soil Conservation for Survival.* Edited by K. Tato and H. Hurni, ISBN 0935734279
• *Erosion, Conservation and Small-Scale Farming.* Edited by H. Hurni and K. Tato, ISBN 3906290700
• Environmental Regeneration in Headwaters. Edited by J. Krecek and M.J. Haigh
*1993*
• *Working with Farmers for Better Land Husbandry.* Edited by N. Hudson and R.J. Cheatle, ISBN 1853391220
*1995*
• *Adopting Conservation on the Farm: An International Perspective on the Socio-economics of SWC.* Edited by T.L. Napier, S.M. Camboni and S.A. El-Swaify, ISBN 0935734317
*1996*
• *Hydrological Problems and Environmental Management in Highlands and Headwaters.* Edited by J. Krecek, G.S. Rajwar and M.J. Haigh, ISBN 8120410483

*1997*
• *Soil Conservation Extension: From Concepts to Adoption.* Edited by S. Sombatpanit, M. Zoebisch, D. Sanders and M.G. Cook, ISBN 8120411897
*1999*
• *Multiple Objective Decision Making for Land, Water and Environmental Management.* Edited by S.A. El-Swaify and D.S. Yakowitz, ISBN 1-57444-091-8
• *Incentives in Soil Conservation: From Theory to Practice.* Edited by D.W. Sanders, P. Huszar, S. Sombatpanit and T. Enters, ISBN 1-57808-061-4
*2000*
• *Reclaimed Land: Erosion Control, Soils and Ecology.* Edited by M.J. Haigh, ISBN 90 5410 793 6
*2001*
• *Response to Land Degradation.* Edited by E.M. Bridges, I.D. Hannam, L.R. Oldeman, F. Penning de Vries, S.J. Scherr and S. Sombatpanit, ISBN 812041942
*2004*
• *Ground and Water Bioengineering for Erosion Control and Slope Stabilization.* Edited by D.H. Barker, A.J. Watson, S. Sombatpanit, B. Northcutt and A.R. Maglinao, ISBN 1-57808-209-9
*2007*
• *Monitoring and Evaluation of Soil Conservation and Watershed Development Projects.* Edited by J. de Graaff, J. Cameron, S. Sombatpanit, C. Pieri and J. Woodhill. ISBN 978-1-57808-349-7

## Special Publications, published by WASWC

*2003:* No. 1. *Pioneering Soil Erosion Prediction – The USLE Story.* By John Laflen and Bill Moldenhauer, ISBN 974 91310 3 7, 54 pp. (available on the website)
*2004:* No. 2. *Carbon Trading, Agriculture and Poverty.* By Mike Robbins, ISBN 974 92226 7 9, 48 pp. (available on the website)
*2008:* No. 3. *No-Till Farming Systems.* Edited by Tom Goddard, Michael A. Zoebisch, Yantai Gan, Wyn Ellis, Alex Watson and Samran Sombatpanit, ISBN 978-974-8391-60-1, 544 pp. (With one CD)
*2009:* No. 4. *Soil and Water Assessment Tool (SWAT): Global Applications.* Edited by J. Arnold, R. Srinivasan, S. Neitsch, C. George, K.C. Abbaspour, P. Gassman, Fang H.H., A. van Griensven, A. Gosain, P. Debels, N.W. Kim, H. Somura, V. Ella, L. Leon, A. Jintrawet, M.R. Reyes, and S. Sombatpanit. Special Publication No. 4., ISBN 978-974-613-722-5, 415 pp. (With one DVD for SWAT stuffs that include free software, plus the WASWC e-LIBRARY)

# Conserving soil and water worldwide - join WASWC
Learn more from http://waswc.soil.gd.cn & www.waswc.org
To join as a member, please write to sombatpanit@yahoo.com

The World Association of Soil and Water Conservation (WASWC) appreciates the financial help from the following businesses:

**Mars Incorporated**

**SonTek YSI Incorporated**

Syngenta

**&**

**SEMEATO S/A**

thus enabling the book to be sold at an affordable price, making the soil and water assessment tool (SWAT) technology spread far and wide for timely application to cope with many threats the world is facing now.